ESCAPE ARTIST

Frontispiece. Harry Perry Robinson, age 37, in 1896, the height of his power and influence in the United States.

JOSEPH McALEER

ESCAPE ARTIST

the nine lives of Harry Perry Robinson

OXFORD
UNIVERSITY PRESS

OXFORD
UNIVERSITY PRESS

Great Clarendon Street, Oxford, OX2 6DP,
United Kingdom

Oxford University Press is a department of the University of Oxford.
It furthers the University's objective of excellence in research, scholarship,
and education by publishing worldwide. Oxford is a registered trade mark of
Oxford University Press in the UK and in certain other countries

First Edition published in 2020

Impression: 1

Published in the United States of America by Oxford University Press
198 Madison Avenue, New York, NY 10016, United States of America

British Library Cataloguing in Publication Data

Data available

Library of Congress Control Number: 2019952901

ISBN 978–0–19–879494–3

Printed and bound in Great Britain by
Clays Ltd, Elcograf S.p.A.

For two remarkable women,
Harriett and Gillian

Contents

Acknowledgements

This book is dedicated to two remarkable women, Harriett Wyndham and Gillian Cook, without whose assistance this biography could not have been written. Harriett, Harry Perry Robinson's only granddaughter (born after he died), has been the keeper of the family history, sharing stories and preserving a treasure trove of scrapbooks, letters, photographs, diaries, and other materials that has proved essential to my research. Gillian, Harriett's cousin, is the granddaughter of Harry's older sister, Mary. Thanks to a simple Google search, I uncovered a letter to *The Times* which Gillian had written in 2009, praising her great-uncle and his work as a correspondent during the First World War. I tracked down Gillian, who opened up access to Harriett and the rest of the extended family. The end result is this biography.

Many other family members offered invaluable assistance. Gillian's son, His Honour Judge Paul Cook, is the de facto family historian, having digitally scanned much of the archive and amassed a huge amount of secondary material. I owe him a considerable debt. Harriett's nephew, Ralph Perry Robinson, offered a repository for the family archive and welcomed me into his home. Ralph's father (and Harry's only grandson), Julian Perry Robinson, shared his insights, as did Jeanette Perry Robinson, granddaughter of Edward 'Kay' Robinson, Harry's beloved older brother. I would be remiss in not also thanking the exceptional spouses: William Wyndham, Michael Cook, and Amanda Perry Robinson.

Much like my subject, I travelled far and wide during the course of this research, and relied on the kindness of strangers, many now friends. David C. Smith, the superb local historian in Minneapolis, is a veritable encyclopedia of city information. I sought out, once again, Jack London experts Jay Williams and Thomas Harakal for their insight. In London, Nicholas Mays guided me through the rich archives of *The Times*. I am also grateful to Tim Dale for his detective work there. Judith Curthoys, archivist at Christ Church, Oxford, and David Rymill, archivist to the Highclere Estate, kindly answered many questions.

In the United States, I am indebted to the staffs of the Huntington Library in San Marino, California; the Minnesota History Center in St Paul; the Newberry Library in Chicago; the New York Public Library; the Butler Library of Columbia University; and the Princeton University Library. In the U.K., many productive hours were spent in the British Library, the National Archives, and the University of Bath Library. The Imperial War Museum offered access to its extraordinary photographic archive.

ACKNOWLEDGEMENTS

Throughout my writing, friends offered invaluable advice and support, as ever, including Rosemary Giedroyć, Brian D. Wallace, and the late, great, John R. Glover. At Oxford University Press, my publisher of record, I am indebted to Luciana O'Flaherty, Kizzy Taylor-Richelieu, and Matthew Cotton. Howard Emmens proved a gifted copy-editor, and Priyanka Swansi a skilled guide through the production process.

Last but not least, my family in Connecticut, including Christina and Valerie, offered, once again, enthusiastic support and a safe haven from which to uncover this grand adventure.

Joseph McAleer

Greenwich, Connecticut
January 2020

Author's Note

Harry Perry Robinson, as the reader will discover, wore many hats during his lifetime. He also used several variations of his three-part name, which posed a genuine challenge during the research process. In print, either as the byline to one of his writings or a referenced subject in a letter or article, he could be identified as one of the following:

Harry Robinson
H.P. Robinson
Harry P. Robinson
H. Perry Robinson
Perry Robinson
Harry Perry Robinson

Or, after 1920, 'Sir Harry Perry Robinson'. For the sake of simplicity, and to distinguish him from his father and his two brothers, he will be known as 'Harry' in this book.

Preface

History is replete with individuals who led extraordinary and influential lives yet who are largely unknown today. Harry Perry Robinson (1859–1930) is one of these, and this book seeks to remedy that oversight. It's not simply the fact that Harry's role in major historical events on multiple continents—from the 1896 presidential election in the United States to the First World War and the discovery of King Tutankhamun's tomb—has been obscured. Nor that, through his extensive writings and observations, Harry validates the Tocqueville premise that the best impressions of a given country are offered by foreigners. Harry's life exemplifies these, but also offers an exciting personal story worthy of Horatio Alger. Here is one man's march through history, a near-epic story of a spectacular rise from an Anglo-Indian childhood to American tycoon; a dramatic fall from grace; and an unexpected ascent again as a globetrotting journalist for the London *Times*. This entertaining saga reads at times like a *Boy's Own* adventure, a tale of pluck that bridged two vastly different eras: the imperial splendour of the late-Victorian/ Edwardian period and the upheaval of the First World War and its aftermath. This was also perhaps the last time in history that a man could live one life, in one country, and then wipe the slate clean and live another life, in another country, concealing his past from his family.

An examination of Harry's life and voluminous writings reveals much of interest. He was, for instance, an eyewitness to the gold rush in the American West in the 1880s, recording the harsh life on the frontier. A self-made publisher, he pioneered the organization of railway workers in America, rallying them to vote for William McKinley as president in 1896. Inspired by his adopted country, Harry took up the concept of the 'Special Relationship' in a provocative book and series of articles, crusading for closer U.K.–U.S. ties to counter the growing German menace and foster world peace. Returning home to England, Harry was the oldest correspondent at the Western Front during the First World War, wrote a widely praised book about the Battle of the Somme, and earned a knighthood for his efforts. He sparked international controversy by condemning the Olympic Games, seeing more harm than good in the competition's inflaming of nationalism. Finally, Harry's role in the 'scoop of the century' has been overlooked; he was the Earl of Carnarvon's right-hand 'factotum' in Egypt in 1923 as the tomb of the fabled boy-king Tutankhamun was revealed. (Whether Harry, who died seven years later, succumbed to the notorious 'Curse' is debatable.)

The world Harry lived in is long past, but it is an age which left much on the table, with issues that resonate to this day. Seen through a contemporary lens, Harry's experiences are eerily familiar. As a young immigrant to the United States he faced discrimination, yet persevered. As a publisher he harnessed the emerging mass media to organize workers into voters, tactics which have characterized elections to this day. While he was passionately opposed to labour unions (a distrust that lingers), Harry was committed to a fair deal for workers and a mutually beneficial relationship with their bosses. The aforementioned 'Special Relationship' was an obsession of Harry's. His determination to wrest Britain away from Europe identifies him as a kind of Brexiteer. Harry called attention to the natural world, advocating for animal protection and condemning destruction of the environment. As his cherished British Empire waned, Harry clung to hopes for a peaceful transition among nations. Finally, readers will sympathize with Harry's struggle as a husband and father to provide for his family and connect with his only son amid a fast-changing culture.

As a young man Harry sought fame and fortune in the New World, exploiting every opportunity, no matter the cost. He was a master of reinvention, and each of the nine 'lives' he assumed to 'escape' from one situation into the next is the focus of a chapter in this biography. First, he is an 'Innocent Abroad', a wide-eyed junior reporter in the New World, whose natural talent for writing leads to a series of big breaks and grand adventure on the Western frontier. Next, as a 'Tycoon in Training', Harry moves at breakneck speed to establish himself as a newspaper publisher in his own right, while engaging in the social life of Minneapolis, becoming an American citizen, marrying well, and acquiring immense wealth. This leads him to Chicago where, as a 'Junior Kingmaker', he dabbles in politics, writes a provocative novel about the labour movement, and plays a vital role in the election of a new president. Then the fulcrum tips, and Harry, despite being at the pinnacle of power and prestige, inexplicably abandons everything (including his wife) and returns home, starting life anew as a 'London Bookman', running a publishing house where he discovers a promising new American author named Jack London. The business, however, is a spectacular failure; Harry loses everything and is forced to start over, becoming 'A Man of *The Times*' as a roving reporter. It proves to be a perfect fit, and Harry travels the globe, often leaving his second wife and child behind. He also writes more novels and a seminal work on U.S.–U.K. relations that wins acclaim on both sides of the Atlantic. Despite his age—55 in 1914—and uncertain health, Harry becomes the oldest 'War Correspondent', emerging with a knighthood and considerable physical and psychological trauma. With bills to pay and a family to support, Harry agrees to be a 'World Traveller' for *The Times*, reporting from America, the French Riviera, and India. And if that were not enough, in 1923 he has the scoop of the new century as a 'Tut Factotum', reporting on the Carter–Carnarvon roadshow in Egypt. Finally, his twilight years reveal Harry as an 'Elder Statesman', a man increasingly out of synch with a changing world, but still full of feisty opinions, setting off a firestorm by calling for an end to the Olympic Games.

Harry's incredible journey unfolds in the context of his equally adventurous and accomplished Anglo-Indian family, headed by a clergyman-turned-editor from whom Harry (and his two brothers) inherited a gift for writing, a charming demeanour, and a strong work ethic. His aunt, Margaret Pennington, was a suffragist and personal friend of both Disraeli and Gladstone. Brother Philip was a dashing foreign correspondent (arrested as a spy in Cuba during the Spanish–American War) and editor of the London *Sunday Times* who abandoned his wife and children for an eccentric Australian gold mine owner nicknamed 'Princess Midas'. Brother Edward ('Kay') gave Rudyard Kipling his first writing job, and later founded the British Empire Naturalists' Association. His sister Valence, an erstwhile feminist, descended into madness and ended her days, according to family legend, living in a barrel on a roadside in Bulawayo, happily greeting passers-by. In fact, each family member is worthy of their own biography.

The youngest of six children, Harry was inspired by his siblings and, in later years, came to their rescue in time of need. As the runt of the litter his life could have unfolded in one of two ways. He could have simply coasted unnoticed through life, resting on the laurels of his family. Certainly no one would have predicted that he was destined for greatness when he graduated from Oxford at the very bottom of his class, with seemingly no direction other than to cast off for a foreign land in search of adventure. Instead, Harry took the other path. His dogged perseverance and strong convictions revealed an unseen maturity and confidence which propelled him forward in the New World, where he stood out as a sympathetic foreigner with unbridled curiosity and a knack for leadership. A newspaper in Albuquerque, New Mexico in 1896 described Harry, then traversing the country as part of the McKinley presidential campaign, as 'one of those blooming British dudes, who find their opportunity in the United States, where there are no vexatious class distinctions to offend their pride. Mr. Robinson is a naturalized citizen with a cockney accent.'[1] In America Harry found his voice and the courage to speak out. He was not afraid to be provocative, and his views on labour, the environment, international relations, and war were remarkably prescient. Yet he could also be reactionary, particularly when fighting for the survival of an Empire that was in twilight, and the world he had known which was disappearing before his eyes.

From the White House to Buckingham Palace, the American West to the Western Front, the sands of Egypt to the shores of India, the board room to the bedroom, we shine a bright light on a grand life lived in history's shadow, filled with the joys of service and the promotion of world peace, as well as the sorrows of a man conflicted, a loner with an inaccessible interior life that kept him from getting close to anyone, even his wife and son. Harry's wanderlust was a blessing and a curse, but it made for a splendid adventure. Fortunately for the biographer, he was a prolific and engaging writer, a keen observer of human nature and events, a latter-day Tocqueville. It is within the context of his lively newspaper articles, works of fiction and non-fiction, diaries and memoirs, and private letters that Harry's story unfolds.

Introduction

The English Family Robinson

When Julian Robinson embarked on a cruise to India in 1845, he packed twelve dozen white shirts. 'Yes, 12 dozen', Harry recounted in his memoir. 'It was sure to take 90 or 100 days at best, and a little trouble in rounding the Cape might easily stretch it to 150 days or more. So, for a bridegroom who was something of a dandy, 144 shirts were none too many. And there was life in India to be considered afterwards.'[1]

Like father, like son. To understand the life and character of Harry Perry Robinson (something of a dandy himself) we need first to examine his father, head of a rather extraordinary Anglo-Indian family. When Julian Robinson, a young curate in Doncaster, married Harriett Woodcock Sharpe, daughter of the vicar of Doncaster and canon of York, in 1844, their sea voyage to India was also their honeymoon. Twelve dozen white shirts were only the beginning. 'What a business was the providing of a *trousseau* for a girl going to India to be married! All the clothes to be made (did not every woman in India look to the last-arriving bride for the latest note in fashions?) and all the toilet articles—six dozen bottles of toilet vinegar, six dozen bottles of lavender water, and everything else to scale', Harry continued. 'For people did not go to India then for a winter's trip, when the voyage alone might occupy 12 months there and back; and whatever of English comforts they wished to have around them in their bungalow must be taken from England.'[2]

Thus began the voyage of a newly minted English Family Robinson, an experience that would shape not only the newlyweds but their offspring. Service to the Empire and loyalty to the Crown were virtues instilled by Julian in each of his six children. Julian's personal motto was '*Droit et Adroit*' ('Right and Clever'), a replacement for the Robinson family motto '*Virtute non Verbis*' ('Deeds not Words'). 'Perhaps he did not think "*Virtute non Verbis*" too well suited to a clergyman. Words, after all, are a good deal to a preacher', Harry surmised. However, always doing good but with a creative flair became a Robinson hallmark.

*   *   *   *   *

Julian Robinson was born in 1819, the son of a property speculator who gambled away his fortune and ended his days as head of the Royal Gardens at Kew. 'While still in that office he is said to have gone more or less insane', his grandson, Harry, recalled. At Bruce Castle School in Tottenham Julian met Percy Florence Shelley, son of Percy Bysshe and Mary Shelley, and they became lifelong friends. Together they went to Cambridge, Julian to Jesus College, Percy to Trinity. Neither distinguished themselves in their studies. 'My Father and Shelley had both narrowly escaped being sent down from Cambridge for bringing down from London a whole Italian Opera troupe to give a single performance', Harry explained. 'Apart from the disapproval of the Authorities, his half-share in the expense, I believe, embarrassed my Father dreadfully to the end of his College days.' Julian spent his holidays with the Shelleys at Boscombe or touring with them on the Continent. 'He seems to have been regarded almost as a ward of the family', Harry noted. After Cambridge Julian became a minister in the Church of England. 'Why he went into the Church at all, I have never been understood nor has anyone been able to expound to me', Harry wrote. 'He did not remain actively in the Ministry for very long.'[3] He was assigned as a curate in Doncaster, assisting the Rev. John Sharpe. There he met and fell in love with Harriett, one of Sharpe's eleven children, two years his junior.

Evidently the Robinson family line owned the advowson to the parish church in Charmouth, on the Dorset coast. Julian, as an ordained minister, was entitled to take up this appointment and living. Harry was perplexed as to why his father turned it down. 'It seemed to me so sweet a spot that I wondered why my Parents preferred the adventures and chances of an Indian Army Chaplaincy in those hazardous days', he wrote.[4] Seeking adventure and the unexpected, we shall see, was a Robinson trait, not to mention the desire to escape. So in 1845, Julian accepted a commission as a chaplain in the Honourable East India Company's Army Service and he and his bride sailed from Blackwall, London. A large party of family and friends saw them off, as recalled Harriett's younger sister, Margaret, who took a shine to Percy Shelley. 'My sister and her new husband had never seen the Polka danced', she said, 'and Shelley and I had to give a demonstration of it in the ship's cabin—not an easy thing to do with a dance that needs so much room as the polka.'[5]

The voyage took five months, and soon upon arrival in India their first child, Agnes Harriett, was born. The Robinsons would have five more children: Philip Stewart (b.1847), Mary Frances (1849), Valerie Aimée (1853), Edward Kay (1855), and Harry Perry (1859). In 1851, Harriett brought her first two children home to England, leaving them in Dursley, Gloucestershire, in charge of a schoolmaster. In 1859, unaware she was pregnant with Harry, Harriett brought Mary, Valerie (known as Valence), and Edward (known as Kay) to England, and all five children were entrusted to the care of a second cousin in New Brighton, Mersey-side. Harry was born on November 30, 1859; the birth was likely at sea en route back to India, although Harry always claimed to have been born in Chunar. Harriett's last journey home to England was in 1861, with young Harry, and she and the six children made their home in Cheltenham. Julian would join them a decade later, upon his retirement.

* * * * *

In India, the Robinsons were based in Chunar, in the North-Western Provinces (Uttar Pradesh today) between Benares and Mirzapur, where Julian served as chaplain at the large military station. The Reverend Julian was a popular figure, often depicted in the local press. 'Of those first years in India I must have heard many stories but all are blotted out by one incident, so rapturous to a child', Harry recalled.

> They were going, my Father and Mother, along some hill-path in the rickshaws of the day, when they met a party of Natives, three of whom were carrying on their backs large baskets full of grapes. My Father thought a grape would be pleasant; so he stopped his rickshaw and, mindful of the price of grapes then in England, handed one of the hill-men a rupee with a request for the value in grapes. Whereupon, one after another, they emptied their baskets on the ground before him. An un-broken rupee was a larger sum of money than, perhaps, they had ever handled in their lives.[6]

It was a period of unrest and uncertainty on the Subcontinent, and in his memoir Harry recounted the story of the family's narrow escape during the 1857 Indian Mutiny, two years before Harry was born. Harriett was on a visit to Mirzapur with her three children, Mary, Valence, and Kay, when trouble broke out.

> There were eleven of them—all women and children—crowded in one vehicle, presumably a gharry. So loaded were they that my sister Mary had to sit on the step hanging on by one hand, with the baby Kay hugged in her lap with the other arm. They drove as fast as might be by night. By day they were hidden in the woods. One night, in the grey of the early morning, they were stopped by an English schoolmaster and his wife who came out of hiding and begged to be taken on board. It was impossible. The horse was worn out, the gharry overloaded, and the Native driver refused.

They must either find another vehicle or make their way on foot to safety. A few hours later they were cut to pieces by Mutineers who came along the road.[7]

Harry recalled visiting his father's church in Chunar while on a visit to India in 1921, his first time back in the Subcontinent. No service had been held in that church for fifty years. The caretaker brought out from storage Julian's books. 'They were to me extraordinarily interesting: page after page, beautifully neat, in my Father's handwriting, sixty five years old', he wrote. 'The earliest entries: each Sunday and Holy day throughout the years with every detail recorded in the ruled columns—the name of the officiating Clergyman, the name of the Preacher, his text, the numbers of the hymns, &c. And through all the long period no name occurred either officiating Clergyman or Preacher, but Julian Robinson. Apparently he never had relief.' Nor, Harry observed, were there any references to 'hints of warfare and peril and the need of steadfastness', which his father must have incorporated in his preaching. 'On its face the record runs as smoothly as that of any dozing English vicarage in a season of unbroken peace', he wrote. Harry added that his father had written a pamphlet on Julian the Apostate, although no copy has survived. 'The writing of it seems to have been a whimsical performance', he noted. 'Inevitably he became known as Julian the Apostate himself, especially when he left the Church.'[8]

To the surprise of many, in 1865 Julian refused an offer to become the Bishop of Calcutta, and at the age of 46 retired from ecclesiastical life to run an English-language newspaper in Allahabad, *The Pioneer*. Harry insisted that his father was not defrocked; he continued to be called 'Reverend', and did occasionally officiate at services. 'As was said of him at the time, [he] "only transferred his preaching from the pulpit to the Editorial chair".'[9]

*   *   *   *   *

The Pioneer was founded in 1865 by George Allen, an English businessman who had made his fortune in tea, boots, and shoes. It was initially published three days a week, then became a daily. It was modelled in format, layout, and typeface on the London *Times*. 'No one has ever questioned that it was to Julian Robinson that its instantaneous success and the great power which it soon came to exercise were owing', Harry recalled. 'George Allen, who furnished the capital, though an excellent business man, . . . had not and never pretended to any literary ability or other qualification for journalism. He was, by all accounts, a gentle, ladylike, unimpressive little man in those days, who, after she came out to keep house for my Father, was extremely anxious to marry my sister

Valence.'[10] They did not marry. Together Allen and Robinson, considered an independent-minded clergyman with similar political views, became known in Anglo-Indian parlance as 'old *koi-hais*: experienced India hands who knew the ropes and held deeply conservative, not to say reactionary, views on all matters pertaining to British rule in India'.

> In the pages of *The Pioneer* they gave voice to both their own prejudices and those of the majority of their readers in northern India: planters, boxwallahs, businessmen, engineers, Europeans in the provincial services, and junior officers in the ranks of the Indian Army. They not only provided the Indian and European news that their readers wanted but went to great lengths to be first with it, employing the best news services available.[11]

Not everything in 'The Pi' was reactionary, however. One article, 'On the Salaries of Native Civilians', supported the efforts of natives who agitated for increased pay and better living standards. 'A plea is made for the natives to be allowed to rise in "civilization," material as well as moral, "ere any thing like a free, friendly intercourse between the dominant and the subject classes can take place,"'[12] the article stated. Within the context of British rule, Julian and other civic leaders were not averse to keeping the peace by improving conditions for all peoples. Liberal views like these, but within the status quo, were passed on by Julian to his youngest son. *The Pioneer* also expanded to include poetry, fiction, and book reviews. In 1877 Allen acquired a rival daily newspaper, the *Civil & Military Gazette*, which, along with *The Pioneer*, were considered 'mouthpieces for British and official opinion'.[13]

'Of course I knew something of the space which my father had for many years filled in Indian eyes', Harry recalled. 'Lord Roberts had told me that he was the greatest man in India in his day; and how often I had heard the same thing from others! If a man had lived in India during the third quarter of the last century and, on meeting him, I hinted at my relationship, the response was always eager and immediate: "What you are not Julian Robinson's son?"'[14] Field Marshal Frederick Sleigh Roberts, 1st Earl Roberts, commander in India and, later, the Boer War, stayed in Julian's bungalow when in Allahabad and they became fast friends. 'It was, indeed, a current witticism that India was not governed from Calcutta but from Robinson's bungalow in Allahabad',[15] Harry noted.

In 1873, Julian resigned as editor of *The Pioneer* and returned to England for good; he was 54 years old, and Harry was 14. Interestingly, his two eldest sons, Phil and Kay, followed in his footsteps. Phil returned to India in 1868, aged 21, to assist his father on *The Pioneer* and dabble in fiction. In 1871 Phil founded *The Chameleon: An Anglo-Indian Periodical of Light Literature*, printed on the same presses as *The Pioneer*. When

Julian retired, Phil briefly succeeded his father as editor of *The Pioneer*, but was happier as a freelance writer and naturalist. He left India in 1877 to join the London *Daily Telegraph* as a war correspondent, journeying to Afghanistan (1878–9), Zululand (1879), Egypt (1882), and Sudan (1885). After a few years as a freelance journalist and editor of the *Sporting Times*, Kay arrived in India in 1884 when he was 29, to work as assistant editor of *The Pioneer*, and later as editor of the *Civil & Military Gazette*. Kay's assistant was a talented young man named Rudyard Kipling. Friends from the start, Kay encouraged his charge to write short stories, which he published. Harry's son, John Bradstreet ('Brad') Perry Robinson (b.1906), recalled the oft-repeated story of Kipling's antics in the *Gazette* office. His Uncle Kay, he noted, 'always kept a large black umbrella in his office. This was because Kipling would suddenly have a brilliant idea and would rush into the Editor's room waving his pen. Pens in those days were full of black ink, and the Editor was always dressed in whites. The umbrella was opened wide as soon as the brilliant idea got through the door.'[16]

After his retirement, Julian returned to India only once, donning his clerical hat to serve as a chaplain to Edward, Prince of Wales, on his Indian tour in 1875–6. While there Julian also filed reports for *The Pioneer*. Among his fellow journalists was George A. Henty, representing the London *Evening Standard* (and who would go on to write nine stirring adventure novels set in India). It is unclear if Julian joined the prince for the entire seventeen-week trip which covered 7,500 miles. Along the way Julian introduced the prince to Christian missionaries and schools, and 'read service' on several occasions, whether in camp or inside a palace. When the principal chaplain, Canon Robinson Duckworth, fell ill with typhoid fever at the end of the trip, Julian was promoted.

A brush with death during a 'tiger-ringing' episode on February 26, 1876 was widely reported in the press. Julian had joined the prince and his entourage, riding elephants in search of tigers to shoot. As documented, 'a tiger charged one of the elephants with great determination, happening, sagaciously, to select that ridden by a non-combatant, the Rev. Julian Robinson, who was officiating as chaplain to H.R.H. Both the mahout and the reverend chaplain were in great danger until the tiger was shot by another member of the suite, Colonel Ellis, from a neighbouring elephant.'[17] An eyewitness, William Howard Russell, the veteran *Times* correspondent, described the scene in greater detail:

> The tiger sprang on the elephant of Mr. Robinson, placing one claw on the rifle, so that he could not fire, and tearing the mahout's leg. The elephant swung around, the tiger fell off, but sprang at the elephant again and clawed it cruelly. It then leaped on the mahout of the elephant carrying

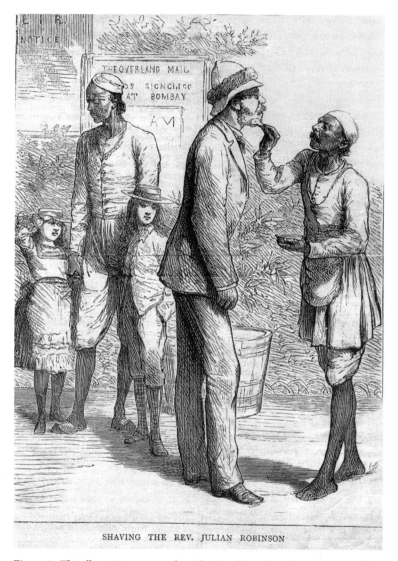

SHAVING THE REV. JULIAN ROBINSON

Figure 1. This illustration appeared in *The Graphic* on April 22, 1876, part of its coverage of the visit of the Prince of Wales to India, during which Julian Robinson served as a chaplain.

Colonel Ellis, and was tearing him down when Colonel Ellis, leaning down over the howdah, fired his rifle, and the tiger dropped, but not till it had lacerated the elephant's ear and the man's knee and leg. Surgeon Kellett dressed the men's wounds, and the injured mahouts and elephants were sent back to camp.[18]

This episode only enhanced Julian's reputation and fame. The next day, Russell noted, 'Mr. Robinson, none the worse for his tiger scare yesterday, read service.' During the course of the prince's tour, twenty-three tigers were shot.

* * * * *

'It was the rule in India at that time that English children born out of there must be sent home to England as soon as they could stand the journey',[19] Brad noted. In 1861, at two years old, Harry left India with his mother for a childhood in Cheltenham. Consequently, he retained few memories of India and of his famous father, who visited England only twice from 1861 until his retirement in 1873. 'With my father I never had more than a slight acquaintance', Harry wrote. 'He comes first into my memory as a very brown person, extraordinarily stubbly to kiss and smelling comfortingly of tobacco; and he piaffed.'[20] Harry explained how his father would trot around the room, imitating a horse's dressage movement (piaffe). 'It was an intoxicating delight to me when this strange brown man, to whom I felt so unaccountably drawn, often so serious, in moments of ebullience would piaffe round the drawing room or, better still, our playroom', he wrote. Even better for the youngster was his father's fondness for 'duchesses', 'ethereal cream puffs' from a bakery in Cheltenham. 'I can still see him, after his first bite, with flicks of cream clinging to that bristly moustache, and hear his voice: "Divine! Perfectly divine!"' Of his mother, Harry recalled a loving presence with a beautiful voice who played the harp. 'I used to as often as I could sit on a stool by her feet, the great golden harp towering above me, while she played and sang. And so it is that I know to a certainty how and with voice it is with their harps that the angels sing.'[21]

By all accounts, Harry's childhood in Cheltenham in what he called 'an extraordinary and tempestuous family' was a happy one, surrounded by his three sisters and two brothers. He recalled, when very young, being admitted to the 'secret female world' when he accompanied his sisters and their chaperones, dressed in 'formidable' crinolines, to their calisthenics class at the Assembly Rooms in Cheltenham. 'Many times have I seen my sisters, then undressing, disembarrass themselves of these stupendous garments, loosening a string at the waist and so letting the whole crinoline slither rattling to the floor', he wrote. They changed into a costume 'that caused me all the trouble', Harry continued, 'costumes in which girls actually showed their stockinged legs up to the very knees'. Harry watched from the gallery, 'the only male person present, while the class, all dressed in the same costume went through their evolutions below'. Suddenly Harry was very popular among the neighbourhood boys. 'It is not surprising that the male youth of Cheltenham became in the slang of the present day "intrigued" and inquisitive, and I, as the only male admitted to the Vestal ceremonies was naturally appealed to for information', he remembered. With his brother Phil presiding over the inquisition, Harry was subjected to an 'exhausted and bewildering cross-examination. What did they look like, these girls? I could only say that they ran about like little mice. And they jumped.'[22]

Of his brothers, Harry was closest to Kay ('my leader, my model, in everything'), only four years older, than he was to Phil, twelve years his senior and away at school ('a gigantic figure, heroic and adorable, to be viewed with some terror but a loving and delicious terror'). The gardens near their home, first in Rodney Terrace and then Montpelier Terrace, provided endless hours of games and hunting for butterflies, along with a cat called Snowball and a pet brown owl named Pausanias. 'To my delight I became increasingly permitted to go with Kay on his birds-netting or butterflying expeditions; and those who know anything of his writing do not need to be told what an admirable field naturalist he was', Harry recalled. 'Together—or he, primarily, and I in imitation—collected almost everything collectible: bird's eggs, bird's skins, butterflies and moths, plants, fossils, stamps, crests, feathers, the names of engines—and probably other things I have forgotten.'[23] From these earliest days Harry would acquire a lifelong appreciation for the natural world.

* * * * *

Harry entered the prestigious Westminster School as a Queen's Scholar in 1872, aged 13. 'As a boy I spent five years of school life in the shadow of Westminster Abbey', he recalled. 'For all those five years I attended, except in the holidays, nine services in the Abbey per week; for we had school prayers there every morning at eight o'clock, and there were regular public services on Saturday afternoon and twice on Sundays besides.'[24] He especially remembered being in awe, 'having just come to London as a country boy', of the service of thanksgiving for the recovery of the Prince of Wales from typhoid in 1872, and the visits of the Shah of Persia in 1873 and U.S. President Ulysses S. Grant in 1877. Harry was a keen cricketer and rose to be Captain (Head) of the school. Not much is known about his studies, except that he won a book prize in classics in 1876. The published collection of Latin verses by Westminster students, *Carmina et Epigrammata* (1877), featured several by Harry. One was called '*Non Clausit Opus*', or 'Not Finishing the Job':

> Look! The bell has rung! The boys go out to play.
> Some anxious to run about, others to play ball.

One of them, alas, homework, unbearable and undone,
Detains. A hateful punishment, taking forever!
In his misery, he envies his companions, and bemoans
His fate, in frustration eating his heart out, and his fingers too![25]

If Harry was describing his own situation, it certainly would not apply to his adult life, as he would become known as a disciplined workaholic, although one who always made time for sport.

Harry followed in his father's footsteps and won a scholarship to Oxford, matriculating at Christ Church on October 11, 1878, to study classics. Brad noted that his father focused more on sport than his studies. 'He had a high reputation as a Whist player, appears in Wisden, and his favourite game was Rackets', he recalled. Harry was a member of the Christ Church Nondescripts, one of the college cricket clubs.[26] Harry recalled a telling incident from his Oxford years. Along with two friends, he went to London one Saturday to see a matinee of *Faust* at Covent Garden. 'We heard the Opera, dined agreeably three-and-sixpenny at the old Criterion table d'hote, and got back to Oxford by a late train in before our College gates were closed', Harry noted. 'It was a highly satisfactory excursion.' The next morning, however, came a rebuke from his father.

Figure 2. Harry, age 17, seated in the front row at right, at Westminster School, *c*.1876.

'The Opera is an entirely gentlemanly taste and I do not criticise you for indulging it', Julian wrote, 'but when your Father is in London, you should not come up even for an afternoon without informing him. I should have been glad to have had the company of yourself and your two friends at dinner.' Not until years later did Harry learn the story of Julian's operatic adventure with Percy Shelley, which nearly had both of them sent down from Cambridge, and no doubt provoked Julian's note to his son. 'His nervousness, when he saw his undergraduate son betraying a <u>penchant</u> for Italian opera, then, is intelligible', Harry wrote. 'But I wish I had known of his Cambridge escapade at the time!'[27]

Harry's academic record was undistinguished. He did pass collections each year, usually with the equivalent of a third-class degree. In the London *Evening Standard* on July 4, 1882, the Final Classical School list was published, and Harry received a Class IV degree, the lowest. To add to the humiliation, the results were alphabetical, so Harry's name was the very last one on the page. He decided not to stay for a Master's degree and pursue a career in the church, despite the encouragement of the Dean of Westminster, Arthur Penrhyn Stanley, who wished that Harry take up the advowson at Charmouth that his father had refused years before. 'It was not until midway in my time at Oxford that I recognised the impossibility of it, and with my refusal, our right to the Living lapsed', Harry noted.[28]

What did Harry gain from his Oxford years? An interesting perspective can be had from Harry's contemporary, Harold Spender (1864–1926), the Liberal Party politician, journalist, and author (and father of Sir Stephen Spender). Harold was at University College and five years younger than Harry. Nonetheless, in his memoir, *The Fire of Life*, he reminisced about his Oxford days. 'I set more store on the social side of that life than on any education that Oxford can give', he wrote, although he obtained a Double First, quite unlike Harry's Fourth. 'The real training for life in Oxford takes place in the many colloquies of youth over their evening pipes, after their day's work is done, whether it be in the schools or on the river. The daily interchange of ideas brought from reading or from the class-room and thrown into the common stock in the college life of a great university can find no parallel as a mental drilling for early youth. There is a freemasonry that lasts all their life among those who have met and talked in their youth by the banks of the Isis or the Cam.'[29] Harry would certainly have concurred.

* * * * *

Twenty-two years old and with an Oxford degree (however undistinguished) to his name, Harry was ready to embrace his future, wherever that lay. Like his father, he had turned away from a safe and secure life in the church, and, following his example, looked to journalism. Through the influence of either his father or his brothers, Harry interned at two London newspapers, the *Daily Chronicle* and the *Pall Mall Gazette*. A full-time position was not in the offing at either establishment, but Harry was there for the experience and the contacts. He was also the only Robinson child in England at the time. Kay was back in India, running the *Civil & Military Gazette* with Kipling. Phil was in America, criss-crossing the country for the *New York World,* and publishing his impressions in book form as *Sinners and Saints: A Tour Across the States and Round Them, with Three Months Among the Mormons* (1882). Each of Harry's sisters, moreover, had returned to India to marry. Two wed civil servants: the sensible Agnes to Thomas Hesketh-Biggs, Accountant-General of Madras, and the brilliant Mary (who passed the B.A. examination at Cambridge long before women were entitled to receive a degree) to Paul Whalley, a magistrate and collector in the North-Western Provinces, in 1870. The youngest (and in time troubled) sister, Valence, married Captain Woodforde Finden, a handsome young surgeon with the 11th Bengal Cavalry Lancers, in 1872.

One would have expected, then, for Harry to look East for his future, as the Robinson family was imbued with the spirit of the Empire and service to Queen and Country in India. He certainly shared the wanderlust and sense of adventure possessed by his father and brothers. Instead, perhaps anxious to strike out on his own as the youngest child, he made his escape in the opposite direction.

1

Innocent Abroad, 1883–1886

In retrospect, Harry's decision to travel abroad in 1883 is not surprising. He was a Robinson, after all, and Robinsons travelled far and wide in search of opportunities to work and serve, not to mention the grand adventure. His father may have retired and resettled back in England, but his two brothers, whom Harry idolized, were having a wild time out yonder. Phil, dashing war correspondent, had just returned from America, a peacetime assignment to travel the country from coast to coast, resulting in a somewhat sensational travel book that lifted the veil on the mysterious Mormons in Utah. And Kay was back in India, following in Julian's footsteps and giving Rudyard Kipling his first big break.

Harry was 23 and anxious to make his mark. But why America, and not India or another part of the British Empire? The answer may have been revealed by Harry in an article he wrote in July 1884 about Spokane Falls, a booming town in Washington Territory (the future Washington State) that was welcoming settlers. 'It is a common theory in the East that the right kind of people to send West are those ne'er-do-wells for whom no matter of use can be found at home, just as it seems to be the fashion in England to divide the utterly good for nothing members of a family between America and the Church, as two fields in which no kind of fool could help getting on', Harry wrote.[1] We know that Harry turned down the offer of a life in the church and a guaranteed income, as his father had done. We also know that he essentially flunked out of Oxford. So did his family, worried about his prospects, 'push' him to take a chance and go to America? It's a likely possibility. Harry's son, Brad, claimed in his memoir that his father made up his own mind. 'When my father was at Oxford, the general assumption seems to have been that he would take Holy Orders with the idea of getting a Beauclerk family living', he wrote. 'When it came to the point, my father said he thought he could do more good by going out to America.'[2]

Harry was not alone in his decision to head to America. Immigration from the United Kingdom rose steadily during the nineteenth century.

Figure 3. Harry, age 23 in 1883, ready to leave for America.

Immigrants from England alone peaked in the 1880s at 644,680, comprising 10 per cent of the foreign-born population of the United States. Irish immigrants comprised the largest group, with 30 per cent.[3] The increase was a result of improved relations between the two countries, but also the vast employment opportunities that lay in the New World. The sense of kinship with the former colonials as well as the common language facilitated adjustment and assimilation, with many regarding America as 'Greater Britain'.[4]

*   *   *   *   *

Thomas Greenwood, in his 1883 tour guide to America, gave the following advice to would-be immigrants (and could have had Harry in mind): 'For unmarried young men, with plenty of energy, and who like work for its own sake, there is plenty of room; and such, with tact, push and principle, the great motto of Abraham Lincoln, would scarcely fail to get on.'[5] America was a thrilling place for a handsome, mannered, curious, ambitious (and unmarried) foreigner in search of adventure. And so in May 1883 Harry boarded the S.S. *Bothnia* in Liverpool, bound for New York. The crossing took eleven days, record time then on the so-called 'Ocean Greyhound'. Harry later recalled that first voyage. 'The staple diet on a crack liner in those days was Irish stew, with soup to

14

precede it, and a good, solid pudding afterwards', he wrote. Mealtime was something of an obsession for Harry, as we shall see. 'In fine domestic fashion we used to work in an extra meal of gruel or bread and milk, like mother used to make, before going to bed; and the reek of the oil lamps, with the smell of engine oil and cookery was all over the ship.' But he marvelled at what was called a 'floating palace', and enjoyed the camaraderie of the passengers and friendships made in the smoking room and at the card table. 'All the other thrilling opportunities for gambles which used to engross us so, as whether the next ship we sighted would be to port or starboard, the number of the pilot boat, whether the pilot would be wearing a hat or a cap, and which foot, right or left, he would land with on deck', he recalled. 'There was so little else to do that everyone in those days kept a log, and in the long days, indistinguishable from each other except by the divine service in the saloon on Sunday and the concert on the last night out, the sighting of a whale or a school of porpoises was an event, and the glimpse of an iceberg made us feel as if we were Hudsons or John Cabots ourselves. There was something of hardihood and adventure in the making of a crossing.'[6] The first thing that met Harry's eye upon steaming into New York harbour (the Statue of Liberty was still three years away) was the tower of the *New York Tribune* building, built in 1875, topped with a clock, the second-tallest building on Manhattan island after old Trinity Church. This would be Harry's place of employment for the next six months. Harry took rooms in the Brevoort House on Fifth Avenue and Ninth Street, a large stately hotel. Clearly, given his first-class travel and now quality accommodations, Harry had some money in his pocket, perhaps provided by his father to give him a good start.

Harry's job as a junior reporter on the *Tribune*, an eight-page daily and the largest circulation newspaper in the United States, came with recommendations from the *Daily Chronicle* and the *Pall Mall Gazette*, both of which hoped Harry would also write the occasional letter home about interesting slices of American life. Founded by Horace Greeley in 1841, the *Tribune* was 'heartily Republican' (which was fast becoming young Harry's politics of choice), pro-Union and anti-slavery, pro-business and anti-strike, and determined to keep a Republican in the White House (Chester A. Arthur was the current occupant) and prevent the Democrats from returning to power. When Ulysses S. Grant defeated Greeley for the presidency in 1872, and Greeley died shortly thereafter, Whitelaw Reid took over the *Tribune*, and would have been Harry's boss and mentor. Although Reid owned the *Tribune* until his death in 1912, he would have a storied career as an ambassador to France (1889–92) and the United Kingdom (1905–12), and was Benjamin Harrison's running mate in the 1892 presidential election, which was won by the Democrat Grover Cleveland. As editor of the *Tribune*, Reid has a reputation for hiring 'brainy writers for likeminded readers' to promote its standing as 'Newspaper as Literature'.[7] In fact, Harry may have encountered fellow Englishmen on the *Tribune* staff and on rival newspapers, as American editors (like Reid) were eager to hire those who could read and write English well and who possessed keen powers of observation. For many it was an easy career choice. Hamil Grant, reflecting on his years as an Anglo-American journalist (which began in New York, like Harry), noted: 'Those who have reached the newspaper offices have, nearly all of them, the same tale to tell, namely, that they had suddenly found themselves without employment and turned to journalism as likely to afford them a chance of using their academic advantages.'[8]

Clearly, for an aspiring journalist like Harry, working at the *Tribune* was a coup and an excellent training ground. Barely in his new job for a week, Harry got his first big break covering the Brooklyn Bridge disaster of May 30, 1883. At that time the longest suspension bridge in the world (originally called the New York and Brooklyn Bridge) with twin towers 268 feet high, it had been opened just six days earlier, on May 24, by President Arthur. Harry would have witnessed the grand spectacle (and perhaps written about it) as 1,800 vehicles and 150,300 people crossed the 1,595-foot span, deemed 'The Eighth Wonder of the World', on the first day. One wonders if he was also caught up in the controversy over the date; by sheer coincidence, May 24 was Queen Victoria's birthday, and the large Irish community, who comprised the majority of the bridge construction workers, felt betrayed and boycotted the opening.[9] Nonetheless, crowds continued to throng the bridge's pedestrian walkways over the next several days. Newspapers reported (perhaps Harry) a rise in disorderly conduct, including horse races and people throwing rocks onto passing boats below, which posed a significant challenge for police. 'Literally, in the aftermath of its opening, the public understood the bridge to be a potential deathtrap', Richard Haw noted.[10]

Indeed it was. On May 30, the eve of the Memorial Day holiday, the pedestrian walkway was jammed with people out for a pleasant stroll. At 4:00 p.m., a rumour spread that the bridge was going to collapse, causing a stampede at the New York side, in which a dozen people were crushed to death on a stairway and hundreds were wounded. Harry was one of the first reporters on the scene, and filed several eyewitness accounts of the tragedy. It was a career-making moment for the young man.

Harry was instructed to visit the police stations, fire houses, and hospitals and write 'pen-pictures' of both victims and survivors, to add to the extensive coverage of the disaster in the *Tribune*. Here are two, published on June 1, 1883:

> The body of Sarah Hennessy, the young bride of seven weeks, was surrounded by many of her school companions and friends, all endeavoring to soothe the agitated mind of her bereaved old mother, at her home, 190 Union Ave. Her face wore a life-like expression, with no apparent disfigurement and her mother said: 'She looks as though she had died from fright more than from any fatal injuries.' Her young husband is almost heartbroken. He wanders aimlessly about, regretting that the first holiday since his marriage should have proved so fatal to his happiness.[11]

> The Oak Street Police Station presented a curious scene yesterday. In one corner of the sergeant's office lay a miscellaneous heap of clothing. There were hats of all sorts and shapes—straw hats, felt hats, stiff hats and soft hats, all battered and all crushed and dusty. Over the railing in front of the sergeant's desk hung a dark blue dress almost uninjured. Boots and shoes there were in abundance. A score of umbrellas and broken canes were stacked in one corner, and handkerchiefs, some of them blood-stained, odd gloves, a child's wee dress, and scraps of feminine apparel, completed the list. From time to time men and women would enter the station in an aggressive sort of manner, generally accompanied by a friend or two, and demand some article, which they stated they had lost in the crowd.[12]

Six years later, when he was based in Minnesota, Harry was interviewed by the *St. Paul Gazette* about that tragic day. 'It is not often that editors are very deeply moved by any pathetic story which is submitted to them for publication, and editors of daily newspapers are the least of all', the paper admitted. But it cited the case where 'the city editor of a great morning paper was moved to tears by the pathos in some "copy" he was reading'. That copy was written by Harry. The article continued:

> The editor of the New York Tribune assigned a reporter to go to one of the fire engine houses where several of the bruised and mangled bodies of the victims had been taken, to write up scenes and incidents. When the reporter reached the place, the friends and relatives of the victims were there, trying to identify the remains of the dead or helping care for the bruised and crushed who were still alive. It was natural that there should be many heartrending scenes, tears, groans and cries of anguish. The reporter spent a half hour at the place and went to the office with half a column of pen-pictures. He turned in his copy, and one or two other reporters sat for a while in the office discussing the affair.

> The city editor chanced to read that copy himself, and when he had finished the tears were running down his cheeks. He called to the reporter who had written it and said: 'Robinson, is this story of the dying woman and her little children true?'

'Those are the plain facts, as I saw them,' was the reply.

'Well, it's a mighty good story,' replied the city editor, 'and it reads like Dickens.'

The story was printed the next morning, and the man that wrote it was Harry P. Robinson.[13]

The story in question was inserted among three pages of coverage on May 31, 1883 in the *Tribune*. At the fire station, Harry described a scene 'certainly sufficient to make women faint and strong men turn pale... There were bloated faces, and eyes circled with dark blue rings, preternaturally swollen; cheeks and faces were covered with blood, and hair was matted with it; foam was exuding from blue lips and clothes were torn and shirts and dresses were in tatters.'[14] The crowd watched as each new victim passed by; 'pale-faced men and women, whose eyes were suffused with tears, and whose lips were trembling with inquiries they scarcely dared to form into words'. Harry proceeded to the hospital nearest to the Brooklyn Bridge:

> Up stairs in the regular wards the scene was more acutely terrible. Shrieks rent the air from those who were writhing in the pains of partial suffocation. Others of the wounded simply lay moaning with pain. The cots were full and blankets and bedding had to be spread on the floors to accommodate some of the injured. In several of the cots lay women and children, unconscious with their lives wavering in the balance. A most touching sight was that of two young children, less than ten years of age, whose sallow faces seemed to speak a half-consciousness of their dreadful surroundings.[15]

For a 23-year-old from a patrician background with little if any exposure to death and tragedy, this was remarkable writing, and the description of it as 'Dickensian' is an apt one. Harry seemed to have inherited the family gift for candid and evocative storytelling, which would serve him well throughout his life. Moreover, one cannot discount the psychological impact on Harry of this tragedy, which remained with him for the rest of his life. Playing on the street below the bridge that day was ten-year-old Alfred E. Smith, son of Irish immigrants and future governor of New York (and Democratic candidate for U.S. president in 1928). 'That was my first view of a great calamity. I did not sleep for nights', he later recalled, remembering how hats, coats, umbrellas, and pocketbooks rained down on the streets below.[16]

The Brooklyn Bridge disaster made headlines around the world, and although newspaper articles at this time did not contain bylines, Harry's efforts did not go unnoticed in the newsroom, and he could expect the best of assignments over the next few months. He seemed to enjoy working on the paper and the camaraderie of his fellow reporters. He was particularly fond of the clam chowder at the stylish Astor House hotel (a favourite of both Abraham Lincoln and Jefferson Davis). For Harry, just starting out, this was the perfect spot to spend his daily lunch allowance. 'It is astonishing, when you know where to go and are not too particular, what a lot you can get to eat for ten cents!' Harry recalled. 'Once in a while, on pay day, we would all of us combine to riot, holding revel on the high stools about those little counters in the Astor House rotunda and wallowing in clam chowder. They have made it, I believe, from precisely the same recipe for some untold number of centuries; it is reasonable to believe that they learned the recipe in the Garden of Eden.' It was, Harry declared, 'what I honestly believe to be one of the most miraculous dishes which has ever been mysteriously revealed to human chef'.[17]

We know from his Oxford days that Harry was a keen cricketer. So he wasted no time in joining the premier club in New York, the Staten Island Cricket Club, whose members included fellow English expatriates. During the summer months this was a popular social scene, and the *Tribune* followed the matches on its sports pages. On June 2, Staten Island beat Columbia College, and Harry was the top scorer with 42 of 139 runs. Harry also played on the club's English team, which competed against the club's American team. On weekends and days off, when Harry was not playing cricket, he travelled to towns in northern New York State and rural New England, visiting families of acquaintances, armed with letters of introduction. He recalled this time as his real 'initiation' to the American people and culture, and the natural kinship with the British. One visit to Vermont was especially memorable, joining a fellow reporter to spend a week at the house of his uncle. 'He was a grand old man, the uncle; and he used to take me out and show me the marks of British bullets on his barn. I never believed in those marks. Nor, I am sure, did he', Harry remembered. But the so-called 'marks' served a purpose: they were 'good enough as a text for lectures on the days when "we fellows whipped you fellows." We became great friends. But how he hated the name "British!"'[18] American Anglophobia stemmed from such century-old memories of Redcoats, but also a protracted sense of colonial inferiority.[19] In any event, the evocation of what he called 'the old Revolutionary prejudice' was a teaching moment for Harry. 'We in England were being brought up in cheerful, if wholly ignorant, friendliness to the United States', he observed. 'It was only on that visit to Vermont that I learned that there could be anything but a natural cordiality between English and Americans. The atmosphere of the *Tribune* office, then strongly "pro-British," had not prepared me for the shock. Yet I knew that that fine old Vermonter, while he hated everything "British," liked me!' Little did Harry know at the time that this would become his life's work, to overcome the misunderstandings and misconceptions between Americans and the British, and to bring the two great Anglo-Saxon nations closer together in the cause of world peace.

*   *   *   *   *

Harry scored a major assignment in September 1883, after just four months on the job: coverage of the completion of the Northern Pacific Railway, opening a route from Minnesota westward to the Pacific Coast. This would become part of a third transcontinental railway line, following the route blazed by Meriwether Lewis and William Clark earlier in the century. If Harry made his mark with the Brooklyn Bridge disaster, this two-month long extravaganza would make his name, showcasing his writing abilities and putting him in touch with influential people. He would come to agree with his brother Phil, who concluded, 'To an insular traveler, it is a prodigiously long journey this, across the continent of America, but I found the journey a perpetual enjoyment.'[20] The trip would also forge a bond between Harry and the railway industry that, unbeknownst to him, would consume his life and career for the next two decades. It would also lay bare Harry's burning ambition to succeed, and his cozying up to wealthy tycoons revealed an opportunist streak.

Harry was part of the official group of journalists from America, Britain, and Germany chosen by Henry Villard (1835–1900), maverick owner of the Northern Pacific, to cover the opening. The German-born Villard, who emigrated to America at age 18 and made his name as a journalist during the Civil War (when he served as a war correspondent for the *Tribune*), had attracted foreign investors to complete the railway line and was keen to show off his achievement. Harry was identified as writing for the *Tribune* as well as for his former employers in London, the *Daily Chronicle* and the *Pall Mall Gazette*. Five trains, furnished 'like a first-class hotel', were chartered to carry the journalists along with 300 V.I.P.s from New York, 2,400 miles across the country to the 'golden spike' completion ceremony on September 8 in western Montana. Distinguished guests included the heads of the Bank of England and Deutsche Bank, members of the British Parliament and the German Reichstag, and engineers and scientists from both sides of the Atlantic. E. H. Talbott, editor of *The Railway Age*, the industry journal of record, also attended, blissfully unaware that Harry would buy his publication and assume the editorship in just eight years. Notably, Queen Victoria turned down the invitation, as did President Arthur, but former President Grant accepted, as did seven governors of states and territories traversed by the new rail line.[21]

Harry's coverage began with the arrival in New York of the German guests on August 25, 1883, and the British contingent on August 28. His writing style was informative but playful. Harry interviewed Heinrich Rudolf Hermann Friedrich von Gniest, the Prussian leader of the National Liberal Party, who admitted that 'his sole reasons for coming were a desire to see America and a longing for rest'.[22] Dr Herman Kreisman, Consul General of the United States in Berlin, noted that the German Government was concerned about emigration to the United States, but, Harry wrote, 'however sorry they might be to see it, it was a fact which has to be faced. He, in common with others of the party, was anxious to see the Northern Pacific lands, and should they be found good there was every reason to believe that German capitalists might invest in them and German immigrants be recommended to settle upon them.'[23] The Germans were wined and dined around Manhattan, visited Coney Island, and took a cruise up the Hudson. 'The decks of the boat were vocal with expressions of surprise at the surpassing beauty of the country', Harry reported, while 'the band of the Liederkrantz Society began playing with an energy that charmed the harps and violins on the passing excursion steamboats into silence'.[24]

The three parties of guests—American, British, and German—departed Grand Central Depot in waves beginning August 28. Harry and twenty-seven journalists left New York the following day, occupying two sleeping cars christened 'Pawnee' and 'Washita'. Overseeing the group was Eugene V. Smalley, a former *Tribune* reporter and author of a recently published official history of the Northern Pacific Railroad, commissioned by Villard. Harry's contact with Smalley would prove significant, as Smalley would become a mentor of sorts to the young man—and persuade him to settle in the West with a job on Smalley's new monthly magazine, *The Northwest*, which was backed by Villard. Among Harry's colleagues on the train were journalists from the Boston *Herald* and *Daily Advertiser*, New York and Baltimore *Sun*, *Harper's Weekly*, *Philadelphia Press*, and *St. Louis Globe Democrat*. Needless to say, as a young Englishman representing the largest circulation paper in America, Harry stood out.

Harry approached his assignment as a grand adventure and travelogue, looking for the human interest angle while recording history as it unfolded. During the stopover in Chicago, he noted on September 2 that 'the citizens are doing everything in their power to make the brief stay of the foreigners a pleasant one. They have been wined and dined.'[25] At every stop, the travellers were mobbed by journalists and well-wishers, 'the English and Americans taking naturally to the operation', but the Germans less so. 'One of them expressed the sentiment of all when he said to a reporter: "For goodness sake, leave us alone and let us rest. America is a beautiful country. You are all first-rate fellows, and sure to become the rulers of the universe; but for the sake of humanity let us alone, we want rest."'[26]

Eventually all trains converged in St Paul, Minnesota, the beginning of the Northern Pacific Railway. Fellow journalist Nicholas Mohr, representing the *Weiser Zeitung* newspaper in Bremen, Germany, was impressed. 'As we disembarked from the train, I was overcome for a moment by a kind of homesickness. Suddenly it came to me just how far I was from home', he wrote. 'For in my imagination, St. Paul was always the *ultima thule*, the last extremity of the northwestern United States, the very last refuge for beings who could find no other spot to take refuge. Now I stood at the train depot of St. Paul, surrounded by a crowd of people who stared at us with genuine interest.'[27] Huge crowds greeted the foreigners, and a four-hour parade featured 14 bands, 829 wagons, 2,213 horses, and, as Harry noted, 'thousands of men engaged in the various flour and lumber mills of the city'. President Arthur made a surprise appearance on the viewing platform, standing alongside former President Grant. Not to be outdone, St Paul's 'twin city' neighbour, Minneapolis, put on its own parade with 30,000 marchers. 'Every effort had been made to surpass the demonstration at St. Paul in the morning, for the people of St. Paul and Minneapolis seem to hate each other as heartily as ever a Guelph hated a Ghieline [*sic*]', Harry observed, injecting humour into his reporting. 'Yet, though the procession was on a splendid scale, though the banquet was irreproachable and the scenery on Lake Calhoun was lovely, it is a melancholy fact that what the guests talked of most afterwards was that President Villard in his excellent speech forgot the name of the town by which he was being entertained and again and again addressed the company as "citizens of Minionopolis," by which it may be inferred the Minneapolitans were not flattered.'[28] Joining the train in St Paul for the journey west was a wealthy business associate of Villard's, Minneapolis streetcar magnate Thomas Lowry. One wonders if Harry made the acquaintance of his millionaire future father-in-law; he would marry Lowry's daughter eight years later.

As the trains headed west, Harry was notably entranced by the majestic scenery, particularly the Badlands of the Dakota Territory ('a country bad by name rather than by nature') and the Rocky Mountains. There's a strong sense that Harry was falling in love with this new country. 'All down the western side the slopes are more gentle and the foliage more varied, the landscape is greener and in the delightful atmosphere which makes us all eat twice as much and sleep twice as much and we feel twice as wide awake and strong during the day as at home', he wrote. 'We envied the brown-faced, broad hatted men who shouted their welcomes at us from the small mountain depots as we passed, for living in such a paradise.' Target practice passed the time. 'At one point on the mountains a member of the party really shot a ground squirrel,' Harry reported. 'All backs were turned to the Rocky mountains while the six inches of mangled fluff was being examined.' He added that skunks were common; when run over by the train, 'many a time has a suffocating smell waked me in mid-sleep; nor will any amount of ventilation purify the atmosphere for some hours afterwards'. Harry found the contrast between the cosseted train passengers and the locals amusing. 'At one place alone, where we stopped, the track was lined with a miscellaneous crowd of brown-skinned western Americans, red man and yellow man, while out of the windows in the train protruded the heads of Englishman and German, and men from the Eastern states, while on the platforms thronged the black waiters and porters of the Pullman cars', Harry wrote. 'Altogether it was probably as strange a mixture as has been seen together for many a long day.' He enjoyed the cowboys: 'those dare-devils of the plains appeared to take great delight in putting their ponies to their highest speed and dashing alongside the train, waving their broad sombreros in answer to the flaunting handkerchiefs from the train'. The Indian tribes and imported Chinese labourers were curiosities; in the briefest of comments on race, Harry observed 'Since we left New York, to say little of Europe, we have passed a good many varieties of man.'[29]

In Grey Cliff the party witnessed the war-dance of 100 Crow Indians, so-called 'savages', upon whose hunting grounds the Northern Pacific traversed. Most of the visitors, Harry noted, came away with a souvenir of a tomahawk or an elk's tooth. 'After the dance so strong was the influence upon the spectators that a large party in one of the trains rolled themselves up in blankets and stuck feathers in their heads and went through the cars, while everyone else was going to bed, yelping and "how! how!" ing the while,' Harry observed, 'so that the leader of the band was not far from being shot by one of the occupants who began to feel creepy and queer about the scalp.'[30] Indeed, the environment and alien cultures had a profound impact upon the visitors from the East— Harry included. 'Put any man who has gone about in thin shoes all his life into a pair of thick Wellington's and he at once becomes twice the man (so far as self reliance goes) he was before', he observed.

Under pressure to file stories, Harry displayed his creativity, writing about 'Northern Pacific Nomenclature'. He began by praising the great divisions of the lands traversed by the Northern Pacific as 'singularly fortunate in their names. Minnesota, Dakota, Montana and Idaho are indigenous words musical in sound and poetic in significance.'

He understood the 'patriotic reverence' displayed in naming the westernmost territory after George Washington, as were towns after Bismarck and Gladstone, given the extent of European immigration to the region. But he lamented the missed naming opportunities in other areas as vast new stretches of land were populated. 'Poverty of invention and lack of imagination are attested by gratuitous imitations such as New-Chicago, New-Buffalo, New-Salem, Detroit, Cleveland, Moscow, Lisbon and Geneva, and by a long series of the Smith-Brown-Robinson order—Youngs, Taylor, Sprague, Kurtz, Steele, Andrews, Dickinson, Dawson, Thomson, Kimberley, Aldrich, Belknap, and so on, until the resources of the average business directory are exhausted', he opined, not to mention some 'artificial French derivatives' in Idaho such as 'Coeur d'Alene'. But the vast Washington Territory—the future state—offered hope, ripe with mellifluous Indian place names such as Tacoma, Seattle, and Walla Walla. 'The great falls of Spokane', Harry wrote, 'have as legitimate if not as musical an Indian name as Niagara.'[31]

'A New Steam Highway Across the American Continent' was the banner headline across the front page of the *Tribune* on September 9, below which was a large map of the Northern Pacific Railroad and its various connections. Harry's article alerted readers that the 'last spike—a golden one' would be driven and the route formally opened. The following day, his reporting was rather straightforward, consisting mainly of lengthy quotations from the many official speeches. Frederick Billings, former president of the Northern Pacific, was especially florid in his remarks: 'There were brave men before Agamemnon. There have been transcontinental roads before this one. There have been last spikes and last spikes, but there never was a more significant last spike driven on the continent than this one; never one which had more work and faith behind it; never one with a greater future before it.'[32]

*   *   *   *   *

The Villard roadshow did not end with the driving of the golden spike. While some of the guests returned to the East, the majority continued on to Portland, Oregon, the Northern Pacific terminus, arriving on September 12, 1883. A two-mile-long parade greeted the guests. Harry quoted one guest on the hospitality: 'Well Chicago treated us well and so did St Paul and every place since then, but we have never been so well handled as this since we left New York.'[33] From Portland, Villard arranged tours of the Oregon and Washington lands as well as a cruise up the coast to Vancouver. The three-week excursion afforded Harry a more intimate glimpse of life on the frontier, and whetted his appetite for more. On September 23, he reported from the town of Walla Walla, Washington, where all talk was about the wheat crop. 'No one can see the country as I have seen it without hesitating to concede any other section a higher rank in wheat production in five years' time', he predicted in his article, which was not published in the *Tribune* until November 4.[34] Amusingly, Harry joined the locals in voting in the local election—even though he was not yet a U.S. citizen. 'My vote was quite illegal,' he recalled years later, 'but my friends (and every one in a small frontier town is one's friend) were all going to vote and told me to come along and vote too. The election, which was of the most friendly character, like the election of a club committee, proved to be closely contested, one man getting in (as City Attorney or Town Clerk or something) only by a single vote—my vote.' The winner was Samuel Henry Piles, an attorney who went on to represent the new state of Washington in the U.S. Senate. Consequently, Harry concluded, 'I have never seen any cause to regret that illegal vote',[35] no doubt as Piles was a Republican.

On September 25, en route back East, the journalists stopped in Butte, Montana, 'to see the largest and most prominent mining camp in the world', according to *The Montana Standard*. Harry joined in and descended into the copper mine and enjoyed the evening's entertainment at the Silver Bow Club. In Helena, he was interviewed by the local *Independent Record* on September 28 as he was a representative from London, 'the money centre of the world—the centre of all enterprise— the fulcrum on which rested the lever of modern improvement'. To the reporter, Harry 'spoke at some length of the impression made upon the mind of an Englishman by his trip through this country. Everywhere he had seen evidences of wealth and prosperity. He could not compare one State or Territory with another; State lines were imaginary lines to him.' This was good news to Helena, which benefited from foreign investment of so-called 'English gold'. Harry pledged that 'he would take back to England the very kindest remembrances of America and her people, especially of the great and generous west'.[36] One wonders if it was here that Harry caught the mining bug—and planned to stay.

*　*　*　*　*

In fact, Harry was already thinking about not returning to England. As he resumed his duties back East on the *Tribune*, he was distracted, contrasting the bustling, noisy, crowded city with the grandeur of the West, its wide-open spaces brimming with hope and optimism. The American character and can-do spirit had impressed him deeply. Twenty years later, Harry reflected on 'the notion that every American is, without any special training, by mere gift of birthright, competent to any task that may be set him'.

The same spirit guides almost every young American who drifts West to tackle hopefully whatever job the gods may send. The cases wherein he has any destiny marked out for him or any especial preference as to the lines on which his future career shall run (except that he may hope ultimately to be President of the United States) are comparatively few. In ten years, he may be a grocer or a banker or a dry-goods merchant or a real-estate man or a lawyer. Whatever he is, more likely than not ten years later he will be something else.

'What is your trade?' is the first question which an Englishman asks of an applicant for employment; and the answer will probably be truthful and certainly unimaginative.

'What can you do?' the American enquires under the same circumstances. 'Most anything. What have you got to do?' is commonly the reply.[37]

So perhaps it is not surprising that when another major story broke out in the West, a gold rush not far from where he had visited, Harry accepted the assignment with enthusiasm. Had he already decided that his destiny lay in the American West? Perhaps, too, Harry had read Mark Twain's 1872 account of his own gold mining adventure with his brother, *Roughing It*. Twain was entranced by the idea of travel ('I had never been away from home, and that word "travel" had a seductive charm for me') and envisioned picking up 'nuggets of gold and silver on the hillside' and becoming 'very rich'.[38] In the end, Twain's account offered not wealth but grand adventure, as Harry himself would soon experience.

Gold rushes or 'booms' were common in the late nineteenth century and often lasted only a year or two in a particular region of the West (until the claims were exhausted). Gold was discovered in the Coeur d'Alene area of Idaho Territory in late 1883, prompting a flurry of excitement and publicity. Heavy snow in the region closed the mining field over the winter. The *St. Paul Globe* reported on January 3, 1884 that 'several companies are already formed, and over 1,000 men are on the spot waiting for the spring to open the region. It is estimated by midsummer that 20,000 prospectors and miners will be in the field. Specimens of ore brought out by prospectors are exceedingly rich.' In the gulches of the north fork of the Coeur d'Alene River, as well as in the Eagle, Pritchard, and Beaver Creeks, $25–$40 per man per day of gold were being panned out, a king's ransom equivalent to up to $1,000 today. Such speculation was a boon to the Northern Pacific, which had the only rail lines in the vicinity. Whether or not Harry had plans to return West, he would have jumped at the opportunity to cover a genuine gold rush. It would also further his relationship with Villard, the first of several wealthy tycoons whom Harry would befriend to advance his own ambitions.

Harry set out sometime in December 1883. While ostensibly he was representing the *Tribune*, which funded his journey, he also took a freelance job with Eugene V. Smalley's new monthly journal, *The Northwest*. Smalley had evidently taken a shine to Harry during the Villard trip and, during Harry's stopover in Minneapolis, offered him the title of 'Western Editor'. *The Northwest*, considered a semi-official propaganda organ of the Northern Pacific (and likely financed by Villard), contained a lively mix of articles on travel and nature, short stories, and practical information for would-be prospectors and settlers.[39] After a few weeks in the Twin Cities, as the Coeur d'Alene area was snowbound and virtually inaccessible, Harry headed West to revisit towns in the vicinity of the gold rush. First stop was a return stay in Walla Walla, where the local newspaper noted that Harry would spend ten days getting acquainted with the town and surroundings. Harry, the paper claimed, 'predicts a very great immigration into this region next year, and says that at the Minneapolis hotel, where he has been living during five weeks lately, Washington Territory was the topic of all the conversation among the guests'. The paper added, 'Mr. Robinson says that if he were to remain permanently in America, he would choose to live in Washington Territory, because of the great activity of its future, and because the climate and other natural characteristics, especially of the western part, so resemble those of England.'[40] This is intriguing, as Harry was already thinking of settling down in the American West, no doubt with Smalley's encouragement. In his debut article for *The Northwest*, 'Walla Walla: The Wheat Metropolis of Eastern Washington', in the February 1884 edition, Harry heaped praise on the town and its location within 'perhaps the richest stretch of wheat-land in the world'.[41] 'The first view of Walla Walla is an unmitigated surprise to the Eastern-bred visitor', he wrote. 'The sudden discovery in the heart of this great waste of their orderly little town, more resembling in its main street some slow-grown New England village than the conventional Western city, with its few months' growth, is like coming upon one of those living frogs which are found embedded in solid rock.' Harry was particularly impressed that in a town of 5,000 people there were three daily and three weekly newspapers. 'No man (and certainly no one who is a correspondent himself) can deny that an indigenous press—in moderation—whether daily or weekly is a blessing to any community, and above all to a young and growing one', he observed. 'It is safe to prophesy that of those who choose Walla Walla in the coming spring to be their future home none will be disappointed or sorry for their selection unless they are terribly hard to please.'

Walla Walla was, apparently, the place to be. The *Courier-Journal* of Lexington, Kentucky, referred to Harry in a January 20, 1884 story about farming in the 'Inland Kingdom', and how people from all over America come, stake a claim, and hope to get rich. The article focused on two young men from Brooklyn, 'innocent of all knowledge of farms, not to mention wild lands', who landed in town with their possessions, including a plough. They hired a man at $30 a month to help them load their four-horse wagon. 'It is of such stuff that millionaires and solid statesmen are made',[42] the article said. The unnamed reporter proceeded to relate that 'my friend H. P. Robinson, who came over from England to see how our country is getting along and to write about it, was also there to load the plow'. Curiously, the Brooklyn duo may have been friends of Harry's, perhaps inspired by his enthusiasm to join him in the West. The article continued: 'That night we talked long over American opportunities, and he [Harry] thoughtfully suggested that the fellow who went to help them at $30 a month and no chance to spend it, may be as rich as the young men themselves if he choose; and so he may.' Such was the American dream! In closing, the story of the hour, the gold strike in Coeur d'Alene, was mentioned by Harry: 'I predict a degree of discovery and enthusiasm in the early spring that will surpass anything in Colorado or California.... Already there are men "wintering" in Portland and in all the comfortable towns between here and the mines, ready to push forward as soon as the weather there will admit of work.'

'Wintering' ended early for Harry, who had returned to Minnesota. On February 23, the *St. Paul Globe* reported that 'H.P. Robinson, a representative of the New York *Tribune*, left this city yesterday for Montana'. For an overview of what Harry faced that winter, we turn to Smalley and his retrospective article for *Century Magazine* in October 1884.[43] 'Of all the stampedes in old times or recent years, the Great Coeur d'Alene stampede of the winter and spring of 1884 was perhaps the most remarkable', he observed.

> The country it invaded was less known than any other part of the Rocky Mountain chain. No roads traversed it; there was not even a bridle trail. To make matters worse, the entire region was covered with a forest growth of cedar, pine, and fir, so dense as to resemble a Hindustan jungle. "Begorra, ye'll find the trees growin' as thick as a bunch of matches," said an old Irish miner, whom I encountered on my way to the region, and he did not exaggerate. To make matters worse, the snowfalls are phenomenal, and the stampede began in the dead of winter, when the snow was from twelve to twenty feet deep in the mountain passes. Yet, in spite of these obstacles, over five thousand men made their way into the heart of the Coeur d'Alene Mountains during the months of January, February, and March. With them went scores of women of a certain class, dressed in men's clothes and hauling their feminine wardrobes on sleds.

Smalley said the desire to get rich quick was as strong as the longing for adventure. 'To be a "stampeder" is to be something of a hero, and the wild life of a new mining camp is full of charms to those who like it', he wrote. 'Even men of education and of intellectual fiber discover a fascination in sleeping on pine boughs in a log cabin, and living on bacon, beans, and dried apples, pawing around in the dirt, and listening to the grotesque tales, the boasting and blarney, and the fantastic oaths of a mining camp.' Such a man was Harry.

* * * * *

Harry's destinations were the twin settlements of Eagle City and Murray along the Pritchard Creek in Idaho Territory, where the first gold strike was made the previous summer. The Northern Pacific stopped 40 miles from Eagle City at Thompson's Falls, whereupon prospectors proceeded on foot, dragging their goods on toboggans over deep snow along makeshift trails in the steep mountains. Eagle City grew tenfold in six months, to more than a thousand residents in February 1884. Among the 'stampeders' in search of riches was the legendary Wyatt Earp (three years after the infamous Gunfight at the OK Corral in Tombstone, Arizona), who brought his wife and brothers and opened a dance hall and saloon called the White Elephant.[44] Molly Burdan, known as 'Molly B. Damned', was the kind-hearted madam of the red light district. Smalley recalled Eagle City as 'a wild, strange settlement' where 'everyone was gay and hopeful'. Of ten buildings or tents, nine were drinking saloons. Lawyers, doctors, and tradesmen followed, all pitching their tents. 'Almost all callings are represented except those of teaching and preaching. There are no children, and Sunday is abolished', Smalley noted, but 'the flapjacks were beyond criticism'. Prospectors panned for gold in the creek and dug for it in the ground. Within six months, Eagle City was pronounced 'dry', and prospectors moved upstream to Murray. Smalley described Murray as 'a hideous half-mile long street of huts, shanties, and tents... A more unattractive place than Murray I have seldom seen... Nevertheless, gold was being shipped out every day by Wells Fargo & Co.'s express, and new discoveries were constantly reported.'

As Harry made his way to the region, he filed his first dispatch on the stampede for the *New York Tribune* on March 1, and it was reprinted in the April 1884 edition of *The Northwest*. Reporting from Miles City, Montana, roughly 700 miles west of St Paul, and 650 miles from Coeur d'Alene—the halfway point on his journey—he spotted his first miners:

Just as the train was moving out of Miles City amid prodigious hallooing and splashing, a wagon came round the corner with half a dozen men in it all up to their necks in bundles of blankets, rubber boots, and buffalo robes. They were a party of old miners who had come by stage from Deadwood, having been in every mining craze of the last thirty years, and were now determined to 'get to Coeur d'Alene, or bust.'[45]

Deadwood, South Dakota, was the epicentre of another famous gold rush of a decade earlier. Harry observed that 'fully three fourths' of his people on the train were similar old hands, not 'tenderfeet' like him, and all were heading now for Eagle City, christened the 'New Leadville' after the Colorado town where gold was also found in 1859. 'Many of them had retired quietly to farming or stock-raising, far away from civilization, and fancied they had quite gotten over all danger of catching gold fever again', Harry noted. 'But here they were, having sold out their ranches and everything they possessed except their blankets and their picks— eager only to get into the mines before the rush set in.' His fellow passengers were a lively bunch, to say the least:

> Altogether it was a riotous car-full, and not such as is usually found on a train from the East. So a gentleman who joined us at Thompson's Falls (which is the easternmost of the various trails into the mines) found out. He was a miner, every inch of him, and a drunken one, too. He burst into the car with a whoop, a whiskey bottle in one hand and a revolver in the other, and planting himself in the center of the gangway, announced himself as the Bamboo Chief and eager to fight the company.

> He doubtless expected to find the car full of mild-mannered Easterners, and must have been astonished when a stalwart miner arose and without a word laid one hand on the scruff of his neck and the other on another part of his person, and carried him bodily, whiskey bottle, revolver and all, out to the platform and then dropped him into a snow-drift.

> Such little incidents (for it was not the only one of the kind) only served to cheer up the company the more, and before Trout Creek (at present the most feasible trail into Eagle City) was reached there was not a miner in that car who was not firmly convinced that he had at last struck the camp where the fortune for which he had washed and dug so hard before was at last to be found.

One can detect the budding fiction writer in Harry in these dispatches. He concluded with a warning to readers: since nothing can be done while snow is on the ground, don't head to Eagle City unless you're setting up a business. Otherwise you'll sit around for weeks and spend your money. 'It is not likely that all the warnings of all the major and minor prophets together would have much effect in stemming the stream which is already flowing in such volume', he observed. 'But if one warning can be of any use, here it is—wait!' Harry did just that, spending most of the month of March in Spokane Falls, one of the many boom towns in the area.

Harry made a circular tour of these towns as he waited for the snow to melt. He dubbed Belknap a 'City of Millionaires' where most of the prospectors were foreigners like him, including Scots who knew how to use Winchester rifles. 'It is a novel experience to live in a city the population of which consists entirely of millionaires, and it is good for one's self-respect', Harry wrote on March 30.[46] On April 20 in Thompson's Falls, which like Belknap was situated at the edge of a fifty-mile mountain trail into Eagle City, Harry marvelled at the astonishing growth of the town:

> When I passed through this place something more than three weeks ago, there was nothing here but the forest primeval. Now there is a town of nearly 2,000 inhabitants; that is, if those can be said to 'inhabit' a place who eat meals at irregular intervals in stray restaurants and spend the nights curled up in their blankets under the neighboring pine trees. And this is how a third of the population of Thompson's Falls live to-day.[47]

Amid some stunning scenery—'the view is one which probably no mountain range outside of the Alps, the Himalayas and the Andes could match'—Harry noted the transience of the place. 'This city which has sprung up here in less than a month may be utterly deserted again in another. Who knows when the other "shortest route" to the mines will be discovered?' In the meantime, Harry noted that of the seventy 'aggressively yellow frame houses' spread about the forest, forty were saloons. Gambling was rampant, with tables set up outside: 'The pine trees drop their cones upon faro-tables, and all day long the road outside the hotel where I am writing this has been blocked by a crowd round a species of roulette table.' Harry delighted in writing about 'what is called in irony the "accommodation" of the hotels':

> Of course in a place which is only three weeks old and which increases at the rate of 500 a week in population, the building fails to keep pace with the growth, and therefore the 'hotels' are all overcrowded. This morning in spite of the early hour—for people out here are most dishearteningly early risers—I had to wait while exactly twenty-seven people washed themselves before I could get a turn at the small tin basin on a chair which was replenished with water from an old whiskey barrel and which each man had to go and empty into the road when he had finished. One towel, moreover, is the allowance *per diem* to the whole crowd.

In what would become a minor obsession of Harry's, he focused on mealtime:

> For breakfast (at which 200 people were served) we had beefsteak, corned beef, pork and baked beans and coffee. For dinner we had beefsteak, corned beef, pork and baked beans and coffee. For supper we had

beefsteak, corned beef, pork and baked beans and coffee; and I can make a pretty shrewd guess at what we will have for breakfast in the morning.

On in the future somewhere—probably at dinner to-morrow—there is a prospect of relief, for soon after dinner today an old, old Indian emerged from the forest staggering under the weight of a fine cottontail deer which was slung over his shoulders. There was an immediate rush toward him from every hotel and restaurant within sight, but as he first appeared exactly opposite our door, our caterer got a few yards start of the others, and before they could explain to the Indian that they were willing to overbid him, he had thrust two dollars and a half into the old man's hand and was dragging him toward the hotel amid cheers. And the prospect of fresh venison has enlivened the hotel enormously, it being expected that a large crowd will be turned away from the doors at dinner time tomorrow.

Setting out on the trail from Thompson's Falls, Harry arrived in Eagle City and published his first dispatch on May 4. He noted the huge number of dead animals that littered the trail, cattle and beasts of burden, and recounted 'the most pathetic sight I have seen... There on a steep mountain side with his legs stretched across the trail lay an old prospector, gray-haired and with a long gray beard, and his face weather-beaten and deeply lined with years of hard mountain work.'[48] Harry's party thought he was dead, but he wasn't. He had been lying there for three days, barely raising himself to eat now and then.

By his side were the smouldering remains of a fire which had been made for him by a passer-by and which each man who passed (he said about a dozen men a day came by) re-made. His only belongings were a little flour, some bacon, a can of beans and a small frying-pan in which he was melting some snow over the fire to make drinking water. He had no blankets or covering for the frosty nights, but that he declared he did not need and refuses our offer of coats and vests to help to keep him warm.

It was a piteous sight—the old man lying there on the bleak mountain side, with above and below and on all sides the level stretch of desolate looking snow sparsely dotted with somber pines and cedars. Below his feet lay a dark, thickly wooded ravine, and beyond that and facing him tier after tier of wild, snow-clad mountain ranges, and the dull April sky overhead. But what could we do but make up the fire, rinse out his frying-pan and replenish it with cleaner snow? On either side of him lay ten miles of country over which it was all we could do to drag ourselves and over which no horse or mule could travel.

Harry noted that work crews were clearing snow and cutting fallen timber on the trail, so perhaps the old man would be rescued. Still, he concluded, 'It will be a long time before those who saw him lying there will forget it. Only two days ago a man died from exposure and the sufferings he went through, having lost his way on this same trail. And yet it is now said to be the easiest entrance to the mines.' Further along on the trail, Harry encountered a happier episode. A prospector's wagon had overturned on the trail, and as a result all subsequent wagons were banned. Instead of feeling sorry for himself, the man made the best of it. He laid out his provisions and set up a makeshift saloon, selling whiskey and cigars to travellers. He earned $6 a day, 'and had found the time pleasant enough sitting on the stump and smoking his pipe all day with six feet of snow piled up around him'.

In Eagle City, Harry could barely conceal his revulsion at the dire conditions in this self-proclaimed 'metropolis' of 1,500 people ('There is a metropolis to every hundred miles throughout the Northwest'). Many had endured the harsh winter in isolated log huts or tents, with fifteen to twenty feet of snow around them. 'The characteristics of the region being so utterly unknown, none of the adventurers knew what they were going to face. None made adequate preparations for the trial', Harry noted.

> One man told me that he lived for two months on bacon alone—no flour, nor beans nor coffee to relieve it, and without any means of shooting the deer of which he saw plenty almost every day. Another on a perilous journey for a new supply of food was forced to struggle on for ten days without provisions of any kind and only kept himself alive by eating the pine moss and sucking snow.[49]

Once the half-starved came to town, Harry noted that 'this is no myth, the generosity of miners. "Never to let a white man want for food so long as you have half a meal ahead," is the standing maxim of camp life.' Unfortunately it had also given rise to a professional beggar class; fully half of the men in Eagle City did not earn a living. Everything cost at least one dollar, including one night's so-called lodging:

> The accommodation consisting generally of a share of a bunk strewn with cedar boughs and a couple of blankets, sometimes of a small canvas cot and blankets, sometimes only of a corner of a floor and a few cedar boughs. A sheet is a thing I have not seen for three weeks, while the arrival of a bedstead in camp would be a thing to chronicle in the newspaper, and the bedstead itself would probably be put on exhibition at one of the saloons.

Harry was not used to this degree of discomfort, even at the tender age of 24. He proceeded to obsess about his meals, as usual, which also cost at least one dollar:

> There are two kinds of meals: the ordinary meal of bacon, pork chop (sometimes on a Monday beefsteak), beans and coffee, which is a dollar, and the extra meal which has two eggs added and costs 50 cents more. Hitherto I have never regarded the potato as a thing deserving of much

respect, but two weeks in camp have altered my feelings with regard to it, and I will never speak slightingly of potatoes again.…

Another vegetable of which one learns to think well out here is the bean—of the Boston baked variety—but for very different reasons. Pork and beans are the quail and manna of this wilderness; and the manna is of distinctly more importance than the quails, for no man ever pretended that he ate pork and beans for the sake of the former.

But Harry was not on holiday, after all. On May 11, he got his hands dirty in an article entitled 'Panning Out Gold: Cleaning Up of a Coeur d'Alene Placer'. This was a sort of primer for readers unfamiliar with the technicalities of searching for gold and working a sluice box. 'It is much like pottering about all day in a hole in the ground up to your ankles in dirty water, and with a long-handled prod and shovel in your hand, with which you scrape and prod and shovel at a dirty surface of rock',[50] Harry explained. 'There is nothing apparently which gold hates more than to be found.' He proceeded to describe the process:

> The claim on which I have been working is perhaps as happily situated as any on the district for working, but even on it two men had found it five hard weeks' work, what with clearing timber, shoveling snow, and drain-ditching, to get the decks cleared for action. Then a gang of four men had worked for five days at clearing a piece of bed rock which is eleven feet down and putting in sluices, and this morning at 6 o'clock when I joined them they were about to begin the sixth.
>
> There had been, therefore, nearly a hundred days' work done on the claim—and hard work too, with ten hours of it to the day—without any hope of, or attempt being made at, getting out a cent of gold, beyond the washing of an occasional panful of soil. No, the gold does not lie about the ground in nuggets with handles to them.

After hours of back-breaking scraping of mud in every nook and cranny, the sluices were cleaned. 'An "Ah!" of satisfaction runs through the party as the gold is exposed lying in shining drifts and hillocks against the riffles in the true bottom of the sluices', Harry revealed. 'How tempting it looks! There is a good deal of black sand and a few pebbles mixed with it, but for the most part it is pure gold in coarse dust and nuggets running as high as three and four dollars apiece.' In the end, the day's labour yielded just 1.5 pounds of gold, for a value of $250, or wages of $2.50 per day per man, 'not half the ordinary wages of labor in these parts', Harry noted. But the men were not discouraged, as a few days later they earned $1,100 ($25,000 today) from a claim nearby, and in the days since Harry wrote his article, another $2,000 as they worked their twenty-acre claim. 'As I tramped back to Eagle City I confessed to myself that in spite of the mud and the water, the heavy rubber-boots and overalls, and all the hard work to be gone through, there remains something undeniably fascinating in mining, and the last half hour of a cleaning up with the first sight of the bright gold makes up for many disagreeable things endured', Harry said.[51] The young man was, evidently, converted. He was uncertain how to break the good news to his bunkmate at the hotel, 'a gentleman from Portland who came out two months ago with an elaborate outfit, has prospected a score or so of miles of country; has sunk eighty-three holes and a good deal of money without finding a color of gold the whole time. Tomorrow he goes back to Portland disgusted.'

Harry remained in Eagle City for nearly three months. On June 20, he filed a disturbing story: 'First Shooting in Camp: Will It Bring Luck to the Coeur d'Alene?' Harry grappled with understanding the lawlessness of the region and its twisted idea of justice. 'Every miner with any pretension to education knows that no camp can be prosperous until at least one man has been shot in its streets', he discovered. 'Prosperity in a mining camp is a kind of mandrake which springs from the blood of murdered men. Not to be aware of this argues gross ignorance in a miner—great want of knowledge of the world.'

> No great public work, it has been said, for the benefit of mankind can, even in civilized countries, be firmly built unless the blood of its best workmen go to cement its foundations; and from the building of the walls of Rome to the building of the Brooklyn Bridge, there have been but too many fatal examples of its truth. The distinctive peculiarity, however, in the case of a mining camp is that no death is of any avail unless it be brought about by a pistol-shot or a knife-thrust.[52]

Eagle City, however, lasted six months without a death; 'this showed, as the miners agree, no small spirit of forbearance in the citizens', despite locals named 'Red-handed Jim', 'Pistol Dick', and 'Quick-shot Sam'. But that had now ended; 'this death was precisely that which is met by three men out of every four who die in new mining camps'. Harry proceeded to recount the story in gripping detail.

> He was a young man of a family well known and honored along the coast (but the society of a camp has but small respect for persons), owning considerable interests in the mines, and having recently made a good sum of money by the sale of a quartz ledge. The man who killed him was known to have the blood of more than one man on his hands already.

> They quarreled about a woman, and the one was shot on the sidewalk where he stood, dying ten minutes afterward with an oath upon his lips. A few feet from him, in the gutter, lay the woman about whom he had

fought, too senseless with drink, as was at once seen, to be of any use as a witness. That was at 3 o'clock in the morning. At 10 o'clock an inquest was held, but the coroner was too tipsy to officiate, and the deputy who took his place was scarcely sober enough to go through the barest formalities of the occasion. Such as it was, however, the inquest was over before noon, and at 3 o'clock the same afternoon (scarcely twelve hours after he was shot) the dead man was buried in a vacant lot in the city.

A lawyer was pressed into service to say a few words of Scripture as the dead man was buried. Harry proceeded to describe the cross-examination of the shooter the next day, with the woman present, 'her rich crimson velvet dress looking strangely misplaced and out of sympathy with the occasion and the place'.

Not much interest was taken in the proceedings, for no one doubted what the result would be. It did not seem to be anybody's business to be particularly sorry for the dead man, and from a purely moral standpoint there is nothing offensive to a miner in the mere shooting of a man. Such code of ethics as the miner has he acts up to scrupulously. But it is a curious code, and in no point more curious than with regard to the taking of human life.

'When I shoot a man I don't expect to be punished for it,' we may frequently hear it said; 'but as soon as I steal a dollar I want to be hanged right off.' Stealing, indeed, is the cardinal crime in the miner's moral calendar; and the most aggravated form of theft is the purloining of another man's gold-dust—the immediate results of honest toil. On the other hand, stealing another man's land—or 'jumping a claim'—is looked upon differently; chiefly so because it requires courage of a certain kind . . . So with homicide; even the worst of 'bad men' (by which is meant men who are always ready to use their pistols) will seldom shoot an unarmed man; and when both combatants have 'guns' in their hands, each is shooting in self-defense. The one who kills the other is not a murderer; he is only the better of the two. In the present case not only was a revolver found in the dead man's hand, but three chambers of it had been discharged. That alone was quite enough to acquit his killer. So the proceedings in the smoky little cabin were watched with only a languid interest.

Harry noted that 'the formal farce' dragged on, and two days later, 'the slayer is drinking his whiskey as usual at his favorite bar'.

It is only three days now since the dead man was alive, but no one talks of him any more. It is only with an effort that the majority of the camp could recall his name. When men mention the affair it is not as the destruction of a life, as the staining of one man's hands with blood and the sending of another man to his last account; it is merely as the 'first shooting in camp,' as an event which is to bring luck to the Coeur d'Alene mines.

It is no wonder that, with dramatic experiences such as these, Harry would be inspired to write short stories. But for now, with a critical article like this, Harry would be *persona non grata* in Eagle City once this article was published in the *Tribune* (intriguingly, not until July 13, three weeks after it was filed). No wonder, then, that this was Harry's last dispatch and he left Eagle City. The *Tribune* in a leading article on July 13 cited Harry's story and condemned the 'travesty of justice' by the 'regular frontier ruffians'. The paper noted that the frontier was a mysterious place ('Where the tides of civilization from the East and West meet, there is yet a good deal of roughness') but change was imminent: 'Happily this kind of thing cannot last long now, even in the mining districts. Communication with civilization by rail and telegraph comes so rapidly that justice soon gets a grip there even on murderers.'

*   *   *   *   *

At some point during his stay in Eagle City, Harry decided not to return to New York, or England for that matter. His time on the frontier had changed him, and he embraced the opportunities that lay in the booming West, just as thousands of immigrants from Europe had before him. With his commission from Smalley, he continued to report for *The Northwest*, while deciding to make his home in Minneapolis, which had emerged as the cosmopolitan gateway to the West and a manufacturing powerhouse specializing in lumber and, especially, milling (hence its nickname, 'The Flour City'). There he also took a job as a reporter on the *Minneapolis Tribune* which, like its New York namesake, was solidly Republican, to Harry's taste. In December 1884, Harry was on the road again, this time to the town of Lisbon in Dakota Territory, where the local newspaper said he was reporting for three publications: *The Northwest*, the *Minneapolis Tribune*, and the *Pioneer Press*, based out of St Paul. Lisbon, the local newspaper reported (a clipping Harry, tellingly, saved in his scrapbook) was 'one of the most promising towns he has seen in the entire Northwest. Mr. Robinson is a very refined and social gentleman whom it is a pleasure to meet.' Heading into Montana, Harry ran afoul of the weather. Years later he recalled 'Christmas snowed in in a train in Montana, where we took exercise in shoveling snow and kept ourselves alive on cheese and crackers, till, late that night, a rescue party on snow-shoes brought relief in the form of canned goods and things more Christmaslike than melted snow to drink.'[53] Clearly, Harry was enjoying himself.

In the *Minneapolis City Directory* for 1885, in his first mention, Harry was listed as 'reporter Minneapolis Tribune' and residing at Judd House, an imposing Italianate mansion in the heart of downtown. It was built in 1874 as the private home for William Sheldon Judd, a lumber tycoon, and was a showcase of design and luxurious fittings, including a central staircase of polished black walnut, double-arched plate glass windows, an observation tower, and a private bathroom, the first in the city. Judd sold the house in 1882, and it became 'the most fashionable boarding house in Minneapolis and the residence of many people of social standing'.[54]

How could Harry, newly arrived in town and not yet a man of means (and likely not to be receiving assistance from home), afford a flat in Judd House, which would have made him the envy of his peers at the *Tribune*? The answer may be more social than financial. Judd House's most prominent resident at this time was John S. Bradstreet (1845–1914), owner of a furniture and design firm and a leading light of the city's fledgling arts and crafts scene. Bradstreet made Judd House the epicentre of society, a place known for lavish parties and intellectual gatherings. He took a shine to the 25-year-old, well-mannered Englishman, a bachelor like himself, and they became fast friends. As such, Bradstreet could have brokered a reduced rent for Harry in Judd House. Years later, Harry recalled his first encounter with the town dandy. It happened by chance; Harry had passed by the windows of Bradstreet's showroom and wandered in.

> As I entered, a tall (yes, quite tall) and thin (decidedly thin) man, imperfectly concealed behind a large mustache, came forward and wanted to know what he could do for me. Well, he could show me things. I couldn't afford to buy anything; but I did want to look, and, if he didn't think me impertinent, I wanted to know what on earth that place was doing in that precise latitude and longitude.
>
> He did not seem to think me impertinent and was as nice as a man could be. He showed me everything as if he liked it, and when he found what a willing, if ignorant, interest I took in it all, he asked me where I was stopping and promised to come and look me up. Incidentally he told me that he was Bradstreet. He looked me up next day—and thenceforward I ceased to feel like a stranger in Minneapolis. No man was ever kinder to a wanderer than John S. Bradstreet was to me.[55]

Bradstreet, as decorator to the wealthy, would have introduced Harry to all the important people, and invited him to all the parties. Harry could have had no better friend. To Bradstreet, a New Englander by birth (and a direct descendant of William Bradford, Governor of Plymouth Colony), Harry was a refined and intriguing link to the Old World and, no doubt, a breath of fresh air in the hinterland. Harry would have been present to console him when the occasional cretin popped in, as Harry recalled: 'An excellent and wealthy citizen of Minneapolis—an admirable man in other ways—who referred to the choice bronzes which Bradstreet was putting into his house, with infinite consideration of every detail of effect, as "them pots."' Harry paid tribute to his new friend in the January 1885 edition of *The Northwest*, writing on the population growth of Minneapolis. 'Just as one can gauge the amount of cultivation in any individual by the style of decoration of the room, or house in which he lives, so one can estimate the level of good taste in the population of any city by the class of furniture and decorative upholstery displayed for sale in its stores', Harry observed. 'A mining camp cannot support an art furnishing company, any more than Paris or New York will be satisfied with a stock in trade of deal tacks and arsenic green wall papers.'[56] Bradstreet, Thurber & Company's store, Harry noted, 'is to-day on a level with any art-furnishing rooms in Broadway or Bond Street. Besides being a witness to the good taste of a section of the people of Minneapolis, such a store is also of immense benefit as a civilizing influence upon the rest, for to one who has never had an opportunity of studying the principles of artistic decoration, a first visit to such a place is a revelation.'[57]

As Harry expanded his horizons, both professionally and socially, he also made his first foray into fiction, following in the footsteps of his brothers Phil and Kay. Moonlighting from his day job as a newspaper reporter, Harry's motivation may have been the extra cash, or perhaps he simply wanted to flex his creative muscles and capitalize on his unusual encounters out West. In any event, his first short story, drawing on his gold-rush experience, was published in the February 1885 edition of *The Northwest* as well as in the local *Pioneer Press*. Entitled 'Yarns of an Old Miner: "3-7-77"',[58] it was recognized by the *Minneapolis Tribune* as a 'very excellent article' written by 'an industrious member of the TRIB-UNE staff'. The story is told from a miner's point of view, as he observes life in a camp named Gulch City. There the camp washerwoman, Mrs Harrington, and a miner called Wiley, provide the entertainment. 'Though she and Wiley always appeared as strangers in public, never speaking to one another, they was pretty intimate, an' used to spend most of their time in each other's cabins', the narrator relates. Their neighbour, Sid Johnson, the most popular miner in Gulch City, gave a running account of the couple's affairs. '"Thermometer way up," he used to say, "crops doin' well," when they'd bin particularly friendly; a "stiff breeze from N.E. A cold day for Mrs. H," when Wiley had bin away at his claim.'

On New Year's Eve, Mrs Harrington is found in the street, shot. She revives just long enough to point at two men standing in the doorway, Sid and Wiley, and shout, 'Johnson did it!' Then she dies. 'Johnson! Sid! the open-hearted, cheery friend of the whole camp! It seemed impossible,' the narrator laments. The next day, Sid is found hanged from a dead tree. '"3-7-77" had done its work quietly enough during the night; an' though everyone in camp felt broke up an' uneasy about it, no one dared to murmur agin the Vigilantes', we are told. In an editor's note, Harry explained that '3-7-77' was the symbol of the Montana Vigilantes, who render justice on their own terms. 'A cardboard, some eight by five inches, with a skull and cross-bones on it and "3-7-77" underneath is the gentle hint which the committee serves on the man whose presence is no longer required in camp', Harry wrote. 'When a man wakes and finds that nailed to his door in the morning, he had better not waste time in asking questions, but devote the next twenty-four hours to getting as far away as possible.'[59]

But the story ends with a twist: Wiley has disappeared. In his abandoned cabin are found letters from Mrs Harrington, addressed to Wiley's real surname, which happened to be Johnson. So when the dying woman fingered Johnson, she probably meant Wiley, not Sid. Vigilante justice, Harry concluded, was not always just. Harry was clearly speaking from his own experience in Eagle City.

* * * * *

Harry's star was rising at the *Minneapolis Tribune*, evidenced by the fact that in addition to news articles he was also writing leading articles, mainly on foreign affairs. His title was now 'News Editor'. For a man of 27 years with very little experience on the world stage, this was a major vote of confidence, and evidence of Harry's growing popularity and ambition, not to mention his strong political views. But his efforts were not without controversy, and were followed by the *Tribune*'s arch rival, the *St. Paul Globe*. Identifying 'Some Noted Characters of Minneapolis', the *Globe* singled out Harry: 'Harry P. Robinson is a very clever young fellow. He writes English editorials for the Tribune, and tells how "we predicted two months ago the British cabinet" would do so and so. He also writes anti-Irish communications for the Tribune and speaks of "American subjects," meaning citizens. That's "English, ye know."'[60] The anti-British, anti-patrician bias is evident in a city with a large Irish population. A glance at the *Tribune* leading articles in 1885 reveals Harry's hand, even though they are unsigned. For the most part, the *Tribune* takes a pro-British, Queen and Empire stance, and, for 1885, was thoroughly opposed to the liberal policies of Prime Minister William Gladstone's government (which fell on June 9, 1885).

Harry's views on Ireland and the Home Rule issue, however, got him into hot water with the local Irish community. On May 16, 1885 the *Tribune* responded to a widely reported incident in the west of Ireland where a much-hated bailiff, having evicted several farmers from their lands, was lured into a trap by his victims, who plied him with drink and then set him on fire. That action, Harry wrote, 'illustrates the medieval and barbarous nature of the lower strata of Irish peasantry'. He argued that education was the only way to counter the agitation and violence resulting from Charles Stewart Parnell and advocates for land reform and Home Rule:

> The oppressor of the Irish people as a whole is no iron-heeled tyrant, but Ignorance. Let the sun of education send its rays through the cloud of barbarian ignorance which hangs over Ireland, for one generation only, and the result will be astonishing. Landleagueism and dynamitism will disappear, the grub will become a butterfly and all race prejudices and present difficulties will vanish. Ignorance is the weight which keeps Ireland down and this must be removed before she can take her place as a responsible country, on the same plane with her contemporaries.[61]

Note that Harry was not advocating Home Rule, but rather Ireland's place as a proud, prosperous member of the British Empire, much as his father, as editor of *The Pioneer*, supported improved educational standards for the people of India (but not Home Rule there). The editorial set off a firestorm of its own in Minneapolis, freely reported by the *Tribune*. 'IRISHMEN INDIGNANT. They jump with both feet upon the "Tribune's" neck' ran the headline on May 18. Members of the Minneapolis division of the Irish National League called for a rally and a boycott of the newspaper, all on account of a 'short editorial'. One of the speakers at the rally was Roger Valle, formerly of the St Paul *Pioneer Press* and no friend of the *Tribune*, who quoted school attendance figures from Ireland to disprove the *Tribune* editorial. He then rounded on the newspaper for employing 'an English dude, so fresh from England that salt water smells on him yet, to write editorials on Ireland. If there is an Irishman that wants to buy such a paper, he deserves all the kicks, insults, obloquy and anything else that the paper can heap upon him.'[62]

Racist threats were bad enough (and not uncommon for the time), and Harry had a thick skin, but a boycott was a real danger to any newspaper, and the *Tribune* would not take this lying down. On May 19 (perhaps by Harry's hand), the newspaper accused the agitators, 'whose ostensible purpose was to injure the TRIBUNE but whose *real* object was to add numbers to what had been a losing scheme in an attempt at landleagueism'. Five Irishmen joined the effort, while twenty-two opposed. Boycott defeated, the *Tribune* declared a victory, and Harry could not resist crowing:

> The strong, sensible Irishmen of Minneapolis, who are represented in all the professions and trades of our city, know too well that what the

TRIBUNE said is true, and they can not be caught by a set of worthless fellows who live not by the sweat of the brow or by any honest labor, but sponge it off the poorer classes, under the guise of benefits to be derived by memberships in some social organization, or the establishment of some league, at one dollar a head. These bummers, having nothing to lose, think 'boycotting' a good scheme to follow.

But we warn them to beware. Suppose the tables should be turned and the TRIBUNE should rise up and call on the citizens of Minneapolis to 'boycott' these agitators and their followers; and suppose these good citizens obey the request? How long would it be before the whole gang would be lodged in the poorhouse? The very men who are threatened with persecution, are the very men who are furnishing aid and support to the same would be 'boycotters.'

The TRIBUNE company today have more than thirty Irishmen in their employ, the private secretary to the general manager being an Irishman who was formerly in Mr. Blethen's law office in Portland, Maine.

How many of these agitators have or have been furnishing bread and butter to the poorer classes of Irishmen in this city? Not one. These fellows who stir up their countrymen by misleading and bulldozing them are not only the very worst enemies of society, but they are the worst enemies the Irish laborer can possibly have.[63]

The General Manager was Alden J. Blethen. The *Tribune* also praised a letter from 'An Irishman', published in the same edition, as eminently sensible and recommended it 'to all of the would-be boycotters who are able to read'. The letter writer admitted there was a lack of wisdom and knowledge in Ireland, and that more could be done. But he opposed a boycott: 'The proposal by the Minneapolis committee to boycott any business house which should exercise its citizen's right to purchase whichever newspaper it prefers, does not, I think, argue much intelligence or civilization on the part of those who proposed or supported such a resolution.'

The *Tribune* tried to put the matter to rest on May 25 by reprinting several past editorials, presumably by Harry, showing its strong support for Irish grievances against the English.[64] For example, in a January 28, 1885 editorial on the Fenian bombing of Parliament, Harry wrote, 'The dynamite plot was a wrong and terrible thing. It deserves only condemnation.' But, he reminded readers, 'England has not a quick sense of justice', and listed a long litany of laws against labourers, Wat Tyler, the Chartists, even the Jews. 'Liberty has had a hard, slow, discouraging struggle in the United Kingdom', Harry observed. 'Until 1869 the Catholics in Ireland were compelled to maintain the established church of England throughout their island. Considering the abominable tyranny of such a law, it is a mark of considerable forbearance that the Irish people had not blown up the whole establishment.' These were strong words. The May 25 editorial concluded with a challenge to the British Parliament that stopped just short of Home Rule:

> It is within the power of England to remove every hovel in Ireland, to re-establish a condition of things that shall bring plenty instead of poverty; that will cover every Irishman with comfort in place of rags, and fill every Irish peasant's home with food where starvation or direful distress now exists. In fact, it is within the power of England to make the Green Isle blossom like the summer rose, where now exist only poverty, squalor and distress.
>
> But that she does not do these things is no proof that they do not exist. That a part of the Irish people are wealthy, educated, and live in comparative splendor, does not disprove the statement that many more are in the very depths of bondage, mentally, morally, and physically. Here then is the gist of the whole case. The TRIBUNE has many times plead the case of Ireland eloquently.

Harry's editorials illustrate his evolving personal philosophy. While he had genuine compassion for the common man, he had no desire for revolution and the violent uprisings of the emerging labour movement. He was a firm believer in the Empire and Britain's right to rule, yet looked for justice and improvement for the peoples in the imperial orbit. Seeking a *via media,* he was a true liberal at heart.

The fact that Harry was cited by demonstrators is a testament to his emerging popularity in the Twin Cities and his prominence on the social scene. This is not surprising since, as a handsome young Englishman not afraid of expressing himself and playing the *provocateur*, he stood out in a city on the edge of the frontier. On November 2, 1886, the *St. Paul Globe* reported on a visit of James Sheehan, a member of the local chapter of the Irish National Land League (Parnell's party, advocate for Home Rule), to the *Minneapolis Tribune.*

> James Sheehan called at the GLOBE office last evening and related a little incident showing how the Tribune is run. In company with a few friends, he was discussing the political situation with H.P. Robinson, of the Tribune, who by the way is an Englishman.
>
> The queen's name was mentioned and Mr Robinson at once removed his hat, saying as he did so: 'I always remove my hat when the queen's name is used.'
>
> 'Are you a voter in the country?' inquired Mr Sheehan.
>
> 'No, sir, I am not,' answered Mr Robinson.

That settled it, and the party left in disgust.

In speaking of the matter Mr Sheehan said: 'That shows what kind
of men the Republican papers are hiring to make our political rules for us,
when a man who has insulted the Irish in the manner Mr. Robinson has
turns out to be a non-citizen, and then wants us to vote his way. It is time
the Irish people stopped and thought over the matter. Do we want to be
dictated to by men who are non-voters and men who doff their hats at the
mention of the queen's name?'[65]

The fact that Harry took a meeting with Sheehan is evidence of his
fair nature. But the foreign alien branding by his opponents during
this boycott campaign must have stung. It would come as no
surprise that Harry, ever practical and pragmatic, had already
taken steps to apply for U.S. citizenship. America would become
his new home.

* * * * *

Harry published his second short story, 'The Crime of Christmas Eve', in
two parts, in the December 1885 and January 1886 editions of *The
Northwest*.[66] Once again he called upon his mining experiences and
rough frontier justice with a story about 'Fortune City' where 'its chief
population is gamblers and its only courts of justice those which are held
at midnight by the men with masked faces who are witnesses, judges, jury
and executioners combined'. Jim Garton is a San Francisco lawyer who
caught gold fever. His new wife insists on joining him in Fortune City.
And so, two weeks before Christmas, 'Mrs. Garton—one of the prettiest,
daintiest, most deplorably inexperienced girls in California—found herself in a log cabin in one of the roughest, whisky-drinkingest, card-
shovingest, and generally toughest and most vigilantesque camps in the
Bitter Roots.'

The Gartons' neighbour in camp is Pete Taylor, 'a bad man in his day'.
He's obsessed with Mrs Garton, while she fixates on Pete's mousy wife.
On Christmas Eve, Pete quarrels with Jim over ownership of the mining
claim, and shoots Jim dead. Back at the cabin, Mrs Garton is worried
sick, and asks two stalwarts of the camp, Judge Grace and Dr Tenney, to
go and look for Jim. They find his body and return to the cabin. 'They
had finally left her with her dead husband in the inner room of the cabin,
with the pine branches and Christmas decorations all around, while a
good old motherly body—a wife of an old miner in camp—sat in the
front room with the tears trickling down her cheeks in sympathy with the
sobs which came from behind the half closed door of the chamber which
held the widow and the dead.'

In the meantime, word travelled fast: 'There was only one opinion in camp as to who was the murderer; and there was only one opinion as to how the murderer should be treated.' So on Christmas morning, the Vigilantes set out for Pete's cabin; covered with a blanket, he neither resists nor speaks. They march him through the darkness to the hanging tree, put his head in a noose, when he shouts, 'Ah! My God!' But it is not Pete's voice; it is his wife's! 'He went away dressed like me, late this afternoon,' she explained, claiming she was willing to die for him 'in expiation of his sin'. Mrs Taylor is marched back to her cabin, but she demands to see Mrs Garton. 'Do not send me away', she pleads with the widow. 'My grief is no less than yours—greater, for I have to mourn for two.' The two become fast friends and set out together for San Francisco—with Judge Grace and Dr Tenney in tow, each hoping to snare a wife. 'If long love-service and patient loyalty can ever win a true second love, the judge and the doctor deserve to succeed.'

The story concludes on a macabre note as the reader wonders what became of the murderer Pete. He might have escaped, or met his fate in the forest: 'Others there were in camp who thought that a human skull, which the coyotes rolled out of the brush next spring, and after mumbling over it all night down the trail through the camp, left it lying at the very door of the cabin he had occupied, was his. Perhaps so; but the All-seeing above knows what penalty he paid in this world for his crime of Christmas Eve.'

Clearly a mildly creepy pattern was evolving in Harry's short fiction that bordered on the supernatural, an emerging genre. Witness Harry's next short story, 'The Curse of Indian Mill', written for the Holiday 1886 number of *The Northwestern Miller*, a weekly trade journal edited by Harry's friend, William C. Edgar.[67] Intriguingly, Harry painted a positive picture of Native Americans. 'There is a tendency just now to do injustice to the Indian—to think and speak more meanly of him even than he deserves', the story begins. 'This may be no more than a natural reaction against the extravagant laudation of him which was so fashionable at one time, and of which [James] Fenimore Cooper will stand to all time as the most conspicuous exponent. None the less—natural or not—it is an injustice.' Harry insists that for every 'lazy, unwashed, blanket-swathed and vermin-ridden being who loafs about the sidewalks of frontier towns, playing poker and drinking whiskey', there are noble Indians who deserve our respect.

The story is set in an old Montana mine, Camp Cedar, now called Indian Mill. The narrator meets his three friends who are mining the quartz deposits. One night an elderly Indian appears. He claims to be the

THE CURSE OF INDIAN MILL.

BY HARRY P. ROBINSON.

HERE is a tendency just now to do injustice to the Indian —to think and speak more meanly of him even than he deserves. This may be no more than a natural reaction against the extravagant laudation of him which was so fashionable at one time, and of which Fennimore Cooper will stand to all time as the most conspicuous exponent. None the less—natural or not—it is an injustice. The lazy, unwashed, blanket-swathed and vermin-ridden being who loafs about the sidewalks of frontier towns, playing poker and drinking whisky, is, perhaps, too low to suffer injustice. But the Red Man can still occasionally be found in the further west with a very considerable share of his native picturesqueness of character yet clinging to him. And it is this more primitive Indian (and he is really the genuine one) to whom the injustice is being done.

Figure 4. The beginning of Harry's short story, published in the Holiday 1886 number of *The Northwestern Miller* of Minneapolis, Minnesota.

last of the Blackfoot tribe. He shouts out a curse on the men and their operations, as they are desecrating the land and the graves of his ancestors, scorned as the usual practice of all white men. 'Before the snow comes again the house that you are to build will be gone, and you three who have caused this thing shall die. By fire and water shall your deaths be—accursed!' And so, one man is drowned, the mill is burned to the ground, and an explosion kills the other two men. The curse has come true! But the elderly Indian is also shot dead. '"Coincidences, only," you say? Perhaps so', Harry concluded. 'You can probably understand why it is that I never look at an Indian now without a certain feeling of awe, in which there is not a little element of fear.'

* * * * *

Socially, Harry continued to rise, and his activities earned mention in the society columns of the *Minneapolis Tribune* and even the *St. Paul Globe*. He was a keen sportsman, and took up the local winter sport of tobogganing as a member of the Makwa Club. In the spring of 1886, he founded the Minneapolis Cricket Club, a first for the city. On July 4, 1886, the *St. Paul Globe* reported with excitement that Harry's team was to meet one from Chicago the next day and 'Minneapolis is to have her first real experience with the English national game'. Interestingly, five members of the Minneapolis Eleven were, like Harry, from England. The *Globe* described Harry, the team captain, as 'known as an Oxford cricketer and played three seasons ago for Staten Island—the strongest club team perhaps in America. Fields point. A change slow bowler.' Alas, as reported the next day, the Minneapolis team received 'a rattling and not unexpected defeat' by a score of 81–47, with Harry scoring 26 runs.

Harry was also excelling at the relatively new sport of lawn tennis. The *Globe* on August 19 heralded the tournament at Hamline University for the 'Championship of the Northwest', noting 'H.P. Robinson of this city will contest'. On August 22, the *Globe* reported that Harry had reached the singles finals, but lost to W.N. Armstrong of St Paul, 6–5, 6–1, 6–2. 'Some very fine returns were made by both players', but 'Robinson was nearly overcome by the heat, and the play waited some time for him when he resumed'.

As 1886 ended, Harry was on the cusp of a big decision: to break away from the life of a reporter/editor to becoming a publisher and editor in his own right, and working for himself. This was quite a career move for a man of 28, an immigrant barely three years in his new adopted country but clearly determined to stake his claim and make his mark.

2

Tycoon in Training, 1887–1894

The *St. Paul Globe* put the spotlight on Harry in its February 26, 1887 edition. 'HARRY ROBINSON, of the Minneapolis Tribune, who has been for some past an ornament to Northwestern newspaper and society circles, will, on April 1, begin the publication of a journal devoted exclusively to railroads and railway men, and entitled "The Northwestern Railroader"', it reported. 'While the date of publication is unfortunate, as indicating a lack of seriousness of the venture, we are confident that if Mr. ROBINSON will exercise his exuberant talent by interspersing dry railway statistics with the charming *vers de société*, in whose composition he is a master, it cannot fail to be a success.'[1]

The *Globe* was no fan of Harry's, as we have seen. But dismissing him as an 'ornament' with an 'exuberant talent' was short-sighted. Harry was a young man in a hurry. Outspoken and ambitious, he was determined to take control of his destiny after just three years in his adopted country. It was clear by now that Harry was making plans to stay in America. His father and brothers had made their mark outside of England, and he would, too. He filed an application to become a U.S. citizen, a major decision not to be taken lightly. He was 27 years old, had made a splash in the Minneapolis social scene, had a wide circle of friends, and had made a name for himself—for better or worse—as a newspaper reporter and provocative editor, as well as a clever writer of short stories. Now he faced the next big step: to work for himself and build a fortune. Harry's ambition could not be concealed, and he was no doubt inspired by tycoons like Henry Villard.

Harry's emancipation from the *Minneapolis Tribune* and *The Northwest* arrived in the form of a brand new weekly paper of his own creation called *The Northwestern Railroader*. It was a smart move, as railways were the engine of growth in the American West, as the Northern Pacific had demonstrated. Railway companies based in St Paul alone employed 64,000 men, with lines emanating 'like the spokes of an enormous wheel', west to the Pacific, north to Canada, and south and east to Chicago.[2]

Harry's new paper would serve as a source of information for owners, employees (from the boardroom executives to the day labourers), and investors, while chronicling the towns and cities linked by the railroads and offering entertainments in the form of short stories and contests. He was determined to make his new paper inviting to all readers, whether they were personally invested in the industry or not. The *Tribune* announced the new venture on February 20, 1887: 'It will appear weekly, and has for its editor and manager Harry P. Robinson, long a valued and faithful member of the TRIBUNE's editorial staff. His talent and experience are the best guarantee for the success of this latest addition to current railway literature.' What is unknown is how Harry financed this new venture, as he clearly had no significant funds of his own. In fact, in later years he would say that he lost all of his savings in a failed claim in the Coeur d'Alene mines. Whether Harry actually invested in the gold rush (given his suspicions in his dispatches to the *New York Tribune*) is open to question; he may have invented this story to promote a self-made-man myth. In any event, someone put up the funds for this new weekly paper, and it is likely that Harry's silent partner was Villard, who had everything to gain from the positive promotion of all things railroad. John S. Bradstreet may also have helped; he was Harry's great friend and certainly a prosperous man.

The first edition of *The Northwestern Railroader* appeared not on April 1, as the *Globe* announced (perhaps Harry was spooked by the article), but the following week, on April 8. Harry was listed as editor and W. P. Hallowell, Jr as business manager. There were offices in St Paul and in Minneapolis, and a call was issued for 'Representatives wanted in all the Railroad and Manufacturing Centres in the country'. Harry offered a declaration and promise in this first edition:

> The financial success of a paper like the NORTHWESTERN RAILROAD-ER must ever be in proportion to its merits. If the NORTHWESTERN RAILROADER rightly represents the interests which it pretends to represent and which it is created to represent, it will succeed as a business enterprise. If it fails to represent those interests, it will fail in a business way. It is the intention of the proprietors of this paper, with the good will of the Gods and the public, to make of it a financial success.

The contents of this first edition set the template for future issues: sixteen pages filled with articles on a variety of railway-related topics, from construction updates to personnel changes. A prize competition offered $25 for 'the best article or short story dealing with an incident (real or fictitious) of Railroad life'. Railroad fables were published, 'in which railroad philosophy and railroad morality are dealt out in liberal weekly doses'. While this looked like a straightforward in-house newsletter, Harry had a bigger goal in mind than an ephemeral journal. He was building community, mindful of the potential for influence in politics and government policy.

Harry's new paper made a splash. The *Tribune* said on April 8 that it was 'willing to certify that it is a journal in every way creditable to the two cities', and that the new publication 'challenges attention and favor by its careful editing and tasty typographical appearance'. On April 13, the *Globe* grudgingly agreed: 'It appears to cover its news field carefully, and in addition presents many features which are certainly valuable and interesting to railroad men.' The paper added that it was 'handsomely printed' and 'for the sake of the able gentleman that has engaged in the enterprise, it is sincerely hoped it will prove remunerative'. Further afield in Montana, it was 'an enterprise that all railroad men in the northwest will take hold of and encourage', according to the *Bismarck Weekly Tribune*. The *Bozeman Chronicle* called it 'a first-class publication' and the *Fargo Argus* in Dakota Territory said it 'is demonstrating that it is a live paper'. The *Mississippi Valley Lumberman and Manufacturer*, published out of Minneapolis, believed it 'fills a really long felt want, belongs to no clique, curries nobody's favor, and therefore is commendable. It is a 16 page paper, neatly gotten up, and is an everlasting credit to the whole Northwest. Harry P. Robinson an A 1. journalist is its editor. The Northwestern Railroader is a success from the start.'

The first six months of the *Northwestern Railroader* were not without its problems. Issues were late and printing quality was uneven. Harry needed an injection of cash to move the operations to a new printing plant. Accordingly, on November 22, 1887 articles of incorporation were filed, 'for the purpose of conducting the publication on an enlarged and improved scale'. The capital stock was valued at $20,000 ($500,000 today), and Harry was one of six investors. His business manager, W. P. Hallowell, Jr, was dropped, and Harry now reported to the other five investors who constituted the board of directors. Two of these were local newspaper men: Col. G. D. Rogers of the *Market Record* and S. W. Alvord of the *Commercial Bulletin*. Intriguingly, the new organization only lasted two months. On January 8, 1888, the *Tribune* reported that the ownership of the *Northwestern Railroader* had changed again, restoring full control to Harry. 'Mr. Robinson made a good paper of the Railroader before, and he will probably do it again. The new firm, which consists of Messrs. J. A. Chater, H. P. Robinson and F. Bateman, proposes to put on a colored cover and increase the size of the paper immediately.'[3] John A. Chater succeeded Hallowell as business manager, while Frank Bateman managed the Chicago office. The *Globe* welcomed the 'new and improved form' which included a yellow-coloured wrap-around cover with advertisements. 'Its improved appearance indicates that its influence is felt and appreciated by the railroad interests of this important and growing section.'[4]

The ownership episode is telling. Harry's confidence in his abilities was supreme, and he was not going to be told what to do by outsiders, even if they were his investors. Nearly a year into publication, he succeeded in controlling his own destiny, and his instincts were right. The *Northwestern Railroader* went from strength to strength. And its self-assured owner was only 27 years old, remarkably assuming a persona and ethos of a tycoon twice his age. Evidently such boldness and chutzpah, judging from Harry's father and brothers, were in the Robinson genes.

*   *   *   *   *

Harry's work ethic was admirable, but he made time for play and social activities, as evidenced in the local papers. He was an active member of the Minnesota Lawn Tennis Club, as well as an eager card player whose preferred game was whist. The *Globe* reported on June 9 that 'Harry P. Robinson is a stout hand at whist and invariably holds the odd trump'. An 1889 newspaper clipping, which Harry kept in his scrapbook, noted his membership in the Minneapolis Chess, Checker and Whist Club, where he is 'the handsomest man in the club, and some say in Minneapolis'.

In fact, the press often harped on Harry's good looks and bachelor status. He was becoming something of a dandy, featured in the society pages about eligible young men and regarded as one of the biggest catches. The *Globe* published an article entitled 'Our Bachelor Bees: Who Are Unwilling to Sip the Honey Sweets of Marriage'. The paper claimed that marriage was not a priority: 'Many of them appear to have an idea that it is not such a brilliant success as it might be, as shown by their own words. This feeling on the part of the young men is a source of considerable worry to the fair maids and eligible young widows of the Flour City, and all are demanding in no uncertain tones to know why this is.'[5] The article proceeded to 'interview' these eligible bachelors, including Harry, who was quoted as saying 'If I can find a pretty heiress, free from faults, I might not object to giving her my name. But she must be very pretty and remarkably wealthy.' Clearly, money was important to Harry, and the irony in the article is apparent in Harry's future choice of bride, the wealthiest heiress in town. Similarly, the *Tribune* ran a very odd article, envisioning what the city's handsome bachelors would look like when they were older. Entitled 'Old Time's Tooth: It Will Gnaw Away at Well Known Minneapolitans With Visible Results', the article included an illustration of the elder Harry, who looked much like the future U.S. President Theodore Roosevelt. 'Harry P. Robinson's appearance will be that of a fine old gentleman with a dignity that may not be approached without a *salaam*', the article proceeded, with a nod to his Indian birth.

> The phrenologist who examines his head at three score and 10 will tell him that he has a head like that of Julius Caesar, save that where Caesar is marked for war he is marked for lawn tennis. A square, firm jaw and chin, a full, rosy face and hair of iron gray will be Mr. Robinson's characteristics. When he has left the office of his railway company of which he is president and chats at a lawn party given in his honor, he will say to the young lady beside him: *Do not marry a butterfly of fashion. I never did. It is singular, but I never could bring myself to do it. I have, however, always found time to mingle in society. It is possible for one to do this and still attend to his secular business. I hold it a sacred duty to play whist at least two evenings in the week.*[6]

Even tongue-in-cheek, people were expecting great things from Harry, and such attention must have fed his (expanding) ego.

In addition to cards, Harry was passionate about a very Minnesotan pastime, tobogganing. He was president of the Makwa Toboggan Club, whose 200 members were, according to the *Globe*, 'the best-known young men of Minneapolis'. He spearheaded efforts to build an enormous, 220-foot long toboggan slide beside Lake Calhoun, near the home of railway tycoon Thomas Lowry (Harry's future father-in-law). Minneapolitans coveted their winter slides, and the rivalry was intense between the Makwas and the other two toboggan clubs in the city, the Crescent Club and the Flour City Snowshoe & Toboggan Club.[7] The *Tribune* reported on January 22, 1888 that the new Makwa slide 'is much superior to any that has been built in Minneapolis before and is probably as fine as any that is in existence in the country'.[8] The toboggan run was nearly a third of a mile, ending in the middle of the frozen lake. A unique feature of the superstructure, 'which has never before been tried in any slide', said the *Tribune*, 'is a wooden house at the top of the slide, elevated some 10 feet above the starting platform, with a front almost entirely made of glass. This is kept warm and ladies and gentlemen can sit here and look straight down the slide, comfortably protected from the weather.' It was all very civilized, illuminated with electric lights, and accessed by trains from the city. The *Tribune* noted that club members wore a distinctive uniform, complete with 'a sash of cardinal'. Members included Bradstreet ('John S. Bradstreet makes his toboggan take the most artistic and negligee poses'); Fred Pillsbury, heir to the flour fortune; and former Minneapolis Mayor Eugene Wilson. The *Tribune*

Figure 5. Harry, age 28, president of the Makwa Tobaggan Club in Minneapolis, wearing the club's official uniform: 'Vine breeches and blouse of French gray heavy woollen cloth, and stockings, toque, and sash of cardinal'. Published in the *Minneapolis Tribune*, January 22, 1888.

included an illustration of Harry and noted that he 'stands on his toboggan, because it is "English ye know"'.

Such was Harry's prominence that the newspapers could make fun of him in a good-natured way. The *Tribune* featured Harry in an April Fool's column: 'Harry P. Robinson sat up ill all night thinking over the report that Tom Lucas was going to take his railroad (on) paper away from him because he was an alien. He is an ail(ing)en yet.'[9] Lucas was a local labour leader. Harry, who was beginning to express his opposition to organized labour, would not have appreciated yet another reference to his alien status. Not surprisingly, he became a citizen of the United States on November 26, 1888. At this time, a requirement for citizenship was a residency in the United States for a minimum of five years, with a 'declaration of intent' filed after two years, followed by a 'petition of naturalization' after three more years.[10] With five years since his arrival in America, Harry qualified for citizenship in the fastest way possible. He knew the decision was essential to achieving success and respect in his adopted country. But in becoming a U.S. citizen he had to forswear the Queen by name (which could not have been easy) and pledge to fight for his new country, if attacked.[11]

* * * * *

Harry's decision to become an American citizen coincided with his next big idea. In July 1888 he proposed a 'Railway Employes [*sic*] Club'[12] with the workers of the Minneapolis & St. Louis Railway, intended for 'mutual benefit and protection against class legislation'. Harry's goal was to advocate for the workers in place of a traditional labour union (which he abhorred, along with all industry leaders at the time, in these fledgling days of worker organization), and to forge a mutually beneficial relationship between bosses and employees that would avoid costly strike action. It was also good business for the *Railroader*, as this became a kind of fan club for the journal, which was growing in popularity (published each week beneath the staff box was 'THE NORTHWESTERN RAILROAD-ER is the official paper of the Railway Employes' Club of Minnesota'). Membership grew: by February 1889 there were 12,000 members in Minnesota, and sister clubs were opening in Wisconsin, Illinois, Iowa, and the Dakota Territory. On November 2, 1888, the *New York Times* wrote about the Minnesota club and its stated position that it was not political, and that opinions to the contrary were 'bitterly resented' by the members. That would, of course, change in time. 'The membership of the organization is pretty evenly divided up between the adherents of the two political organizations, and their votes are likely to be cast without reference to any other consideration except individual party attachments', the paper observed. 'Yet, there is no denial that the members will favor, like all others, the men and policies which are most likely to benefit them in their occupations.'[13] Without a doubt. The *Times* proceeded to quote Harry, in his capacity as publisher of the *Railroader*, on this subject, and Harry did not mince his words regarding the current electoral campaign for state governor:

> I know the facts well, as I have published a report of every meeting held, and I give you my word of honor that no attempt has been made through the club to prejudice one single vote in favor or against either Wilson or Merriam; nor will any attempt be made. The club as a club has no interest in the Gubernatorial election. Set that down as the first fact in regard to the club. The organization has no interest in either party, and will not attempt to injure or help either candidate.
>
> The next point to set down is that it is not a movement of the railroad corporations. It is a movement of employes for the benefit of employes. It was started among shop hands in the Minneapolis and St. Louis and Milwaukee and St. Paul shops in Minneapolis. The railroad employes have come to the conclusion that it is time to organize for their own protection, just as every other class of men have done, and they are doing it. It is a permanent organization, not started for this campaign or any other campaign. The power of the organization will be just as formidable if used against a railroad company as it would if used against a political candidate.

This was a bold statement, although in the end the members of the club did vote to support the victorious Republican candidate for governor of Minnesota, William Rush Merriam, over the Democrat, former mayor Wilson, casting Harry's sincerity in doubt.

With the Employes Clubs expanding and garnering attention, Harry decided to broaden his horizons on a national stage with a new publication, 'Our Railroads: Being a Presentation of Facts and Figures, Showing the Value, Earnings, Profits and Present Condition of the Railroads of Minnesota and the Northwest'. Harry observed that the principal audience for the 20-cent pamphlet were not just railway employees but also residents and workers in small towns and rural neighbourhoods, who sought to discover 'in the simplest form possible that there is nothing mysterious about the organization of a railroad company and the building of a railroad'. The pamphlet was praised in *The Northwest* in March 1889 by Harry's old friend, Eugene V. Smalley, as 'a careful digest of facts and figures showing the value, earnings, profits and present condition of the railroads of Minnesota and the Northwest', and a pamphlet that 'should be in the hands of every intelligent man who proposes to talk, write or vote upon the railway question'. 'Our Railroads' was reissued and updated annually.

The publication, however, was not without controversy. This was not just a simple compendium of facts and figures, allowing readers to draw their own conclusions. Rather, Harry had an agenda (as demonstrated in his Railway Employes Clubs) that the growing campaign at the government level in support of railroad regulation must be stopped. In the second edition of 'Our Railroads', published in 1890, he threw down the gauntlet:

> Now, supposing for one instant that it is possible that the people, as a whole, are not interested in the welfare of the railroads and their maintenance on a safe basis of operation; supposing, for an instant, that they could look on with indifference, so far as their personal interests were concerned, and see the commerce of the country suffering from insufficient train service, tracks in bad repair, and inadequate equipment; supposing that they do not care if all the lines in the country are absorbed by five or six gigantic systems—supposing all this, and considering only the few millions who are immediately interested, is it, firstly, the part of political expediency to compel these men to combine together, their hands against every man's, for the protection of their rights and their homes; and, secondly, is it the part of justice to deprive them of the returns on their capital and their labor, and to confiscate their property? Do we need more anti-railroad laws, or do we not?

Harry had, in just a few years, become the voice and even conscience of the railroad industry in America, straddling the fine line between supporting the bosses and advocating for the workers. While the *Tribune* praised the second edition for its 'lucid analysis', the *Globe* was swift in its condemnation:

> It appears to be republished at this time in its present shape because the subject of railroad legislation is before the public. Its final sentence is a rhetorical inquiry, 'Do we need more anti-railroad laws or do we not?' And the pages which precede this outburst are filed with figures and a strife of words that the railroads of the Northwest are in a desperate condition through no fault of their own, and that the only way to save their lives is to let them do their own sweet will, however much the public may suffer. In other words, Mr. ROBINSON has presented to the public in his brochure what we take to be the railroads' side in the existing controversy, and the reasons why they think that they ought to be left alone.[14]

Indeed he did, and Harry could no longer conceal his true agenda. The *Globe* proceeded that there were only two ways of looking at this: that 'the author does not know what he is talking about' or 'that he deliberately disguises and misstates the facts':

> In partisan zeal [he] omits the story which would work against his case, draws false inferences from admitted premises, perverts the established principles of railroad law, and, in order to bolster up a cause which must rest on the shifting sands of desperation if it needs such a defense, commands

everybody to forget his own experience and his own powers of reasoning and adopt a style modeled on the methods of 'Alice in Wonderland.' These are frightful alternatives, but every reader of Mr. ROBINSON'S book must choose one or the other.

Needless to say, Harry did not take this attack lying down. He sent a long letter to the *Globe*, which was published on January 31, 1891. He resented being called a liar and claimed the editorial writer was misinformed: 'It is the practice of the old maxim, familiar in the courts of law, "When you have no case, abuse the opposing counsel." '[15] He insisted his statistics were correct, drawn from official sources, and challenged the *Globe* to investigate: 'A very large question of the public welfare is at issue. Would it not be more in consonance with the position of the GLOBE as a moulder of public opinion if it were to inquire for itself into the facts, and recommend our legislators to do the same, that public opinion might be moulded aright, and that our laws may be based on the truth and on consideration of public interest?' The *Globe,* on the same page, took offence at Harry's 'bitterness of spirit', and claimed it never called him a liar. 'This paper maintained its wonted urbanity and courtesy. Mr. ROBINSON'S mistake is but another example of the readiness with which men misunderstand what is said to them or of them, and teaches that it never pays to feel hurt until one is quite sure that a wound has been received.'

If the *Globe* thought this would dissuade Harry from his path, it was surely mistaken. Personal attacks had no effect on his surprisingly thick skin. Indeed, Harry used the pages of the *Railroader* to express his strong views on strike action. The paper, he wrote in the June 27, 1890 edition, 'has never been uncertain or half-hearted in the expression of its opinions on the question of strikes'. Regarding a current strike action on the Illinois Central Railroad, Harry noted, 'We have a great many readers among Railroad employes of all grades—not a few among those who are now at this writing "out" on the strike in Chicago—and to them and to all employes who read this paper we say that the present strike, like almost every Railroad strike of recent years of any magnitude, is a folly and almost a crime.' He said he was 'almost weary of quoting' statistics from the U.S. Commissioner of Labor that in six years, strikes had cost the workingmen of America $55 million in lost wages, of which $25 million was 'wasted on strikes which failed utterly and for which there was no recompense whatever'. Interestingly, although Harry was opposed to strike action he admitted that it could be justified, but only as a last resort:

> To make a strike justifiable there must be, in the first place, no room for question that the cause of the employe is right and the cause of the

employers wrong. In the second place, every other resource—of argument—of overture—of arbitration—must have been tried and failed. In the third place the striking force must be so strong that as soon as the strike takes place, the employer must yield.

Under no other circumstances can the interruption of the public business, the injury to the public property, the hardship to the strikers themselves and to their families and to all those other workingmen in allied trades who are thrown out of work, be justified or excused...

We trust and believe that the time is coming when the workingmen of this country will refuse to be led by the nose by a gang of politicians and walking delegates; when they will come to understand that they are disloyal to the interests of their employers, of themselves and of their families when they surrender their independence at the nod of a worthless 'chief' or 'master' workman, and that they are degrading the dignity of labor which they claim to be organized to uphold.

These were powerful words, and reaction was swift. In the July 4, 1890 edition Harry shared a letter from 'evidently not an educated man' who inquired as to why the *Railroader* 'is so d—d down upon strikes and strikers'. Harry thought he had made himself perfectly clear in the previous issue, but provided a rehash on the reasons. He concluded with a profound accusation: 'The whole system of political manipulation and wire pulling by which strikes are brought about in the labor organizations by men who are chiefly seeking their own comfort and aggrandizement and to whom the honest working man sacrifices his manhood and independence, is immoral in principle and injurious to the community in practice.'

One wonders where Harry acquired such strong convictions in so short a period of time. He doubtless wished to prevent the violence and bloodshed caused by labour movements in Europe which, at times, veered dangerously close to revolution. In any event, with talk like this, Harry would be favourably noticed by the railroad owners, even though his primary concern was a fair deal for railroad workers. His sought-after *via media* would prove a fine line to walk.

*   *   *   *   *

In his capacity as publisher of the *Northwestern Railroader*, Harry made a point to travel as widely as possible outside of his coverage area, to make contacts and observe industry trends and developments. He was always looking for ways to increase the appeal and national visibility of his newspaper. He did so in dramatic fashion by hitting the road to annual conventions around the country, and issuing a *Daily Northwestern Railroader* on location. For the Master Car Builders' and Master

Mechanics' Conventions, held in New York and Virginia, Harry travelled with six men and a thousand pounds of equipment. 'In the last four years we have not failed of success and hereafter if the Conventions should be called to meet at Vladivostok or at the Cape of Good Hope, we should not fail to be on hand and to publish the DAILY NORTHWESTERN RAILROADER at 7:30 every morning', he predicted on June 27, 1890. 'We win each year the respect and congratulations of the Railroad men of other sections of the country and show to the people of the East and the South that "Northwestern Enterprise" is something more than a name.'

One such trip included a stop in Washington, DC, in June 1890, and provoked an extraordinary news story which Harry clipped and saved in his scrapbook. Entitled 'Uncle Sam's Simplicity: How a Northwestern Man, Once a Subject of the Queen, Rolled on the White House Grounds', the article (source unknown) is a delight, and worth reprinting here in its entirety:

> The simplicity at the American capital strikes foreigners very forcibly by the contrast with their own countries. This was illustrated the other day when Harry P. Robinson of Minneapolis, editor of the Northwestern Railroader, was in this city.
>
> Mr Robinson was once a loyal subject of her majesty, the queen, and when his home was in old England he often used to visit the capital, where all the dignity and pomp of everything impressed him deeply.
>
> When he saw for the first time the White House, with its grounds open to all, he at once remembered the queen's palaces, with their red-coated officers on guard, and the pomp attendant of royalty.
>
> It was a summer Sunday afternoon that he saw the White House first. The grass was green and the sunshine twinkled through the thick-leaved trees along the walks. The gates to the grounds were wide open. No guards or watchmen, or even one of the district policemen, were in sight. The outer door opening from the portico of the house was ajar. The windows in the chambers of the house were open. Sparrows hopped on the front steps, and some colored children came up the walk from the state building on a Sunday afternoon romp.
>
> Mr Robinson again thought of the Buckingham and its red-coated guards. He has of late become an American citizen, and his first sight of his adopted national capitol pleased him. D. W. Meeker, who is associated with him in the Northwestern Railroader, was with him.
>
> 'Say, Meeker,' said Robinson, 'you can't imagine how different all this is from the home of the queen. You couldn't get within sight of her front door without passing from two to five guards and going through all manner of formalities.'

'Yes, this reminds me very much of the grounds around Lake Harriet,' said Meeker. 'If they had a band and some motors it would be as free and easy as it used to be out at Tom Lowry's pavilion.'[16]

'Say, Meeker,' replied Robinson, 'this is so informal that I believe I could lie down and roll right here on the lawn of the president of the United States, and nobody would find any fault.'

'Very likely you could,' said Meeker, 'but you haven't the nerve to try it.'

Mr Robinson, however, was not in a mood to be challenged, and he was so taken with the idea of rolling on the White House grounds that he did so. It was right beside the walk on the north side of the house, within easy sight of Secretary Blaine's house[17] and in plain view of such pedestrians on Pennsylvania Avenue as happened to be there. Robinson stretched at full length, and rolled and stretched on the grass like a child.

'You couldn't do that around any of the queen's palaces,' he said as he got up. 'I rather like the style of this government, too.'

Clearly, the world was Harry's oyster! One gets a sense of his playfulness and *joie de vivre*, as well as his growing affection for his adopted country.

*   *   *   *   *

It is remarkable that, as busy as Harry was in running his publication and building up his reputation, he still found time to dabble in his new hobby: writing fiction. His literary ambitions took a big leap forward in February 1889, when the *Atlantic Monthly*, arguably one of America's finest literary journals, published his new short story, 'The Gift of Fernseed'. This was a bold move on Harry's part, to make the transition from publication in a small provincial paper like *The Northwest* to a prestigious national journal, and is evident of his growing self-confidence as a writer. Harry was in esteemed company: the same edition of *Atlantic Monthly* featured 'The Tragic Muse' by Henry James. An unattributed newspaper clipping which Harry kept in his scrapbook was florid in its praise: 'Mr. Robinson, in addition to his gifts as a graphic narrative writer, is a graceful versifier and wields as well a trenchant controversial pen.' Thanks to his time in Coeur d'Alene, the paper noted that Harry had 'gathered a knowledge of the geography of that new region and of the Indian character that has assisted him to plots of stories several times since'.

Indeed, 'The Gift of Fernseed' continued to mine the setting and experiences of Harry in Idaho, with a supernatural twist that was becoming his trademark of sorts. It is the story of Arthur Sayce, 37, born in

New York and educated at Columbia College, a well-travelled doctor on an extended hunting trip to the Pacific Northwest. In telling his fantastic story, he assures the reader that he is quite sane: 'In my life I have known but little sickness, and have never been subject to fits, faintings, trances, delirium, or hallucinations of any kind. It is impossible that I can have been deceived in any of the sensations which I experienced in the events that I am about to describe. However incredible the following narrative may seem, it is the simple, sober truth.'

Arthur arrives at the (real-life) Coeur d'Alene Mission, where in addition to five cabins and the mission itself, there's an Indian tepee and four 'Indian bucks'. But they are friendly natives, according to Father Francis, the priest who heads the mission. One, called Tsin-shil-zaska, is a medicine man. He resents Arthur because he drew his Winchester rifle on their first encounter; Arthur also seems sceptical of the medicine man's talents. After a long and unsuccessful excursion bear hunting, Arthur returns to his cabin, strips off his clothes, and takes a bath. As he is standing 'mother naked', Tsin-shil-zaska bursts into his cabin. Arthur is embarrassed, although 'the Indian has, in the matter of nudity, no sense of what we are pleased to call the proprieties, and I doubt whether the medicine man had any idea of the awkwardness which, however illogically, I could not help feeling'. The Indian has brought a potion to the so-called 'Man-with-the-rifle', to prove his knowledge of medicine, and insists that Arthur drink it. This is madness, of course, but the Indian challenges his honour: 'Will the man who was brave the first time be a coward the next?' So Arthur concedes, and the Indian departs.

The reason for Arthur's nakedness is soon apparent. After feeling giddy, exhilarated, dizzy, and then nauseous, he realizes 'there is only one word by which I can describe the process which then seemed to be going on in me—the process of *disintegration!*' The potion has rendered him invisible and helpless; he cannot be seen, nor is he able to touch or move objects, or communicate with Father Francis when he comes to his cabin. The priest organizes a search party for the missing man. As Arthur watches, only animals can sense his presence. '"The dogs howl with icy breath/When Azrael, Angel of Death,/Takes his flight through the town." The quotation from the Koran came into my mind, and then a sudden horror seized me—*Was I dead?*'

Arthur never gives up hope, and falls to his knees, praying 'as only a man in the supremest agonies can pray. From that moment I have never ceased to be devoutly thankful for the sustaining hope which was always with me. I arose from my knees full of confidence.' He leaves the mission and goes to the Indian camp, where he witnesses a wild 'Dance of Death', a prelude to the planned murder of poor Father Francis. Arthur stays by the priest's side, and watches in horror as the Indian arrives, knife in hand. Suddenly Arthur reappears, in full nakedness, to wrestle the enemy to the ground and stab him to death. The story closes with Arthur making a desperate search in the forest for this 'drug of properties entirely new to science'. It would be, he says, 'the fable of Gyges' ring translated into the language of prescriptions: "the gift of fernseed" in the hands of every qualified pharmacist in the United States!' The Ring of Gyges was a magical artefact mentioned in Plato's *Republic* which granted its holder the power to become invisible at will. Similarly, legend holds that fernseeds—spores of ferns—grant invisibility. Harry's story ends with Arthur pledging to make this search his life's quest, and encouraging readers to do the same.

Clearly, 'The Gift of Fernseed' marked a significant advance for Harry in terms of storytelling. It was also quite daring: a foray into science fiction (eight years before H. G. Wells's novella *The Invisible Man*), with the added titillation of nudity. He decided this time to use his mining experiences as a backdrop, not as essential to the story. The natives are portrayed in a bad light, a change for him. Also, being published in the *Atlantic Monthly* was a coup, offering wide national exposure, especially as the story was also syndicated in newspapers such as the *Baltimore Sun*.

In September 1889, Harry published his second story in the *Atlantic Monthly*, 'The Gold Heart'. He wrote this in January, but did not mail it until May 15, presumably after an inquiry from the journal due to the positive reception of 'The Gift of Fernseed'. For this story, as for 'Fernseed', Harry earned $65 ($1,600 today), a sizeable sum.

Not surprisingly, 'The Gold Heart' was also set in the mining region and had a strong supernatural theme. The narrator, working his claim on Eagle Creek 'in the first days of the Coeur d'Alene mining craze', admits his ignorance of 'the superstitious veneration with which so many of the Northwestern Indians regard the symbol of the heart'. Anything heart-shaped is avoided, we are told, and a heart traced on a boulder or tree stump marks a place of great solemnity, such as the death of a warrior in battle. Unaware of the superstition, the miner dislodges a huge, heart-shaped gold nugget 'worth something more than six hundred dollars', and is elated, not terrified. 'My first sensation was that of one who sees a miracle happen', he recalls. 'This was incomparably the finest nugget that I had ever seen...I rubbed it and polished it; held it out at arm's length to look at it; laid it down, and drew off a few paces to admire it. Then I kissed it.' He digs deeper at the spot of his magnificent find, only to recoil in horror as he unearths a skeleton of an Indian man. 'The Gold Heart, I had no doubt, had been clasped in the dead man's hand when he was buried.'

The miner returns to camp and shows the nugget to his partner, Alfred, who had a half-share in the claim, and therefore the gold. They draw their cots together in the lodging house, 'large tents which looked like hospital wards', and sleep with the precious find between them. When they awake the next morning, the nugget has vanished. 'There was nothing to be gained by making an uproar about it', the narrator says. 'There was no police in Eagle City then, and if the gold had been stolen we were more likely to catch the thief by saying nothing than if we raised a hue and cry in camp. So we said nothing.'

A month passes, and the duo, with a third man, Charles, in tow, leave Eagle Creek on a hunting trip. At night they hear a noise. Thinking it a bear, Charles fires—and kills an Indian. In the native's hand is the Gold Heart. 'And it came to me that this was how the other had lain—on his back, with his legs out straight, his right arm bent on the breast and his left extended, and the hand clutching the nugget', the narrator relates. Baffled, but pleased, they board a boat and head downstream. While fishing, the boat overturns. The water is not deep, but all of their provisions are swept away—including the Gold Heart.

The story fast-forwards several months. The narrator, after touring the Pacific Northwest, is on a Northern Pacific train bound for Minneapolis. Just outside the town of Glendive, Montana, the train derails, and eight people are killed (a plot point that would surely not have pleased Villard).[18] Our narrator helps to extricate the survivors and comfort the injured. As he pulls a dead man from the wreckage, he discovers in the man's hand— the Gold Heart. 'The man was never identified, and I know no more how the nugget passed from the bottom of the Coeur d'Alene River to his hand than I know how it made its way from my bag to the Indian whom Chapman killed on the mountain-side', the narrator relates. 'The Heart, with the other properties saved from the wreck, of course passed into the custody of the Northern Pacific Railroad Company.' The narrator puts in his claim to the nugget, only to be informed that he has none.

The following summer, he returns with Charles to the Pacific Coast, where they witness a horse-racing competition between two Indian tribes, the Yakimas and Umatillas. He is impressed at the level of gambling: 'both tribes bet recklessly, so that one lives in poverty and the other in affluence for the next twelve months'. Atop an amassed pile of valuables was—the Gold Heart. The Indians quarrel over the precious item, and one is slain. The authorities are summoned, the murderer surrenders, and all is peaceful. But the Gold Heart is nowhere to be found. 'We had not stolen it', the story ends. 'Nor have I heard of or seen it since.' The *Atlanta Constitution* in Georgia praised Harry's story and even wondered if there was any truth to it: 'For the lovers of the queer—

not green goods, but stories—this romance of the wild west will have unusual attractions. It occurred, or is said to have occurred, in the northwest.'

In March 1890, Harry expanded his fiction horizons further with a children's story in *St. Nicholas*, 'An Illustrated Magazine for Young Folks', published in New York and London. The story was called 'On a Mountain Trail'. It follows the narrator, Jack, and his companion, Charlie Gates, as they ride on horseback between Livingston, Montana and Gulch City, 50 miles away, with a load of camp supplies. They are stalked by a pack of grey timber-wolves, also called 'black wolves'. They are heard but not seen, shadows in plain sight, perhaps forty of them. 'To me, and I think to everyone who has seen it, that silent, persistent, haunting presence is the very embodiment of ruthlessness and untiring cruelty', Jack relates. 'There, in the twilight and shadow, was the same silence, the same indistinctness, the same awing impression of motionless speed, the same horror of the inevitable, in that pursuit by the wolves.' He fires his gun until he is out of ammunition, but is unable to disperse the pack. Jack and Charlie then fashion a bomb from sticks of dynamite and toss it in the wolves' direction. 'A moment later and the air and the earth shook around us. I was still standing, clutching the low side of the sleigh, and the concussion threw me upon my face', Jack says. 'The stillness that followed was intense, but I thought that I heard, from the direction where the wolves had been, one broken, muffled howl.' The duo arrive safely in Gulch City with a big story to tell. Two years pass, and Jack notes that locals still speak of the section of the trail that had to be rebuilt, where travellers 'still turn out of their way for a minute to look at "Giant Hole," and to kick up out of the weeds and brush that had grown around it the skull or part of the skeleton of a wolf'.

What is especially interesting about Harry's story is the subject matter. The hero's name, Jack, and the encounter with wolves brings to mind the best-selling author of the American frontier, Jack London. In 1890 London was in the seventh grade and working in a cannery in Oakland, California, some thirteen years away from writing *The Call of the Wild*. Since Harry would discover London and act as his first overseas publisher in 1902, the parallels are striking. The *Los Angeles Times* on March 2, 1890 praised Harry's 'stirring' story which 'will enlist the fullest attention of its readers'.[19]

Harry returned to the supernatural with 'Medusa', published in *Westward Ho!*, a new Minneapolis-based monthly magazine, in its inaugural issue in November 1891. The magazine was edited by Dr Albert Shaw, a colleague of Harry's on the *Minneapolis Tribune* and an academic who went on to edit an American edition of the *Review of Reviews*. Harry had written this story in August 1889, but it was sent to, and rejected by, the *Atlantic Monthly*, *Scribner's*, *Century*, and finally *Harper's*. Sending it to *Westward Ho!* was probably Harry's last resort.

In this bizarre story, Mrs Edith F. Tierce of New York City visits an English politician who subsequently drops dead. The man's private secretary, the narrator, is entranced by the mysterious lady and falls in love, even though, at age 35, he was resigned to bachelorhood. 'A bachelor's life is an inchoate existence; a species of half-life at best—"like the odd part of a pair of scissors," as Benjamin Franklin said', he observed. 'But now the picture of a home rose frequently before me, altogether pleasant to contemplate—a home in which two wonderful black eyes smiled at me across the breakfast table-cloth in the morning and were waiting to meet mine as I looked up from my reading in our sitting room at night.' Harry was 32 in 1891, but 30 when he wrote this—and certainly marriage was on his mind.

The narrator is visited by a crippled man with a story to tell. He, too, had fallen madly in love with this mysterious lady, following her all over Europe. In Oxford he called on her at the Old Mitre Inn every morning, and proposed to her in the cloisters of Christ Church. But she was not the marrying type. As they sat on a bench in Magdalen College gardens, she attacked her paramour, who survived, but was severely paralysed. The lady vanished. The narrator thinks it a fantastic story, and continues to woo Mrs Tierce. But death seems to follow the lady, and when her servant drops dead, the narrator rushes to her side. In an amusing aside, Harry notes that this meant cancelling plans to attend the theatre with another couple, 'John Bradstreet and his wife'.

The story ends with the narrator proposing marriage to Mrs Tierce, seemingly hypnotized by her beauty and her intense gaze (akin to the Medusa of Greek mythology whose gaze would turn men to stone). 'I felt my whole being concentrating itself in—merging itself into—drowning in—her eyes. A strange feeling of intoxication possessed me; or ecstasy.' He appears to be a goner—until the cripple springs into the room, exclaiming, 'I hope I am in time!' He was, and the narrator is horrified at the appearance of his beloved, slumped on a sofa: 'I could liken her to nothing but some blood-sucking thing; some human leech or vampire, torn from its prey, quivering dumbly with its unsated appetite.' The two men escape. A week later, Mrs Tierce is found dead in her flat. Soon afterward, the narrator discovers he is the beneficiary of the estate of James Livingston, a.k.a. the crippled man.

Given its dark tone, akin to Gothic horror, it is perhaps no surprise why 'Medusa' was turned down by the leading fiction journals. Harry clearly enjoyed revisiting his Oxford days in this story, and the reference to Bradstreet (who never married) was playful. The *St. Paul Globe* called Harry's story 'striking.' But it did not seem the work of a man who was about to propose marriage.

*　*　*　*　*

In many respects, 1891 marked a turning point for Harry, his coming of age as a public figure and a man. 'Our Railroads' was child's play compared to Harry's next move, which combined his growing interest in science fiction with political advocacy. 'Federal City: Being a Remembrance of the Time Before St. Paul and Minneapolis Were United' was a 36-page pamphlet written by Harry but published anonymously, signed 'An Optimist' and dated 'Federal City, Minn., March 15th, A.D. 1916'—twenty-four years in the future. An introductory note read, 'It is the hope of the writer that this short retrospective while being found, perhaps, not without interest merely as a historical narration, may also be discovered to contain some lesson—or at least a hint—which may be of value in our own times.'

Harry's effort, distributed in March 1891, was his personal response to the 1890 U.S. Census controversy raging between the Twin Cities of Minneapolis and St Paul. Population was a sensitive subject, as it affected new investment in commerce and industry, as well as representation in the state legislature and Washington.[20] For years Minneapolis and St Paul had been growing closer in totals. On June 17, 1890, U.S. marshals from St Paul stormed the census office in Minneapolis, claiming fraud, and arrested seven enumerators. Never mind that St Paul had been accused, during the 1885 census, of counting graves in its cemeteries to boost its population total. Minneapolis eventually came out on top over St Paul in the 1890 census: 164,000 to 131,000.

Harry was not the first to propose that the future for the Twin Cities lay in amalgamation. But he turned to science fiction to raise the subject in a creative, inventive way. He imagined a single urban district called 'Federal City'. In his pamphlet he reminded readers that 'twenty-five years ago Federal City did not exist. What is now East Federal City was St Paul, and West Federal was Minneapolis. And neither, apparently, had any serious idea of ever becoming anything else.' All that changed, he related, was the first 'inter-urban electric line' which linked the two cities in December 1890. Such rapid transit (in reality built by his future father-in-law, Thomas Lowry) played a major role in bringing the two rivals together.

Federal City, the pamphlet purported, had become a utopia of sorts based on 'the legal right of individuals and corporations to combine to prevent excessive competition . . . The voice of a million people must be listened to.' Boards of Trade and Chambers of Commerce were united. The new city consolidated all liabilities, and the refunding of debts generated interest which paid for new public works, benefiting all. It used its increased influence in the state legislature 'wisely and without selfishness' to pass a 'Female Emancipation Act', giving women the vote. Clearly enjoying himself, Harry pushed his future vision to the limits. In 1916, a citizen of Federal City is president of the United States. Canada has been annexed, so Federal City is the principal trading partner with the new American state of Manitoba. A 'Great European War' boosted the local economy (fortunately this was the 'Last Great Battle of the World', with peace ensured by a Treaty of Constantinople). And Federal City has expanded eastward to the Great Lakes, making Federal City a maritime powerhouse. 'Receiving in tribute the commerce of the St. Lawrence and the Gulf of Mexico, Federal City will have an industrial empire greater than has ever been subject to one city since the days of Imperial Rome', Harry predicted. He concluded his vision with a nod to the naysayers who still opposed the idea:

> The great forces of nature which run from generation to generation, never play us false. Their action is certain; and he who can see them in their full current, not distracted by the accidents of the day, need never doubt where they will lead to. Before a city is built or a people grows, its destiny is written on the face of its land. And it was set down of old that here between the Mississippi and the lakes should arise one of the great cities of the world.

One cannot underestimate Harry's sheer audacity in writing and distributing this pamphlet. A citizen of Minneapolis for barely five years, he thrust his hat boldly into the ring with a vision that was daring and provocative. It was a star-making turn. 'Federal City' was a sensation and a bestseller, and for once rival newspapers were in agreement. The *Globe* said that 'no publication of local interest has yet appeared which so entirely deserves to be read by everybody in both St. Paul and Minneapolis. And every one who reads it once will read it again and wonder who the author is.'[21] The *Tribune* agreed, noting that 'the little work is not only entertaining but suggestively instructive, for it contains many economic, social and political hints calculated to start a train of profitable reflection in the thoughtful mind'.[22] The *Northwestern Miller* observed 'It has a lesson to teach and does it well and briefly. Citizens of both cities who are broad enough to forget foolish pleasures will read it with pleasure and profit, but the ancient party hacks will regard it as a foolish, treasonable and abhorrent thing.'[23] Even the *New York Times* chimed in: 'It will be admitted on all hands that if consolidation will keep them quiet Minneapolis and St. Paul ought to be consolidated.'[24] It was not long before Harry's name leaked out, and the *Globe* reported on April 30 that 'Harry Robinson, the author of "Federal City," has made a good thing out of it. The sales were large—the result of judicious advertising—and the profits correspond.'[25] The *Globe* added that Harry 'is at work upon a second brochure of entirely dissimilar character', but that apparently was not issued.

It turns out that 'Federal City' was not Harry's original idea at all, but was suggested by Thomas Lowry himself. Lowry (1843–1909) was one of the most powerful businessmen in Minneapolis and president of the St Paul, Minneapolis & Sault St Marie Railway. In 1891 he founded the Twin City Rapid Transit Company, which ferried 100,000 passengers daily on 400 electric streetcars between Minneapolis and St Paul (ironically, Lowry's initial business partner was Henry Villard, who withdrew early on due to financial difficulties). On July 15 the *Chicago Tribune* paid tribute to Lowry's publicly expressed passion for unification of the two cities (under the headline, 'Paul Will Wed Minnie'), noting that the name once suggested for the united city was 'Lowryville'. Of 'Federal City', the paper noted, 'As Mr. Robinson is to be married to Mr. Lowry's daughter in a few weeks the public easily ciphered out that Father-in-Law Lowry has inspired the book.'[26] We know how Harry pandered to tycoons, and 'Federal City' would have stood him in good stead.

Clearly, Lowry had big plans for his future son-in-law, and thoroughly approved of the engagement of his eldest child, Mary, to the bright young publisher and friend to the railroad industry. Precisely when the courtship began is unknown, although both Harry and Bradstreet (Lowry was a big client of his) were among the sixty guests celebrating 'Miss Lowry's recent entrance into society' at the fashionable West Hotel, reported by the *Tribune* on April 19, 1891. Mary was only 19 years old and relatively unknown to the social scene; Harry was 32. The engagement was officially announced in the *Tribune* on May 5:

Harry P. Robinson is receiving congratulations from his friends on his engagement to Miss Mary Lowry. The engagement has just been announced, and was something of a surprise to friends of both parties. Miss Lowry is the eldest daughter of Thomas Lowry, and is one of the most universally admired of the season's debutantes. Mr. Robinson has a wide circle of friends in the Twin cities. He was educated at Oxford university, England, and after coming to Minneapolis was for a long time connected with the editorial department of the TRIBUNE. He is now editor of the Northwestern Railroader, but is better known through his literary productions. The latest of them is the pamphlet "Federal City." He is a regular contributor to leading periodicals, and has made quite a reputation as a writer of fiction. The date of the marriage has not been announced.[27]

The *Globe* wrote on May 10 of 'an engagement that is exciting considerable attention. Miss Lowry but recently entered society. From the first she has been a favorite, and has made a large circle of friends. Mr. Robinson is also widely known, both in society and in the literary world.'[28] The *Anoka Union,* a newspaper published north of Minneapolis, applauded the union, tongue in cheek, noting that 'editors invariably make better husbands than any other fellows in the world. They appreciate womanhood thoroughly. They love, admire and most of 'em obey the lady of their choice always.'[29]

Given how the marriage will unfold, one wonders at this moment about Harry's motives. Was he truly in love? We have seen his unbridled ambition, and how he cosied up to men of wealth and influence. A match with the daughter of the richest man in Minneapolis would bring great rewards. An unattributed newspaper clipping Harry pasted in his scrapbook noted, 'Editor H. P. Robinson, of the "Railroader," is said to be engaged to the daughter of a six times millionaire. He is a bright newspaper man and brings to these shores some of the ozone of the prairies.' Harry may truly have loved his future wife, but the engagement also opened many doors—including a very large one in a major city.

Just weeks before the wedding, Harry dropped a bombshell: he was purchasing *The Railway Age*, the venerable industry publication based in Chicago, for a whopping $75,000 ($2 million today) for the entire capital stock. It is likely that Lowry footed the bill, perhaps as part of his staggering $200,000 wedding gift ($5.5 million today). The actual purchase price may have been higher. The deal was finalized on September 1. E. H. Talbott, president and managing editor of the *Railway Age* since its inception in 1876 (and whom Harry had met eight years earlier on the Villard expedition), would retire. Furthermore, the *Railway Age* would merge with the *Northwestern Railroader*; the consolidated publication, based in Chicago, would be called *The Railway Age and Northwestern Railroader*, and its first edition would be published on September 15, 1891. Harry was president of the new 'Consolidated Railway Publishing Company', with a capital stock of $150,000, with Horace Hobart as vice president and H. M. Wilson as secretary. Harry and Hobart (a fifteen-year veteran of the *Railway Age* and widely respected in the industry) would jointly serve as editors. The Chicago *Inter Ocean* newspaper noted on September 5 that 'the only fault to be found with the new arrangement is that the new paper will have too long a name'.[30] Harry saved several unnamed newspaper clippings in his scrapbook. One read, 'Mr. Robinson is, easily, the leader of the young railroad journalists of the country, and is to be congratulated upon this enlargement of his sphere of action. The Railway Age has long been regarded high authority upon railroad questions, and the same may be said of the Northwestern Railroader. The combination of the two will result in a thoroughbred that cannot be distanced.' Others were more cynical, tinged with jealousy. 'It is a peculiar fact that Mr. Robinson, when he took hold of the Northwestern Railroader, did not know a semaphore from a brakeman's lantern', ran another. 'He made many amusing mistakes at the outset of his career in railroad journalism, but perseverance and tact have finally landed him at the top of the ladder.' Finally, this: 'We should smile, Harry. When a newspaper man marries a rich man's daughter and finds a check for $200,000 among the wedding presents as you did the other day, congratulations are of course in order. May you live long and prosper and your consolidated newspaper flourish like a circulation liar's dream.' A cynical comment, but true, as Harry's financial future was now secure.

* * * * *

Lowry's wedding gift to Mary and Harry was just one of the sensational details splashed across newspaper pages coast-to-coast of 'the largest and most fashionable wedding ever held in the Northwest' (so said the *New York Times*). The couple were married on September 23 at 7:30 p.m. at St Mark's Church in Minneapolis. Mary's younger sister, Eleanor ('Nellie'), was maid of honour, and Bradstreet was groomsman. Coverage in the local newspapers the next day was extensive. The *Tribune* reported on 'the tall and slender bride, whose robe of satin fell away in a sweeping train, while the bridal veil, but half concealed the pensive face and downcast eyes'.[31] She carried a prayer book made in London, presumably a gift from Harry. The *Globe* noted that 'inside were the representatives of most of the influential social people of the Northwest, and two immaculate white-gloved policemen at the door marked the line of demarcation between the invited and the uninvited'.[32]

A reception followed for an astonishing 1,400 guests at the Lowry mansion. A special train had transported guests from Boston, New York, Montreal, and Chicago. Phil was the only Robinson family member to come across for the wedding; it is uncertain if he brought his erstwhile girlfriend, Alice Cornwell, a.k.a. 'Princess Midas', the Australian gold mine owner. Phil had only recently gave up the editorship of the London *Sunday Times*, of which Cornwell was the proprietor, and his sensational divorce to his wife Sarah was finalized in 1889. The *Minneapolis Journal* set the scene:

> It was a glimpse of some fair visionary land; it was a big beauty bee hive. Electricity, that modern wizard, had been summoned to take a prominent

THE GROOM.   THE BRIDE.

Figure 6. Harry and Mary on their wedding day, September 23, 1891. Harry was 32 years old; Mary, 19. Published in the *Minneapolis Journal*, September 24, 1891.

part in the happy affair and he responded right royally, too. He transformed the home into a bower of light and made each window a mirror of brilliancy. Driving out Hennepin av., the sight of the house made one think of the stories of elves and goblins who created palaces of light for brides and grooms to live in and suggested that those days were realized. Hundreds of carriages filled the streets for blocks around. Even the electric cars were stopped for a time and at least 1,000 people filled the sidewalks and literally covered the lawns up to the house.[33]

The *Tribune* agreed that the Lowry mansion was 'beautiful far beyond description', with grand floral arrangements adorning every room. The gardens were transformed into 'an enchanted fairy land where brilliantly costumed figures flitted back and forth and sweetest music enticed the muses to the dance'. Upstairs was an elaborate display of wedding gifts 'which no more costly or numerous had ever greeted bridal couple. A marquiesse ring set with colored pearls and diamonds was the gift of the groom, and the choicest wares of the world had been poured in abundance from the hand of plenty at the feet of these two. A wonderful old necklace with a stone of priceless value came from the Canadian Pacific railroad and was surrounded by a crowd of admirers throughout the evening.'[34] The *Inter Ocean* estimated that 'the wedding, it is said, having fully cost $20,000 [$550,000 today]—the Lowry–Robinson marriage was by all odds the most important social event in the history of Minneapolis or of the Northwest'.[35] The *Tribune* added that the happy couple departed the next day for Chicago, 'to a new home in another city, and for a season will live at the Auditorium in Chicago, till a suitable residence shall have been found'. The honeymoon was postponed until the spring, as the groom had much work to do at his new job.

∗ ∗ ∗ ∗ ∗

Chicago in 1891 when the Robinsons arrived was booming. Nearly twenty years after its 'Great Fire' (legend had it that Mrs O'Leary's cow kicked over a lantern, starting the blaze that consumed one-third of the city), the 'Windy City' had rebounded into the capital of the Midwest, nexus of railway lines (boasting that one-twenty-fifth of the railway mileage of the world terminated in Chicago, serving thirty million people), and the country's largest producer of beef and pork (the slaughterhouses were notorious).[36] Chicago attracted a new class of entrepreneurs as well as bankers and attorneys, and had just surpassed Philadelphia as the second-largest city in the United States, after New York. With them came culture and money, and it was called the 'Gilded Age' for good reason. There were 24 daily newspapers and 260 weeklies. Chicago annually sent 20 million pounds of periodical literature through the mails, more than Boston, Cincinnati, New Orleans, Buffalo, and Baltimore combined.[37] Trade journals like the *American Commercial Traveler*, the *Northwestern Lumberman*, and Harry's *Railway Age* extended their reach far beyond Chicago. 'If one wanted to know where to buy or sell something—anything—one could find the answer more easily in Chicago than anywhere else in the Great West', observed William Cronon.[38]

Newly enriched by his marriage, and backed by his powerful father-in-law, Harry was well positioned to succeed in this rarified world. The Robinsons received a warm welcome into Chicago society. Just before Christmas, Mrs John Davidson, wife of the president of Davidson and Sons, marble dealer and importer, gave a luncheon for twelve 'in honor of Mrs. Harry Robinson, née Lowry, formerly of Minneapolis', as reported by the *Inter Ocean*.[39] In attendance were the wives of some of the biggest names in Chicago, including Mrs Charles L. Hutchinson, wife of the president of the Art Institute museum; Mrs J. Ogden Armour (meatpacking); Mrs R. L. Henry (lumber); Mrs O. B. Tennis (flowers); and Mrs W. J. Bryson, wife of a warden of the Episcopal church. Mary's head must have been spinning as the ladies sought to court the Lowry heiress, all 19 years of her.

Although the prominent ladies at the luncheon had grand homes on Prairie Avenue, a wealthy enclave just south of downtown, Harry and Mary chose a different neighbourhood for their new residence: the so-called 'Gold Coast', north of the city centre, and along the waterfront of Lake Michigan. This was a newly developed area by the *nouveau riche*, with large mansions and terraced houses. 'There are more miles of detached villas in Chicago than a stranger can easily account for', Julian Ralph observed in 1893. 'As they are not only found on Prairie Avenue and the boulevards, but in the populous wards and semi-suburbs, where the middle folk are congregated, it is evident that the prosperous moiety of the population enjoys living better (or better living) than the same fraction in the Atlantic cities.'[40] Some of the homes survive to this day. There was no uniform architectural style to speak of; rather, it seemed as if each owner was out to impress and outdo his neighbour in size, stone, and flourishes. ('The contrasts in architectural design evidence among Chicago house-owners a complete sway of individual taste',[41] Ralph added.) The largest mansions (settings for the most lavish parties) were built by the publisher of the *Chicago Tribune* and the lumber titan James Charnley from a design by a young architect, Frank Lloyd Wright. The Robinson home at 570 Division Street was a modest three-story home with a large back garden. But within a year, Mary and Harry moved a few doors away to no. 18, Astor Street. Astor Street was *the* address for the rich and famous (named for John Jacob Astor, one of the wealthiest men in America). Among the prized possessions in their new home was a Mehlin grand piano, shipped from Minneapolis. Mary was an accomplished pianist and often invited to play at parties and weddings of friends. Similarly, Harry moved the *Railway Age* offices to a new 16-storey building called the Monadnock Block ('Monadnock' is a Native American word meaning 'mountain'). The tallest load-bearing brick building ever constructed, it was intended to evoke the monuments of ancient Egypt with its soaring geometric shafts. It certainly commanded the downtown area, and when it opened in 1891, it was the premier office address.

On April 13, 1892, Harry and Mary set off from New York on the White Star Line's S.S. *Teutonic*, bound for Liverpool and a belated two-month honeymoon in England. 'Mr. Robinson was anxious to take his wife on a visit to his fatherland, and his intention is to return home in time for the conventions in June', reported the *Neodesha Register* of Kansas (Harry's reputation had spread far and wide) on May 6. What is not mentioned is that Mary was now four months pregnant.

This would have been an especially happy time for the couple, and Harry would have been excited to introduce his bride to his parents and siblings. While in London Harry paid a memorable visit to Liberty's, where he and Mary were no doubt shopping for fabrics for their new home. 'On coming away I stopped to ask some question about the duties on the things which I had bought and intended taking to America', Harry recalled, years later. 'It was the first intimation that the man to whom I spoke had had that I was from America; and the first question that he asked was if I knew a Mr. Bradstreet.' The exchange is telling for the interplay between the Old World and the New:

> He could not remember the name of the town where Mr. Bradstreet lived, so I furnished it. 'Ah, yes,' he said, 'of course. Is it not a remarkable place for such a man to be in? Could he not get much wider recognition in New York, for instance?' Undoubtedly he could; but, after all, I suggested, the place for a missionary was among the savages.
>
> I was a savage myself, I explained, and it was entirely owing to Mr. Bradstreet's labors that I was fitted to come into Liberty's shop and buy the things that I had been buying. There were, I added, a few thousand other people like myself, new customers of Liberty's, potential or actual, who but for Bradstreet would still be going to places where they sold nice mid-Victorian articles with red plush in them. I think he understood.[42]

The Robinsons remained abroad until the end of June. Mary then spent most of the summer at home in Minneapolis, where she gave birth to a girl, Beatrice Harriett, in August (the exact date is uncertain). The choice of name was a tribute to Mary's mother, Beatrice Lowry, and Harry's mother, Harriett Robinson.

*   *   *   *   *

By 1893, Harry would have been the envy of his peers. At just 33 years old, he had a powerful position as owner and editor of the nation's leading railway publication. He had married a wealthy heiress and had a beautiful daughter. The future was indeed bright for this emerging tycoon, and between now and the end of the century Harry's star would continue to rise. He was certainly beholden to Thomas Lowry, his father-in-law and a significant player in the railroad industry. By footing the bill to purchase *The Railway Age*, Lowry would hope to ensure a sympathetic voice. He need not have worried. Harry and his father-in-law were in agreement over protecting the railroad owners from government regulation and interference. One way to ensure this was to elect sympathetic politicians. That meant building a base of voters among the railway employees, and here Harry brought an ingenious idea to the table: start a political movement, if not an actual party.

Harry made his first overt move into the political arena with an article in *The North American Review*, a prestigious journal, in May 1893. Entitled 'A Railway Party in Politics', he expounded upon the Employes Clubs already formed, and the potential for influence, showing that he had significantly revised his initial view that the clubs were not political in nature.[43] The impetus for the article was the present threat to owners and employees by proposed legislation to regulate rates and operations. 'It is easy to see how much strength such a party, if formed, would possess', Harry speculated. 'According to the reports of the Interstate Commerce Commission, there were in the immediate employ of the railways of the United States a year and a half ago 749,301 men—all or nearly all voters—which number has now, it may be assumed, been increased to about 800,000.' He added that there were 1.25 million shareholders in railway properties in the U.S., and an estimated one million more people in trades and industries immediately dependent upon the railways for their support. 'These three classes united would give at once a massed voting strength of some three millions of voters', Harry wrote. 'The financial backing and the commercial and political strength of which the party would find itself possessed from its birth would be practically unlimited.'

Having teased readers with the possibility, Harry then pulled back, noting that 'experience has impressed upon railway men the unwisdom of "the corporations" appearing in politics'. If a formal political party was, therefore, unlikely, Harry claimed that an informal one already existed, noting the results in state elections where Employes Clubs were active. Such activity, Harry insisted, was bipartisan; in Minnesota in 1890 the club threw its support behind Republicans; in Iowa in 1891 it was given to Democrats. 'A railway party is therefore already in existence, but it is scattered, decentralized and incoherent', Harry said. 'It has no recognition from the railway interests themselves—meaning by that "the corporations"—or their officials. On the contrary, a number of the heads of the railway companies regard the movement with profound distrust. None the less it has strength, and the potentiality of much greater strength. And, moreover, though accidentally only, it is working forcibly in behalf of railway interests as a whole.' That was a sound idea, Harry reminded readers, as gross earnings of the railway companies in 1891 were $2 billion, or six times as large as the U.S. Government. Hence, Harry asked, 'Are the railway presidents and managers right in their apparently unanimous opinion that the regulation of railways by the State (or by the States) has grown to be a persecution or confiscation of their property? Are the railway employees justified in believing that Granger legislation [regulation of railroad shipping rates more favourable to farmers] is robbing them of their means of living?' Once again, Harry was linking the owners with their employees, creating a united front, however unlikely that may have seemed.

Needless to say, Harry's article made quite a splash. The *Minneapolis Tribune* said that it was 'carefully written' and 'ought to be appreciated by Eastern stockholders'. But the *St. Paul Globe* called it a sham in a scathing editorial. 'The GLOBE is in a position to know that Mr. Robinson has not had access to the best sources of information. It knows that the plan did originate in the office of the president of one of the principal railway companies, and the movement was inaugurated by one of his staff.'[44] Thomas Lowry, presumably. 'The purpose was to use the employes as cats-paws, just as they used their conductors to get the anti-scalper bill passed at the last session. The ostensible purpose of the organization was to secure the appointment of an expert rate man on the railway commission of the state.' The *Inter Ocean* was also sceptical of Harry's intentions. 'The history of railroad strikes shows very plainly that the employes and the stockholders do not stand together, but far enough apart to regard each other with the suspicion of a readiness to take every advantage', it noted. 'It may be that these 3,000,000 men have a common interest but if Mr. Robinson can convince them of it he will be able to use it to better purpose in preventing strikes than in organizing a new political party.'[45] Ironically, that would prove Harry's main intention.

In the meantime, Harry had a growing business to run. As majority owner of stock in, and president and editor of, *The Railway Age and Northwestern Railroader*, Harry's responsibilities expanded well beyond publishing the largest-circulation weekly railway paper in the country. He was a book publisher of tomes related to the industry, including *Compound Locomotives* by A. T. Woods, and *The Biographical Dictionary of Railway Officials of America*. He also published informative pamphlets, such as *The Protection of Railroad Interests* by James F. How, vice president of the Wabash Railroad, described as 'brief, pointed, suggestive, and an earnest appeal to railway managers to stand together against demagogic encroachments upon the rights of railway property'. Harry launched a new biweekly paper, *The Railway Surgeon*, in June 1894, the house organ of the National Association of Railway Surgeons.

*   *   *   *   *

Tragedy struck Harry and Mary in the summer of 1893 when Beatrice Harriett, their daughter, died on August 13, barely one year old. Whether she was a sickly child, or if her death was sudden and unexpected, is unknown. We do know that she died one thousand miles west of

Chicago, in Colorado Springs, Colorado, with her parents by her side. The family may have been there on holiday, or, more likely, they went there in search of a cure. Colorado Springs was an emerging destination for hospital sanitaria and the treatment of tuberculosis. The *Minneapolis Tribune* broke the news on August 14, noting that Beatrice died at 2:30 a. m. 'The family have the sympathy of a host of friends in this city, in their heavy affliction.' The following day, the *Tribune* reported that the child's remains had arrived in Minneapolis, and the funeral would take place at the Lowry residence. The death of her child started a downward physical and mental health spiral for Mary, who soon returned to Colorado Springs to convalesce. Over the next several years she would be in and out of sanitaria.

In January 1894, Harry received a letter from his father, Julian. Now 75 years old and in failing health, Julian began with a plea for forgiveness in his response to a recent letter from Harry. '*Non sum qualis eram* [I am not what I used to be]', he wrote. 'Guiding a pen is by itself rather hard and laborious work with me, but to write anything with vision and purpose in it is simply beyond me.' Amid relating brief news of Harry's mother and siblings, he asked about Mary, whom he met during the honeymoon visit in 1892. 'I am truly happy to hear that the improvement in your dear wife's health still continues', he wrote. 'She seemed to me a bright example of the best womanhood—amiable, intelligent and very fair to look upon. Give her my sincere love and homage. Such women are of the very salt of the earth.' Indeed, Mary was improving, although she remained in Colorado Springs, where Harry joined her for Christmas. In January Mary's mother and sister came to stay; Nellie would meet her future husband, Percy Hagerman, there. On March 1, while in Colorado Springs, Harry started work on his first novel, as he noted in his journal.

At this time Mary became pregnant again. Julian responded to the good news in a letter to his son on August 24, 1894. 'The news that Mary was at Chicago again with you, and that she had fond expectations for November, were very comforting', he wrote. 'I pray God that she may be allowed to remain with you this winter, and that the arrival of a little one, to replace the dear child which you lost, may complete the happiness of your home.' The fact that Mary had returned home to Chicago was indeed good news, although Julian's hope that she would remain there suggests that Mary might have been on some sort of hospital regimen in Colorado Springs.

* * * * *

As we know from his time running the *Northwestern Railroader*, and his association with industry leaders, Harry had no patience with railway strikes, which he found ineffective and ultimately damaging to the workers who were often goaded into participating by nefarious union bosses or disrupters. So when the notorious Chicago Pullman Strike of 1894 happened in his back yard, with corresponding violence and blood-shed (reminiscent of European clashes), Harry, fearing the worst, was ready to respond.

The strike began on May 11, 1894 when workers of the Pullman Palace Car Company in suburban Chicago walked out to protest a reduction in wages. The newly formed American Railway Union, led by Eugene V. Debs (who had supported a successful strike action against the Northern Pacific Railroad, forcing the company into arbitration over wage cuts), stepped in to support the workers, and called for a nationwide boycott of all Pullman trains. Strike action spread to 250,000 workers in 27 states, sabotage caused $80 million in damages, and 30 people were killed in riots. After two months, President Grover Cleveland called in the military to run the railways and crush the strike, which collapsed.

In August 1894, the *North American Review* published four articles under the banner 'The Lesson of Recent Strikes'. Harry contributed one, along with General Nelson A. Miles, head of the U.S. Department of the East (who commanded the troops mobilized to put down the Pullman Strike); Wade Hampton, U.S. Commissioner of Railroads; and Samuel Gompers, president of the American Federation of Labor, founded in 1886. A common theme of all four articles was the condemnation of violence and attacks on property, and the solution of problems by peaceful means—on both sides. 'Let us not blow down the beautiful arch of our sovereignty—the hope of humanity, the citadel of liberty, independence, the temple of happiness for all mankind',[46] Miles wrote. Hampton called Debs and his cronies 'designing demagogues' who led the workers astray. 'For the unscrupulous leaders, who, at a safe distance from danger, exposed their unfortunate dupes to probable death and to certain ruin, no condemnation can be too emphatic, no punishment too severe',[47] he wrote. Gompers, an English expatriate like Harry, took the workers' side, naturally. 'It may well be asked, if the state refuses to deal out some degree of justice and guarantee protection to labor, what interest has the laborer in the state?' he wrote. 'We must insist upon the right to organize, the right to think, the right to act; to protect ourselves, our homes, and our liberties, and work out our emancipation.'[48] Gompers, who repudiated socialism, favoured peaceful negotiation, as he worked to convince the American public that organized labour was a respectable and responsible component of the establishment (which is why the American Federation of Labor did not support the Pullman Strike and its ensuing violence).[49]

It was up to Harry to pull it all together as the recognized national advocate for the railroad industry. He began sensibly, providing some perspective. 'It is as old as Plato (and therefore presumably older), that though revolutions break out on trivial occasions, the underlying causes are never trivial', he wrote. 'They arise *out of* small things, but *about* great ones.'

> The grievance of the men at Pullman—the question whether they should receive 25 cents more or less for a day's labor—was not the cause of the strikes and riots which followed. It was only an excuse for precipitating a conflict which had been already decided upon, and which must have come sooner or later.

> Those who have been in any measure conversant with the currents of thought in what are known as 'labor circles' have seen the clouds that were gathering, not only for months past, but for some years. Had the country not encountered the financial depression of the last twelve months,[50] their breaking might have been delayed for some time yet. But it was a question of time only. The storm could not have been finally averted.[51]

Harry reminded readers that the recent action was not a general railway strike, but a Pullman-specific strike. The majority who walked off their jobs had no connection with Pullman nor any grievances; rather, they were part of a plot by labour leaders against all classes of employers. 'The strike was primarily a demonstration of force on behalf of organized labor against the general social conditions of the country', Harry observed. 'It was only accidental that it occurred on certain railways.' Harry's intention was clear: he wanted to protect the railroads (and their owners) from being branded a cause of strike action (however guilty the Pullman Company may have been). Harry concluded with a dire warning to the American people, and in particular certain members of Congress sympathetic to the strike organizers. 'They knew that they were embarking upon rebellion. The word had no terror for them, because, as we have seen, they believed themselves to be strong enough to win', Harry wrote. 'The movement itself is not strictly a movement of anarchy, though it would have all the forces of anarchy upon its side. That it is a conspiracy against the public peace there can be no question.' Harry was talking about treason, and issued a clarion call for concerted action to stop the proposed revolution in its tracks. 'Forewarned is forearmed', Harry insisted.

> While listening to the pleas of labor agitators and the champions of organized labor—whether in the press or from the platform, in legislative halls or from gubernatorial chairs—it is well that the people should know and remember that it *is* rebellion which these organizations contemplate. It is revolution which they hope to attain—by peaceful means, if may be; by force, if must. The ear of the country is always ready to hearken to the cry of the workingman. The heart of the country is tender and quick to be touched

by the tale of the wage-earner's suffering. But the country cannot afford to be kind or soft-hearted to treason.

Let no man flatter himself that these latest strikes are no more, and bear no deeper significance, than other strikes which have gone before. Former disorders have been but sporadic outbreaks, resulting from local causes. This last is the development of a deep-seated malady, a cancerous growth, which has been deliberately implanted in the social system of the country, and has been fostered there till it has struck roots, which will not be torn out without the rending of tissue and the spilling of blood. Its existence is a menace to the nation.[52]

Harry did not mince his words, and coming from the head of the *Railway Age*, this condemnation of socialism and warning about treason certainly carried weight. Needless to say, not everyone was impressed. The *Minneapolis Tribune* expressed alarm over Harry's judgement, reminiscent of those 'who think that labor so thoroughly organized and disciplined that it must be feared as a sort of Frankenstein born of hard times and unrestricted immigration . . . Proof ought to be forthcoming if such a vast conspiracy really exists'.[53] The *Chicago Tribune* also thought Harry unduly alarmist. Men like Debs and his union members 'are cherishing vain hopes. The American commonwealth cannot be converted either by peaceful or violent methods into a Socialistic State.'[54]

Harry would not back down, and was quick to condemn the report of the commission appointed by President Cleveland to investigate the Pullman Strike. The commission was led by Carroll D. Wright, who was the first U.S. Commissioner of Labor, serving from 1885 to 1905. When the report was issued in November 1894, Harry published an open letter to Wright in the *Railway Age*, which was also published in *The Forum* in January 1895 under the dramatic title 'The Humiliating Report of the Strike Commission'. Restating his analysis in the *North American Review* and his warnings about anarchy, Harry was appalled to discover no similar denunciation in the official report. 'For all the treason, the violence, and rebellion, the Commissioners have no word of condemnation—the strife was simply over the handling of Pullman cars!' Harry wrote. 'There is not one word of praise for those who in the time of peril upheld the dignity of the nation and the sanctity of the law; but there is abundant vituperation of the "rank injustice" of corporations and the "unlawful and dangerous combinations" of the "monopolies" against the "rights of labor".' It is perhaps not surprising that Wright, as Commissioner of Labor, would want to seek a middle ground. Furthermore, Harry was amazed that the commission praised the leaders of the strike for their 'dignified, manly, and conservative conduct in the midst of excitement and threatened starvation', conduct that was called 'worthy of the highest type of American citizenship'.

> What was this 'dignified, manly, and conservative conduct?' It was the conduct of the strikers at Pullman—their conduct in failing for several weeks so far to overstep the restraints of law as to demand the intervention of the military. That they took part in rioting and violence later, is forgotten. That because 'until July 3' they refrained from such extremity of lawlessness as to compel their suppression by military force—for this their conduct is 'worthy of the highest type of American citizenship.' Verily, if American citizenship knows no loftier ideal than this, the time for despairing of the Republic has almost come.

Needless to say, Wright was not pleased, writing to Harry, 'I have examined the points you attempt to make against the commission and find that every material position taken by you is false, while our own positions are in the main clearly substantiated by the evidence taken. I believe the report of the commission to be thoroughly impregnable as to every material statement of facts.'[55] Case closed, but Harry had taken a bold and prominent stand, and industry and political leaders had taken notice. Now he would further his cause in a new and unexpected direction: a novel.

*   *   *   *   *

As the controversy waned, Harry was in mourning, again. In Chicago, Mary gave birth to a boy on October 9, perhaps one month premature. Christened Julian Thomas (after his parents' fathers, Julian Robinson and Thomas Lowry), the baby died within hours. Harry accompanied his son's body alone the next day on the train to Minneapolis, where he was interred at Lakewood Cemetery next to his older sister. The *Minneapolis Tribune* noted on October 13 that 'only the child's father and members of the mother's immediate family were present'. The grief must have been unimaginable, especially for Mary, alone in a Chicago hospital. And the strain on the three-year-old marriage was growing. From this point onward, Mary and Harry would spend less time together. Mary was frequently in Minneapolis or Colorado Springs, while Harry, his star rising, was often on the road to New York, Washington, and further afield.

3

Junior Kingmaker, 1895–1899

'I have climbed to the top of the greasy pole', Benjamin Disraeli famously declared in 1868, when he became prime minister for the first time. By 1896, with a best-selling novel on a hot topic—labour—and a successful campaign to elect a Republican president under his belt, Harry could say the same. Through sheer ambition, dogged perseverance, and unmistakable charm, Harry had come a very long way in a short time, excelling as a journalist, editor, publisher, novelist, and, shortly, a kind of kingmaker, not forgetting his marriage into a prominent family and entrance into society. At 36 years old, he was the envy of his peers, and would have considered being called a 'Republican henchman' (as one newspaper branded Harry) as a badge of honour. He was also a master of surprises, and his first novel, *Men Born Equal*, was as unexpected and provocative as was his pamphlet, 'Federal City', and wound up placing him on the road to the White House.

Harry's novel represented a departure from his short fiction to date, as it had nothing to do with the Wild West, mining camps, or the supernatural. Rather, it had a 'ripped-from-the-headlines' flavour, since it was a romance set against the world of big business and organized labour, and featured a strike action not dissimilar to the Pullman Strike. After all, he finished the book during the early days of that strike, and the opinions he expressed in public permeate its pages. It was a brilliant move on Harry's part: it represents the fullest expression of his views on labour and the working man, and an attempt to bring those views to a much wider audience outside of the railroad industry. Harry's novel, moreover, joined a growing number of so-called 'strike novels' published on both sides of the Atlantic in the 1880s and 1890s. Inspired perhaps by earlier popular English novels such as *Sybil, or The Two Nations* by Disraeli (1845), *Mary Barton* by Elizabeth Gaskell (1848), and *Hard Times* by Charles Dickens (1854), these American novels by mostly lesser-known authors like Harry served to raise the alarm among readers of the social dislocations which accompanied industrialization, using a genre that was becoming a popular form of expression. Their calamitous message was far from subtle. 'Perhaps because they were unused to severe social upheavals [unlike Europeans], Americans regarded them with terror', noted Anita Clair Fellman. 'Strikes, with their accompanying violence, would dredge up the scum lying at the bottom of American society and release it to pollute the social atmosphere.'[1]

Harry wrote the 155,000-word novel in just three months, and sent the manuscript to Houghton Mifflin in Boston, one of the country's pre-eminent publishers, on July 15, 1894. Houghton Mifflin published the *Atlantic Monthly*, so Harry had a connection there. But it was rejected and returned on August 9 by Herbert R. Gibbs, editor. (Ironically, in 1899 Gibbs would green-light *The Son of the Wolf*, the first book by a new author, Jack London, whom Harry would publish in England.) 'We have tried to put ourselves in your attitude, so that we might read the book not only conscientiously and thoroughly, as you requested, but also sympathetically', Gibbs explained. 'The topics which form the staple of the book, apart from the romance, are of great importance and their intelligent discussion is always interesting.' Gibbs, however, was not confident of 'securing for it a measure of success which would be satisfactory to you and to us'.[2] It is surprising that Houghton Mifflin rejected the book, as the subject matter was timely and the novel would generate publicity for the entire list. But Gibbs was being charitable: the reader's report, written by Horace Elisha Scudder, and signed off by the publisher himself, Henry Oscar Houghton, is more revealing. 'Mr. Robinson, brother to Phil Robinson, wrote a few years ago a clever story for the Atlantic—The Gift of Fernseed, and when he wrote about this new novel of his we encouraged him to send it', Scudder noted, with an interesting nod to Phil. 'It turns out to be a somewhat showy, shallow piece of work, with some superficial excellence. The author has taken advantage of the attention drawn to strikes, especially as connected with politics.' Scudder concluded that Harry's personal opinions were far too strong. 'Mr. Robinson has tried to do two things, to tell a story and to show the folly of much of what is called the labor movement', he observed. 'Unfortunately he fails really to penetrate the difficulty of the situation and gives his treatment a partisan air. He does not convince and makes the reader impatient at his weak handling of the subject; his story, meanwhile, is a transparent one, with conventional people, and can scarcely be ranked even as second rate.'[3] Of course, novelists are expected to have an opinion, but the conclusions of *Men Born Equal* veered too far to the right for Houghton Mifflin. Indeed, as much as Harry insisted he was non-partisan, his efforts were always in support of the Republican cause.

Undeterred, Harry dispatched the manuscript to another prestigious publisher, Harper & Brothers, in New York on August 12, 1894, and it was accepted for publication on September 29. Harry was joining a venerable publication house which featured the likes of Henry James, Stephen Crane, and Arthur Conan Doyle. His contract offered the standard royalty of 10 per cent, and publication was set for February 1895. Harper's described the novel in its advertisements as 'A strike in a Western town furnishes a point from which evolves a story which will attract all interested in social and political questions. With the theme a love story is interwoven, and the strike itself provides incidents of the most absorbing character.'

* * * * *

Men Born Equal is, in essence, Harry's own story. The hero, Horace Marsh, is 'emphatically a good-looking fellow', about thirty, the son of a clergyman. He had 'gone through Harvard creditably', spent two years in Europe, and migrated to a Western city in the United States, 'confronting life soberly with a reasonably correct estimate of its requirements and responsibilities' (one wonders if Harry was paying a compliment to his brother-in-law by naming his hero 'Horace', or referring to himself with the letter 'H'). Horace is a lawyer with an interest in politics and a burning desire to change things for the better. His partner in the law firm is 'General' Harter, a sleazy character who has dreams of becoming governor of the state.

Horace falls in love with Jessie Holt, whose father runs a great steel works and an electrical railroad company (read: Mary Lowry and her father). Thoroughly ignorant of politics (unlike her father), Jessie believes the working man has been mistreated, and Horace initially sympathizes. Horace speaks at a Democratic Party political meeting on the rights of labour, but party members are opposed to his ideas. With Harter's connivance, they put out a false interpretation of Horace's speech, implying that Horace is an enemy of the people. Horrified, Jessie wants nothing more to do with her boyfriend, and turns her attention to another, Marshal Blakely. Amid the drama Horace strives to clear his name. When strike action hits the Holt concerns, Horace discovers how union bosses prey on the common worker for their own selfish means (read: the Pullman Strike). He joins the Republican Party, as it is anti-strike. Overall, Horace is committed to the betterment of the working man, but also to a belief that the businessman is doing the best he can—and that means loyalty and sacrifice from his employees, not going on strike. Harry depicts unions as brutal, wicked—and treasonous, as he had written in articles previously.

There are multiple subplots in the novel that would not be out of place in a Victorian 'triple-decker' novel, including an out-of-wedlock pregnancy, several suicides, and a murder mystery. Escapism aside, Harry's primary intention was to express his strong opinion on the current state of the country. He was not at all subtle, much like the novel's title. Horace speaks for the common man. 'It was the cause of those who were in bondage in Egypt, and it was the cause of the black man in the South. It is the cause of the voiceless millions all over the world and of every age—or if not voiceless, they might as well be so, for they are spent with labor and weak with lack of food, and their voices reach only to ears that are deaf, on which they beat in vain.'[4] He insists that solutions can be found, so long as opposing parties find common ground—and resist violence, especially in the form of strike action. 'This country is within a measurable distance of anarchy today', he predicts in typically alarmist fashion. 'In the older countries now the revolution is on the road to working itself out with the bomb and the firebrand and the knife. Surely we, in this country of freedom, can find a better way! We have scorned before the precedents of the ages, and we can once more. It is only lack of such leaders as might win the victory by peaceful means that throws the multitude back on its ultimate and one certain resource of violence.'[5] Harry was determined to keep the flames of revolution in Europe away from his newfound country.

Harry's refusal to compromise on the subject of unions shines through in *Men Born Equal*. As a strike looms, organized by labour leader August Wollmer, Horace convinces a sceptical Jessie that all is not well in her father's business, and that his employees deserve a better deal. Jessie's eyes are opened wide: 'Now for the first time some definite recognition of the immensity and reality of the terrible problem came to her. It seemed as if a great cloud had settled over the earth, and beneath it opened an abyss, black and fathomless, full of writhing, struggling men and women—"one-half of mankind against the other half."'[6] (One hopes Mary Lowry Robinson did not feel the same way about her own father's employment practices.)

When Horace makes his big political speech, he appeals not to party loyalty but to unity of employer and worker and their common goals. 'We are not the heirs to the estate of any party, but to all our nation's history', he proclaims. 'Let us remember the wrongs done only as warnings to us in the future; let us cherish whatever is good for an example for our guidance. We can take no backward step. All the glory that is gone, though living with us yet, is but a preparation for the greater glory yet to come.'[7] Harry's optimism was clearly bubbling over. But Horace is soon humiliated by his own Democratic Party leaders and union bosses, and seeks greener pastures. Horace's self-revelation and perseverance are remarkable:

> Somewhere, though it slumbered deep, the American people must have a conscience. Somehow it could—and would—be touched. They did not understand as yet; they did not see. They were too busy with other things. But if there is one lesson which is writ large in the history of the nation it is that when once the people are awakened and see and understand, they will have right. Had all the manhood and truth left the race in the course of one generation? Under the lash of the labor union, had the working-classes indeed become but this mob of rioting, drunken fools whom Wollmer juggled with? Had the iron of the ward machine so eaten into the soul of all classes that the whole people were no more than these puppets that Sullivan made to dance?
>
> It could not be. When the trumpet had called before, the nation had answered. And somewhere the same stern fibre was in the people—the people whose fathers and great-grandfathers had followed Washington and Grant.[8]

Indeed! When the strike erupts, the militia is called in (as during the Pullman Strike), resulting in the deaths of scores of innocent, misled men. Jessie is horrified that blood is on her father's hands. Horace comforts her with strong words:

> 'The blood is not on your father's head—nor yet on the beads of the mass of the men. It is a handful of leaders—it may be only one man or a dozen men—who stand between the employers and the men, and will not let them know the truth. These leaders make their living by the work. They saturate the men with false teachings—teachings of the tyranny of capital, and making them believe that the employer is their natural enemy. Many of them, foreigners who have already drunk in the doctrines of the bomb in Europe, are only too willing to lend their ear to the same teachings here. And of the rest, some, hearing no other side, come in time dully and passively to acquiesce in what is told them, and the others, conscious of their own individual weakness when opposed to the organization of the unions, keep their peace, and dare not speak.'[9]

Jessie despairs, wondering how this will end. Horace insists it will only end through education, and prosecution of wicked labour leaders. 'In time the nation and the world will recognize that the man who, as a leader of a labor order, persuades men to strike and to riot is as criminal in his anarchism as the men who, under the shadow of the red flag, openly advocate the use of dynamite for the destruction of society', Horace predicts, labelling labour leaders as 'the most dangerous criminals—far more destructive of society than the man who commits an individual murder'.[10] He tells Jessie that, one day soon, the American people will rise up and herald a new era, 'when the government of our country is made again in fact what it ought to be, the noblest government of earth, instead of what it is, one of the clumsiest and most corrupt'.[11] Amid rainbows and sunshine, Horace and Jessie live happily ever after, with Horace now a card-carrying member of the Republican Party.

*   *   *   *   *

Despite its provenance as a political novel with sharp opinions on the American labour scene by a foreign-born author, reaction to *Men Born Equal* was uniformly positive. The *Pittsburgh Daily Post* said that 'Men never are born equal, to be sure, but Mr. Robinson refers to no personal equation, but to equality in the eye of the law. It is written by the editor of a railway journal, in a position to see the inside of his subject.' The *New York Times* agreed: 'Mr. Robinson has a thorough acquaintance with political conditions in the United States, and the lesson he wishes to inculcate is an excellent one.' The *St. Paul Dispatch* regarded the novel as 'a clarion call to rouse the people from sleep'. 'Entitled to a distinguished place in American Fiction', deemed the *San Francisco Chronicle*. The *Brooklyn Daily Eagle* said 'it is thoroughly up to date in its gossip and discussion of political, psychological and sociological matters'. The *Minneapolis Tribune* took great pride in 'the first notable contribution to the fiction of 1895' by a former favourite son: 'The acceptance by such a firm as Harpers of a work of this length by a new writer and the placing of it on the market as the first book of the year, is no small compliment to Mr. Robinson.'[12]

The rival newspapers in Harry's new hometown were evenly divided on the merits of the novel. The *Inter Ocean*, noting the novel is 'full of thrilling incidents, lofty sentiment, and is not confined to the labor problem', observed 'Another young Chicagoan has written a book that will attract much attention and a good deal of criticism from the so called labor-leaders . . . Mr. Robinson may call himself a prophet again for he predicts the time when laboring men will refuse to allow dictation from leaders who are not of themselves.'[13] This was Harry's intention. But on the same day the *Chicago Tribune*, while asking 'Has a novelist of the first rank arisen in Chicago?' largely denounced the book. 'Although the name of Chicago (curiously enough) is not once mentioned in the novel "Men Born Equal," the reader is sure that it treets [sic] of this city before he has gone far in the first chapter', claimed the reviewer, who had no love for Horace, noting 'the hero is no hero at all':

> Horace Marsh does nothing heroic. He starts out with fine sympathies with the masses, and he is converted (or perverted, as the reader chooses) to the

classes (as Mr. Gladstone would say) by what? Well, to be frank, by his love for a rich girl. Horace Marsh is an honorable man, but he is not the stuff of which heroes are made. As for his lady love, Jessie Holt, one will try to regard her type of the fashionable lady of Chicago whose carriage wheels roll daily toward the relief of suffering.[14]

The reviewer called out Harry's intention: 'If this novel "Men Born Equal" could be scattered among the laborers of Chicago it might doubtless do good work in making them more contented with their lot, and in making them distrust the interested leaders who often fatten on their misfortunes. They would find that Mr. Robinson preaches directly at them ... One is afraid, however, that "Men Born Equal" is one of those luxuries which the masses must do without.'

Claims that Harry's novel was based on real life and real people may explain the great pains that he and his publisher took to distance the novel from the Pullman Strike, perhaps for fear of libel action. The *Railway Age* ran advertisements for the book and offered it for sale direct to readers. It also issued a clarification on March 1, presumably written by Harry:

> So closely is the general trend of the Chicago strikes of last summer and also of the street railway strike in Brooklyn followed in the story that critics in the daily press show a disposition to refuse to believe that the book was written before those events. As a matter of fact it was written in March, April and May, 1894, and was ready for the publishers when the A. R. U. strike in Chicago broke out. It was at first intended to issue it last fall, but Harper & Bros. decided to hold it until the beginning of the year, when the flood of holiday literature was out of the way. The book is a romance—a tale of love and incident; but the dark background of the strike gives the setting. In so far as the story has a moral, it preaches a lesson of sympathy with the working man and of condemnation of the professional labor agitator and strike leader, as well as of the unscrupulous local politician of the day.

On a visit to Minneapolis, Harry insisted to a *Tribune* reporter that his novel was fiction, not fact. 'The critics have treated me very kindly and the publishers seem to be satisfied', he said, 'and if well-meaning people would only stop identifying the characters in the book with living people, I should be happy'.[15] Harry's insistence bordered on exasperation. 'There is not a line of conscious portraiture in the entire volume', he added. 'An accidental resemblance may have crept in here and there, in an isolated trait or two, but it was totally unintentional, and I suspect that every story writer finds such accidents unavoidable.' When Harper's issued a second edition of *Men Born Equal* in November 1895 it included a message from Harry, repeating this assertion. But critics weren't buying it. The *Chicago*

Tribune stated, 'In a prefatory note the author states that, contrary to general belief, his story was written some months before the Debs strike— a fact that shows Mr. Robinson in the light of a literary prophet.'[16]

Did *Men Born Equal* sell? *The Bookman* claimed it was one of the 'top-selling' books in the country, ranking third in the St Louis market, after *Sans-Gene* by Sardou and *Bonnie Brier Bush* by Ian Maclaren. The most popular books were *Trilby* by Gerald du Maurier and *Woman Who Did* by Grant Allen. But according to records of Harper & Brothers, it was only a modest success, selling 1,340 copies in its first two months, earning Harry a royalty of $167.50 ($4,600 today). By November 1895 the book had a second printing but sold only 220 copies, earning another $27.50. In comparison with other Harper authors, Arthur Conan Doyle's *The Adventures of Sherlock Holmes* sold 11,118 copies between June 1894 and April 1896, earning Conan Doyle $2,501.55 ($69,000 today). Fellow journalist and war correspondent Richard Harding Davis's *The Princess Aline* sold 7,500 copies from November 1894 to May 1895, earning $1,406.25.[17] If Harry's novel was not a commercial success, it did nonetheless make headlines, and Harper's would have welcomed the publicity.

*   *   *   *   *

Mary was not present to share in her husband's good fortune. As *Men Born Equal* was published in March 1895, she sailed for Europe with her father and brother. After a stop in London, they continued on to Paris, where Mary's mother and sister had spent the winter. While in London, the Lowrys called upon Julian Robinson, who recalled the visit in a letter to Harry, dated April 5. 'The Lowry party are here again for a too brief time', Julian wrote. 'They are, one and all, nicer and more loveable than ever. You <u>are</u> a lucky fellow. <u>Your</u> marriage must have been "made in heaven."' Presumably Harry had not shared his concerns about Mary with his father. Julian also praised *Men Born Equal*, as Mary had lent him her copy while she sojourned in Paris. 'I was delighted with it, really delighted with it', he wrote. 'I feared that the interest of the story would be smothered under the weight of grave description. But you have driven your horses well abreast. Your serious views are lofty, humane and patriotic, and your story does not suffer a bit—it is extremely interesting.' Julian only found one fault, but a happy one: the title. 'It is *splendide mendax* [nobly untruthful]. It misrepresents, <u>happily</u>, the nature of the work.'

The Lowrys sailed to New York in early May. Harry met their boat and returned with them to Chicago, while Mary continued on to Minneapolis with her family. In the meantime, Harry kept busy with his business, travelled widely about the country (in Georgia in October, the *Atlanta Constitution* hailed his arrival as 'one of the best known editors of the industrial papers in this country' and 'in the front ranks of fiction writers of the day'[18]), and published another short story, this time in *Scribner's* magazine in the November 1895 edition. 'The Story of the Late War in Europe' offered a parable about greed with Harry's signature science-fiction twist (with parallels to 'Federal City'). James Gollerson, millionaire president of the Great Western Provision Company, is fretting about lost profits resulting from the financial panic of 1893. He also laments that peacetime is not good for business, asking, 'Why do not Germany and France get at it again?' His right hand, Arthur Branty, suggests he start a war, which would correspondingly raise prices for all commodities. And so Branty enlists the help of a shady detective, Brane, to stir things up in Europe. Lo and behold, tensions rise between the two countries, Britain gets involved, and America, happily neutral, reaps the rewards. 'From her isolation, America looked on', Harry wrote. 'Her markets began to rise. The price of wheat went up until speculators said that it was "like old times again."' The story ends abruptly on a hopeful note: the Emperor of Austria and the Russian Tsar have intervened to stop the conflict and keep the peace. Harry does not offer details, only stating, 'How the war cloud, when even on the point of bursting, passed away is matter of history.' Was it Harry's intention to show how good men could be misled, and so easily? Or how interdependent and fragile the world's markets were, and how easily a war could start? Reaction to Harry's story was positive. The *Salt Lake Tribune* praised its 'remarkable plausibility'.

* * * * *

The holidays brought family celebrations, and a health scare. The *St. Paul Globe* reported on December 15, 1895 that the Thomas Lowrys were in New York City, at the Holland House, celebrating their twenty-fifth wedding anniversary. 'There was a quiet little family celebration last evening, attended by Mr. and Mrs. Harry P. Robinson and Miss Nellie Lowry.' But the *Minneapolis Tribune* on January 4, 1896 reported that Mary was 'dangerously ill' in Washington, DC. She must have been visiting the city with Harry, perhaps on holiday. No details were given of her illness, but Mary recovered quickly enough to attend the wedding of her sister, Nellie, to Percy Hagerman of Colorado Springs, held at the Lowry residence on January 22. Nellie met her future husband ('highly esteemed as one of the influential young business men', the *Tribune* noted the following day) while visiting Mary at the sanitarium in Colorado. The wedding was much less grand than her sister's. Oddly, the bride had no attendants; Mary was not the matron of honour. The Robinsons gave the happy couple 'decorated French china', and guests danced to the music of a thirty-piece orchestra. Following a honeymoon in 'Old Mexico', the couple made their home in Colorado Springs.

Family matters consumed Harry thanks to a long and newsy letter from his brother Kay on February 24, 1896 updating him on his siblings. At this time, Harry, youngest of the six children, was also the wealthiest, thanks to his marriage. As such, his less fortunate siblings were often contacting him for money. The greatest cause of concern at the moment was Harry's sister, Valence. In 1872 Valence married Army Surgeon Woodforde Finden, and they had three children: Aimee (b.1874; lived only ten days) and two boys, Eric (b.1875) and Leyton (b.1879). But the marriage was strained, and Valence's mental state was increasingly unstable—in fact, there were questions about Leyton's parentage. By 1881 Eric and Leyton were living with their Finden grandparents. In 1890, Valence, now a widow, married another physician, Frederick Mercer. In 1892 she was admitted to an asylum in Norfolk, and by 1895 was living on her own in London, divorced from Mercer and penniless.

Valence's current state was a cause for concern for her siblings. 'I have several times lately asked both the Father and the Mother, as well as Mary, for news of her: but they all seem inclined to change the subject whenever I mention her name', Kay wrote. 'Her position must have changed for better or worse.' Apparently Kay had an idea to send Valence to live with Harry in Chicago, but reconsidered. 'I think it would be a mistake to send her out before you come in the summer and so I have not suggested this to her but have asked whether she thinks it would be cheaper for her to live where she is or (2) to chum with the Mother or (3) to live for a while with Phil and Alice, if they were willing.' The last of these sounded very unlikely, given the scandalous nature of their romance, as well as their own financial state. 'On Phil's finances, there is a leakage somewhere: and I have just succeeded in pulling him and Alice out of a hole they had got into through his shifty ways of doing business', Kay reported. 'If I had not interfered and persuaded the man to whom he had given a promissory note to accept terms, the whole scandal would have been out in the courts and the newspapers. Phil behaved disgracefully throughout: but he evidently has no money just now.' Nor, indeed, did Harry's parents. Harry had been sending money for Valence, via Kay, who had given her only £1 of the £4 Harry sent, reserving the rest for future expenses.

Kay himself was in even worse financial shape. He had only recently returned to England after a stint in India running the *Civil & Military Gazette*, and was seeking work as a journalist. 'My position is just now

Figure 7. Harry's mother, Harriett, age 82, with her daughter Valence, age 49, in the garden of Harry's home, The Wigwam, in West London in 1902. They are knitting items to sell to make ends meet.

very helpless', he wrote. 'I have screwed out every possible penny to pay the first year's instalment of hire-purchase (£66) for our furniture and all day long I am worrying about the ways and means of getting along until the end of April. After that I see my way a little better, but at the present moment a cab fare would mean bankruptcy.' Kay had also been supporting his wife's widowed sister and her children. 'I tell you now in confidence in order that you may understand how little I, who have two women and six children dependent upon what I earn by the pen and who use the pen so indifferently, can do to help with either the Mother or Valence. I have, however, hopes of striking out one day: and meanwhile I could occasionally assist.' Mary, Harry's eldest sister, was better off; 'the only one of the family who can always, I suppose, produce a ten pound note: but then there are probably reasons why Valence did not apply to her. Mary always takes eccentric views of her friend's affairs, and probably sympathises with Mercer!'

Kay concluded that support from Harry was 'the only hope: and living for solitary women is so cheap in England that the amount which you would spend in Val's passage would keep her going'. Kay proposed a payment of £100 per year (£13,200 today) from Harry which would support Valence and their mother. 'With the proceeds of Mother's fancy work and whatever Valence might earn in the same way or in other ways, they would be able to live comfortably, decently and happily in some nice country-place.' Left unsaid was the fact that Harry's parents, Julian and Harriett, were now living apart, as Julian (it appeared) had taken a mistress.

It is not known if Harry sent the money; presumably he did, as he had the financial means to do so. Nor do we know if he ever seriously entertained the idea of inviting the increasingly unstable Valence to come to America to live with him. Still, Harry loved his family, and with the death of his two children and a growing estrangement from Mary (who was away in Minneapolis for months on end), he must have been homesick and sympathetic to the plight of his siblings and his parents.

Kay's letter coincided with one from his now-famous protégé, Rudyard Kipling. Harry mined his own acquaintance with Kipling for the *Railway Age* when, on March 7, 1896, he featured hitherto unpublished verses. This showcased a unique connection between the acclaimed English author (*The Jungle Book* and *The Second Jungle Book* were issued in 1894–5) and the Minnesota 'Soo' Railway, shorthand for the Minneapolis, Sault Ste. Marie and Atlantic Railway, of which Thomas Lowry was president for many years. 'When the Soo line was being built—which was in the days before Rudyard Kipling began to attain the full measure of his present fame—there chanced to be in the northwest a small school of Kipling worshipers who were also railway men', Harry wrote. These men formed a reading club (Harry might have been a member) and scoured English journals and Indian papers for work by their favourite author. Even the line managers became fans. So, Harry related, 'When the time arrived for naming new stations on the Soo lines east, one was called "Rudyard" and another "Kipling."' The year was 1890, two years after Kipling published *Plain Tales from the Hills*, his first collection of short stories. Word got out to Kipling—presumably by Harry—and the author wrote to Frederick Underwood, the Soo general manager, expressing his thanks and enclosing a poem written especially for the occasion—but not for publication. Harry published the poem '"Rudyard" and "Kipling"' for the first time, 'with the author's consent', including the verses 'For who the mischief would suppose | I'd sons in Michigan?' Harry included photographs of the two 'sons' (stations), which he also shared with Kipling, who found his 'great twin brethren' rather 'smallish and coldish at present' (it was winter, after all) but said he hoped they would grow to be 'good and lusty cities'. In a private letter to Harry, Kipling quipped about the photographs, 'I don't think you display much respect for my kids. If you had to take them why didn't you wait till summer instead of showing them up to their poor little feet in snow. They look all froze up.'[19]

* * * * *

Family worries may have been on Harry's mind in 1896, but he had bigger items on his plate. This was a presidential election year, and the Republican Party was making a major push to retake the White House after the second term of the Democratic President Grover Cleveland. The campaign was shaping up to be a battleground over a single issue, the economy (given the financial panic of 1893), and whether to maintain the gold standard for the money supply, or to expand the supply through the coinage of silver. The gold standard was an issue of paramount importance to the railroad industry; bimetallism would lead to inflation which might help farmers and miners, but the urban cost of living would rise, meaning higher prices and lower wages for city dwellers, including railroad workers. The campaign pitted the Republican governor of Ohio, William McKinley, against the Democratic congressman from Nebraska, William Jennings Bryan.

It is clear that Harry was now well known across the United States. He had achieved this prominence carefully and methodically, via the *Railway Age*; his novel, *Men Born Equal*; his articles and short fiction in popular magazines; and, of course, the runaway growth of the Railway Employes Clubs. Any or all of these would have attracted the attention of the Republican Party, as McKinley and his team plotted a path to the White House. Harry's initial contact with McKinley appears to have been a result of his leading article 'The War on the Wage-earner' in the July 17, 1896 edition of *Railway Age*, which he sent to the candidate. 'Most certainly the arguments presented by you must appeal with great force to those employed by the railroads of the country; and I congratulate you on the position you have taken', McKinley wrote to Harry on July 25, from his home in Canton, Ohio. 'I am glad that you have put yourself in direct communication with Mr. Hanna.'[20] Businessman Mark Hanna was McKinley's maverick campaign manager and veritable kingmaker, who used his personal wealth and business acumen to propel his friend to victory.

The article in question represented a departure for Harry's paper in its starkly partisan tone. Truly, by 1896 Harry was a committed, converted member of the Republican Party. It was precipitated by Bryan's nomination at the Democratic National Convention, held in Chicago, and his famous 'Cross of Gold' speech on July 9, 1896, which Harry witnessed. ('You shall not press down upon the brow of labor this crown of thorns; you shall not crucify mankind upon a cross of gold.') 'For twenty years The Railway Age has strictly refrained from meddling with questions of party politics', Harry began. 'Now, however, there has arisen in political affairs a crisis which does intimately concern every railway man—concerns him not merely as a citizen in common with all other citizens, but also more personally and peculiarly as a wage-earner in the service of one of the greatest industrial institutions of the country.' To Harry, Bryan and the campaign for free silver represented 'a war on the wage-earner':

> The free coinage of silver in this country would shake our commercial and industrial fabric to its very foundations. It would bear with especial hardship on all earners of wages or salaries in industrial pursuits. It could not fail to reduce the number of employes in the service of the railways. It must compel reductions in wages. At the same time (if the silver men themselves are to be trusted) it would increase the price of everything which those reduced wages would have to buy. Therefore it seems to The Railway Age that there can be no topic of greater interest to railway men of all classes— no subject which can be more rightly within our province than the political issue which is now dividing the country. In spite of the precedents of twenty years we believe that it is now not only permissible for us, but that it is our duty, to enter the field of politics and to use whatever strength we may have to prevent railway men from being led away to their own destruction.[21]

With that in mind, Harry pledged to be the resource for voters in November. 'We earnestly urge all railway employes who are in any doubt as to the rights and wrongs of the silver question to address inquiries to us', he wrote. 'If any silver man advances an argument which you are unable to meet or do not know how to answer, refer it to us. If there is any question of fact or of reasoning on which you are uncertain and need light, ask The Railway Age. We promise to meet every question fairly and simply—to give truth in such terms as cannot be misunderstood.' A man's very livelihood was at stake. 'No railway man can vote for free silver without voting against his own bread and butter', Harry insisted. 'If for one moment it seems to you otherwise it is because you have been misled as to the facts and do not understand the truth.' Harry was assuming the role of a (very junior) kingmaker, determined to use the press as a weapon.

With an established power base in the *Railway Age* and connections all across the country, Harry was invited by Hanna to join the Chicago headquarters of the Republican National Committee, which was managed by a young lawyer named Charles G. Dawes (who down the road would become vice president of the United States and ambassador to the United Kingdom). Securing Illinois's delegates was considered vital to a McKinley victory, and the Chicago office became a hub of activity. Dawes informed McKinley on August 1 that he deliberately selected his office managers 'from business associates', like Harry, 'and not from politicians'.[22] With the New York headquarters handling fundraising, Dawes's primary role was educational, and fitted in with the 'blanket' media campaign devised by Hanna to inundate the country with the Republican Party's platform. 'The aim would be to build the base by expanding the ranks of the faithful through political education', explained Robert W. Merry, 'at a time when significant immigration was bringing new voters into the political process'.[23] For innovations such as these, McKinley's campaign is often called the first modern presidential campaign, and Harry was right in the centre of it. With a $2 million budget (four times as much as Bryan's entire campaign, with $500,000 spent on printing alone), Dawes and the Chicago office headed a massive voter education drive, building the base by supporting 250 speakers in 27 states and dispersing up to 250 million pieces of literature (pamphlets, brochures, posters, buttons, and favourable newspaper articles, in a dozen languages) into a country of 15 million voters—or 18 pieces for every voter. The mail room in the Chicago office employed 100 people, and railroad cars loaded with materials left the city daily.[24] Harry was a big part of this effort, as head of the Railroad Publicity Department. Essentially, he carried on his oversight of the Railway Employes Clubs while coordinating their activities with Dawes's master plan. 'This was an important department, and he was a success', Dawes recalled of his friend. 'Robinson was a young man of intense nervous energy, which was never misdirected but employed always constructively.'[25] Actually, Dawes was the younger man, 29 years old in 1896; Harry was 37. Harry's 'intense nervous energy' is an apt description; driven and forever on the go, Harry was, in modern parlance, 'wired'.

Harry would have divided his time between the Republican headquarters and the *Railway Age* office, which was now in full elect-McKinley mode. Starting with the July 24 edition and continuing weekly until October 30, Harry ran a special eight-page 'Sound Money Supplement' in the *Railway Age*. This was chock-full of information, articles, and even cartoons about the free silver question. Harry was going all out to educate his readers. The first supplement began with a call to action: 'RAILWAY MEN! You have before you an opportunity such as has rarely been given to any class of men in history—the opportunity to be the controlling influence in saving your country. There is no state in the Union in which, if you vote as a unit, you cannot turn the scale in any

SCENE IN THE HEADQUARTERS OF THE RAILWAY MEN'S M'KINLEY CLUBS.

Figure 8. A Chicago newspaper, *c.* September 1896, illustrated the frenetic activity in Harry's *Railway Age* office during the McKinley campaign.

ordinary election.' Harry insisted that 'his is not a question of Republican or Democrat, but of your own protection as wage-earners. Organize for the preservation of sound money—in defense of your own wages—in support of the country's prosperity and the country's honor!' He proposed a 'Railway Men's Sound Money Club' on every railroad in the country, organized along the lines of his Employes Clubs. 'If you, who read this, are personally willing to take hold of the work of organization in your locality and the work of educating your fellows for their and your own benefit, write to The Railway Age, Chicago. Until the central organization of the Railway Men's Sound Money Club is perfected, we will send you all the information and literature you require, free.' Harry insisted the future was at stake. 'Let railway men of every class act together', he said. 'It is as noble a cause as ever man put his hand to. Organize now and work, and when November comes and free silver is defeated, the people will know that the railway men did their part nobly for the country's salvation.'

And so Harry launched a national movement. By the next edition, July 31, 1896, Harry was able to provide pocket rulebooks for Sound Money Clubs along with membership applications, all in an effort to facilitate foundations. The formal structure included dues for members, officers, regular meetings, and voting rules. It also stated that the movement must be open to everyone, and not directly affiliated with any one party—although obviously McKinley was the preferred candidate. All clubs would be linked to the Central Organization of Railway Men's Sound Money Clubs, headed by Harry, and together they would cooperate for the good of the common cause. The *Railway Age* printed letters from across the country from readers eager for information. 'Will you please send me some of your literature on the gold question? I can put it where it will reach a good many inquiring minds', wrote an official with the Illinois Central Railroad in Cherokee, Iowa. From the Coudersport & Port Allegany Railroad in Pennsylvania: 'Although young myself, this being my first year to vote, I will do all in my power to organize a club and help put down the craze which threatens us, so please send me some literature and information regarding the proposed club.' From the Missouri Pacific Railway Company in Little Rock, Arkansas: 'Quite a number here want to see United States money, like our flag, respected and honored everywhere.'

Campaign materials took creative forms. The *Railway Age* distributed gold and silver coloured 'dollar' medallions to the Sound Money Clubs across the country. Printed on the silver one was, 'This kind of a dollar is good only when limited and exchangeable for gold.' The gold one read, 'This kind of a dollar passes unlimited on its merits anywhere on earth.' Years later Harry recalled receiving a letter written on a torn half of a railway worker's time card. It said, 'DEAR SIR—There is sixty-five of us here working in a gravel pit and we was going to vote solid for Bryan and Free Silver. Some of your books [i. e. campaign leaflets, etc.] was thrown to us out of a passing train. We have organized a Club and will cast sixty-five votes for William McKinley.' Harry observed, 'So far as those sixty-five were concerned our chief interest thereafter lay in seeing that the existence of that gravel-pit was never discovered by the enemy. A faith which had been so speedily and unanimously embraced might perhaps not have been unassailable.'[26]

Not surprisingly, Harry's movement attracted attention—and controversy—as he took to the road and travelled about the country to preach the Sound Money gospel. The *Albuquerque Morning Democrat-Journal*, a pro-silver newspaper in New Mexico (traversed by the Atchison, Topeka and Santa Fe Railway), condemned 'The Railway Bulldozer' in a leading article that ridiculed Harry in particular:

Mr. Harry P. Robinson, of the "Railway Age," has been commissioned by Mr. Hanna to bulldoze the railway employes of the country into support of the republican ticket, and he is now traveling around the country in his luxurious private car telling the common people in the employ of the roads how they have to vote. Maybe some of them will vote as Master Harry commands, and maybe they won't. The Railway Age has always been the organ of the railroad wreckers, and has no more sympathy with the working people on the railroads, or anywhere else, than Mark Hanna himself, and it would be impossible for Mr. Hanna to devise a more effective plan for driving the railway men of the country away from his ticket than he is now carrying out in sending the editor of this organ around the country on a bulldozing mission.[27]

Harry (who probably did travel around in style) took attacks like these personally. Witness the *Minneapolis Tribune,* which interviewed Harry on August 9, 1896 on a visit to the city. Harry claimed he was the victim of a 'personal assault' by a rival paper, the *Minneapolis Times,* regarding his Sound Money Clubs, and wanted to set the record straight. 'The article alleges that our campaign is simply a plan for coercing the employes which has been adopted by the railway managements', Harry told the *Tribune.* 'The accusation is absurd. I started the campaign without consulting a single person, railway manager or otherwise, inspired solely by the conviction that the free silver campaign is, before everything else, a war on the wage-earner, and believing that The Railway Age was better able to reach the railway employes of the country and put them on their guard than any other instrumentality, person, organ or party.'[28] Harry's veracity is somewhat questionable, as he certainly worked in close collaboration with the railway companies and may have floated the idea before his announcement. In any event, he proceeded:

On my first appeal, the railway men arose in response all over the country. We were flooded with calls for literature, not from railway officials, but from employes in the shops and offices, from engineers, brakemen, firemen and men of all grades. The thing developed with such amazing rapidity that I had to put myself in touch with the national Republican committee, and since then we have acted entirely with the co-operation and advice of that committee.... It is a perfectly plain proposition. The railways cannot possibly increase wages under free coinage. They will pay at most the same number of dollars as they pay now, and each dollar will be worth only half as much. The railway employe who votes for free silver votes to cut his own wages in half.

Harry also granted an interview to the *Minneapolis Times.* 'Some of the editors of The Times know me personally too well to take any stock in the statement that when I swung my paper and myself into the present political campaign, I did it at anybody's dictation or suggestion', Harry said. 'I wish to say most emphatically that my present campaign was inspired by no railway officer or management, nor anyone but myself and that, with the backing of the national republican committee, I propose to fight it through till November when I honestly believe that 90 per cent of the railway men of the country will vote for sound money.'[29] Harry may have appeared disingenuous—his effort was clearly aligned with the Republican Party—but the tactic worked. The *Chicago Tribune* noted of Harry's efforts on behalf of sound money, 'The articles were entirely non-partisan. They "took" with railroad men, and soon requests were pouring in for reprints of the series as they appeared.'[30] The newspaper claimed that more than 4,000 workers of the Chicago, Milwaukee, and St Paul Railroad were now Sound Money Club members.

* * * * *

The turning point in the Sound Money campaign occurred early in September 1896. To mark Labor Day (a national holiday created in 1894 by President Cleveland following the Pullman Strike) on September 7, Harry sent a telegram to McKinley at his home in Canton, Ohio, where the candidate received his supporters:

> The Hon. William McKinley: As a bit of good news for Labor Day, I take pleasure in informing you that the number of railway men's sound-money clubs now organized has reached 300, with an aggregate membership of 120,000, and the ball has only started rolling. HARRY P. ROBINSON, Editor of the Railway Age.[31]

This publicity was a savvy move by Harry, as news of the telegram spread like wildfire in newspapers across the country. The *Globe-Republican* in Dodge City, Kansas, expressed amazement on September 24 that 'when we remember that thirty days prior to the above date, there existed only one railway McKinley club, we can begin to realize the growth of the movement and the rapidity with which railway men all over the country have rallied to the support of sound money and good government'. The *Los Angeles Times* on September 10 called the movement 'An Army for Maj. McKinley' that was growing at a breakneck pace, and labelled Harry 'the father of his remarkable movement':

> The clubs in this movement are scattered from Massachusetts to California. The majority of them, however, are in the Mississippi Valley, where they will do the most good. Many of the organizations have glee clubs, marching clubs, ladies' auxiliaries, etc. Some have adopted an official button, and many are doing missionary work among other classes of citizens. In Minnesota the clubs have united in a State league. On every hand there is abundant evidence of intense earnestness and infectious enthusiasm.

On September 19, Harry joined 6,000 Sound-Money railway men and telegraphers, on eleven trains, representing every railroad running into Chicago, on a free, 700-mile round trip pilgrimage to Canton to meet with McKinley at his home. The *Inter Ocean* the next day reported that the group came 'for the purpose of personally pledging to the Presidential nominee of the Republican party their support'. The procession to the McKinley residence was more than one mile long, and when Mr and

Mrs McKinley appeared there was a five-minute ovation. McKinley gave a stirring address, stating 'The railway is the mightiest factor of modern civilization':

> I cannot conceive of a more potential force in our politics this year than the men who traverse this country from one end of it to the other ... The signals of danger to public safety and honor are as quickly and faithfully heeded by you as the danger signals which your roads have established for the safety of life and property committed to your care. The perils which lie along the path of the Nation's progress you would help to remove as you would remove those along the track of the mighty railroads you operate. I welcome the railroad employes of this country as allies in this great contest for the country's honor and the country's flag.[32]

The *Inter Ocean* noted 'Great applause and cries of "We will!"' along with 'tremendous cheering'. A front-page cartoon depicted McKinley on a wagon wheel as 'The new hub of the Universe'; one of the six spokes was labeled 'Railway Employees' (spelled correctly), along with Farmers, Iron-Workers, Veterans, Business Men, and 'Everybody'. Clearly, the railway industry was now an electoral force to be reckoned with. Workers returned to Chicago with souvenir splinters from McKinley's front porch or fence and, most importantly, unbounded enthusiasm for the Republican ticket.[33]

A very public spat erupted when Hanna appointed Richard C. Kerens to head the campaign's new Railway Department, overseeing Harry, who was the natural candidate for the top job. Kerens, a native of Ireland who served as a colonel in the Union Army during the Civil War, was based in St Louis, Missouri, where he was active in railroad construction. The *Pittsburgh Press* on September 28 claimed that Harry was perturbed and that he and Kerens would clash. 'Mr. Hanna will be back in Chicago within the next few days', the paper reported. 'Immediately upon his arrival the employes at the headquarters predict that open hostilities will begin between Mr. Kerens and Mr. Robinson.' The same story was syndicated in newspapers across the country. The *St. Louis Dispatch* on September 29 claimed the situation had apparently become intolerable:

> Harry Robinson of the Railway Age, who has been directing the work among the railroad men, felt aggrieved at Col. Kerens' selection. Mr. Robinson has been active in the organization of anti-silver clubs. As soon as he had many of them in fine working order Col. Kerens was placed in charge. Naturally, Mr. Robinson felt warm under the collar and he has raised a storm about the ears of the Missouri Colonel ... Mr. Robinson has thus far declined to give way and the Missouri member of the National Committee is put in the ridiculous attitude of barking up a persimmon tree after the

possum has escaped. Monday the row between the Colonel and Mr. Robinson grew so heated that the former went over to New York, leaving Mr. Robinson in temporary possession of the field. When he returns from New York, however, hostilities will be resumed and what the outcome will be the factions in Missouri cannot foretell.[34]

Clearly, this was getting out of hand. Harry was quick to debunk the controversy in interviews with both Chicago newspapers on October 2. The *Tribune* claimed Harry's denial was 'emphatic' and noted that 'Mr. Kerens' work is entirely in the East and Mr. Robinson will continue his activity in the West'. The *Inter Ocean* quoted Harry directly: 'The story is ridiculously false... So far from quarreling we are all working together most cordially. The movement is so tremendous that we need all the helpers we can get. If Mr. Kerens is superseding me, I should like about a dozen more superseders of the same kind.'[35] Harry was magnanimous, but knowing his ambition, he was bound to be disappointed. But there was a job to be done, and Harry predicted that 90 per cent of the 800,000 railroad workers in the country would vote for McKinley.

On October 23, the Sound Money Supplement opened with a warning: the vote was close, and the enemy was getting desperate—and more devious. 'Be on your guard', Harry warned. 'It is not necessary now to say much more about the kind of campaign which the other fellows are conducting. It is a campaign of falsehood and trickery.' As an example, Harry published a letter from a railway worker in Iowa. 'I learned to-day that the silver element were coaching about two hundred ex-railroad men with the intention of sending them out over the road making a personal canvass and distributing their literature to each employe that is supposed to be in the doubtful list, and that they are to be sent out at once', he wrote. Harry warned, 'If our information is correct these men will go out in gangs, in couples and individually. There may be 20 or 100 in one place at the same time... Believe nothing—listen to nothing! You have made up your minds. Let no falsehoods or lying stories make you weaken at the last moment. Stand firm!'

Indeed, behind the scenes, the intensity of the campaign was taking its toll. The *Railway Age* office was flooded with hate mail. 'They came by every post and in every form, ranging from mere incoherent personal abuse to threats of assassination', Harry recalled. 'Hundreds of them were entirely insane: many hundred more the work, on the face of them, of anarchists pure and simple. A large proportion of them were written in red ink, and in many—very many—cases the passions of the writers had got so far beyond their control that you could see where they had broken their pens in the futile effort to make written words curse harder than they would.'[36] The letters were put in a receptacle called by office staff the 'Chamber of Horrors' or the 'Hell Box'. 'Before the end of the campaign, capacious though it was, it was crowded to overflowing, and hardly a document that was not as venomous as human wrath could make it', Harry said. He recalled that 'in the organs of free silver we have been called almost everything from a "flea in the hair of a railroad dog" to "a bronze toad."' Harry shared a few examples. A reader from Umatilla, Oregon, claimed 'Anyone that will distribute such reading material is either a blamed idiot or else the biggest liar and scoundrel on earth. Perhaps railroad men have more sense than you give them credit for.' And this one, directed to Harry from Kedron, Arkansas: 'I presume that you are either a lunatic, or Mr. Mark Hanna has paid you a sufficient sum to enable you to pose as one. Have you not sense enough to know that you could not change one workingman from his honest opinions?' Needless to say, such insults would have only strengthened Harry's resolve.

On October 24, Harry organized a 'Sound Money Day' in Chicago, featuring a parade of 25,000 members from Illinois, Kansas, Iowa, and Missouri, complete with lavish floats illuminated with incandescent lights. Harry obtained McKinley's blessing for the event, and the reviewing stand featuring Hanna and Dawes and their wives as well as a large delegation from Ohio. On October 28, Harry was in Grand Rapids, Michigan, for another parade of 2,500 men. The local newspaper reported on an 'able address on the money question by Editor Robinson', who was at pains to say 'I am not a politician or an orator.'[37] Harry was interviewed by the paper. 'In this campaign Bryan is like the man who tied his horse in front of a saloon and went in and took several drinks', he explained. 'When he came out he mounted his horse with his face the wrong way, and when asked about his position said he did not know which way he was going. Bryan is on backwards with his face toward the White House and his horse is going the other way just as fast as half a million railroad men can yank it.' Clearly, Harry did not mince his words, evoking the start of the Civil War:

> The shadow that has hung over this country until the last few weeks is as dark as the one in '61. I was in that hall in Chicago when Bryan was nominated ... I have heard Bryan refer to the 'enemy's country.'[38] In this land there is no enemy's country. It is all one land bound together by railroad tracks, which have made the west to blossom as the rose. The railroads having built the country are not going to see it destroyed, and an Appomattox is only six days ahead.

On October 30, in the last *Railway Age* before the election, the Sound Money Supplement issued the 'LAST CALL'. Harry's writing was especially florid:

> When the victory is won on Tuesday next you will have contributed more than any other class of the people to the salvation of the country. It is not

only that your votes alone will have swung several stales. The influence which you have wielded individually in converting others has been tremendous. Above all, the magnificent example of the Railway Men's Sound Money Clubs as organizations has been an inspiration to the citizens of every state.

SOUND MONEY SUPPLEMENT.

VOL. XXII.   CHICAGO, OCTOBER 30, 1896.   No. 18.

LAST CALL.

RAILWAY MEN:

When the victory is won on Tuesday next you will have contributed more than any other class of the people to the salvation of the country.

It is not only that your votes alone will have swung several states. The influence which you have wielded individually in converting others has been tremendous. Above all, the magnificent example of the Railway Men's Sound Money Clubs as organizations has been an inspiration to the citizens of every state.

It is matter of history that in 1861 when Abraham Lincoln called for troops the employes of the railways responded almost as one man. It will be matter of history hereafter that in 1896, when the nation was again in peril, it was the railway men who answered first and most unanimously to the country's call.

Ninety per cent of the railway men will vote on Tuesday next for sound money, for national prosperity and national honor. Why not the other ten per cent? If you know any silver man among your fellows, seek him out now. Reason with him once more at the last moment. Make one final appeal to him—an appeal to stand by you and by his country.

To you who have already made up your minds we do not say "Stand Firm." It would be an insult to suppose that your determination could be shaken—an insult to your intelligence and your patriotism. But plead with the others! Those who are not with us are against us only because they do not understand and have not seen the truth. They can yet be won. Let every railway man who knows a waverer, or one who seems to be opposed to us, reason with him between now and election day, and let the railway vote of the country be not 90 per cent, but *unanimous* for sound money and against repudiation and shame.

It is hoped that all club secretaries have received the "Appeal to Voters" sent out this week from central headquarters, and have given it prompt and full attention. It is a case wherein co-operation and unanimity are needed, and every club must remember that it is only one link in a chain and that every other club in the country is relying on it to do its duty.

Club officers are requested to give special attention to the matter of having men at all polling places who know the club members, to help them in any way that they need help.

The Railway Men's Sound Money Clubs are strictly non-partisan. Their one and only object is to save the country from the threatened curse of the free coinage of silver. Democrats have been as welcome in the clubs as republicans, and members are at liberty to vote according to their consciences and their reasons as they see fit. It should not be forgotten however that a vote for the sound money democratic national ticket is only one vote against free silver, wh'le a vote for the republican national ticket is two votes against it. A democratic vote for McKinley not only takes a vote away from Bryan, but it adds a vote to the strength of the man who is going to beat him.

When the clubs were organized they were organized to exist only until the grand ratification meeting to celebrate the victory at the polls. It has been suggested from several quarters that all clubs designate the same day—Saturday, November 7—as ratification day. Clubs will of course be guided by local conditions; but if this can be done, it would be a fitting wind up to one of the most remarkable and honorable movements that ever took place in any political campaign.

Not only vote yourself, but see that every man whom you can reach or influence votes also. Vote as early in the day as possible.

Figure 9. The cover of the special edition of *The Railway Age and Northwestern Railroader* issued just before the U.S. presidential election.

It is matter of history that in 1861 when Abraham Lincoln called for troops the employes of the railways responded almost as one man. It will be matter of history hereafter that in 1896, when the nation was again in peril, it was the railway men who answered first and most unanimously to the country's call.

The *Railway Age* reproduced a sample ballot paper, instructing readers how to mark it properly.

* * * * *

McKinley was elected the twenty-fifth president of the United States on November 3, 1896. While the popular vote was closer than expected, 7.1 million to 6.5 million (51 per cent to 47 per cent), McKinley won a landslide in the Electoral College, 271 to 176 (224 were needed to win). The message in the *Railway Age* of November 6 was euphoric: 'Well, the American people is still sound at heart, thank Heaven! And now let us turn our attention to helping along the good times that are coming.' In the November 13 edition, Harry compared the vote from thirty clubs, representing more than 100,000 members, against the total vote in each of their communities, and identified a definite swing. 'We do not claim that the railway men alone did all this work. There were not enough railway men there by their votes to do it', Harry noted. 'When we find this amazing change in the vote wherever railway men were congregated and we do not find an equal change at other points in the same state or district, what are we to conclude? We can conclude only one thing, viz., that the railway men were the staunchest, truest class of men in the country, and that to them more than any other body of men the gratitude of the nation is due.' Indeed, railway workers were among those in the so-called 'ultimate swing bloc' in the Gilded Age, the labourer vote, which McKinley and his allies courted relentlessly with great effectiveness, through the Sound Money agenda promising jobs, good wages, and rising prosperity.[39]

Harry elaborated on the election outcome in the January 1897 edition of the *North American Review*, in an article written just after the election and entitled, 'The Railway Vote in the Campaign'. Analysing the data, he revealed that 'it is certain that not less than 80 per cent., and probably over 90 per cent., of the railway employees' voted for McKinley. Of these 800,000 voters, 50 per cent had previously voted for the Democratic candidate—and, in fact, may still consider themselves Democrats. 'These men voted as they did avowedly as railway men', Harry noted, predicting, 'We now have to reckon with an entirely new factor in American politics':

The votes of certain races—the German vote, the Irish vote, the negro vote, the Scandinavian vote, etc.—have long been recognized as distinct entities in the political world. There has also been the agricultural vote, and the mining vote has had great power in certain States. Outside of these few grand divisions, politicians have heretofore lumped all the wage-earning classes together in one conglomerate 'labor vote.' That can never be done again. In this election the so-called 'labor vote' has split within itself, and the immediate and most important result of that cleavage is the emergence of the Railway Vote.[40]

And it was entirely Harry's doing. He reminded readers that the campaign was 'a war between all the forces of discontent on the one side and of law and order and respect for established institutions on the other. The railway employees deliberately declared that their part is the part of law and order and that their welfare rests on the maintenance of our institutions.' This bode well for the future, Harry claimed. 'Hereafter whenever the forces of Socialism rise turbulently to the surface—whenever Anarchy raises its head against the government—whenever again sectionalism and Communism and discontent unite together in conspiracy against constituted society—the American people can rest assured that the best brain and sinew of the workingmen of the country are on the side of righteousness', he insisted. Clearly, Harry considered this election to be about much more than sound money, but the very future of the Republic, spared the disturbances taking place across the Atlantic Ocean.

On November 20, 1896 Julian Robinson wrote to his son, offering 'only a poor and tardy compliment on the resource and energy you showed in the Presidential contest, and a congratulation on the success of the cause you espoused. I should like to be assured that your exertions have been fully recognized by those whom they benefited.' Bursting with pride, he added, 'There is one trait in your character from which I confidently augur for your great ultimate eminence: it is that, "whatever your hand findeth to do, you do it with your might."'[41] Similarly, in his scrapbook Harry pasted an article from an unnamed newspaper which was published after the election. The writer singled out Harry, a 'Republican henchman', for his influence on electing McKinley, dubbed 'Napoleon', and referenced Harry's statistical analysis of the votes. 'Col. Robinson certainly worked up the "agony" in favor of sound money, and if there be one editor in the country who deserves well of his party, certain it is that man is Col. Harry P. Robinson, of Chicago', the article ran. 'May he get his full measure of party reward. To the victor belong the spoils, is sound Republican logic.'[42]

Indeed, what would be Harry's 'reward'? Surely the McKinley campaign, from the president-elect on down to Hanna, Dawes, and even

Kerens recognized the tremendous work that Harry did in rallying the railway workers, many of whom crossed party lines in casting their ballots. Several of Harry's potted biographies over the years, as well as family legend, claimed that President McKinley offered Harry an ambassadorship. In 1927, a documentary produced by the London *Times* said this about Harry: 'He was Chief of one of the Departments of Mr. McKinley's Campaign in the great Free Silver fight of 1896, being subsequently offered a foreign Mission by Mr. McKinley, which he declined.'[43] Harry's obituary in the London *Times* on December 22, 1930 was more specific: 'When the Presidential election was over, the Republican Party chiefs wished him to remain in politics, and he was offered the Legation at The Hague, but refused.' Even Brad insisted this in his memoir, noting that McKinley 'always said it was my father who got some sense into their heads', persuading railway workers to vote Republican, 'and that was why he was the only Englishman ever to be offered an American ambassadorship (McKinley wanted him at The Hague)'.[44] But there is no evidence to support this claim. As early as February 6, 1897, in the *St. Paul Globe*, local attorney Stanford Newel was tipped as the new ambassador. The *Globe* noted that Samuel R. Thayer, a Minneapolis attorney, had held the post from 1889 to 1893, appointed by President Benjamin Harrison. 'This has given the Republicans of Minnesota the feeling that, in the distribution of foreign posts, they have a claim; and there has been a strong movement in favor of the selection of Mr. Newel as minister to the Netherlands. This state is certainly entitled to such recognition, and the new president could not make a worthier choice.'[45] Minnesota had a large immigrant Dutch population. Newel, also an attorney, was the former chairman of the Minnesota Republican Party and was a delegate to the Republican National Conventions of 1884 and 1892—in the latter, the only Minnesota man who cast a vote for McKinley, then seeking the party's nomination. The mystery deepens with a letter from John Addison Porter, secretary to the new president, to Harry on April 5, 1897. McKinley had assumed office on March 4. 'The President directs me to acknowledge the receipt of your communication of the 1st instant, and to assure you that any endorsements you may give an applicant for office will have careful consideration',[46] Porter wrote. What could this have been about? Did Harry put in a good word for Newel, whom he would have known in his Minnesota days? In any event, Newel's nomination was sent to the U.S. Senate on May 5, and he was approved.

So the question remains: was Harry ever offered the post? Over the years he did not dispute the story that he was. If true, then why did he turn it down? Perhaps he was reluctant to give up the company and power base he had built up in Chicago. Or perhaps he was unwilling to leave America, mindful that Mary would likely not join him. But if false (which is more likely), Harry's endorsement of an untruth over the years casts a shadow on his character. Whatever the reason or the truth, it was now business as usual. Harry remained head of the *Railway Age*, albeit with a much raised national profile. He remained active in the newly formed National Sound Money League, created, according to the *Brooklyn Daily Eagle* on February 24, 1897, to 'disseminate views of leading thinkers on financial questions against the theory of bi-metallism and in favor of the gold standard'. Eugene V. Smalley was the league's secretary; Harry was the representative for Chicago and a member of the executive committee. The League organized conferences around the country and issued a monthly journal called *Sound Money*. Harry's portrait was featured on the cover of the October 1897 edition. He was praised for stepping into the breach when Bryan won the Democratic nomination. 'In this emergency Mr. Robinson discerned an opportunity to render national service by organizing the railway men in behalf of the sound money cause', the article ran. 'The vigor and enthusiasm with which Mr. Robinson and his associates conducted this railway campaign baffled the free silver designs and held the railway men where they rightfully belong—on the side of sound money and national honesty.'[47]

Harry joined Mary in Colorado Springs for Christmas, where they celebrated with the Hagermans, who had just welcomed their first child. Harry returned on his own to Chicago, where early in 1898 he moved into an apartment closer to his office. This could indicate that his marriage was further breaking down, as Mary was rarely in Chicago anyway. In fact, in 1898 Mary was under the care of a doctor at the Glen Springs Sanitarium in Watkins Glen, New York. Dr Thomas J. Carney, on staff there, later told the *Chicago Tribune* that he remembered treating Mary, and that 'Mr. and Mrs. Lowry frequently visited her there. She had told him, he said, that she married a man of the name of Robinson, who was employed by her father, but she was not happy.'[48] Of course, Harry did not work for Lowry (at least not directly), but this much was certain: the marriage was in trouble.

* * * * *

In the meantime, Harry threw himself into his work. Early in 1898 the Chicago Sound Money League, headed by Harry, produced an extraordinary publication, 'The U.S. Patriotic Almanac', which was distributed free with the *Chicago Tribune* and other prominent daily newspapers in America. It was chock-full of presidential portraits and quotes, statistics about wages and labour, the complete text of the

Constitution—and snippets about the gold standard. Clearly, this was an expensive effort to further align financial policy with patriotism and the American way. On January 18, 1898, the *Philadelphia Inquirer* thought the publication, 'to advance the interests of the gold standard with country people', was a 'fairly successful device', even though 'we had supposed the silver question to be dead'.

The almanac continued Harry's good will with the McKinley Administration, and on February 2, Harry had an appointment at the White House, joined by his old friend and colleague, Smalley. This was the first time Harry met McKinley in person and, tellingly, Mary was not with him. Harry jotted ten pages of notes on the meeting on hotel stationery which were akin to a transcript and show McKinley's pleasure with Harry and the work he did in the campaign. The conversation is all the more remarkable considering that, just eight years earlier, a giddy Harry was rolling about on the White House lawn.

'Mr. Robinson, I am glad to have the pleasure of meeting you at last', McKinley opened the meeting.

'Mr. Robinson did great work in the campaign, Mr. President', Smalley said.

'I know it.'

'We tried anyway, Mr. President', Harry said, 'and I am afraid at times I was something of a burden to you in my excessive zeal.'

'There could not be any excess of zeal—at least in my opinion', McKinley replied. 'You also did as able work as was done in the campaign.'

'And I think, Mr. President', Harry continued, 'they are organized "for keeps,"' referring to the Railway Sound Money Clubs. 'We can call on them again when needed. Indeed I am planning to do so.' He shared with the president plans to invite two men from each of the 500 clubs to Chicago for a rally, and invited McKinley to speak. The timing would coincide with the start of McKinley's re-election campaign in the autumn, as the long road to the 1900 presidential election began. McKinley agreed, noting, 'I certainly would not run away from men who worked so hard for me.'[49]

Following their meeting with the president, Harry and Smalley attended a reception. McKinley introduced Harry to the First Lady as 'one of my friends'. Harry also met President and Mrs Sanford Dole of Hawaii (the United States would soon annex Hawaii in July 1898) and assorted members of the cabinet. Clearly, Harry was star-struck. In 1901, after McKinley's assassination, he recalled the former president fondly. 'It was impossible to underrate the strength or the curious mental sanity of the man', Harry wrote. 'I do not expect ever to meet a man of more impressive presence, at once so unaffectedly attractive and so full of dignity. From his photographs the world is familiar with the somewhat Napoleonic face; but photographs do not give the colour or the stead-fastness of the warm grey eyes, nor the charm of bearing and manner.'[50]

Not much time would pass before Harry had to call upon the White House again, this time on a personal matter: his brother Phil had been captured in Cuba as the Spanish–American War intensified, and Harry appealed for his release. It seems Phil had spent several weeks in New York City in March and April 1898, covering the heightened tensions between the United States and Spain as a freelance reporter for the *Pall Mall Gazette*. As a seasoned war correspondent, Phil would have been in demand by the London papers. Spain declared war on April 23; the U.S. two days later. Harry met up with Phil in Washington on May 9, when Phil visited the British Embassy to receive his press credentials to travel to Cuba. To his wealthy brother Harry, Phil presented his hotel bill in New York, which included seven weeks' board, whiskey, beer, cigars, and cigarettes. Harry bid his beloved brother farewell, and Phil made his way to Key West, Florida, the launching point for Cuba. From the Hotel Key West, he wrote to Harry. 'I have been baffled and bushed beyond description. Everybody afraid to help one. Three tries made but all failures. However starting tonight to fail or succeed.' Enclosed in the letter was $100. 'If you are well at the moment it reaches you send it to Alice c/o I.H. Davies, 15 Tavistock Street, Covent Garden.' 'Alice' was Alice Cornwell, his lover; the address was, intriguingly, Phil's London publisher, Isbister & Co. (the firm Harry would run less than four years later). 'If you are not', Phil proceeded, 'keep it against what I owe to you. Goodbye. You have already wished me luck and a couple of days ought to tell me whether I am there.' Phil attached a list of personal items he was leaving behind 'in case of accident', including '3 cases of papers and some laundry'.

Phil did eventually make the crossing, joined by another British reporter, H. J. Whigham, representing the London *Evening Standard*. They approached Cuba on an English-chartered steamer, then lowered themselves in a small boat to row ashore. They were captured in Matanzas, on the north coast of Cuba, and thrown in jail. Needless to say, this was the stuff of high drama and national headlines, and Harry rode to the rescue of his big brother, as evidenced in a sheaf of letters Harry kept in his scrapbook. On May 31, he telegrammed William R. Day, Secretary of State, in Washington. 'Phil Robinson reported captured Matanzas. Is British subject, war correspondent Pall Mall Gazette. He is my brother. It is case for intervention of British Embassy. I have wired Pauncefote.' Julian Pauncefote, 1st Baron Pauncefote, was the British Ambassador to the United States. 'As his brother I beg to invoke your offices in his behalf', Harry wrote to Sir Julian. 'He went to Cuba intending to make his way direct to General Blanco's headquarters, expecting to be received by him as war correspondents of neutral papers always are received by the commanding officers of armies of civilized powers.' Ramón Blanco Erenas Riera y Polo, 1st Marquis of Peña Plata, was the Captain-General of Cuba and sworn enemy of the United States, who pledged to arrest all foreign reporters who set foot in Cuba. 'He is in no way subject to treatment as a hostile, but as the representative of the *Pall Mall Gazette* and a British subject is entitled to all consideration and courtesy', Harry continued. 'I gather from the dispatches this morning that he is regarded in the light of a prisoner of war, and I trust that you will make the necessary representations through the proper channels.' Harry also alerted the offices of the *Pall Mall Gazette* in New York, and wrote to John Addison Porter at the White House, enclosing his messages to Secretary Day and Sir Julian. 'I do not know that there is anything to add to this. I presume the less interest that is shown by the government of United States in the matter the better', Harry wrote. 'None the less, if the President has any such kindly feeling towards myself as would prompt him to make any confidential communication to Her Britannic Majesty's representative on the subject it will be a favor that will be appreciated by Yours very sincerely.' In other words, Harry was calling in a favour. Porter replied on June 3, noting that 'both of these communications have been laid before the President for his information. Hoping that the result of your efforts will be in accordance with your wishes.'

The newspapers had a field day with the story. Harry told the *Inter Ocean* on June 1 that he feared for Phil's safety as he was 'arrested as a spy'. Phil's intentions were pure, Harry assured the paper; his object was 'reaching the Spanish army and reporting the war from the Spanish side, believing that after the defeat of the Spanish forces the real news would be on the defeated side'. In its June 2 edition, the *Pall Mall Gazette* refuted claims that Phil was a spy, and downplayed Phil's surreptitious method of arrival in Cuba. 'It was obviously not Mr. Robinson's fault that he landed in the way he did; people who go to Cuba nowadays, apparently, have to get ashore the best way they can, and every correspondent cannot obtain the luxury of an escort from a British gunboat when he wishes to enter a port of one of the belligerents.'

After one week in jail, Phil and Whigham were released and told to leave Cuba immediately; they did so on the British cruiser *Talbot*, bound for Jamaica. Writing to Harry on June 12, Kay expressed his relief over Phil's release but also his exasperation. 'What on earth will he do in Jamaica? I dare say that question will have been answered before you get this: but it seems a hopeless kind of fiasco so far', Kay wrote. 'I am awfully sorry for him, because he is too old to rough it: not too old in years, but too old in health and habits.' Phil was 50 years old.

No sooner had Phil been released than he wrote about his adventure in rip-roaring style. His article was syndicated in newspapers across the United States, and published in England in the October 1898 edition of *Good Words*, the monthly journal of Phil's publisher, Isbister & Co.[51] 'Our little boat is lowered into the water, and we take our places, Whigham at the oars, I astern, and then our kind friends lower down to us a pail of drinking-water, some biscuits, a pot of jam, a tin of beef, and our flags—three Union Jacks and a table-napkin (as a flag of truce), and then after a hearty hand-shake and "Good luck to you" we shove off', Phil wrote. Waving that napkin furiously saved the men from gunfire from Spanish patrols on shore. To Phil's delight, they reached land without incident, and persuaded local children to show them the way to the Hotel du Louvre. 'A single child shouting at us "Americano!" might easily have cost us our lives', Phil recalled, 'and later on we gathered from the officials that they considered our successful audacity in arriving at the hotel unharmed almost as remarkable as our arrival on the island.' After a bath and breakfast, the dynamic duo was arrested. Their 'capture' was relatively painless. One can only imagine Harry's reaction at this silliness; while he admired his older brother, he would not have condoned such reckless behaviour (nor having to foot the bill).

Family matters intruded again. On December 15, 1898, the *Chicago Tribune* reported that 'Harry P. Robinson of Chicago sailed for England yesterday on the White Star line steamer Cymric in response to messages from London informing him of the serious illness of his father, the Rev. Julian Robinson'. Julian and his wife, Harriett, were estranged (for reasons unknown), and Julian had been homebound for some time. His children now gathered by his bedside. Harry adored his father, and he would have been deeply touched by the letter Julian wrote to his eldest child, Agnes, and her husband, Thomas, on December 9:

> It seems pretty clear that I shall never see you again in this world. And by way of farewell I want to say that you and Tom have always been the perfection of goodness to me everywhere in all the relations of life and I bless you both for it with all my heart. May God himself bless you and yours now and ever through our loving Saviour Jesus Christ. It will be a comfort to you to know that I shall die in perfect trust and confidence in God's mercy, through the Saviour Jesus Christ. Goodbye. God bless you. Daddy.

Kay, presumably with Harry's help, informed Agnes on December 20 that to counter his father's 'marked diminution of vitality and strength' they put him on an (intriguing) diet of port and Bovril.

Harry returned to America early in the new year. Kay informed him of Julian's death on February 4, 1899, via telegram: 'Father died peacefully today'. He was 81 years old. One of Harry's prized possessions was the last book Julian read before he died: *The Biglow Papers* (1864), a collection of short stories by the American writer and pacifist James Russell Lowell. Harry inscribed the volume, 'This book was the last that was handled and read by my father, Julian Robinson, before his death. It was constantly within his reach in his last days.' Julian's will, which he filed on December 31, 1898, was probated on February 27, 1899. Apart from a watch and chain bequeathed to his widow, Harriett (which upon her death would be given to Kay), and his clothes to his landlady, Julian left everything to a 'Miss Annie Loveridge' of Notting Hill, who was also the executrix. Her relationship with Julian—romantic or otherwise—is unknown.[52]

*   *   *   *   *

As the century drew to a close, Harry continued to plough his solitary furrow, as Mary spent weeks on end at her parents' home in Minneapolis. Curiously, Harry was not present when President and Mrs McKinley visited Minneapolis on October 12, 1899 and had lunch at the Lowry residence. Mary was there, playing hostess (as Mrs Lowry was away) to a retinue of Cabinet officials and newspaper reporters, as well as local businessmen including John S. Pillsbury. Even her brother Horace was present. The next day, the *Minneapolis Tribune* noted that Mrs McKinley had taken ill (she suffered from epileptic seizures) and spent most of the time in an upstairs bedroom. The luncheon 'was as informal a gathering of men who are prominent in business life, letters and politics, as was consistent with the occasion...The ladies did not participate, though they were given the choice of lunching with the gentlemen.'[53] Harry's absence may be a further indication that he had made up his mind to end his marriage.

The year came to a close with a long and newsy letter from brother Kay, who was concerned that Harry was ill. 'We all hope that by this time you are all right again, and the children want me to thank you in anticipation for the museum things'—presumably Christmas presents. Once again, he hit his brother up for money; 'I am, however, really hard up owing to my beastly illness and if at any time soon you are able to lend me some money, it will be wonderfully welcome. By midsummer I calculate to get things straight and to repay you soon after; but I am terribly harassed now.' Kay also updated Harry on Valence. She had been discharged from an asylum in Middlesex, and 'she is quite sane now, according to the doctors'. But Kay reiterated that Valence could not go on begging, and the family must rally to her aid. 'We must look forward to the burden of her support for a long time; and the best way would be for all of us to contribute £1 a month. Mother will do this, so will I, so will Phil, so will Aggie, and if you will do the same it will make just enough for her to live upon, provided that she has not the handling of the money. Will you then, if you agree, begin sending your contribution at once?' Mother had already sent her £1 and Kay had given Valence 10 shillings to buy clothes. We know that Harry had sent money before, and was now being asked for more.

Speaking of Mother, Kay noted that he had averted a near-disaster from Harry's recent letters. Apparently Harry, in his ill state, put his letter to his brother Phil in an envelope addressed to his Mother, and his Mother's letter in the one to Phil. Fortunately Kay's wife Flo had opened the letter before Harriett saw it. 'Then came a telegram from Phil who had discovered his half of the mistake, and so the letters have been sorted out and mother happily prevented from discovering that Alice Cornwell is still with Phil! She has always had a suspicion: and your mention of "Alice" would have confirmed it.' So Mother was in the dark about her eldest son's continued dalliance with 'Queen Midas'. Phil at this time had changed his name to Frederick Stennard Robinson, presumably to avoid creditors, and was living at an undisclosed location.

Harry was his family's lifeline—but all that was about to change along with the century as he turned his own world upside down, planning his boldest escape yet.

4

London Bookman, 1900–1905

If there is a fulcrum in Harry's life story, it is the year 1900. As the new century dawned, everything changed. There was no good reason for Harry to abandon his life in America, return to England, and reinvent himself as a book publisher and discoverer of new authors like Jack London. At 40 years old he had amassed a fortune (albeit through marriage) and a power base, was a friend to the U.S. president, and a recognized national leader in a vital industry, with the respect of both owners and employees. He was akin to a celebrity in Chicago and Minneapolis. He was a published author with a provocative novel and several short stories to his credit. And he was immensely fond of his adopted country, a proud and active citizen for a dozen years. He had everything to gain by staying the course. Instead, he gave it all up, seemingly out of the blue. Why in the world would Harry turn his back on his wife and his career and board the Cunard liner *Lucania* in New York on February 10, 1900, bound for Liverpool and a new life in England?

Even his closest friends were puzzled by Harry's move. William C. Edgar had known Harry since the Villard expedition in 1883, and published his articles in *The Northwestern Miller* and, from 1906, *The Bellman*. Edgar offered a glimpse into what happened in his appreciation of Harry in 1931, after Harry's death. 'As the result of convictions of duty which did him the greatest honor, he determined to eliminate himself completely from his existing environment', Edgar observed. 'To many of his friends his action appeared unnecessary and Quixotic, but to him it was a matter of simple duty and characteristically he did it simply.'[1] And so, Harry disposed of his interests in America and returned to England, after seventeen fruitful years. Evidently his U.S. citizenship then lapsed, and his British citizenship was restored.

What did Edgar mean by 'convictions of duty'? Harry had no urgent reason to leave the country nor his livelihood in Chicago. Granted, the strains on Harry's marriage were evident since the death of his second child in 1894, and the physical and psychological toll it took on Mary, who was increasingly away from her husband. His marriage may have been on the rocks, but surely the Lowrys would have preferred the status quo to the public scandal of a divorce. Adding to the mystery is Harry's 1927 biography for the London *Times*, which stated that 'in 1900 he returned to England and for domestic reasons resumed residence there',[2] implying that Mary eventually joined him, which she did not. For some apparent (and good) reason, Harry had to do the 'honourable' thing—and leave.

Family legend, however, tells a very different story. Both of Harry's grandchildren (born after Harry's death) recall with great conviction a story that their father Brad told that Harry was 'forced' to leave America by the Lowry family; specifically, by Mary's 'two' mean-spirited brothers. Mary only had one brother, Horace, who was younger and rather innocuous. In any event, the story was told that these 'brothers' had addicted Mary to morphine, driving her insane, and for that reason commanded that Harry leave the country, for good. Of course, this story is as implausible as it is fantastic. Granted, Harry was beholden to Thomas Lowry, who put up the funds to purchase the *Railway Age*, setting up Harry's success. But eight years had passed, and Harry was now well established in his own right, and apparently on good terms with his in-laws. This might have started as a marriage of convenience, but there's no evidence Harry did not love his wife; he certainly was supportive of Mary's absence from home and her many stays in sanitaria (which were not likely due to drug abuse, although she may have received drug treatments). It's just as improbable that Harry would have abandoned his wife in her hour of need. Divorce, furthermore, would have been anathema to the son of a clergyman, although two of his siblings, Phil and Valence, had divorced, and his parents were separated at the time of Julian's death.

In fact, Phil's sensational divorce from his wife Sarah may have indirectly inspired the family legend regarding Harry. Phil and Sarah married in 1876 in Bombay. They had two children, Edith and Guy; a third child, Maud, died in infancy. In 1884 Sarah was granted a divorce on the grounds of Phil's cruelty and his adulterous relations with two women. Given Phil's notoriety as a war correspondent and author, the scandal made headlines as far away as Australia. Over the next eight years, the exes were frequently back in court over unpaid alimony and child support, as well as child custody and visitation issues. According to court records, at one point Sarah accused Phil of drugging her with morphine and having her confined to a lunatic asylum. This raises the question: could Harry have co-opted a version of this shocking tale as an excuse to tell his family in America why he left Mary?[3]

The surprising answer to what really happened would reveal itself in a few years. For now, Harry took full advantage of one of the last times in history when a man could wipe the slate clean and start his life anew, keeping his past hidden from his family back in England. Harry must have had a good reason to peddle yet another untruth (which casts even more shadow on his character), as he embarked on his ultimate reinvention.

* * * * *

We know very little of Harry's movements upon his return to England in February 1900 until he takes up his new career as a book publisher in November 1901. What is especially interesting is that there was no press coverage of his departure from Chicago, nor of the sale of his interest in the *Railway Age*. Surely one or the other would have prompted a newspaper headline. Instead, Harry slipped away, almost unnoticed. He remained on the masthead of the *Railway Age* as its 'Editor' until the April 26, 1901 edition. The following week, the paper reverted to its original title, from *The Railway Age and Northwestern Railroader* to simply *The Railway Age* (which is still published today, although based in New York). Again, there was no mention of Harry's role or departure, even as his name was dropped from the masthead. There was also no news of a divorce from Mary, for there was none: they were still married, if separated by an ocean.

Brad recalled in his memoir that his father arrived in London and 'was very ill, nearly dying at Garland's Hotel in the Strand'.[4] Harry then moved in for a while with Phil at his home, 'Mortivals', in Takeley, Essex, about 40 miles north-east of London. Phil was now dying, possibly of syphilis, and was in hiding, either from creditors or for fear of scandal, with his lover, Alice Cornwell. A 1901 census document listed the residents of Mortivals as 'Frederick Stennard Robinson', a.k.a. Phil, as head of the household; his 'wife', named 'Anne' (really Alice); their daughter Myrtle (Dorothy, born illegitimate in 1889); a stepson, Fred, aged 22; and Harry, listed as the brother, an employer, and a publisher of books. Phil's 'disappearance' was assisted by his two brothers. He even kept his whereabouts from his two legitimate children, Guy and Edith, perhaps to avoid further payments to his ex-wife. But Phil was no recluse, and when able, would travel to London with Harry, meet up with Kay, and spend time at the Savage Club, a rather raucous gentlemen's club whose members included G. A. Henty and the future King Edward VII. Brad recalled that the club would host 'Robinson nights' when all three brothers 'would send the members into paroxysms of

Figure 10. Harry, age 42 (at left), with his brothers, Phil, 54, and Kay, 45, at Mortivals, Phil's house in Essex, in 1901. Harry lived with Phil when he returned to England. Phil was in hiding from creditors and had assumed the name 'Frederick Stennard Robinson'. He died one year later.

amusement and incredulity by the astonishing variety of adventures and information which the brothers produced'.[5] Perhaps it was over drinks in the Savage Club with Phil and Kay that Harry concocted his story about Mary and her 'drug addiction' to explain his departure.

It was an interesting time for Harry to be back in England. He recalled the death of Queen Victoria on January 22, 1901, after sixty-three years on the throne. 'It seemed as if the heart of London stopped beating', he wrote. 'I had arrived in England from the United States but a short time before, and that evening I saw men walking in the streets with tears running down their cheeks, women sobbing hysterically without concealment, strangers stopping one another merely to look in each other's faces for a moment, to shake their heads, say a word or two and pass on. All England was as a child that had lost its mother and groped blindly for comfort.' Harry watched as the gun carriage bearing the late monarch passed through the London streets, 'while millions of her subjects stood silent and bareheaded in the February air, and over all were the sobbing, sobbing, sobbing of the funeral music and the booming of the great guns which from far away told of the stages of the royal progress'.[6]

For Harry, the profound commemoration of Victoria's death was juxtaposed with a bizarre story of another demise on the other side of the Atlantic. On March 22, 1901, Mary Lowry Robinson was reported dead in a boarding house in New York, an apparent suicide. It was a case of mistaken identity, of course. Mary was in Baltimore, Maryland, staying with friends, when she sent a telegram to her father: 'Just received a telephone from New York in regard to a suicide. Told them that you had no relative by the name of Robinson except myself. — Mary L. Robinson.' Thomas Lowry shared this with reporters, and the following day made a statement to the press, including the *Minneapolis Journal*:

> 'This is one of those unfortunate things which demands a denial when sense and propriety would seem to warrant a parent in ignoring them,' said Mr. Lowry this morning. 'The statement is not only untrue but unkind. Mrs. Robinson is a guest of Dr. Rickards and his wife in Baltimore. She is not under his care. Her health was never better. My daughter is looking after her four children. Mr. Robinson is in Europe at present, and during his absence my daughter is visiting Dr. Rickard's family. I saw her last Saturday, and had a talk with her last Tuesday by telephone.'[7]

Why Mary was taking care of another couple's children is unknown. It is interesting that Lowry noted that Mary was not under the care of this mysterious doctor (possibly untrue) and was in good health (also questionable), and that she was still married to Harry, which was true. Harry's description as 'in Europe at present' implied that he was there on business and would soon return. He would not. Nonetheless, the story made headlines across the country. The woman in question was called Lillian Robinson and, like Mary, had a husband in Chicago.

One year later, Mary was back in the headlines. A syndicated story picked up by multiple newspapers on May 16, 1902, announced that 'Mrs. Harry P. Robinson, daughter of the multi-millionaire street car magnate, Thomas Lowry, has startled her friends in Minneapolis by giving up her position to become a professional nurse. She is the wife of Harry P. Robinson, of Chicago, proprietor of the Railway Age.' Apparently, Mary had just taken a job as a nurse at a Minneapolis hospital.[8] 'When asked her reasons for giving up a life of luxury for that of a nurse Mrs. Robinson said: "Reasons? Oh, there are none. I simply love the work, that is all."'[9] Luxury did follow Mary in one sense; 'One of the fashionable dressmakers of the city has made six handsome uniforms for her. Although the style and pattern are of the regulation model, the material is the richest and the caps and aprons are of sheer linen and lawn.' The article is telling in many respects, not the least of which for the rare glimpse which it provides into Mary's psyche. Mary was definitely bucking social conventions by taking a job, as the heiress of a fortune and a married woman (if only in name). One wonders if this position was part of her therapy as she recovered from whatever ailed her. The article concluded, 'Harry P. Robinson is at present in London, where he is engaged in literary pursuits and in the publishing business, still retaining his interest in the Railway Age. He left Chicago over a year ago.' Unbeknownst to the reporter, evidently, Harry was no longer connected to the *Railway Age*. And the newspaper did not question the separation of the two, nor did it seek out Harry for a comment about his most unorthodox working life.

*   *   *   *   *

Overseas, Harry was making headlines of his own. As William C. Edgar explained it, 'His first attempt to start afresh was to invest his capital in an old-established publishing business in London, of which he became the managing director.'[10] That business was William Isbister & Company, Limited. The firm was founded as Strahan & Company in 1858 by Alexander Strahan and William Isbister. When Strahan dropped out due to financial difficulties, the name changed to Isbister in 1874. This prestige publishing house issued devotional works and books for children as well as works of the leading writers of the day, including Anthony Trollope, Mrs Oliphant, and Augustus J. C. Hare. It also published several prominent literary periodicals, including *Good Words* (founded 1860), the *Sunday Magazine* (1864), the *Argosy* (1865, edited by Mrs Henry Wood of *East Lynne* fame), and the *Contemporary Review* (1866).

Harry's introduction to Isbister must have come from his brothers. Phil published two natural history books with Isbister: *Birds of the Wave and Woodland* (1895) and *In Garden, Orchard and Spinney* (1898), and was a regular contributor to *Good Words*, as was Kay. As such, both brothers may have been privy to the news that Isbister was in financial trouble. In 1891 an extraordinary general meeting of the board of directors passed a special resolution that the firm be 'wound up voluntarily'.[11] It was not, but publishing at the turn of the century was a cut-throat business, and competition for authors—and readers—was fierce. New firms were transforming the industry with one-volume novels (instead of the traditional 'triple decker') at cheaper prices to encourage book buying rather than borrowing, backed up by extensive publicity. Namesake firms founded by William Heinemann and

Algernon Methuen led the way, as did magazine publishers such as George Newnes. Older firms like Isbister lacked the volume and the resources to attract popular authors, whose book sales financed those of lesser-selling writers.

Harry had experience as a magazine publisher and, cash in hand from the divestment of his American holdings, saw an opportunity to establish himself back in his homeland. He also needed a job. Isbister had seen better days, but Harry apparently saw potential in its revitalization. Negotiations opened in October 1901, and at a meeting of the Isbister board on October 19, a special resolution was approved: 'That the conditional agreement made between JEROME N. BANKES, Esq., on behalf of the Company on the one part, and H. PERRY ROBINSON, Esq., of the other part, now read and submitted to this Meeting be, and the same is hereby, approved and confirmed.'[12] And so Harry became the managing director of the company with a majority ownership stake. A formal announcement of Harry's position was made in *The Bookman* in November 1901. 'We have great pleasure in presenting our readers with a portrait of Mr. H. Percy [*sic*] Robinson, the new manager of Messrs. Isbister and Co.' The journal *Literature* on November 16, 1901 mistook Harry for a Cambridge graduate but noted that 'He founded in the States several commercial journals which have been extremely successful'. Harry, moreover, was expected to shake things up: 'It will be gratifying to English publishers to learn that Mr. Robinson returns to London convinced that the methods of the best English houses are the soundest methods he can adopt, and that he has no intention of attempting any revolutionary changes in the house of Isbister. Preparations are being made, however, for a busier season next spring than the firm has known for years.' In *Caxton's Magazine* for January 1902, Harry was included in a symposium on 'Modern Book Printing', along with H. G. Wells and Eden Phillpotts, among others. Harry pledged to improve upon the 'sobriety' that characterized the covers of English books, compared to the 'extremely ornate' American covers, which offered a distinct advantage in sales. 'The ideal we are trying for at present is a combination of a charming outside and a well-printed inside', Harry said. 'Having the latter, we are adopting some American ideas as to cover designs, which, we believe, will make the English book as attractive externally and far superior internally to the general run of American publications.'[13]

Harry also pledged to reinvigorate Isbister's magazines, which still had a wide circulation and could be used to advertise the book list. The cover of the *Sunday Magazine* was freshened up, and a prize competition was introduced to *Good Words* to mark the coronation of Edward VII. The Christmas 1901 edition of *Good Words* invited 'British subjects from all over the world to compete for three prizes of £50, £15 and £10, respectively, to be given for the three best Coronation Odes'. The response: 1,084 entries from all over the world. The judges were three Isbister authors: Stopford A. Brooke, Edmund Gosse, and William Canton. The winners were published in the 80-page special Coronation section of the July 1902 edition. First prize went to the Rev. Lauchlan MacLean Watt, Presbyterian Minister of Alloa, Scotland. His ode concluded, 'Great shall that monarch be, | Great on the shore, and the sea; | And the nations near and far | Shall see his star, | And know that the day of darkness now is done, | And wait for the rising sun, | That bringeth the days to be.' As hoped for, the press picked up on the results. *The Times* on June 19 noted that 'many of the compositions, as was to be expected, do not deserve even the name of poems, but they represent an exhilarating outburst of patriotic sentiment'. Harry was so pleased that he announced a new competition for 'Songs of the Empire'.

Harry had no qualms about self-promotion in his magazines. He wrote a long article for the November 1901 edition of *Good Words* entitled 'The American Presidency—Mr. McKinley and Mr. Roosevelt'. Illustrated with election pins, banners, and cartoons (possibly from Harry's personal collection), Harry wrote of his great affection for McKinley, who had been assassinated on September 14, 1901, and sought to reassure readers that Theodore Roosevelt would be a strong leader and a friend to England. 'What we would chiefly have cause to fear would be the presence of a little man, a mean man or a weak one in the President's chair, and Mr. Roosevelt is none of these', Harry wrote. 'He may be hot-headed and masterful but we cannot pretend to wish that he should not be a patriot and a believer in the destiny of his country. He is a man of brains as well as strength and in the hands of such the peaceful relations of the two countries should be secure.' In June 1902, *Good Words* published 'The Gift of Fernseed', first published in the *Atlantic Monthly* in 1889.

* * * * *

To succeed in publishing at this time, a firm gained attention by signing up big names or promising new authors, and by holding on to existing authors, lest they be poached by larger houses with better contract offers. Harry solicited two literary giants, the newly knighted Sir Arthur Conan Doyle, and family friend Rudyard Kipling, both of whom turned him down. 'Alas, my life is so cram full that I can take no more into it, much as I should have enjoyed a chat', Sir Arthur wrote. Kipling also declined, saying that he, too, could not take on 'extra work'. Notably, Harry raised the royalty rates for several of Isbister's authors, including the literary critic Stopford A. Brooke. Brooke was rather startled to receive a rise, writing to Harry 'Miracles will never cease—that a publisher should of his own accord raise a writer's royalty from 12½ to 15 per cent is utterly unknown in my experience. I need not say how willingly I take advantage of this most marvellous event. I am very much obliged to you.' Brooke, author of *Tennyson: His Art and Relation to Modern Life* (1894) and *English Literature from the Beginnings to the Norman Conquest* (1898), was under contract to Isbister for *The Poetry of Robert Browning*, published in September 1902. Harry's generosity was also quite shrewd: in addition to currying favour he was sending a message to his authors that Isbister was still a viable concern.

By far Harry's biggest gamble was signing an unknown young American author named Jack London. In 1902 London was still one year away from his breakout novel, *The Call of the Wild*. But he had published in America two collections of his Yukon-based short stories, *The Son of the Wolf* (1900) and *The God of His Fathers* (1901). Neither sold particularly well but they were critical successes. London was emblematic of the American can-do spirit which so appealed to Harry, who may have read his works before departing America. Harry wrote directly to London in February 1902, saying that Isbister had just acquired the rights to *Son of the Wolf* and also wished to publish *God of His Fathers*. London, accustomed to flattery, would have been delighted by Harry's letter. Harry hoped that London would see, in his words, 'some propriety in continuing as far as possible your connection with the house which is now preparing to gamble on your first work when it must be very much of an experiment with the English public'. He promised London that the firm would 'make a success of it' and pledged, 'We shall hope to have whatever future work you are putting out. We wish to express our admiration of the power with which you write and it is our intention to push your books strongly in England, believing that they deserve success.'[14]

Harry's excitement over introducing a new author is evident in the pamphlet he prepared to publicize *God of His Fathers*, the first Jack London title published by Isbister. 'Mr. London has established himself as the apostle of the Klondyke, doing for that dreary region what Mr. Kipling has done for India', Harry began. 'The natural impulse of many of Mr. London's admirers, in these days when personal preference for the writings of one author over another is too often allowed to do duty for honest criticism, is to call him the Kipling of the Klondyke; but that is hardly doing justice either to him or to Mr. Kipling. There is plenty of room for both, each in his own sphere.' It was clever of Harry to tie London to Kipling, then at the height of his popularity. He proceeded

ISBISTER & CO., LIMITED.

GOOD WORDS.
SUNDAY MAGAZINE.

TELEGRAPHIC ADDRESS:
"CONTEMPORARY, LONDON."

15 & 16, TAVISTOCK STREET,
COVENT GARDEN,
LONDON, W.C.

ISBISTER'S
SCHOOL BOOKS,
PRIZE BOOKS,
&c.

OFFICE OF MANAGING DIRECTOR,

February 18th, ____ 190 2

Dear Sir,
We have within the last few weeks put your book "The
God of His Fathers" on the English market, having taken it from
Messrs McClure, Phillips & Co. We have also bought the rights
in "The Son of the Wolf" from the English house to whom Messrs
Houghton, Mifflin & Co. had parted with the English rights. We
are now writing to say to you that (as we have already informed
Messrs Houghton, Mifflin & Co.) we shall hope to have whatever
future work you are putting out. We wish to express our
admiration of the power with which you write and it is our
intention to push your books strongly in England, believing that
they deserve success.

As a commercial matter we believe it will be to your
advantage to see that your future books also come into our hands
on this side. We also hope that you will see some propriety in
continuing as far as possible your connection with the house
which is now preparing to gamble on your first work when it must
be very much of an experiment with the English public. It may
perhaps be as well to explain that the undersigned has lived in
the United States for some 15 years' and is not unfamiliar with
mining life. Personal considerations have largely swayed us in
our determination to take hold of your work in earnest, and to
do all that we can to make a success of it. Apart from that let
me say again that there is a very sincere admiration for the
quality of your writing.

With best wishes,

Yours very sincerely,

Mr. Jack London,
962, East 16th Street,
Oakland, California.

Figure 11. Harry's first letter to the new American author, Jack London.
Source: Huntington Library, JL 17246.

to appeal to readers to give London a chance: 'It is a barren country and bleak existence that Mr. London depicts, but it is illumined by many of the things that make life endurable—comradeship, self-forgetfulness, and sacrifice, the surpassing love of women, and the loyalty of men. Mr. London tells the thing as he knows it with a force that goes home.'

God of His Fathers and *Son of the Wolf* each sold less than 1,000 copies for Isbister, a disappointment at a time when 500 copies were needed to cover production and marketing costs. Harry sought to reassure his new client. 'You probably know something of the extreme difficulty of introducing a new writer to the English market, especially a non-English writer, and while the above numbers may seem small to you, we are entirely satisfied and have every confidence that you will ultimately get a large public here, which you undoubtedly deserve', he wrote.[15] But reviews were excellent. On May 17, *The Publishers' Circular and Booksellers' Record*, the principal trade publication, declared, 'We do not wish to be patronising when we say, with emphatic conviction, that Mr. London has a future before him. He has power of so rugged a nature, flashes of insight of so startling a character, and pathos so elevated in tone that he compels instant recognition at the hands of all careful readers.' And *The Spectator* stated on February 22, 'He may tell us that neither the laws of God nor man hold beyond 50° N., and that God never meant the land of frozen snow for living purposes; but he shows us men with as much chivalry, poetry, loyalty, and living faith, among his miners as are to be found in the gentlest latitudes and most civilised communities.'

At the same time Harry was courting London, believing him to be the next great American author, London was also being pursued back home by George Brett of the much larger publisher Macmillan, the American branch of the venerable English house. Macmillan published some of the biggest names of the day, including Henry James, Mrs Humphry Ward, Winston Churchill, and Owen Wister, the 'father' of Western fiction. In an unusual move, London decided to engage both publishers, granting Macmillan his American rights and Isbister the foreign book rights, which included publication in Britain, 'Colonial editions' for the rest of the English-speaking world, and foreign translations for sale in Europe. Brett was opposed to the Isbister connection, considering Isbister to be an inferior concern that could not offer the exposure of one of the larger, more established firms in England, with which Brett wanted to do business. But as London explained in a letter to Brett, Harry 'ploughed the ground, he was the first to plough it, and he ploughed it well ... He was the first to take me up in England; he has performed the labor of introducing me; in order to introduce me well he had foregone immediate profits, sinking them into the publishing, with the idea of building up greater mutual profit for both of us; and because of all of this he looked upon my future work as honestly his to publish. I may say that he agrees to give me the same royalties, whatever they be, that I receive in America.'[16] And for Harry, this was the opportunity to prove to the bigger and more established firms that he could handle a rising star. London was delighted by Harry's attention and flattery, and author and publisher struck up a good rapport. He was pleased that *God of His Fathers* had been well-received. 'It seems that you on your side of the water have caught my underlying motive better than the average American reviewers caught it', he wrote.[17] He expressed a desire to visit

England: 'I have long since made up my mind to see England and the Old Countries (I have started twice, but never succeeded in making it). And some day I hope to walk into [your offices at] No. 16 Tavistock Street and shake hands with you.' Within a few months, he did just that, during his time 'underground' in the East End of London for his non-fiction exposé, *The People of the Abyss*.

* * * * *

Harry adapted well to his new position, bringing his solid work ethic to bear and making the rounds of industry circles and clubs, hobnobbing with peers and rivals at parties thrown by *John Bull* magazine, for example. For a small general publisher like Isbister, variety was the spice of life. The goal was to publish as many interesting titles as possible to appeal to all classes of readers—and price points. In September 1902, apart from Jack London, Isbister promoted *Three Men* by Maxim Gorky, along with two curious non-fiction books, *The Snow Baby: A True Story with True Pictures of the Only White Child Ever Born So Far North*, by Josephine Peary, her mother (capitalizing on the hoopla over Admiral Peary's North Pole expedition); and the peculiar *Life and Love Letters of a Dwarf: Being the Memoirs of the Celebrated Dwarf Joseph Boruwalski, a Polish Gentleman: Containing a Faithful and Curious Account of His Birth, Education, Marriage and Reception in the Principal Courts of Europe*. Nepotism was not a problem for Harry, and he freely published books by Phil and Kay, knowing that they both needed the money: Kay's *My Nature Notebook* (1903) and *In the King's County* (1904), and a children's book by Phil, *Bubble and Squeak: Some Calamitous Stories* (1903). Of the latter, 'These short sketches of animals are written by a devoted student of wild life, and he has a particularly engaging literary style, too', wrote the *Manchester Guardian*, 'so that we are sorry that he did not invent some better name for his work'. And then there was *Tales by Three Brothers* (1902), a collection of short stories by Phil, Kay, and Harry. This was a long-gestating project, first suggested by Kay to Harry in 1898, with the hopes that an American publisher might be interested. Advertised as 'A volume of stories of adventure and mystery in all parts of the world, sometimes weird, always striking, and entirely out of the common', *Tales by Three Brothers* had the distinctly science-fiction flavour that the Robinson boys favoured. The brothers dedicated the book to their mother: 'To Harriett Woodcock Robinson, now in her eighty-third year, these tales are affectionately inscribed by her sons.' Oddly, the author of each story was not identified, but included were three of Harry's previously published efforts: 'The Gift of Fernseed',

A JOHN BULL DINNER PARTY:

Key:—SIR W. B-B-NS-N; SIR CR-CHT-N BR-WNE; MR. A. W. À B-CK-TT; SIR L-W-S M-RR-S; SIR W-LT-R P-CE; Mr. P-RRY R-B-NS-N; MR. M-X B-RB-HM; SIR J-HN C-CKB-RN; CANON T-GNM—TH SB-RE; REV. A. C-R-L P-RS-N; MR. C-MPT-N R-CK-TT, M.P.; MR. A. P. GR-VES; MR. E. M-J-L-R; MR. H-RRY F-RN-SS; MR. ADK—N K-SS; MR. W. J. B-LL, M.P.; RT. HON. W. I. P-RRIE; MR. P-RCY FR-NCH; MR. L—S WA-N; MR. A. C. G—LD; MR. ARTH-R R-CK-TT; MR. EM-RS-N B—NBB-DGE; SIR H-R-CR T-J-N; DR. P-RQUH-RS-N, M.P.

Figure 12. *John Bull*, July 23, 1903. Harry is seated at centre, in profile; standing next to him is Max Beerbohm.

'The Gold Heart', and 'Medusa'. Reviews were good, although critics did point out that most of the stories were not new. *The Spectator* observed on November 8, 1902, 'None of the stories are worth remembering, but they are all worth reading when one has nothing else to do.' *The Athenaeum* on December 13, 1902 offered special praise for 'The Gift of Fernseed' and Harry's depiction of invisibility: 'Not Mr. H. G. Wells himself was able to paint its possible horrors more tellingly or more convincingly.' The reviewer continued, 'In the best sense this is a British book. It is unpretentious, and its authors do not vaunt their knowledge of the outlying corners of our dominions; yet it may be doubted whether even Mr. Kipling could concentrate in one volume more varied aspects of life and strange happenings in widely separate portions of the Empire. It is a book to be read, and to be kept.'

The good notices for *Tales by Three Brothers* and the acceptance of *Bubble and Squeak* would have consoled Phil, who was dying. He passed away at home on December 9, 1902, recorded in *The Times* as 'Frederick Stennard Robinson', following 'a long and painful illness'. He was just

54 years old. Both Harry and Kay took Phil's premature death hard, as they idolized their older, adventure-loving brother.

* * * * *

Jack London had emerged as the star of the Isbister list, and Harry was determined to hold on to him as rival publishers took notice and London's fame grew. But cracks in the relationship began to appear early in 1903, for economic reasons. At this time, a small publisher like Isbister could either import printed books from the American publisher to sell overseas, or purchase unbound sheets and have them bound as needed in England, both options considerably less expensive than setting type themselves and printing locally. However, the American publisher would charge fees and royalties on sheets and books sold. And Macmillan, one of the premier American publishing houses, was not inexpensive. It also dictated other terms in the foreign edition, in terms of physical size, appearance, and number of illustrations. These up-front costs impacted Isbister's bottom line. Harry informed London on March 31 that 'our present loss on Mr. J. London's books is £102 ($510)', or £12,100 today.[18]

Harry had high hopes that London's ambitious new novel, *The Call of the Wild*, would be the sales bonanza that Isbister desperately needed. But something went very wrong. At the end of May 1903, Brett expressed his concern to London as *Call of the Wild* was set to be published on July 15 and Isbister had not yet responded to Macmillan's offer. 'You see I wanted to follow your wishes and still offer the book to Isbister, although I would have preferred to bring it out through another London house', Brett wrote on May 27. 'If they do not reply within the next few days I think I shall, unless you have very strong objections to having another London publisher, try and put the book into the hands of another English concern.'[19] By early June, with no reply from Isbister, Brett offered the novel to a major rival, William Heinemann Ltd. Suddenly Harry was faced with major competition from another publisher in England, one even larger and with considerably greater resources at its disposal. And Heinemann had the better Jack London book to sell. Published in July 1903, *Call of the Wild* was a blockbuster, and has never been out of print.

What happened? The mystery was finally solved in a letter from Harry to London on August 24, one month after publication of *Call of the Wild*. 'Of course you know that another house is publishing "The Call of the Wild" over here and I suppose you know the story of it', Harry wrote. He claimed he was stricken with diphtheria and unable to answer any of his correspondence. 'I am sorry because I think the book will sell and I should like to have had the pushing of it', he wrote. 'However, it was one of those acts of a kindly Providence which there is no arguing about.'[20] It does seem strange that no one in the Isbister office noticed Brett's appeals while the managing director was stricken with a deadly disease. In fact, Harry's health would never be the same after this crisis, nor indeed would his relationship with Jack London.

Harry's other preoccupation in 1903 was the launch of a new 1d. weekly magazine called *The V.C.* This was vintage Harry: an upbeat and unabashedly patriotic paper. The name was based on the Victoria Cross, awarded for gallantry 'in the face of the enemy' to members of the British armed forces. Kipling was a natural choice to assist with the new paper, but, once again, he turned Harry down. 'I am afraid that about the last thing in the world to move my enthusiasm would be a new paper', he wrote to Harry. 'I have been present at the birth and mourned over the death of too many. Ninety nine out of a hundred start with a jump, and live as long as three months; then the men who put their money in it expect immediate return and make life hectic for the editor. There's a row and recriminations.... I am very sorry but new papers are things I am very much afraid of.' Kipling's words would prove to be prophetic, as the *V.C.* lasted just eleven months—which may be why Harry saved the letter in his scrapbook.

Published every Thursday, the first issue appeared on April 23, 1903, appropriately St George's Day. Advertisements heralded 'A new paper that appeals to everybody. A Paper of the People. Read it and feel better. A Pennyworth of Happiness. An entirely new kind of paper.' Harry hired as editor Harold Begbie, a journalist, poet, and author (*The Handy Man, Common Heroes, The Story of Baden-Powell*) who had worked as Kay Robinson's assistant for the popular nature column 'By the Way' in the London *Globe*. The first issue set the tone for the paper. 'We have chosen the title "V.C." because to all mankind . . . these letters stand for the quick eye, the cool pulse, the daring brain; for grit, for pluck, for chivalry, for honour; for all those bracing qualities which go to make up the hero', Begbie wrote. 'It is to record brave actions—actions which contradict the going-to-potmaniacs—that "V.C." has come into existence.' He was quick to state that this was not a journal of militarism nor the glorification of war. 'There are many kinds of courage, and "V.C." seeks to honour as well the beggar-boy as the soldier, and as well the sempstress as the sailor. Courage on the high seas, courage on the battlefield, courage in the flaming factory, courage deep down in the falling mine; the courage of the poor; courage wherever found—this is what "V.C." exists to chronicle.' The *V.C.* defied anyone to mock its mandate. 'If there is anybody to whom courage does not appeal, it is to that unfortunate creature, the limp, backboneless, *blasé* and decadent *poseur* of Smart Society. It will be our business, if only for diversion, to whip this ninny as often as occasion serves. We don't like him; we think he occupies too big a place on the world's stage, and we hold that he is something of a corrupting influence.' The first issue announced the 'V.C.' Prize Awards, 'half-a-guinea each for the six best paragraphs relating tales of heroism, self-sacrifice, pluck, endurance, and chivalry in every class of the community'. These snippets were always inspirational and relentlessly sunny. For example:

> During an important football match at Groton School, in America, it was noticed that young Roosevelt, son of the fearless President, looked pale; he was advised to stop playing, but refused. At the end of the game it was found that for the last part of the time he had been playing with a broken collar-bone. Not long ago he had fought every boy who would fight him, and had beaten all except one: perhaps he managed to beat that one since. This is the strenuous life in embryo.[21]

Contributors in the first year featured a who's who of military heroes and adventure writers on both sides of the Atlantic, including Boer War standouts Lord Roberts (a family friend) and General Baden-Powell; Admiral George Dewey, hero of the American navy during the Spanish–American War; and even Jack London.

The *V.C.* got off to a roaring start. The venerable *Advertising World* noted that the first number had an initial order of 100,000 copies but orders kept coming in, until 250,000 were printed. As such, the *Advertising World* predicted a 'great success' for this newcomer 'dealing with the brighter side of life', noting 'the general control and supervision is in the hands of Mr. H. Perry Robinson, the managing director of Isbister & Co., Ltd., who is a gentleman of proved ability as a newspaper conductor. In all departments the new paper is strongly controlled and neither money nor enterprise are being spared in the venture. We confidently predict a great success for the latest penny paper.'[22] The poet and great imperialist Sir Edwin Arnold, an Isbister author, offered his congratulations to Harry in a personal letter. 'A publication which will present to its readers only the noble, the heroic, the self-sacrificing, the glad, the hopeful and the courageous aspects and events of human life, deserves the welcome and the good wishes of every right-minded person', he wrote. The *V.C.* found its way to all corners of the Empire as well as America. The *New York Times* on May 9, 1903 noted Harry's U.S. background, stated that 200,000 copies of the third number had just been sold, and observed, 'Its tone is high, and the spirit in which the paper is edited reminds the reader of President Roosevelt's "Strenuous Life." Negotiations are on foot to publish an edition of "V.C." in the United States.' That never happened—perhaps because of Harry's illness.

The *V.C.* was also a good vehicle to advertise Isbister books and its authors, which were earning critical praise. Robert Barr's novel *Over the Border* was serialized in *V.C.* before being published in book form. *Wolfville Days*, by a new American humourist, Alfred Henry Lewis, was hailed by the *Daily Telegraph*: 'Bret Harte seems to have bequeathed his mantle to the author of this remarkable little book of sketches of life in Arizona.' This was another example of Harry's pursuit of new American authors. *The Adventurer in Spain* by the popular Scottish novelist S. R. Crockett was illustrated with photographs by the author, who carried his camera 2,500 miles on mule-back. It was also serialized in *Good Words*. *The Hill of Trouble* by Arthur C. Benson featured 'stories mystical, medieval, and supernatural.' *The Light Invisible: Tales of a Visionary* by Robert Hugh Benson ran into four editions. *Gulliver Joe* by 'Jonathan Quick, Dean of St. Rattricks' (pseudonym for Cecil Eldred Hughes and Harold Begbie) was a parody of Swift's *Gulliver's Travels* satirizing the Right Hon. Joseph Chamberlain. *To-day* called it 'an uncommonly joyous little volume'. A riff on encyclopedias, *Wisdom While You Wait, being a Foretaste of the Glories of the 'Insidecompletuar Britanniaware'*, by the authors of *Lives of the 'Lustrious*, had its first edition of 18,000 copies exhausted on publication day. *The Sketch* on March 18 gave it a rave: 'One of the most genuinely funny books it has ever been my lot to come across.'

The November 12, 1903 edition of the *V.C.* included an excerpt of Jack London's *People of the Abyss*, prefaced by an explanation as to why 'one of the grimmest books ever published in fair England' was in a magazine as sunny as the *V.C.*:

> The book is a stimulus to action, and as such we welcome it. Not a page of it but charges the idle citizen with guilt, not a line but smites the conscience of the wicked sensualist. We would that the contemptible people who call themselves Smart Society would have this book dinned into their peevish souls from waking to sleep-time. And we pity the man who reads this book and does nothing to realise his citizenship for the poor and them that have no helper.

Provocative prose, but effective. Harry had included a similar defence as a preface in the published book. Of all of the London titles published by Isbister, *People of the Abyss* was the most sensational, given its criticism of human suffering and squalor in the East End of London, seemingly unnoticed by the ruling class. Yet it also marked a turning point for

Harry. Not only was this the end of his personal relationship with Jack London, who had moved on to Heinemann, but its popular success was not enough to stave off Isbister's bankruptcy.

*   *   *   *   *

'After three years of vain effort, this enterprise proved unsuccessful and the concern was liquidated', William C. Edgar noted. Harry 'had lost his capital and three years' time, but not his courage'.[23] On January 25, 1904, a meeting of the Isbister board passed the following 'Extraordinary Resolution': 'Resolved, That it has been proved to the satisfaction of this Meeting that the Company cannot by reason of its liabilities continue its business and that it is advisable to wind up the same and accordingly that the Company be wound up voluntarily.'[24] George T. Brown, one of the directors, was appointed liquidator. *The Bookseller* published the announcement on February 8. Two months later, another announcement: the assets of Isbister were acquired by Sir Isaac Pitman & Sons for the sum of £7,250 (£875,000 today). Harry was out; Brown would continue to manage the Isbister business until it was fully absorbed into Pitman, perhaps best known for religious-themed books and for the invention of shorthand by its founder.

Why did Isbister fail? We know that the company had registered for bankruptcy before, in January 1891, but continued in business until Harry came along in October 1901. Within three years, it was all over. Did Harry overextend himself? He learned the hard way that earning a profit as a book publisher was not easy, and reflected on the experience a few years later. He noted that, to generate a profit, a novel had to sell six copies to every one of a biography or book of memoirs, as the latter could be sold at a higher price than a six-shilling novel. 'I was for some years interested in an English publishing house, which put out a good many very successful novels', Harry recalled in 1909. 'But we made seven thousand five hundred dollars more clear profit out of one two-volume life of an archbishop than we did out of any novel. Every year the great individual prizes in the publishing field, to author and publisher alike, are the important biographies or books of travel and not the most popular novels.'[25] That work was *The Life and Correspondence of William Connor Magee* by John Cotter MacDonnell, published at an enormous 32 shillings in two handsome red volumes by Isbister in October 1896, running to a second printing that same month. Magee was the popular Archbishop of York. While Harry could point to several publishing successes, including the *V.C.*, profits were insufficient to cover liabilities. Unlike his work in Chicago with the *Railway Age*, which had little competition and a captive market, in England Harry had to face publishing houses with bigger lists and far more resources at their disposal. His failure and the loss of his capital and livelihood were a heavy blow.

The first casualty of the new Pitman regime was Harry's beloved *V.C.* In March, Begbie was out as editor, and the paper changed its name to *V.C. and Competitions*, focusing more on contests than stories. It folded in July. The Isbister book list and name, however, continued through 1904, until it was fully absorbed by Pitman, benefiting from contracts initiated by Harry. In fact, one of Isbister's big books of 1904 was *My Recollections* by Princess Catherine Radziwill (1858–1941), Polish aristocrat and daughter of the Russian General Adam Adamowicz Rzewuski. It was published in October, long after Harry had left the firm, at a high price of 16 shillings, given the likely upper-class audience and the expectation of profit. Harry worked on the book in 1903, and some of his correspondence with the eccentric lady survives, offering a glimpse of his management style. His decision to sign the princess was typical of the desire to gain from expected publicity from this controversial figure, despite the rather exhausting time and effort required to appease a demanding author (shades of Jack London).

The princess first made contact with Harry on August 4, 1903, in a letter sent from jail in Cape Town, South Africa. She had served a sixteen-month sentence for forging Cecil Rhodes's name on a promissory note, a sensational crime that made headlines around the world. Evidently she had stalked Rhodes in the years before his death in 1902, falsely claiming that they were engaged. Rhodes spurned her, and she accused him of loan fraud. The case went to trial, Rhodes was exonerated, and the princess went to jail. 'Dear Sir', the letter began, 'I am leaving this place on Saturday 8th August, [travelling by] steamer and here in London about Sept 1st. I shall call on you as soon as I get in town. In the mean while please keep any letters or wires you may receive for me addressed to your care, and don't mention my arrival to any one.'

My Recollections is a gossipy romp through the Imperial courts of Germany and Russia, with observations such as that Bismarck did not like to dance at weddings, 'his immense head with its sharp outlines appearing almost like that of a bulldog'. Amid anecdotes about parties and balls and numerous aristocrats, the princess devoted most attention to her meeting with Disraeli. 'I had, of course, against Disraeli the prejudices which I was bound have as a Russian; he appeared to my eyes the incarnation of everything that was bad, evil, and destructive. I detested him a parvenu, and as the man who had humiliated and defied my country', she wrote. 'But when I met him my prejudices melted away like snow in the sunshine. A more fascinating personage than the late Lord Beaconsfield has never existed.' The last chapter is about Rhodes, whom the princess recalls fondly. 'When, after all that I have endured and suffered, I think of him, and remember all he did, the generous instincts that really existed in him, I seem to forget these sufferings, and my resentment melts away, leaving only room for passionate regret', she wrote. 'He deserved a better fate than he got, and he ought not to have had such an unutterably sad and lonely deathbed, one from whence the two great things which sanctify those of humbler people—the Church's blessing, and a woman's love—were alike absent. He deserved, above all, to have had better friends.' She blamed Rhodes's handlers for turning him against her. 'Whatever some people may think, he had trusted me, and he had been led to think I had wronged and betrayed him. Had I done so, I would indeed have been a vile creature.' The London *Globe* called the chapter 'a queer compound of admiration and spitefulness'.

Indeed, critical reaction to *My Recollections* was decidedly mixed. An Isbister advertisement on October 1904 cited William Thomas Stead's *The Review of Reviews*, which named *My Recollections* one of the best books of 1904, calling it 'One of the most charming and fascinating volumes of the kind ever written in the English language. She has the wit and style of the French and the romantic imagination of the Slav.' Stead's opinion may have been coloured by his appearance in *My Recollections* as one of the princess's friends. Mrs Humphry Ward was more critical in her (unsigned) review in *The Times Literary Supplement*. She noted that, for a book called *My Recollections*, 'It is not, perhaps, surprising that the Princess has failed to "recollect" the only incident in her career which is publicly on record—namely, that on April 30, 1902, after an exhaustive trial at Cape Town, she was sent to prison for two years for forging the name of Mr. Rhodes to various large bills.'[26] Ward admitted that the book was well written, especially the account of the assassination of Tsar Alexander II, but asked, 'Knowing what we do of the Princess's career, the question is, of course, constantly present to our mind: How far can we believe her? With regard to the greater part of the book the question is not, perhaps, after all, of much importance. It is not all history, and it may be largely fiction.'

Harry's extant correspondence with the princess jumps to October 1904, with the book about to be published. Harry received a letter from George T. Brown, the solicitor who oversaw the liquidation of Isbister. It seems that both Harry and James S. Blankensee, the princess's solicitor, were owed money. Apparently Harry had loaned the princess £25 (£3,000 today) when she was in financial distress, and she promised to repay it from her book advance. Harry wrote to the princess, now living in Paris, about the problem. She was mortified, and assured Harry she would write to Isbister to pay his £25. The fact that this sum was so important to Harry is an indication of his financial state at this time. The princess was not happy at her treatment by the new Isbister regime: 'We are a little at daggers drawn with them, as I think that they did not act quite fairly towards me, and eliminated from the book a lot of things which I would have liked to leave in it', she wrote. Presumably this was done for fear of libel action. Still, she claimed 'upon the whole the book has been wonderfully well received, and so far I have seen, the only paper which made it the subject of a violent personal attack against me, has been The Times, and I would give much to find out who has written the article, as I have got certain suspicions about it. Have you got the possibility of finding out?' Harry was not about to expose Mrs Ward and risk antagonizing *The Times*. She then teased an idea for a new book, 'a volume of recollections of the Russian Court which though in the same style as the one just published will far exceed it in interest', and was in search of an editor (hint, hint). But under no circumstances would she let Isbister have it. Finally, she requested, 'Will you please write to me and address me as the Countess Rzewuska, my maiden name under which I am living at present.'

In his reply, Harry sympathized with her plight and offered to help. 'I am not surprised at what you tell me in regard to their treatment of your book after I left', he wrote. 'Any criticism of anything that they might do would come from me with a very bad grace and their judgement is probably better than mine; but I had already heard from another direction that they had again revised your M.S. and had cut out many things which I had decided to leave in. Very probably, as I say, from a publisher's point of view, they were right, but I can understand that it would be annoying to you.' Harry asked for an outline of the new book, and whether the princess had offered it to any publishers yet. The sense is that Harry was not offering to edit the manuscript but to act as the princess's literary agent (a more lucrative prospect): 'I will be glad to see if I cannot place it for you to advantage.'

In her reply, the princess was delighted. She reiterated that 'I did not like the way Isbister treated my book, especially the snobbishness which presided at certain alterations, which would certainly have harmed no one. They wrote to me about another volume, but I replied that I had already made other arrangements, to which they answered that in that case they considered the matter at an end.' For the new book, she proposed 'a more serious work' on the reign of Tsar Alexander III. 'I am very well au fait on that subject, as I had plenty of opportunities to know more than did the general public. Of course gossip should play an important part in the book, and a certain amount of amusing anecdotes would be related, the whole work would contain about 100,000 words.' The princess was more than *au fait*; while at court she had an affair with General Peter Alexander Cherevin, a trusted friend of the tsar. Her letter also revealed that Harry had still not been paid his £25, but thanks to 'a good deal of money' from the death of an uncle, 'a selfish old miser who never gave a penny to anybody', the princess said she could now make amends. 'This means I expect to repay to you immediately after New year the £25 which you so kindly advanced to me when I was in such dire distress. It was a real God send, that death.'

By early January 1905, poor Harry had still not received his £25. 'I have unfortunately been away and ill or you would have heard from me before', Harry wrote on January 9. 'On the other matter, of the payment to me. Do I understand that I am to look to you direct or to Isbisters or to your Solicitors? I need it perhaps more than you imagine.' Times were tough for Harry. He added that he had spoken to Gerald Duckworth, a prominent new publisher, about the princess's book idea, and that he would like to see the manuscript. 'They are not one of the biggest firms but they do their books well and I know that authors have nothing but good to say of them, and Mr Duckworth himself is a gentleman and a charming man to deal with', Harry said. In two years' time Duckworth would issue the publishing sensation of the new century, *Three Weeks* by Elinor Glyn. The princess sent an immediate reply. She had been unwell, too, and had not written a thing. As for Harry's money, 'I am enclosing here a note to Isbisters about your £25, and hope it will lead to something.' So it was back to being Isbister's—Pitman's— problem. The princess proceeded to denigrate her publisher (again), as they refused to accept an offer for a French edition: 'When I told them about it they coolly replied that they did not care to have the work translated as it might spoil the sale of the English edition. Now I think this is quite silly, for certainly the people who would read the book in French would not do so in English.' This was perhaps an indication that Pitman had not recouped its investment. 'They are horrible people', she concluded. Harry, clearly exasperated, put an end to this nonsense, telling the princess she would hear directly from Duckworth. In a private letter to Duckworth, Harry apprised him of the situation, and the fact that the princess had nothing to show so far. He also asked to be removed from the correspondence:

> Would you mind writing to her direct? I have no desire that she should come to regard me as her literary agent, to whom she can fire off M.S.S. when she pleases to be placed. Princesses, I think, get into a way of thinking that

they can command services as a matter of course; but, having made the introduction, I would rather drop out of sight, unless I can be of use at any time in straightening out any difficulty which may arise. She is, I think, inclined to listen to my advice.

She should be addressed, by the way, not as the Princess Catherine Radziwill, but as the Countess Rzewuska (you need not try and pronounce it) which is, I believe her maiden name and under which she pleases at the moment to believe that she is living incognita.

It is not known whether Harry ever received his £25. And the princess's new book, *Behind the Veil at the Russian Court*, was not published until 1913—and by Cassell & Co., not Duckworth (but still priced at 16 shillings). It was published under the pseudonym 'Count Paul Vasilli', one that the princess had used previously when writing a number of gossipy articles about the Russian Court. Cassell advertised the book as 'Banned by the Russian Censor' and having 'created quite a stir in Diplomatic Circles'.

*   *   *   *   *

The year 1904 was a time of momentous change in Harry's personal life—and not because of his strained relations with the princess. On June 18, in the Fourth Judicial District Court in Hennepin County of the State of Minnesota, Mary filed a petition for divorce. Harry was required to respond within thirty days. Mary's action clears up the mystery surrounding Harry's departure—and would debunk another family legend: that Harry was a bigamist.

In the complaint, Mary said she was 32 years old and had resided in Minneapolis now 'for more than two years past'. Harry, the defendant, was 44. They cohabited as husband and wife from September 23, 1891 'until on or about February 1st, 1900'. They 'have no children living'. It proceeded:

That on or about the first of February, 1900, said defendant willfully, wrongfully, and without any cause, pretense or justifiable reason therefor, deserted and abandoned this plaintiff and went to England, his native country, and has ever since continued to reside, and still resides, at the City of London, in England; and since said desertion has contributed nothing to the support or maintenance of plaintiff in any manner or to any degree whatsoever; and that said desertion and abandonment has been continued until the present time; and since said first of February, 1900, plaintiff has not seen defendant, nor have they lived or cohabited together as husband and wife.[27]

Mary's claims are puzzling. We recall that during the alleged suicide episode in March 1901, Thomas Lowry mentioned Harry as Mary's husband, and that he was on business in Europe. When Mary took up her job as a nurse in May 1902, she was still referred to as Harry's wife. And yet she claimed 'abandonment' since February 1900. Also, for the daughter of a multi-millionaire to plead poverty was a bit disingenuous. Nonetheless, Mary swore all as true before the judge.

On July 6, 1904, Harry was served the papers at his modest West London home, which he called 'The Wigwam', in Hampton Wick. But papers filed in court in Minneapolis on August 23 reveal that Harry chose not to respond. The thirty-day period to answer had passed, and on August 24 the judge gave an ultimatum: 'That September 12th, 1904, is a reasonable time after the personal service of said summons and complaint within which to allow said Defendant to appear and answer in said action, and that if no answer is filed on or before said 12th day of September, 1904, said action may be heard and determined as on default.' Still, Harry did nothing. So on October 4, 1904, a judge found that 'Plaintiff is entitled to judgment dissolving the bonds of matrimony'. Mary was present with her attorneys; 'The defendant did not appear, but made default.' And so they were divorced, after thirteen years of marriage. Incredibly, not a word of the divorce was printed in the local newspapers, another sign of the power of Thomas Lowry to keep the matter quiet.

Harry's great-grandnephew, His Honour Judge Paul Cook (great-grandson of Harry's sister Mary), suggested that at this time an accusation of abandonment was probably the quickest and easiest way to end a marriage. 'I don't think "abandonment" is harsh', he observed. 'Better than infidelity or violence or drinking. Also, it might have been the easiest ground to prove.' Harry's lack of reply, he added, 'was probably pragmatism. The marriage was over. Mary was on the other side of the world. What was to be gained by battling over honour?' The court documents, moreover, put to rest worries that Harry was a bigamist, as his descendants wondered if he had ever been legally divorced.

So at the end of 1904 Harry found himself with no wife and no job, apparently no savings, and in questionable health. He was also mourning the death of his mother, Harriett, on August 2, 1904, in Brighton. She was 84, and with her passing Valence, who had been living with her, moved in with Harry. While the now-bachelor Harry would have appreciated the company, and the opportunity to help his troubled sister, Valence was often ill and in bed. Still, she would have been a distraction. A postcard from Minneapolis arrived just before Christmas from John S. Bradstreet. 'Best wishes for 1905, old chap', he offered. Bradstreet mentioned a mutual friend, with whom he shared Harry's news about the divorce. 'All broken up when I told him.'

Still, neither Harry nor his ex-wife wasted much time in heading to the altar again. Mary was first to tie the knot, only seven months after the divorce was final. Her engagement to Dr Gustav Schwyzer, the handsome resident doctor at the hospital where Mary worked as a nurse, was announced in the *Minneapolis Journal* on February 4, 1905. Swiss-born Schwyzer emigrated to Minnesota in 1897. This was his first marriage; he was 37, Mary, 33. 'The fascinations of the hospital nurse are proverbial, but in fiction it is commonly the grateful patient who weds his nurse', the article began. 'Minneapolis has developed a charming hospital romance of a different kind that would be interesting without regard for the position of the principals, but whose prominence adds a touch to the story.'[28] Mary had advanced in her training to become an operating room nurse, and the surgeon was often Dr Schwyzer. 'The deft, silent, white-capped nurse who aided him was Mrs. Robinson', the paper continued. 'Starting from his admiration of her skill and capability as a nurse, Dan Cupid found no obstacle to leading the brilliant young surgeon on to personal admiration, which has culminated in today's announcement.' Shades of a Mills & Boon romance. The *Journal* concluded 'This culmination of Mrs. Robinson's career as a nurse will be a great surprise, as it was supposed when she left the hospital that she intended to take up at once the private practice of her profession.' What is astonishing, of course, is the lack of mention of Mrs Robinson's first marriage, to a man who was quite a name in the Twin Cities. Mary and Gustav were married on April 20, 1905, at the Lowry residence. Mr and Mrs Lowry were the witnesses, and only the immediate family was present; as the *Minneapolis Tribune* noted the next day, 'The service was solemnized as simply and quietly as possible', perhaps mindful that this was Mary's second marriage.[29] They planned a two-month honeymoon in Europe.

Needless to say, Harry made no mention of Mary's remarriage in his handwritten daily diary, as he had made no mention of the divorce.[30] But an entry on February 7, 1906 is revealing: 'Heard from Mr. Lowry in Arizona.' This is the first of several references to the Lowrys over many years, including visits with family members when Harry is back in America. This further debunks the family legend of a forced separation of Harry and Mary. It must have been amicable, otherwise Harry would have had no further contact with his in-laws. Thomas Lowry may have realized in 1900 that his daughter loved another man, Dr Schwyzer, and wanted children. We know he was fond of his son-in-law, and so may have asked him to slip away quietly—perhaps with a financial incentive. Harry, after all, was unhappy and also wanted a family. The fact that they all apparently remained friends after the divorce suggests that the separation was carefully arranged, not the sensational tale which Harry told his family and friends, perhaps to save face.

As Mary re-wed, Harry was advancing his own romance with a Miss Florence Tester, nineteen years his junior. In his diary for July 11, 1905, Harry outlined in pencil, 'Flo approves my scheme'. This understated remark was related perhaps to honeymoon or future living arrangements, for just a fortnight later, on August 1, they were married in St Pancras Church in London (presumably a Service of Blessing, as Harry was divorced). Present were Kay and his wife, Flo; their daughter, Grace; and Florence's father. The honeymoon was a modest one in Llanishen, Wales, a suburb of Cardiff.

In his memoir, Brad wrote at length about his father's marriage to his mother. He believed Harry was motivated by a desire to put down roots and establish family traditions, much as his own father, Julian, had done, and to succeed this time. 'In my father's case a strong impulse may have come from the disastrous experience of his first marriage', Brad noted, 'his second wife, my mother, being as completely different as possible from the first'. Florence was the daughter of an inspector of the London & South Western Railway. 'Railway men were the aristocrats of the wage-earning world at that time', Brad said, 'and he may have personified the English Yeomanry which my father was determined should be the source of his next wife (if any) after his disastrous experience with the daughter of the Chicago meat King'. Brad was misinformed about Thomas Lowry, of course, but the point is a valid one. Brad proceeded to describe the courtship:

> He first encountered her at a regatta on the Thames—at Richmond, I think, not Henley (regattas were very popular just after the turn of the century)— and my mother was extremely pretty, lively and amusing with a beautiful figure and an excellent dress sense. My father could well have been bowled over. She was engaged to a young man in Australia at the time, but neither she nor my father seem to have bothered about that.

> My mother's father, however, may well have bothered about it a lot. He was a man of stern principles, with a big black beard. He certainly disapproved of his daughter marrying a divorced man, and although he consented to be a witness at their wedding, he would never meet or speak to my father thereafter.[31]

Ironically, Florence's parents were also mismatched; he was a humble ticket collector, she the daughter of landed gentry whose father disapproved of the marriage and disowned her. Brad noted that he only saw his black-bearded grandfather once, when he was six years old and Harry was away on assignment for *The Times*.

Brad concluded that the marriage was a good one, even though his parents came from very different backgrounds. 'My father was invariably very kind to my mother, and she was not merely devoted to him but adored him', he wrote. 'My father was a man of high station; he was well-known to a great many people not only in England but in other parts of the world... He was a brilliant talker, with a quite astounding memory for knowledge. He played all sorts of silly games with me and other children.'[32] This time, it seems Harry married for love, not money, and this union would bring a degree of happiness and normalcy which he had not experienced since the early days of his marriage to Mary, some fourteen years earlier, not to mention a much-hoped-for child.

*   *   *   *   *

Newly married with a wife to support (and no rich father-in-law), it was time for Harry to redouble efforts to secure full-time employment. One can only imagine the psychological toll this took on him. Essentially he was starting over, at 46 years old, seeking a job as a journalist, much as when he went down from Oxford 23 years earlier. Then, as now, he was broke. Unlike then, he was not now in the best of health. Life after Isbister meant relying on his strengths as a writer, seeking freelance work while looking for a salaried position. He set his sights high: *The Times*. He had already written a freelance news article on February 16, 1905, entitled 'American Ship Subsidies and Great Britain', warning that the U.S. sought to wrest from Britain her supremacy of shipping lanes, once shipbuilding began in earnest to make up for the setback of the Civil War. 'When the steamship lines are established the American banks will be quick to follow', he predicted.[33] For this article he earned £9. Harry paid several visits to Printing House Square, nurturing contacts. On March 9 he wrote to Charles Frederic Moberly Bell, the managing director, mistakenly under the impression that *The Times* was launching a new evening paper. His humility and earnestness are striking:

> The Editor of The Times has recently accepted and published some of my work and more recently (I only received the books yesterday) has contacted me with books to review for the Literary Supplement. I have had rather a wide newspaper experience, though, as it has been more in America than in England, of late years at least, I am not at present well-known in the London press. I believe I would be a very useful man to the new paper and would immensely like the opportunity to prove it. I write to you as I have had the pleasure of meeting you, as you may remember, but should be very glad if I could have an interview with the Editor or whoever is again hiring the staff of the new paper.[34]

Bell had founded the *Literary Supplement* of the newspaper in 1902 and, despite Harry's error, offered him work as a reviewer. Mostly he was given books on American history and natural history. His first review was of *The History of North America: Volume VI: The Revolution* by C. W. A. Veditz and B. B. James, and appeared in the July 21, 1905 edition. 'A century is not a long time in the life of a nation, and the Republic it yet almost too young for its citizens to be able to write the history of even its earliest years with entire dispassionateness',[35] Harry observed. In another edition on September 22, he reviewed five books in a single, 3,400-word article, including *The Basis of American History 1500–1900* by Livingston Farrand.

As brother Kay started work as editor of a new illustrated penny weekly, *The Country-Side*, a 'weekly organ for all nature lovers' in support of his new foundation, the British Empire Naturalists' Association, Harry wrote a sample article for *Country Life*, which led to a commission for a fortnightly column called 'Wild Country Life'. Harry wrote about flowers, birds, insects, and animals with a passion and enthusiasm not expressed since his childhood in Cheltenham. 'If you have a liking for wild-beast fights', he wrote in the September 2, 1905 issue, 'any corner of your garden where the common garden spider abounds will at this time of year afford you as thrilling a morning's entertainment as ever set the people of old yelling round an amphitheatre'. He enjoyed poking fun, and his sense of humour was evident in his exasperation over the 'reckless adaptation' in America of confusing names. 'There are "black birds," which are, indeed, birds, and blackish, but bear no likeness to their English namesakes', he observed on September 22. 'There are "robins" as big as thrushes, all because they happen to have a tawny breast; there are "partridges," which are, in truth, ruffled grouse or colins.' Indian names added to the confusion: 'The Indian musquash soon degenerated into musk-rat, though the exigencies of polite trade are now bringing the old name into use again. The lady who buys a collarette in Regent Street of "genuine musquash sable" might hesitate about the purchase if the article were labelled "musk-rat skin."'

But the literary highlight of 1905 was the publication of Harry's second novel, *The Life Story of a Black Bear*, published in September by Adam & Charles Black in London (as part of its 'Animal Autobiographies' series) and (ironically) Macmillan in New York (evidently George Brett bore Harry no ill will). Clearly Harry was being responsible, using his talent as a fiction writer to earn money while seeking a full-time position as a journalist. Told from the point of view of a bear, this charming book was a considerable departure from the content and style of *Men Born Equal*, having much more in common with Jack

London and *Call of the Wild* (published two years earlier). Like London, Harry had written a book ostensibly for children, but laced with issues on wildlife conservation and the environment for their parents. Harry mined his first-hand experiences in the American West, especially among prospectors in Idaho, for a parable about the disappearing frontier. He set the tone in the introduction:

> There is always tragedy when man invades the solitudes of the earth, for his coming never fails to mean the destruction of the wild things. But, surely, nowhere can the pathos be greater than when, in the western part of North America, there is a discovery of new gold-diggings. Then from all points of the compass men come pouring into the mountains with axe and pick, gold-pan and rifle, breaking paths through the forest wildernesses, killing and driving before them the wild animals that have heretofore held the mountains for their own.[36]

Harry was writing from experience. 'Here in these rocky, tree-clad vastnesses the bears have kinged it for centuries, ruling in right of descent for generation after generation, holding careless dominion over the coyote and the beaver, the wapiti [elk], the white-tailed and the mule-eared deer.' But change comes when winter ends and the spring thaw begins. 'The hills ring to the chopping of axes; and the voices of men—a new and terrible sound—reach their ears. The earth, soft with the melting snows, shows unaccustomed prints of heavy heels.'[37]

Bears, Harry insists, are peace-loving and naturally friendly. From his perch in the Rocky Mountains, Wahka, the ursine title character, is overly curious about the strange humans and their new gold-mining town. When his sister Kahwa is held captive, he struggles to make sense of it. 'I wondered why they should have wanted to catch her at all. We had no wish to do them any harm. We were nobody's enemy; least of all was little Kahwa. Why could not men live in peace with us as we were willing to live in peace with them?'[38] But when Kahwa is killed, Wahka's heart hardens. 'I had borne man no ill-will whatever, and would have been entirely content to go on living beside him in peace and friendliness, just as we lived with the deer and the beaver. Man himself made that impossible, and now I no longer wished it. I hated him—hated him thoroughly.'[39] Wahka would have killed man, but was afraid of his 'thunder-sticks'. So he and the bear colony are driven out, in search of a new home, for man was here to stay. 'They were wiping out the forest: the animals that lived in it had vanished: the very face of the mountains was changed, so that I could not tell the spots that I knew best; and I was sure that we could never drive them out again.'[40]

143

The story ends profoundly. The timeline advances two years with Wahka, captured, in a cage, part of a travelling circus.[41] He has accepted his fate, despite a profound sense of loneliness and a longing for the past. 'At night sometimes, when the wolves howl and the deer whistle, or the whine of a puma reaches my ears—all caged, I suppose—the longing for the old life becomes almost intolerable. I yearn for the long mountain-slopes, with the cool night-wind blowing; and the stately rows of trees, black-stemmed and silver-topped in the moonlight; and the noise of the tumbling streams in one's ears, when all the world was mine to wander in.'[42]

Clearly, *The Life Story of a Black Bear* was, to Harry, much more than a children's fable. It offered a powerful reminder of the devastation of the forest and wildlife which was going on in frontier areas of the world, especially in America. Harry was a conservationist at heart, much like the current American president, Theodore Roosevelt.[43] The *Evening Standard* predicted a wide audience for Harry's book. 'It is a volume that boy or man will read with interest, for not only does it give, in popular form, the life-history of the black bear but it is written in language that appeals at once to the man who loves reading good books more for the sake of the writing than for the work itself.' The *Aberdeen Press and Journal* suggested, 'Any parent who wishes to find out whether his children take an interest in animals should place this book in his hands: the boy who stops reading it without reluctance may at once be declared to have no interest in natural history.' Although sales figures do not exist, *The Life Story of a Black Bear* was reprinted twice, in 1910 and 1913, making this the most successful of Harry's novels.

Harry ended the year 1905 on a positive note in his diary: 'Things look better and I feel better than I have for two years.' He began 1906 with, 'Started a reform by rising in time to breakfast at 9 sharp!' despite suffering from neuralgia. By February he could declare, 'The most writing work of the year.' As Harry changed hats, yet again, the future looked a whole lot brighter.

5

Man of *The Times*, 1906–1913

Harry threw himself into his search for work with the drive and enthusiasm of a man half his current age of 47, a time when most men would have been already established and settled comfortably in their chosen profession. As he lobbied for a full-time position at *The Times*, he had also written, seemingly without effort, yet another novel—his third, which he provisionally entitled *The Diary of a Honeymoon*. This light-hearted tale about deliriously happy newlyweds was clearly autobiographical, reflecting Harry's new life with his new wife, Florence. It was serialized in *C.B. Fry's Magazine* in eight parts from April to November 1906, alongside works by two of Harry's acquaintances, Harold Begbie and Jack London. Harry did not use his real name as author but 'J. Blundell Barrett', the main character's name, instead. He perhaps wanted to test the waters for this decidedly different type of novel—and protect his reputation as a 'quality' writer before *The Times*. In a clever promotion, the magazine took ads in the 'Personal' column of the *Daily Mail*, one a day from March 20 to 23, featuring fictitious messages between the husband and wife of the story, J.B.B. (Jack) and Euphemia. One read, 'J.B.B.—Have found "Diary of Honeymoon" in "Fry's Magazine." Funniest thing I've read—EUPHEMIA.'[1]

The series was not published in book form until May 1911, revised by Harry and re-titled *Essence of Honeymoon* (which sounds like a perfume) and now published under Harry's name. The publisher in America was Harper & Brothers, who sixteen years earlier had issued Harry's very different first novel, *Men Born Equal*. In London, the novel was published by Heinemann (with evidently no hard feelings about *Call of the Wild*), on a distinguished list which included *The Dop Doctor* by Richard Dehan; *Zuleika Dobson* by Harry's friend, Max Beerbohm; *The Secret Garden* by Frances Hodgson Burnett; and *Juggernaut* by E. F. Benson. The novel was serialized in *Harper's Bazaar* over three months from April to June 1911. 'Come, now, for a fresh perspective— idyllic happiness with the appropriate background of fragrant hedgerows and hay-fields, cottage gardens aglow with old-fashioned posies, and smooth, green English lawns—wander forth with Jack and Euphemia on their honeymoon', ran the *Harper's* ad. 'In these pages there is good fun, good company—and the spirit of youth.'

Essence of Honeymoon is extraordinary for several reasons. First, the style was quite unlike anything Harry had written to date. There was no underlying message or agenda to this novel, as there was in *Men Born Equal* and even *The Story of the Black Bear*. Instead, it is a bit of froth, a breezy, silly, utterly disposable romantic novel, much in the vein of a popular author like Robert Hichens. As *Essence of Honeymoon* is filled with veiled references to Harry's real life, one can assume that the sweet, devoted heroine is based on Florence. Autobiographical references abound. The hero, Jack Barrett, an Oxford man (as was Harry), has married the considerably younger (as was Florence) Euphemia Torkington of London, and they depart for the Welsh mountains (as did the Robinsons) for their honeymoon. The account of their romantic sojourn is told from Jack's point of view. On arrival at their Welsh cottage Jack sweeps his wife into his arms and they kiss, overseen by the housekeeper:

> 'It is almost too loveliful to be true!' continued Euphemia (and on her lips the word is one of the prettiest I know), as she came close to me and, with a long sigh of content, drew my arm round her waist.
>
> 'Breakfast is ready, ma'am!'
>
> Neither of us had heard Mrs Bradford step out on the veranda, and we started guiltily apart.
>
> 'Do you think she saw us, Jack?' whispered Euphemia.
>
> As she had not been six feet away while we stood in the full blaze of the morning sunlight, I thought it quite probable that she had, and I said so.
>
> 'Well, I don't care if she did,' said Euphemia. 'Why shouldn't I kiss my own husband, any-how?'
>
> 'It is a practice,' I said, 'much more common than novelists would have us believe.'[2]

Jack proceeds to chronicle their days in episodic form: meeting the locals, walking in the village, playing golf together, going shopping. 'This is the charm of shopping with a woman, and I begin to understand why they enjoy it so much', Jack explains. 'When a man goes shopping it is to buy a certain article; he enters a shop to buy it, gets it—or does not, as the case may be—and comes out again. When a woman enters a shop she has not the smallest idea what she will bring away with her. That is on the knees of the gods.'[3] Hence, a shopping trip to purchase buttons and gloves ends up in the acquisition of a sheepdog (Harry and Florence had a real one, named 'Bob', early in their marriage[4]).

Euphemia is goodness personified. On her twenty-fourth birthday, she proposes, 'I should like to go out and make all the world as happy as we are'. She begins by giving money to beggars in the street. To Jack, somewhat set in his ways, this was a revelation: 'There is no such thing as being happy except by giving happiness to some one else. There is no other road to happiness; and that road is certain. I had to wait until I was married to Euphemia to find this out.'[5] Harry was no doubt describing his bride.

After the honeymoon, the young couple settle in a cottage in Suffolk (not dissimilar to the Robinsons' Cambridgeshire cottage which was connected to Florence's family). Euphemia takes to domestic life and is a superb cook, far better than the 'ordinary English cook of the mid-Victorian type ... She can make curries (not English curries, nor yet those mockeries which are served at some London restaurants as "made by a native cook")—real curries—three or four of them. She knows the right use of pistachio nuts in a pillau; she has sounded to the depths the possibilities that lie in green peppers, and—final triumph of the true chef—has mastered the mysteries of soy.'[6] Harry presumably knew all of these culinary dishes from his family's Indian background.

In the end, *Essence of Honeymoon* is a ringing endorsement for marriage. 'How can people talk the nonsense that they do about ceasing to love one another after one is married? How can two people stop loving if *they* are *they*?' Euphemia exclaims. 'So long as I don't do anything wrong, you can't help going on loving me, can you, Jack? And you'll never do anything wrong, so I shall just go on loving you more and more.'[7] Even though we know little about Harry's second marriage, he clearly made his intentions clear with this novel. He was married to Florence, they were happy, and their marriage would endure. He was determined to succeed this time, despite the failure of his first marriage, and those of his parents, his brother Phil, and two of his sisters, Mary and Valence.

Reviews were generally good for *Essence of Honeymoon*. In America, the *New York Times* noted that 'the book depends for its charm largely on witty exaggeration, but there is some very true and natural humour in it. As a book for a vacation hour, at any time or season, it is highly commendable.' *The Boston Globe* said the 'consistently wholesome humor' that was 'by no means mushy' was a refreshing change of pace. 'In view of the awful problems which so many writers nowadays evolve from matrimonial matters, it is a distinct relief to get the fragrance of orange blossoms uncontaminated by the miasma of the divorce court', the reviewer said. 'Some may call the book reactionary. Progressive persons may sigh for something nerve wracking. But the normal person will welcome this volume as a whiff from summer meads.' British critics agreed. *The Scotsman* promised 'a good deal of amusement will be got', noting 'Their great ambition is to deceive onlookers into the belief that they are an "old married people," but they fail from the first and at every turn, chiefly because they are so much in love with each other that they cannot help showing it.' The *Croydon Chronicle* said, 'There is, of course, a lot of sentiment in this book, but it is not of the character to get on one's nerves.'

It is unknown whether Harry ever intended to write a series of novels about Jack and Euphemia. In America, *Essence of Honeymoon* sold nearly 1,500 copies, a modest number, earning him around $250 ($6,650 today) in royalties.[8] It went out of print after one year. Perhaps this is why *Essence of Honeymoon* would be Harry's last work of fiction.

* * * * *

Essence of Honeymoon was a one-off experiment by Harry. He was a journalist and chronicler by nature, not a natural-born novelist. Indeed, his talent was on full display when, in July 1906, he signed on to write a weekly column in a new Minneapolis-based publication, *The Bellman*. The founder and editor was William C. Edgar, editor for twenty years of the *Northwestern Miller*, and one of Harry's oldest friends. The *Minneapolis Tribune* heralded the new weekly on May 18: 'There seems to be room for a clean, readable Saturday paper.' It noted the column from London by Harry, showing he still had name recognition. Clearly, by agreeing to write this column Harry had no hard feelings about America and his former life in Minnesota.

Harry's column was called 'Echoes from Bow Bells'. For the next three years he offered a weekly window for residents of the Twin Cities on doings in Britain and the Empire, while showing just how much the U.S. and U.K. had in common, much like Alistair Cooke would achieve decades later with his 'Letters from America' series. There was a healthy mix of gossip and serious topics. The first column dealt with the popularity of American songs in Britain: 'Perhaps stage lyrics are not art or literature; but a step of some importance has been taken if Englishmen generally are coming to believe that Americans can beat them at song writing.' Harry wrote often of his passion for golf. On August 11 he recalled the favourite parlour game of 'Who are the three greatest men in the world?' Once it was Bismarck, Gladstone, and Li Hung Chang; then Cecil Rhodes, Wilhelm II, and Joseph Chamberlain. Now he suggested Edward VII, Theodore Roosevelt, and (still) Chamberlain. Germany was fast falling out of favour: 'It is Germany that we really want to shut out;

and all Englishmen would like to see Great Britain and the United States peacefully dividing the commerce between them.' By turning away from Europe and aligning himself with America, Harry was proposing a new alliance that was coming to be known as the 'Special Relationship'.

On the domestic front, Harry was chronically ill, unable to sleep for an entire week with chest pains that forced him to write by hand in bed, rather than at the typewriter. At this time rushing to the doctor was not the custom; instead, one simply retired to bed until the worries passed. Florence was also frequently sick, but she had good reason: on October 21, 1906 in Little Shelford, Cambridgeshire, where the Robinsons kept a cottage, Florence gave birth to a son, John Bradstreet Perry Robinson. There can be little doubt of Harry's joy, although it was not expressed in his diary. Florence spent the next two weeks in bed, assisted by a nurse. The baby was christened on December 9; the godparents were his namesake, John S. Bradstreet, and Kay's daughter Grace.

Suddenly blessed with a wife and son and about to turn 47 years old, Harry must have entertained serious thoughts about providing for his new family, something he did not have to do in Chicago when married to an heiress. Having renewed his relationship with Edgar via *The Bellman*,

Figure 13. Harry, age 47, and Florence, 28, with their infant son, John Bradstreet Perry Robinson, born October 21, 1906. In his album, Harry wrote underneath this photograph, 'All three of us'.

Harry had another offer from his friend: to run the European desk of the *Northwestern Miller*, based in London. Flour and grain exports to Europe were a significant source of income for mills in Minnesota. Harry wrote to Edgar on November 30, proposing a salary of £1,000 (£119,300 today) a year, an enormous sum (considering the average annual salary at the time was around £75 [£8,900 today], although this was for a common labourer and not someone higher up).[9] Clearly, Harry wished to return to the days when he was married to a Lowry heiress. But one week later Edgar turned the tables, sending Harry a cable inviting him to move back to Minneapolis instead and take over the *Northwestern Miller*. The following day, Harry entered in his diary, 'Cabled Edgar asking $1000 moving bonus and $6000 salary.' At this time $6,000 was nearly £1,000. Then, on December 8, 'Edgar cables 'Terms Prohibiting'. The very fact that Harry considered uprooting and moving his new family to his old hometown confirms there were no hard feelings with the Lowrys. One wonders what might have been had the Robinsons moved to America in 1907. In the end, Harry would take up the European Manager position for the *Northwestern Miller*, starting with the March 27, 1907 issue, but only as a short-term proposition. As the year closed, Harry recorded in his diary, 'The best year of the last half-dozen. Press receipts £321' (about £38,000 today), although this was still well-short of his £1,000 goal.

*   *   *   *   *

Before taking up his temporary post in London for the *Northwestern Miller*, Harry was asked by Edgar to come to Minneapolis for a consultation, his first time back in America in seven years. He did so in good stead. Yes, he had had a huge defeat with Isbister, but in the three years since the bankruptcy Harry was turning his life around. He was published widely as a freelance journalist, at home (*Times Literary Supplement*, *Country Life*, *Fry's*) and abroad (*The Bellman*). He wrote a well-received children's book. He had married and produced a son. Moreover, he had renewed his ties with America and was becoming something of a goodwill ambassador, encouraging closer ties as he worked on a major non-fiction project on the topic.

Harry's trip was nearly postponed due to Brad's illness. On February 7, 1907 he reported that the baby was sick and had a 'rupture'; Brad had an operation in Cambridge on February 11. Harry departed on February 17, despite noting in his diary that he was 'anxious' about Brad. Aboard the S.S. *Etruria* for what was his thirteenth transatlantic crossing, Harry sat at the Captain's table and played a lot of bridge. He saw the ship's doctor about his knee: 'had it iodined and bandaged'. He landed in New York on February 24. In Minneapolis on March 5, he lunched with Edgar and accepted the London job at £3 a week, considerably less that the £1,000 a year (£19 a week) he had asked. That same day, he met Horace Lowry, Mary's brother, another sign that relations were good. One wonders if Harry saw Mary, or visited the graves of his two children. Intriguingly, the *Minneapolis Tribune* interviewed Harry on March 17, catching him in Chicago on his way back East. Readers, the paper said, were interested in what Harry had been up to. 'Mr. Robinson was in a specially happy frame of mind, although anxious to get back to England, where he has lived most of the time since disposing of his interests in the Chicago trade publication', the article said. 'He is married again and has a son who is named John Bradstreet Robinson.'[10] This was the first public mention that Harry and Mary had divorced, although by 1907 he had long since disposed of his *Railway Age* 'interests'. The article proceeded:

> He spoke enthusiastically of his home, which is in one of the London suburbs, and which he secures at a rental that would seem ridiculously low in this country. He has three servants, but as they can be employed in England at $50 a year, or thereabouts, his retinue is not as expensive as might be supposed.
>
> 'The changes in Minneapolis are simply wonderful,' he said. 'I could not but help notice the wonderful progress that city is making, and although I am happily situated in London I will always have pleasant memories of Minnesota.'
>
> It is understood that Mr. Robinson spends most of his time writing for the newspapers and magazines.

Boasting of a London home with three servants, Harry projected an air of prosperity, although in reality he struggled to maintain the lifestyle he had grown accustomed to (and refused to give up). Before leaving New York, Harry had a meeting at G.B. Putnam's Sons, the eminent publishing house. For the past year he had been working on a major non-fiction book about America, and presumably this meeting was to sign a contract. It is surprising that Harry did not approach Harper & Brothers, Houghton Mifflin, or even Macmillan. He arrived in Liverpool on the S.S. *Carmania* on March 24.

Harry's trip to America after a seven-year absence was fodder for several columns in *The Bellman*, as well as for his non-fiction book. What struck Harry most was the innate optimism of the American people, 'the conviction, the unquestioning confidence, that, whatever comes, the future is safe. Out of all the chaos and present ferment, there will come stability.

The people may seem to be at a loss for the moment: but it will strike the right trail again.' He contrasted this with Europeans:

> What is so conspicuous in the faces of the American people—just the ordinary crowd upon the streets—is that curious look of wide-eyed hopefulness. You are so accustomed to it that you do not notice it. When you go abroad you find the English, the German and the French masses dull and heavy-featured. You must stay abroad for some years before that dullness ceases to seem to you the natural aspect of mankind in the lump. Then, returning to America, you are struck by the extraordinary alertness and direct self-confidence of gaze in the eyes that meet yours in the streets. And that is a memory that lives and grows more vivid.[11]

Clearly, Harry's time in America was transformative, and he missed it. He would share his fondness and enthusiasm in his forthcoming book. He signed a contract with Putnam's on June 19. 'On the whole a good year', Harry wrote in his diary on December 31, 1907. 'Flo and baby well. Trip to America. Won car and prizes. Total income £814.2.10.' Boosted by the sale of the car won in the *Pearson's Magazine* competition, the *Northwestern Miller* job, and book reviews, Harry's income had increased considerably over 1906, nearing his magic number of £1,000.

*   *   *   *   *

Harry's last edition as the European Manager of the *Northwestern Miller* was on May 6, 1908. He was succeeded by C. F. G. Raikes, imported from the St Louis office. In the issue Edgar thanked Harry, who 'has been acting as a temporary representative...but his other engagements are such that he is unable to give his entire time to the office'. It is uncertain what Harry's other engagements were, apart from his work as a freelancer for *The Times*. Edgar may have decided that Harry was not a good fit for a very technical job, or Harry may have simply been bored. No matter: he was poised to have his biggest success as a writer to date, one that would set up his career as a journalist and pundit for the rest of his life.

   In July 1908, G.P. Putnam's Sons published simultaneously in London and New York Harry's major non-fiction book, *The Twentieth Century American: Being a Comparative Study of the Peoples of the Two Great Anglo-Saxon Nations*. This long-gestating project was Harry's master work, inspired by his American experience which convinced him that the two great imperial powers, formerly at odds, had to work together in the interests of world peace. Towards that goal, 'my desire is to contribute, if possible, something towards the establishment of a better understanding between the two peoples by correcting certain misapprehensions which exist in the mind of each in regard to the other', Harry explained. Hence, *Twentieth Century American* was a kind of primer for Englishmen of everything American, from politics and the economy to race relations, women, sports, and even humour. Like Kipling, Harry was convinced that the peace of the world depended on the two great Anglo-Saxon nations: Britain (with her empire) and the United States. Although Harry was not the first to take up the cause of the so-called 'Special Relationship' that exists today ('Bismarck was reputed to have said that the most important fact of the nineteenth century was that Great Britain and the United States of America shared a common language'[12]), he approached the concept with *brio*, insisting he was uniquely qualified to write with authority. 'I have lived in the United States for nearly twenty years, under conditions which have given rather exceptional opportunities of intimacy with the people of various parts of the country socially, in business, and in politics', he stated in the preface. 'Wherever my judgment is wrong it is not from lack of abundant chance to learn the truth.'[13]

Inspired perhaps by works like Charles Dilke's *Greater Britain: A Record of Travel in the English-Speaking Countries* (1868) and W. T. Stead's *The Americanisation of the World or the Trend of the Twentieth Century* (1902), among others, Harry's immediate motivation for this project was a fellow Englishman, H. G. Wells, who had just written sceptically on the subject in *The Future in America: A Search After Realities* (1906). Wells expressed strong doubts about the United States as a world power, although he concluded that America could emerge as the best hope. 'In spite of my patriotic inclinations, in spite, too, of the present high intelligence and efficiency of Germany, it seems to me that in America, by sheer virtue of its size, its free traditions, and the habit of initiative in its people, the leadership of progress must ultimately rest',[14] he wrote. Harry responded strongly to Wells's distinct lack of enthusiasm in *Twentieth Century American*. 'Mr. Wells looks superficially upon the country as it is to-day and finds society more chaotic, distances larger, sentiment less crystallised than—*mirabile!*—in the older countries of Europe, and is plunged in despair', Harry wrote. 'Nothing but a little more experience would enable Mr. Wells to see the national feeling of the American people.'[15] Given Harry's extensive time in and study of America, his book was the more credible. It was bold of Harry to take on Wells, but it would have brought *Twentieth Century American* more publicity, even notoriety.

Anglo-American solidarity was essential, Harry began: 'An alliance between Great Britain and the United States would secure the peace of the world.'[16] Any longstanding prejudices stemming from independence must be cast aside as America was now taking the lead. 'A child is rightly

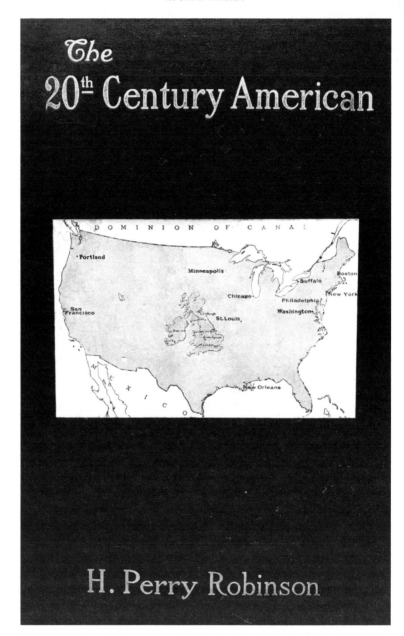

Figure 14. The striking cover of Harry's non-fiction book, published by G.B. Putnam's Sons in 1908, reminded readers of the disparity in geographic size between the United States and the United Kingdom.

forbidden by his nurse to make acquaintance with other children in the street; but this child has grown to manhood and gone out into the world to seek—and has found—his fortune',[17] Harry observed. The tipping point was the Spanish–American War, which 'brought the people suddenly into contact with the things of Europe and widened their horizon...The quarrel with Spain did but furnish, as it were, a definite taking-off place for the leap which had to be made'.[18] Britain and America, moreover, reached common ground over the war, as they did over the Boer War and the Boxer Rebellion in China, going far to mend fences over Britain's sympathies with the Confederacy during the American Civil War.

Slowly and methodically, Harry made his argument that, given their connected history, background, and values, Britain and America had nothing to fear from sharing the world's stage, seeing as America was now building an empire of her own. 'Two brothers will commonly be aware only of the differences between them—the unlikeness of their features, the dissimilarities in their tastes or capabilities—yet the world at large may have difficulty in distinguishing them apart', he explained. 'While they are conscious only of their individual differences, to the neighbours all else disappears in the family resemblance.'[19] Indeed, the closest soil to America was British in nature: Canada. 'One of the chief lines of railway from New York to Chicago passes for half its length over Canadian ground; the effect being precisely as if the Englishman to go from London to Birmingham were to run for half the distance over a corner of France', Harry noted. 'It is difficult for the Englishman to understand how near Great Britain has always been to the citizen of the United States.'[20] However, he admitted that history was to blame for suspicions and misunderstandings on both sides. The Englishman, he insisted, 'cannot expect the American to feel towards England as he himself feels towards the United States. The American people came in the first instance justly by its hatred of the name "British," and there have not since been at work any forces sufficiently powerful to obliterate that hatred, while there have been some operating to keep it alive'.[21]

Accepting the need for an alliance as a given, Harry proposed that the two peoples must come to understand each other better, already facilitated by the rise in tourism between the two countries over the past thirty years. So he delved deeply into the differing points of view of both peoples, noting common traits and misunderstandings, in humour, art, sport, politics, commerce, even attitudes towards women. Of the latter, Harry noted that, much like the eponymous heroine of Henry James' *Daisy Miller*, 'the average American girl acquires when young a self-possession and an ability to converse in company which Englishwomen only, and then not always, acquire much later in life'. Harry found such self-assurance refreshing, but rejected the common English belief that American girls are 'forward' and, therefore, possess the corresponding vices. 'That the girls of to-day are any less womanly, in all that is sweet and essential in womanliness, than any generation of their ancestors, I for one do not believe',[22] he wrote. Harry's style is evident here: provide information, debunk false assertions, and seek common ground.

Similarly, Harry noted that a class structure exists in America, but mobility is greater. 'While in America all classes exist, they are not fenced apart, as in England, in fact any more than they are in theory', Harry observed. The American people, he added, '"comes mixed"; dip in where you will and you bring up all sorts of fish'.[23] Harry praised the optimism of the American people, and the notion that a person could aspire to be anything, even president of the United States. But this trait of 'extraordinary resourcefulness and versatility', he insisted, was inherently Anglo-Saxon. 'The colonial Englishman develops the same qualities in a not incomparable degree', Harry observed. 'The Canadian and the New Zealander acquire a like unconquerable soul, but the Englishman at home is not much impressed thereby, chiefly for the reason that he is almost as ignorant of the Canadian and the New Zealander as he is of the American, and with the same benevolent ignorance.'[24]

Harry's mission was to eliminate such 'benevolent ignorance.' The way forward was through education and interaction. Harry applauded the Rhodes Scholarships, begun in 1902. He appreciated the diaspora, Englishmen like himself who lived and worked in America, claiming they assimilated better and supported the American way of life more than other immigrant groups:

> The American people ought cordially to cherish Englishmen who come to the United States to live, if only for the reason that they have never organised for political purposes. In every election, all over the United States, one hears of the Irish vote, the German vote, the Scandinavian vote, the Italian vote, the French vote, the Polish vote, the Hebrew vote, and many other votes, each representing a *clientele* which has to be conciliated or cajoled. But none has ever yet heard of the English vote or of an 'English-American' element in the population.

> It is not that the Englishman, whether a naturalised American or not, does not take as keen an interest in the politics of the country as the people of any other nation; on the contrary, he is incomparably better equipped than any other to take that interest intelligently. But he plays his part as if it were in the politics of his own country, guided by precisely the same considerations as the American voters around him.[25]

Harry insisted that the present generation of Americans had learned the lessons of the past, particularly in terms of big business and corruption.

'They live under a new social code', he wrote. 'They have nothing like the same opportunity for successful dishonesty and immeasurably greater chance of punishment, whether visited on them by the law or by the opinion of their fellows, if unsuccessful or found out.'[26] But he admitted that prejudices take a long time to die out. As an example, he cited English goods versus American goods, with a nod, no doubt, to his friend Bradstreet:

> I had lived in the United States for many years before I ceased to cling to the notion—which I never hesitated to impart cheerfully to Americans when occasion offered—that though American workmen turned out goods that served their purpose well enough, for really sound and honest workmanship you had, after all, to come to England...
>
> A Sackville Street tailor begged me to leave in his hands for a few days longer some clothes which he was pressing for me, made in a far Western State, in order that he might keep them—where they then were—hanging in his work-room as an object-lesson to his men in how work ought to be done.[27]

On race relations, Harry condemned the 'barbarous and disgraceful' incidents of lynchings of blacks in the American South. However, recalling his days in Idaho, where he had first-hand experience of the extreme justice meted out by teams of vigilantes to maintain order among the lawless, Harry understood the plight of the Southerner. 'Many of those people who in London (or in Boston) are loudest in condemnation of outrages upon the negro would if they lived in certain sections of the South not only sympathise with but participate in the unlawful proceedings',[28] he noted. While Harry believed that white rule was essential (agreeing with Kipling on the 'White Man's Burden'), he was sympathetic to possibility of peaceful coexistence. 'There is no reason to believe that the two races cannot live together comfortably even though the blacks be in a large majority', he wrote, 'but there must be no question of white control of the local government and of the machinery of justice'. Indeed, Harry believed that granting the vote to black people in the United States was a mistake, as it only heightened tensions between whites and blacks. He spoke from experience of the Empire, and knew that his British readers would understand. 'The English have wide experience of native races in all parts of the world and they have not yet found the problem of living with them and of holding at least their respect, together with some measure of their active good-will, anywhere insoluble.'[29] The acknowledgement of a problem was Harry's hallmark: he was determined to shine a spotlight, even if he could not propose a solution, to provoke debate.

Harry concluded his book with a reality check and a desperate plea for peace. He admitted that there had always been the threat of another war between the United States and Britain. 'The danger of such a war is greater, perhaps, than the people of either country recognises, certainly greater than most Englishmen imagine', Harry wrote. 'The people of England do not understand the warlike—though so peace-loving—character of the American nation. It is just as warlike as, though no less peace-loving than, the English, without the restraint of that good-will which the English feel for the United States; without, moreover, the check, to which every European country is always subjected, of the fear of complications with other Powers.' But threats must be put aside in favour of a higher purpose: counter Germany:

> Beyond all this—apart from, and vastly greater than, the considerations of the interest or the security of either Great Britain or the United States—is the claim of humanity. The two peoples have it in their hands to give to the whole world no less a gift than that of Universal and Perpetual Peace. It involves no self-sacrifice, the giving of this wonderful boon, for the two peoples themselves would share in the benefit no less than other peoples, and they would be the richer by the giving. It involves hardly any effort, for they have but to hold out their hands together and give.

> It matters not that the world has not appealed to them. The fact remains that they can do this thing and they alone; and it is for them to ask their own consciences whether any considerations of pride, any prejudice, any absorption in their own affairs—any consideration actual or conceivable—can justify them in holding back.

'That such an alliance must some day come is, I believe, not question-able', Harry insisted. 'That it has not already come is due only to the misunderstanding by each people of the character of the other ... Eng-lishmen and Americans only come to a realisation of their resemblance when either compares the other critically with a foreign people. Foreign-ers, however, see the likeness when they look at the two together.'[30]

* * * * *

Reaction to *Twentieth Century American* was strong, and in some cases polarizing. The London *Morning Post* said Harry followed in the foot-steps of Alexis de Tocqueville and, more recently, H. G. Wells and Henry James, but given his in-country experience had far more credibility. 'It remained ... for a citizen of the United States familiar with the politics, the educational systems, and the intimate life of the two peoples to describe the American people as they appear to themselves, and more particularly as they appear to themselves in comparison with the other great branch of the Anglo-Saxon race', the review said. 'It is this task which Mr. H. Perry Robinson attempts, and we may say goes very far to accomplish, in his work.' The London *Daily Mail* was more sceptical. 'An alliance between the two branches of the Anglo-Saxon race would, Mr. Robinson thinks, ensure the peace of the world. If that be so, it is certainly most desirably; but perhaps, after all, Mr. Robinson is too optimistic.' Indeed, the *New York Times*, while generally praising Harry's book, struck a cautious note: 'In the eyes of Germany and possibly of Europe, our entrancing league of peace would be a league of aggression and conquest, and would be resisted or attacked as such. Before we undertake to enforce upon the world a "Pax Britannica-Americana," let us look coolly at the chances of ending our career in a sort of Armageddon.' This was six years before the outbreak of war. The *San Francisco Chronicle* called Harry's work 'a masterly valuation and criticism of the American people and nation to-day...While he does not hesitate to score our frailties unmercifully, he shows a hearty appreciation for our virtues, and is less of a pessimist than many a native-born citizen, recognizing in the evils of the day and their exposures a healthy moral growth, a building up rather than a tearing down.' The reviewer especially liked Harry's praise of American women: 'High tribute is paid by this author, who finds in them an adaptability, a power of expansion not prevalent among the English.'

Clearly, Harry was riding high with the positive response to *Twentieth Century American*. He soon learned that one of his biggest admirers was none other than the legendary Alfred Harmsworth, Lord Northcliffe. On October 19, 1908, Northcliffe wrote to Harry's publisher, George H. Putnam, from his New York hotel (a letter Harry preserved in his scrapbook). 'I am greatly indebted to you for the interesting book "Relations between England and America" which I have almost read', he wrote. 'If Mr. Perry Robinson is on this side I would like to see him when I return from Canada at the end of next week. The matter with which he deals is practically most important in the world to day.' Harry was not in New York, so presumably met Northcliffe back in London. Anglo-American relations were a passion for Northcliffe, the publishing impresario who founded the *Daily Mail* and the *Daily Mirror*. Northcliffe had just acquired *The Times,* for which Harry continued to write book reviews. In his diary on January 16, 1909, Harry noted that his prospects had improved, 'due to American book and Northcliffe's good opinion'. Indeed, Northcliffe himself would secure Harry's future with *The Times*.

Intriguingly, only a year before, Harry was one of Northcliffe's staunchest critics. In *The Bellman*, he excoriated the man and his practices, aligning him with the worst excesses of William Randolph Hearst, the father of 'yellow' journalism in America. The occasion was Northcliffe's defeat in a libel suit brought against the *Daily Mail* by William Lever and the Sunlight Soap Company. The *Mail* had accused Lever of building up a monopoly to keep the prices of his goods high, which he denied. The £50,000 award (£5.7 million today) was insufficient, Harry wrote on August 10, 1907. 'It is a pity that the sum was not large enough to compel the Daily Mail to cease publication', Harry wrote, 'but much will have been gained if it has taught it such a lesson as will make it observe some measure of decency in its attacks on individuals and private concerns hereafter'.[31] He condemned the *Daily Mail* in no uncertain terms:

> It merely has no standards, civil, literary, ethical or patriotic. It has no traditions, no guiding principle but the love of sensationalism. It provides its readers with new thrills and shocks each morning; and he who reads it, and it only, for a month will have no conception of what has really happened in the world, no continuous survey of the progress of events. Yet it is probably read by more people than any other six morning papers put together; and what, in the course of years, its influence has amounted to in the intellectual debasement of the people and the corruption of their moral sense, it is impossible to calculate.

Harry called Harmsworth's appointment to a baronetcy and then a peerage 'an altogether deplorable and calamitous thing' for an awful man. 'No man can spend his life in work which makes for unrighteousness and go himself unpunished', Harry predicted. Of rumours that Northcliffe would buy *The Times*, Harry wrote in his November 23, 1907 column, 'Such a thing in the view of any one who has respect for the traditions of English journalism would be nothing short of a national calamity.'[32] And yet, aligned on the single issue of Anglo-American cooperation, and eager for a full-time job at *The Times*, Harry set aside his animus for Northcliffe, and they would become the best of friends, however hypocritical that may have seemed.

Kay and his family joined Harry and his family for a very happy Christmas. Perhaps inspired by his book, Harry arranged for some Yankee dishes to be included in the Christmas dinner, with mixed results, as he conveyed in *The Bellman*. 'There was, it is true, a conspicuous lack of enthusiasm over PettiJohn's breakfast food', a bran-based cereal invented in Chicago (and presumably a favourite of Harry's), 'but succotash did better; though I am not sure whether it was the thing itself that was popular or only the name. Cranberry sauce with turkey, or, indeed, with anything, had a great run, especially with the younger members of the party, while opinion was divided on sweet potatoes.' But the 'real triumph', Harry said, were the baked beans, so long as they were not served with tomato sauce. 'The ordinary baked bean of commerce, the familiar, comfortable Sunday-breakfast bean was received at each appearance with acclamation. It was a great day for Boston.'[33]

Harry was in a good mood. His finances were looking up, and for the first time since leaving America, his annual income exceeded £1,000. And Harry and Florence were planning their first trip abroad, to the Canary Islands. This would be a working trip for Harry, to gather fodder for articles. To generate spending money, and pay for two £30 steamer tickets to the Canaries, Harry wrote ferociously for nine days from January 16 to 25, 1909. He proudly listed his week's output in his diary: 'I wrote: 5 Bellman letters, 1 Bellman Book Sketch, 1 Wild Country Life, 4 Daily Mail articles, 1 City Life Review, 2 Times Reviews, 1 for Kay.' The last was, presumably, for *Country-Side*. Harry had no qualms now about writing for Northcliffe's *Daily Mail*; money was money, after all.

The Robinsons sailed on the S.S. *Patani*, without Brad, arriving in Tenerife on February 2. Harry wrote about the experience in a series of travelogue articles in *The Bellman* in March and April. He played a lot of golf, admired the black-eyed women, and explored the peaks, valleys, and craters. While there, he received word that Thomas Lowry had died in Minneapolis, aged 65. His son-in-law, Dr Gustave Schwyzer, attended him at his deathbed, along with Mary (who was still called 'Mrs. Harry P. Robinson, wife of the former editor of The Railway Age' in Lowry's *New York Times* obituary). Six months earlier, Harry had been asked by Edgar to write a tribute for *The Bellman*, as Lowry's health was failing. His glowing article was yet another affirmation that his break with the Lowry family was an amicable one. He affectionately called his former father-in-law 'Tom'. 'His mere existence was a public blessing and his place can never be filled; for their remains no other like him', Harry wrote. 'He was more like Abraham Lincoln than any man whom America has seen in this generation.' He noted how 'in those dark days' of the financial panic of 1893, 'it was only Wall Street's confidence in Tom Lowry that stood between the Northwest, or certainly between Minneapolis, and wreck…It rested solely on Wall Street's knowledge of the man'. He called for a statue of Lowry, which was eventually erected in 1915. 'So strong and yet so tender-hearted, so just and yet so generous, endowed with such great gifts yet quite unspoiled by them, it will be long before there is another like him', Harry concluded. 'Of such men nature makes but few and when one dies his departure is the common loss of humanity, even of those who never heard of him. The world is poorer by one whose acts and influence were all for good.'[34] The family must have been delighted by Harry's tribute.

* * * * *

In 1909, perhaps prompted by his new friendship with Northcliffe, Harry finally made the leap from occasional contributor to *The Times* to the category of 'Special Writer'. This was not yet the hoped-for full-time position, but it paid well, and the assignments catered to Harry's love for natural history and animals. His series 'Studies in the Zoological Gardens' featured two articles every month from May to December 1909. Harry knew the London Zoo well, as he was on the board of directors (along with Kay), and often took his son Brad along on visits. 'My father and his brother Kay were of course active Fellows and knew a lot of the keepers', Brad recalled. 'This meant that when I was taken there, I used to get snakes wound round my neck or be given young crocodiles to hold. Fellows in those days got tickets which admitted their families on Sunday (when no one else could get in).'[35] With this series Harry clearly enjoyed himself, combining a detailed description of the animal in question with personal observations and humorous anecdotes. For example, in his debut article on May 15, 1909, Harry discussed 'Lions':

> In the lion house one may see any day the eyes which look so indifferently on the men and women who come and go before the cages light up with sudden savagery as some small child toddles alone across the floor. The truth is that the lion has learned that men and women are not for him; but this smaller creature—nice antelope-size—soft and helpless, presents itself to the royal mind as easily killable, and as being not impossibly excellent eating.[36]

Harry's hidden agenda, moreover, was to counter a growing movement that held that keeping animals caged in zoos amounted to cruel punishment. Quite the contrary, zoos were a vital educational and conservation resource, Harry insisted in his first article. 'It is doubtful whether the majority of animals are not better off in the Zoo than ever they could be in their wild state', he wrote. 'Certainly they have the chance of living longer; and there must be much peace of mind in the assurance of regular meals and great comfort in the freedom from the necessity of having to go out every night to catch your dinner, with always a considerable likelihood that you may fail to catch it.'

Harry moved on from elephants, rhinoceros, and crocodiles to buffaloes and Great Apes. He admired the ostrich, whose plumage was adopted by royalty around the world. 'As each ostrich egg is equivalent to about two dozen eggs of the villatic fowl, the possibilities of omelette in a well-furnished ostrich nest are evidently considerable',[37] he observed. Harry concluded with a wonderful anecdote:

Perhaps man would have been more courteous to the ostrich if the ostrich had insisted more punctiliously on its dignity; but it is not proud. With a finely catholic appetite, it does not hesitate to beg—or swallow—pence from the humblest visitor to the Gardens, so that in course of time the bird may become a perambulating savings bank. An ostrich has been known to pick up and swallow bullets coming hot from the mound. One which died in the Zoological gardens had by assiduity accumulated ninepence-halfpenny in coppers; and Cuvier[38] found inside another metal odds and ends to the weight of almost a pound. Yet another is recorded to have died possessed of a silver medal and the cross of an Italian order, both of which may be assumed to have been more valuable to the original owners than to the bird, for though the ostrich may have a coat to its stomach, as a writer pointed out at the time, it can only be regarded as, at best, an indifferent surface for display.

Perhaps encouraged by *The Times*, Harry pitched his collected articles as a book to publishers. G.P. Putnam's Sons declined, but Heinemann, publisher of *Essence of Honeymoon*, accepted. *Of Distinguished Animals* was published in November 1910, in time for the Christmas sales season. Dedicated to Brad and featuring more than fifty 'photographs from life', the book was well received. The *Illustrated Sporting and Dramatic News* praised Harry's writing on December 3 as 'sprightly and amusing. This is, in fact, an excellent book for young people as well as "grown-ups"; and the boy or girl who would probably be bored by the duller pages of a serious natural history will find in "Distinguished Animals" a great deal of information couched in light and readable form, and illustrated by a capital series of photographic reproductions.' Further afield, the *Sydney Morning Herald* in Australia on January 14, 1911 noted 'the treatment is of a very popular type ... It is interesting and well produced'.

*   *   *   *   *

Harry had good reason to celebrate over the Christmas holidays. He noted in his diary on Christmas Day, 'Heard from Chirol saying <u>Times</u> want me to go to U.S.' Ignatius Valentine Chirol was the director of the Foreign Department of *The Times*. After years of writing reviews for the *Literary Supplement*, and following the success of his 'Zoological Gardens' series, Harry was now being offered a full-time salaried position, commencing July 1, 1910. To Harry's glee, he would be based in Washington, DC, part of Northcliffe's concerted effort to enhance the reporting presence of *The Times* in America. Harry met Chirol for breakfast on December 30 to hammer out the details, which Chirol recapped in a letter on New Year's Eve. The plan was to have Harry leave England around May 1, 1910, travelling East so as to visit Japan, the Philippines, and Hawaii before landing in San Francisco. Once in America, Harry would make his way to Washington, where Florence and Brad would join him. Chirol offered £175 to cover the cost of the ticket, plus £275 for expenses. For a man who had just turned 50, not in the best of health, and having to move his family overseas, this was an ambitious undertaking. But Harry was never one to resist a challenge, nor a chance to feed his wanderlust, and the future looked very bright indeed. 'Have received the Times letter telling me to go to America via the Pacific', he wrote in his diary on New Year's Day. 'I thank whatever God there be.'

Charles Frederic Moberly Bell, The Times managing director (who helped negotiate the sale of The Times to Northcliffe in 1908), confirmed Harry's appointment in a January 8, 1910 letter. 'From your arrival in San Francisco you will act as our special correspondent in America, will travel about America when necessary and have your headquarters in Washington where you will co-operate with Mr. [Arthur] Willert who is our resident correspondent in Washington', he wrote.[39] 'From the 1st July 1910 your salary will be calculated at the rate of £83. 6. 8. per month and all expenses travelling in America will be at our charge.' A guaranteed annual salary of £1,000 would have been a windfall for Harry and his newfound family. Bell concluded, 'In this formal letter I will only express our very great satisfaction at having secured your valuable services.' In his January 9 reply from the Cambridgeshire cottage, Harry was excessively florid in his appreciation and praise:

> To the formal acknowledgment of your letter (which is enclosed) I wish to add a more personal expression of thanks for the great kindnesses which you have shown throughout our negotiations.
>
> I have been accustomed, for many years before I first contributed to the paper, to say, in expressing my admiration of The Times, that one of its chief claims in one respect was that it was always such a gentleman.
>
> It has been a delight to find how completely the spirit which manifests itself in the paper seems to possess everybody who has anything to do with its guidance. I do not think that any one could enter in any work with more earnest enthusiasm that I now have, or with a fuller sense of personal obligation to those with whom he is becoming associated.[40]

Before setting off around the world, Harry was given another assignment by Bell and Chirol: travel to the West Indies to report on the Royal Commission headed by Lord Balfour of Burleigh, which was investigating trade relations between Canada and the Caribbean with an eye on improving transportation and telegraphic communications. Harry's articles would feature in the annual Empire Day Supplement in *The Times* on May 24, 1910, in line with Northcliffe's desire to pay more attention to various regions of the Empire and their connection to the Crown.[41] One wonders whether Bell and Chirol also wished to test Harry with a rigorous overseas assignment before setting him loose on the rest of the world. Harry was an experienced writer, granted, but it had been some time since he was a roving newspaper reporter.

With Bell promising to write to the White Star Line 'asking for their good offices', Harry set sail on January 12, 1910 on the S.S. *Oceanic* with Lord Balfour and other members of the Commission. After a few days in New York and lunch at G.P. Putnam's, he sailed to Jamaica on the Royal Mail Steam Packet vessel *Clyde*. Over the course of six weeks, Harry followed the Commission around the Caribbean, visiting Cuba, Puerto Rico, Martinique, Dominica, St Lucia, Barbados, Grenada, St Kitts, and Antigua. While making notes for his *Times* articles, Harry also wrote a multi-part travel series for *The Bellman*.[42] Returning to England on March 21, Harry spent much of the month of April writing up his articles. His progress was interrupted by the death of King Edward VII on May 6, a day Harry happened to be in Paris. 'Very hard to believe that the King is dead, here in Paris!' he wrote in his diary. 'Everybody mourning.'

The death of the monarch added poignancy to the celebration of Empire Day on May 24. The new King, George V, insisted that the festivities continue, and *The Times* thoroughly agreed. 'There is, at such a moment as this, a heightened consciousness throughout the Empire of its devotion to the Throne', stated the leading article of the Empire Day Supplement. The Crown held together the Empire, a 'compact of different races, different creeds, and different systems of government...No other symbol, not even the Flag, could thus focus and embody an allegiance as diverse as that which is owed to the King.'[43] The sixteen-page supplement included five pages dedicated to the West Indies, along with sections on Canada, India, Egypt, and Australia. Harry wrote the lion's share of the West Indies articles, with a byline of 'From Our Special Correspondent with the Royal Commission Lately in the Islands'. Across sixteen articles, Harry offered his impression of each island, commenting on agriculture, tourism, finance, wildlife, food, poverty, even race relations. Harry was a firm believer in King and Country, a patriot to the end, so his articles were always geared towards support of the Empire. 'It is worth remarking, too, that both black and coloured are everywhere loyal to Great Britain', he noted in a typically rosy outlook ('coloured' referred to those of mixed blood; it was not the pejorative as used in the United States).[44] His signature style is evident: informative yet engaging. What stands out most amid a dizzying array of facts and figures is Harry's eye for the unusual and the humorous. 'One of the first discoveries of a visitor to the West Indies will probably be that he has a good deal to learn about the mere pronunciation of the names of the places which he goes to see', Harry wrote. 'The Leeward Islands, for instance, are not "Looard" nor "Leward" Islands, but straightforwardly Lee-ward, as they are written. Dominica is Domineeka.'[45] He noted that 'the ultimate contempt of the colonial is perhaps reserved for the tourist who writes Barbados with an "e" ("Barbadoes"). Or even "the Barbadoes," as if it were a plural like potatoes or tomatoes.' He is consistently entranced by the beauty of the islands and the friendliness of the people. 'We are all familiar with the colouring of picture post-cards on which the tints are all too vivid to be real', he observed. 'Yet many a time, when lying off one of the islands, it may be Dominica or another, passengers on dock will say, one to the other, "There! That is the exact colour of the post-cards!"'

We know that Harry enjoyed good food and drink, and for him the West Indies were a gastronomic delight. 'An edifying volume waits to be written on the beverages of the West Indies', he wrote, focusing attention on the 'Swizzle' cocktail, 'which is to say beaten, as with an egg beater, into a froth'. There were various types, some deadly. 'Among the miscellaneous Swizzles to be met with in the islands, one which would require special analysis is that which Antiguans have invented for the destruction of their friends, which contains a teaspoonful of so of *Crème de Cacao*. It is a theme which would require some subtlety of treatment.'[46] Regarding supper, Harry had his fill of turtle and shellfish. 'Gastronomically there are better foods than dolphin', he wrote, 'but, from an aesthetic and emotional point of view, it would not seem as if, after eating flying fish and dolphin, there could be many more worlds to conquer. The only fitting course to follow should undoubtedly be mermaid.'[47]

*   *   *   *   *

Two days after Empire Day, Harry bid farewell to Florence and Brad and departed Victoria Station, bound for Marseilles. There he boarded the S.S. *Moldovia* for the journey East. This would be the longest period of time away from his new family, but Harry showed no signs of distress (which was perhaps his biggest character flaw). In fact, he never seemed to mind being by himself, with his natural wanderlust as his companion, and he thoroughly enjoyed the grand adventure of travel. Perhaps owing to his new assignment, Harry gave up his column in *The Bellman*, which was renamed 'Westminster Chimes' and taken up by fellow English author Herbert Westbrook, a friend and collaborator of P. G. Wodehouse.

Transiting through the Suez Canal, Harry arrived in Colombo on June 11, Singapore on June 18, Hong Kong on June 22, and, finally, Manila on June 28. The *South China Morning Post* made note on July 13, 1910 of 'Mr. H. Perry Robinson, the special correspondent of the "Times" of London, who recently passed through here en route to Washington'.

Harry spent a month in the Philippines, travelling to multiple islands and surveying the country, much as he did in the West Indies. Oddly, his eight-part series of articles did not begin in *The Times* until October. Harry's reporting was connected to his new American assignment, as the United States had acquired the territory from Spain after the Spanish–American War, and was the focus of significant American investment. Curiosity in Britain was high about America's new imperial experiment. 'The mission of the United States is to civilize the islands and make them prosperous, not to write poems about them or to paint pictures',[48] Harry observed. He marvelled at the engineering works, including the building of roads and bridges, and the expansion of forestry and agriculture. He was especially impressed by Baguio, the 'summer capital' which was transformed into a mountaintop resort accessible by an 'astonishing' American-built road. 'Nothing, perhaps, has been done in the Philippines more characteristically American than the creating out of chaos a summer capital on these mountain tops', he wrote. 'In much the same way did Kubla Khan decree him pleasure-houses. So far, the 24 miles of automobile road, which is fairly near completion, have cost about five million *pesos,* or roughly half a million sterling.'

Unlike his rather playful West Indies articles, Harry's reports from the Philippines were more serious in tone, reflecting the political issues at stake as America came to terms with what it meant to be a colonial power like Britain. Harry was not afraid to voice criticism. 'The one paramount question in the Philippines is that of the permanence of American rule', he observed.[49] He acknowledged the growing calls for independence, and the restlessness of the locals as to how long the American 'occupation' would last. 'America is not to be their motherland', Harry noted, 'but only their foster motherland.' Harry said that uncertainty and indifference were taking a toll. 'There is already grumbling enough in America at the expense of maintaining the Philippines', Harry noted. 'The time is at hand when the people of the United States will have to consider seriously whether what they are now doing in the islands is not either too much or too little.'[50] In this sense, he insisted, America could learn from the British experience in India. 'No one will be slower than the Englishman who has seen something of British Colonies elsewhere to consent to the statement that the United States is making a failure here', he observed. 'It would be a blessed thing for the world if there could be established some circulating system by which the entire American people could be pumped in sections out to the Philippines, held there for a while till they understood something of what Colonial work and an Empire mean, and then pumped home again.'[51] A greater understanding of Filipino life would lead Americans 'to sympathize with the work which Great Britain has done, and is doing, in the world', leading to Harry's dream of Anglo-American cooperation worldwide in the cause for peace.

From the Philippines, Harry returned to Hong Kong, writing in his diary on August 1 that he was 'pleasantly idle'. He proceeded to Japan, then Hawaii, landing on August 28. Like the Philippines, the Hawaiian Islands were another recent acquisition by the United States. The front page of the *Honolulu Star-Bulletin* on September 5, 1910 featured a banner headline, 'London Times' Washington Correspondent is in Honolulu'. The article stated that Harry had spent six weeks in the Philippines 'studying the conditions there. As the result of his inquiries he has nothing but admiration for the manner in which the administration of the islands is carried out. The officers who are responsible for the work are zealous and clean, and it is a pity, Mr. Robinson considers, that the officials at Washington do not render more assistance.'[52] Hawaiians had as much at stake as did Filipinos in raising awareness overseas. The article proceeded, 'Mr. Robinson is sanguine that ports of the Philippines will yet provide the summer resorts of the Orient. In support of this Mr. Robinson points out that Manila in the middle of the summer has a better climate than Hongkong, Shanghai, and other parts of China and Japan.'

Oddly, Harry seems to have written only one article on Hawaii for *The Times*, a travel piece on 'The Nuuanu Pali. The Great Battlefield of Hawaii', published on December 22. 'Every visitor to Honolulu is expected to go immediately on his arrival to see the Pali', Harry reported. 'In an hour he will be back in town, a trifle exhausted, perhaps, but conscious that he has successfully "done" one of the historic sights of this part of the world.'[53] Apart from describing the scene of the bloody 'Hawaiian Battle of Hastings' that installed Kamehameha as king, Harry offered tourist advice on golf (the Oahu Country Club boasts 'probably the best nine-hole golf course between the California coast and the Mediterranean'), automobiles ('commonly high-powered and luxurious'), and the proliferation of Japanese, who comprised nearly half the population. 'The *click, click* of wooden shoes heralds the approach round a bend in the road of a party of Japanese women, half of whom carry on their backs doll babies which have evidently been picked off a Christmas-tree.' Harry did not venture into politics or American rule, as he did in the Philippines, evidently more pleased with the situation in Hawaii.

Harry landed in San Francisco on September 19 and immediately 'cabled Times for money', as indicated in his diary. 'Two days much worried over <u>Times</u> money', he continued. A reprieve came with £100 on September 22. While there he took in the sights, including Muir Woods, and dined at the Bohemian Club, one of Jack London's hangouts (although there is no evidence he and Harry met). Harry sent a postcard to Brad, writing, 'Hurry up! Daddy's waiting!' and giving his new work address: 'The London Times, 801 Munsey Building, Washington.' Harry boarded a train west on October 1, destination Chicago, then transited to Minneapolis. There he met up with his old friend Bradstreet and had dinner with Horace Lowry, Mary's brother. 'Mpls [Minneapolis] most cordial and members of the family especially', he wrote in his diary on October 7. On October 12, he lunched with his former mother-in-law, Beatrice (no doubt offering condolences on Thomas Lowry's passing), and then boarded a train for Washington. He was met at Union Station on October 13 by Willert, his new colleague in the Washington bureau. One week later, Florence and Brad arrived, along with a governess named Jean.[54] They secured rooms at the Hamilton Hotel at $250 per month. On Brad's fourth birthday on October 21, the Robinsons and Willerts paid a visit to the Washington Zoo.

* * * * *

While Harry was en route east, Valentine Chirol dispatched a memorandum outlining his expectations for the revamped Washington bureau. 'It was felt that THE TIMES had not yet acquired in the United States the position which one might reasonably hope for it', Chirol observed. 'Something could, of course, be done by making our American news and our interpretation of American current events, through our Washington correspondent, sufficiently interesting to attract the attention of Americans travelling or residing in Europe.'[55] Prompted by Northcliffe, Chirol was anxious that *The Times* become as well known in America as it was in Europe. 'But our Washington news, however excellent, must have lost its bloom by the time the Paper itself reaches the United States', Chirol noted, 'and one cannot expect Americans, of all people, to study with care Mr. Willert's appreciation of quickly-changing situations at least a week after date'. This was where Harry, 'an able writer of experienced judgment', came in:

> In order to enlist the permanent interest of American readers, the only course, in my opinion, is to deal with the larger problems of the United States, and especially with the great economic, industrial, financial, labour

and racial questions which play so large a part there, on such broad lines that Americans will look to THE TIMES for an authoritative treatment of them which they do not find in any of their own papers. Work of this kind must be attractive in form and weighty in substance; and it will require the undivided energies of an able writer of experienced judgment.

As far as it is possible to judge beforehand, Mr. Perry Robinson appears to be well equipped with those qualifications. I think he understands thoroughly the nature of the work expected from him, and when he was consulted as to what he considered the best place to make his headquarters for the purposes of that particular kind of work, he stated emphatically that it could be nowhere else than Washington, as Washington is the only place in the U.S. where, owing to the presence of the Central Government and of the Legislature, one comes into contact with the leading people from every part of the country.

From his base in Washington, Harry was expected to travel at least three months in the year, 'gauging, especially in the Middle and Western states, the trend of public opinion on the larger questions in which the whole country is interested'. While Willert would focus on news articles ('We do not look to Mr. Perry Robinson for news'), Harry would 'devote himself exclusively to the writing of special articles such as form one of the most valuable features of THE TIMES. He will, moreover, be able to supply a certain amount of work on literary, dramatic and artistic subjects which Mr. Willert is not particularly well qualified to deal with.' Chirol predicted the men would not clash and would work well together: 'I do see obvious advantages in their being in close touch and having frequent opportunities of comparing notes and exchanging their views.' Chirol hoped the situation would last, but was making no promises. 'It may be that the scheme will not work out as successfully as I anticipate, but I hope that it will be given a fair trial', he said. 'It seems to me very important that, for the first year at least, Mr. Perry Robinson should be given the opportunity which he desires of establishing relations for himself in Washington.' Chirol's words were prophetic, as Harry's term would, in fact, last less than one year.

The Robinsons' first Christmas in America featured a familiar face: Percy Hagerman, Harry's former brother-in-law, visiting from Colorado. Florence was evidently well aware of the Lowrys and their clan and, apparently, did not mind the continued contact with Harry's exes. On December 31, Harry wrote in his diary, 'A good and eventful year, with West Indian trip, voyage around the world, settling in Washington. Thanks be again!'

Per Chirol's instructions, Harry began filing stories for *The Times* (as 'Our Special Correspondent in America') on a variety of topics, from the mortality rate in the U.S. (at 15 deaths per 1,000, the lowest in history) and social unrest (noting the growing divide between the *nouveau riche* and the poor, especially in the West), to stories about forestry and conservation efforts. Writing on the railroad industry, Harry encouraged shareholding to build public interest and support of corporations, which were often regarded as the enemy. Harry journeyed to British Columbia to examine the lumber and mining industries. While in Seattle, he was robbed, noting in his diary on March 24, 1911, '$90 taken from my room during night'. His suitcase was lost on a train to Minneapolis.

Harry's most prominent contribution to *The Times* in his new position involved an extended visit to Utah and an analysis of the Mormon Church. The April 1911 trip was prompted by a recent wave of anti-Mormon protests in London, due to a rather successful proselytizing campaign by Mormon missionaries in England. In 1910, there were 82 Mormon churches in London alone, with 80,000 members. Some 300 missionaries had visited 63,000 homes, resulting in 963 converts being baptized, and more than 500 emigrating to Utah. Some feared that these departures were forced, that young English girls were actually kidnapped and thrown into Mormon 'harems' in Salt Lake City as a prelude to polygamous marriages. Winston Churchill, then Home Secretary, conducted an inquiry.[56] *The Times* ran several articles on the Mormon Church, including on the practice of polygamy, which was meant to have ended as a condition of Utah statehood in 1896, but many believed persisted.

The *Salt Lake Tribune* on April 30, 1911, in an article headlined 'Special Commissioner of London Times Here', welcomed Harry. 'The paper wired him to come to Utah and make a thorough investigation of the subject. Mr. Robinson declines to be interviewed on the ground that it would be a breach of ethics for him to talk at this time. He expects to be in Utah about a month.' Newspapers across the state followed Harry's progress. The *Ogden Standard* invited Harry to state his position:

'It is against our ethics to state just what we are going to do,' said Mr. Robinson, 'but I can say that I am going to the bottom of the subject in every way possible. The subject of Mormonism, it would seem, has caused considerable trouble in London, and the Times wishes to get at the facts as they really are. I have copies here of the magazines in which articles have appeared and will investigate the allegations in detail. I expect the work to require four or five weeks. I desire to learn the facts absolutely as they are and to give my paper the absolute truth.'[57]

It is interesting that Utah newspapers did not connect Harry with his brother Phil, and Phil's not very flattering account of the Mormons in his 1883 book *Sinners and Saints*. Harry no doubt had his beloved brother in mind as he travelled about the state.[58]

Harry had quite the scoop for *The Times* in an article published on May 1, 1911. The president of the Mormon Church, Joseph F. Smith, nephew of the church's founder, Joseph Smith, handed Harry a statement for publication in order to 'counteract the misrepresentations now being made in England and in the hope to establish the truth'.[59] In 1904 Smith had reiterated the ban on polygamy, applied it worldwide, and made it grounds for excommunication. The irony is palpable, as Smith himself had six wives and forty-eight children. Nevertheless, Smith told Harry that, in the nine years so far of his presidency, 'no man in the church having one wife has been permitted to take to himself another'. He hoped to impress, 'through *The Times*, upon the English people the extreme desire of the leaders of the Church for an exhaustive and dispassionate investigation'. A leading article in the same edition reiterated Harry's claim that the 'remarkable' document was 'official to the fullest extent', adding, 'It is written with a judicious moderation of tone which is well calculated to appeal to the sense of justice of the British people, and it breathes a spirit of earnestness, simplicity, and truth.' However, *The Times* noted that Smith's declaration was not retroactive, as Smith himself had admitted in 1906 to 'unlawful cohabitation' and having five wives (in addition to his 'legal' wife) and was fined $300. 'The character of a witness is very material when he invites us to consider his unsupported statements', *The Times* noted. Oddly, the *Salt Lake Tribune* agreed: 'There should go along with this statement of President Smith's the fact that he is living continuously with five women as his wives; that he has announced his determination to continue so to live; that he admits that this conduct of his is a violation of the Manifesto as interpreted under oath by himself; that he admits that it is a distinct violation of the law of the State.'[60] In any event, Harry's reportage stirred up a hornet's nest and made him, like Phil, *persona non grata*; he was doubtless happy to leave the state.

* * * * *

For reasons unknown, Chirol's hope that Harry and Willert would be a 'dream team' for *The Times* in Washington was not realized. On June 17, Harry sailed to London for meetings at Printing House Square. He returned to America, where he spent the summer with the family in a rented cottage in Kerhonksen in the Catskill Mountains of New York

State, a popular place to escape the Washington heat. In his memoir, Brad, who was nearly six years old at the time, recalled this three-month summer stay as a halcyon time. 'We had a clapboard house on a hillside above the village', he said. 'We had chipmunks nesting in our gatepost, we had skunks in the garden, and an apple orchard, a peach orchard and an apricot orchard. When we walked in the woods, we were rattled at by snakes, and all along the paths and on the rocks in the open spaces there were Indian signs. There were very few people in the hills—a few farmers in the valleys—and the Indians had really only just gone.'[61]

On July 11, 1911, Reginald Nicholson, who succeeded Moberly Bell as manager of *The Times* (Moberly Bell died at his desk on April 5), wrote to Harry, confirming their June conversation that his Washington assignment would end in October. The exact reasons are unknown. Harry seemed to get on fine with Willert, but he may have found the cross-country travel arduous. Or, he may simply have preferred that his young family live in England. Or, indeed, he might have been fired. In any event, Nicholson stated that Harry would continue to work for *The Times* 'under the instruction of the Editor and his assistants' at rate of £4 a column, with a minimum guarantee of £500 a year. 'On these terms we are perfectly willing for you if you so wish to contribute to foreign newspapers or to monthly periodicals in this country but not to any daily or weekly newspaper', Nicholson said.[62] Five hundred pounds was half the guaranteed salary of the Washington position. Was this Harry's idea, or was he essentially demoted by *The Times*? It is difficult to say, although Harry may indeed have been feeling the strain of the constant travel; his diaries contain frequent references to his physical condition, often requiring several days' rest in bed. One thing is certain: from this point on, Harry would never be free from financial worries, as he struggled to maintain a certain lifestyle for himself and his family.

Harry left for England one month earlier than Florence and Brad, arriving in Liverpool on October 19. With his change in circumstances, he moved the family out of their small house, The Wigwam, and took rooms in Sandringham House on Sydenham Hill, at '6 ½ guineas a week with 10/6 extra for fires'. It was time for the Robinsons to economize, but without sacrificing a good address. Florence and Brad arrived home on November 24. In his memoir, Brad recalled the move to Sydenham, adjacent to the Crystal Palace in South London, an area 'lined with large or very large Gothic mansions inhabited by very successful businessmen. It was said to be one step below Muswell Hill for the rising Jewish families, and indeed there were a number of very well-known commercial figures on the ridge.'[63] These included Elizabeth Lazenby of

Lazenby's Sauce, akin to Worcestershire sauce, and James Crossley Eno of Eno's Fruit Salt, the popular household remedy. Brad noted that many residents were refugees from the Franco-Prussian War of 1870, including Lieutenant-Colonel Francois Armand Maurice Georges Duault, who would become young Brad's pen pal during the First World War.

Brad also recalled the day when, walking with his mother on the ridge, they spotted a 'For Sale' sign in front of one of the smaller detached houses, named 'Ashmore'. 'We waited to read the name of the house agent on the board, and then my mother said, "Come on, we must run and telephone Daddy." She got my father at <u>The Times</u> office and he got the house agent who gave him the name of the man selling it, from whom my father got first refusal that evening.'[64] That man was Colonel Ian Campbell of the Argyll and Sutherland Highlanders, whose father was head of Reid, Pye, Campbell & Hall, one of the largest importers of Bordeaux wine. The house, according to Brad, was a gem. 'It stood on a very steep hillside, with three storeys in front and four at the back. From the dining room windows at the back, the whole panorama of London was laid out, with Big Ben on the left-hand edge and Tower Bridge at the right. Behind, the garden sloped down in three tiers.' The real prize, to a youngster like Brad, was the fact that a branch of the London and South East & Chatham Railway ran under the garden in a tunnel on its way to the Crystal Palace. 'The mouth of the tunnel was only a few feet below the bottom of the lowest tier of our garden, and on both sides as it went in there were big embankments with rabbits and wild flowers', he recalled. 'We could see at least half a mile of the double track at its curved towards us from Forest Hill station.' Brad pointed out that the neighbours were not 'rich tycoons'. On one side was Sir Edward Clarke, the barrister who defended (unsuccessfully) Oscar Wilde at his 1895 trial. On the other side was Professor John H. Plumb, the Cambridge historian, 'an erudite character who used to make obscure jokes to me through the fence'. Down the road was 'a family of Guinnesses' with four sons, whose father played golf with Harry, 'year in, year out and had a silver cup made to record their wins'.[65]

It is interesting that, despite Harry's change in circumstances at *The Times*, he took the new house on Sydenham Hill, and still employed four servants: a full-time housemaid and cook, and a part-time gardener and a general handyman, who hauled coal, cleaned boots, polished the doorstep, and the like. Despite the financial hardship, Harry was determined to maintain a certain way of life and respectability. Still, behind the scenes he was forced to watch his expenses closely. An extraordinary document exists, dating from this time, which took the form of a contract, handwritten by Harry and signed by both him and Florence. It consisted of ten promises made, all in an effort to trim expenses. These were:

1. Both servants must take 25 per cent less pay.
2. We must have <u>no</u> guests to stay in the house.
3. No casual entertaining. No theatres. No outing for pleasure costing over 2/-. No taxis. Only 3rd class travelling.
4. No wines, spirits, or cigars.
5. Neither you nor I must have one single new article of dress.
6. No newspapers except <u>The Times</u>, <u>Punch</u> and one feminine weekly.
7. If any golf, no caddies, and only on the Sydenham course.
8. No Christmas, birthday, or wedding presents.
9. Rigid economy in food: no soups, entrees, sweets (candies) or fruit except from our own garden (beyond what you think necessary for Brad's health): only joints, plain puddings and simplest food.
10. Strict economy in coal, gas and electric light.

Of course, the Robinsons could have simplified their lives even further, but that was not Harry. For him, these were extreme measures, but ones that could be taken without the risk of public humiliation (by a certain class, of course). He was especially fond of wine, and took great pride in his appearance. He would not give up his beloved golf, and he would still retain his servants, saving Florence from domestic chores. For a woman, Harry's restrictions would be especially hard, including the ban on new clothes. It is likely that Florence disapproved of this unusual agreement, but deferred to her husband as a loyal spouse. In his diary, Harry kept an accounting of the servants' wages. The cook earned £27 a year; the maid, £22 a year. The gardener was paid 4s. 6d. a day; the handyman, 2s. 6d. a week. Presumably these were the reduced wages. The goal now was to exist on £800 annually, down from £1,000. Pets were spared, of course, and the Robinsons had two, a cat and a dog. The cat, called 'Nickie', was named after Reginald Nicholson, manager of *The Times*. 'Mr Nicholson came to dinner and of course asked what the cat's name was, and I replied correctly, "Mr Nicholson,"' Brad recalled. 'My father got out of the difficulty by revealing that our dog was named after a famous editor of the paper, Mr [George Earle] Buckle, which shewed that we were immortalizing, as it were, famous <u>Times</u>' characters.'[66] Close call indeed.

* * * * *

In his new position at *The Times,* Harry went where needed, either at home or abroad. He satisfied his twin passions for sport and world affairs when he became the beat reporter for the 1912 Olympic Summer Games, the Sixth Olympiad, held in Stockholm, Sweden from July 6 to 22. The fledgling Olympic Games would become a minor obsession of Harry's. He arrived on the scene on June 28. Britain's poor performance in these Summer Games would become a *cause célèbre* and spark nationwide soul-searching. Among the 27 participating nations and 3,000 athletes, Sweden won the most medals, 65 (including 24 gold medals), followed by the United States (63, but with 25 gold medals, one more than Sweden). Great Britain was a distant third with 41 medals, only 10 of which were gold. Britain had topped the medal count at the previous Olympics, held in London in 1908. Harry credited American wins to the seriousness of the Olympic movement in the United States and the focus on training, not to mention the amount of money spent on the athletes. It was a matter of national pride, which he found distinctly lacking in the British effort. 'The man who is to beat the Americans this year must not only be a great athlete, but he must have undergone a through and scientific course of training; and in this the Americans are, of course, pre-eminent', he wrote. 'Not even the Swedes (and they have an American trainer) have had anything like the care lavished on them that has been spent on the Americans.'[67] Harry noted that the amount spent was unknown, but 'we do know that the SS. Finland, which brought the athletes and their admirers across, cost over £20,000. We also know, by authority, that at least an equal sum was spent on other items. The contrast with our happy-go-lucky ways and the ineffectiveness of our British Olympic Council is almost ludicrous.' Training became a major issue with Harry. 'The American athletes have lived together on board the steamship Finland and have been under strict discipline', he wrote on July 19. 'Each man, it is believed, went into each race with a definite understanding as to how he was expected to run it, the instructions, of course, taking into account the character of the opposition to be encountered in the individual event. The results have been evident.'[68] The British athletes, on the other hand, were on their own. 'One of our University runners told me that from the day when he was asked to come to Stockholm no single individual had said one word to him, by way of advice, on the subject of training', Harry revealed. 'He added that he would probably have been extremely annoyed if any one had presumed to do so. These conditions and this attitude of mind are, of course, unthinkable to the Americans.' As a result, 'Our men have run largely by the light of Nature. Their tactics on the path have been those of children pitted against experts and veterans.' Harry noted that the problem was not limited to track and field events, but other sports such as swimming, tug-of-war, fencing, and wrestling. He concluded, 'I think I am safe in saying that there is neither any British athlete here, nor any British visitor who has taken any interest in the matter who does not consider that the way in which our affairs have been managed has been a mere farce.'

Harry clearly relished his role as provocateur on a subject that was of keen national interest. *The Times* endorsed his opinions in leading articles, promoting the idea first suggested by Sir Arthur Conan Doyle that a single British Empire team be fielded for future Olympics. 'Without wishing to encroach on the legitimate pride of our great self-governing Dominions, South Africa, Australia, and Canada (which has still to come into the scoring) are naturally at least as much a part of "England" as, let us say, the Sandwich Islands are a part of America', Harry wrote on July 9. 'Though "England" at present stands only third in the list of competing countries, the British Empire is, at the end of the first period of the Games, comfortably in the lead.'[69] Needless to say, the International Olympic Committee was thoroughly opposed to the idea of a 'United Empire' team, which was never adopted.

Returning home from Stockholm, Harry had lunch with Lord Northcliffe on July 28. Conversation focused on the Olympics, Britain's third place finish, and the controversy whipped up by Harry over the lack of training and overall commitment to the British athletes. Northcliffe had a keen interest in the Olympics; he had donated £16,000 to the cash-strapped 1908 Games in London, and was anxious that Britain continue to make a good show. The following day, Harry's article in *The Times* rehashed what he called the 'executive incompetence and mismanagement' of the British Olympic Committee.[70] 'England has, in truth, been the Mother of Sports', he wrote. 'In the eyes of the world we have lost our supremacy; we have forfeited the reputation so long enjoyed, and are no longer regarded as the men that we were.' The fundamental issue at hand, Harry continued, was the cherished British ideal of amateur sport versus the new Olympic reality of the professionally trained athlete.[71] 'We have been pre-eminent in the field of sport in the past; but a new tribunal with new standards has been set up, and if we cling to our old traditions we must be content to be ranked by that tribunal not first or even second among the nations,' he predicted. Although Harry was now among those who questioned whether the Olympics had been a force for good and peace among nations, withdrawal was out of the question (for now, at least). 'We may regret that the Games were ever instituted. But, if we withdrew from them now, we should inevitably be regarded as having done so in petulance and under the mortification of defeat.' *The Times*, no doubt egged on by Northcliffe, endorsed Harry's views in a leading article,

'The Moral of the Olympic Games', on July 29, calling for reform. 'The real fault lies in public apathy', it stated.

> Our Correspondent's article will leave no one who reads it in any doubt of the nature of the reform required. It is not necessary, we may say at once, to turn our athletes into the slaves of some particular pursuit and thereby to pervert our national ideal of sport. We can do a great deal better in the Olympic Games without resorting to extreme measures of that kind. But we have to recognize that it is pointless to stake our national reputation in international competitions without creating the mechanism in this country which such competitions require. Two things are wanted—a determination to organize properly, and funds. At present it is hardly an exaggeration to say that there is no organization at all.[72]

Conan Doyle, in a letter to *The Times* on July 30, endorsed the call for reform and said it all came down to money. 'Can we not find among our rich men some one who will make the Games his hobby and be the financial father of the team?', he asked.[73] Sir Cecil Spring-Rice, Ambassador of Great Britain to Sweden, wrote directly to Harry. He enjoyed meeting him during the Games and thanked him for raising awareness of the problem. 'Evidently we are more virtuous and the finer sportsmen, but as you say it's not because we are virtuous but because we are incompetent', he wrote on July 30. 'And if we go in for it we must go in with a will.' He added, 'Please insist on the necessity of lodging and feeding and supervising our men in a proper manner. I daresay you noticed how we went off towards the end—what you say about this matter is most important.' Harry had reported that the majority of British athletes in Stockholm had lost weight, in some cases more than a stone. 'For men in training they were quite improperly nourished.'

The matter continued to simmer in letters and articles on both sides of the Atlantic for the rest of the year. Harry decried claims in American papers that English athletes were 'the worse losers on earth'. *The New York Sun* devoted an editorial on September 1 to 'the puerile complaints of the letter writer'—Harry—noting 'As the American athletes are always winners in the Olympic track and field events year after year uniformly and decisively, there must be merit in their performances, so let the carping critics carp, British or Continental'.[74] By the time the British Olympic Council issued its report on September 19, *The Times* appeared to grow weary of the controversy, lending some perspective. 'The fact that two nations (one of which was the organizing nation) stand in front of us seems to have been given far more importance than the fact that behind us stand Germany, France, Austria, Italy, Russia, Finland, and many others', Harry wrote. 'And this consideration suggests that too much emphasis may be laid on concrete successes as apart from general well-doing.'[75]

Harry's efforts would bear fruit the following year. In August 1913, *The Times* started the ball rolling with a donation of £500 towards the £100,000 public appeal for a fund that would improve the instruction of sport in schools and underwrite the Olympic team for 1916. 'A wider and less slipshod physical training of our boys and young men cannot fail to improve the physique and manhood of the people', Harry wrote in a leading article on August 18.[76] 'There is also the consideration that the national reputation is more deeply involved than perhaps we care to recognize in the demonstration of our ability to hold our own against other nations in the Olympic contests.' Girls, moreover, must not be forgotten, 'for the part which women play in the Olympic contests is too seldom recognized'. The irony, of course, is that the 1916 Olympics, scheduled for Berlin, were cancelled due to the war.

* * * * *

When Harry wasn't starting fires in condemnation of the British Olympic Council, he was writing articles on a wide variety of subjects, and continuing to review books for the *Literary Supplement*. In the leading article for the Printing Number on September 12, 1912, Harry reminded readers that an enormous amount of toil and sweat was required to produce a daily newspaper that is discarded when read. Consider, Harry wrote, 'the thousands of men who daily burn themselves up, giving usually under conditions of intense and exhausting strain the best of their strength and brain to producing what to the general public serves only to beguile the idle moments of a day. None of the ancient gods was so insatiable as the Molech of the modern Press whose altar fires never go out and who calls daily for his sacrifice.'[77] Working on a newspaper was a sacred vocation to Harry, and such florid praise no doubt helped him in making yet another plea for more money to Nicholson. 'The time seems to have come for me to ask you to take up in earnest the sad case of my inadequate income', he wrote on October 8. Harry said that the 125 columns of published articles did not represent the full extent of his work behind the scenes 'of night and day work', in particular for special supplements such as the Printing Number. 'My work is scattered through various Departments and Supplements and Special Numbers that it is, I believe, more useful in the aggregate than it appears.' But his current minimum salary of £500, based on £4 a column, was inadequate. 'My own situation is that I have to earn some £800 a year. I cannot possibly go on for another year living as to three-eighths of my expenses on an extremely meagre capital', he wrote. 'I am extremely reluctant (and I think it would be bad policy for The Times to compel me) to earn a portion of that outside.'[78]

Nicholson knew he had a star in Harry, but he was not going to increase his salary by £300. He was not an unreasonable man, however. In a reply on October 10, he proposed paying Harry a bonus of £100 each for two supplements. 'In the future, in addition to your salary we propose to remunerate you from time to time for your work on the various supplements', he added, 'but I must ask you to leave the actual amount on the different supplements to my discretion as it must vary in accordance with the work entailed in each case'.[79] In any event, Harry's earnings for 1912 were now £700, leaving him £100 short of his goal.

Mindful of the need to supplement his income, Harry returned to writing his weekly column in The Bellman, under the new title, 'Westminster Chimes'. On March 15, 1913, he praised the success of Selfridge's department store, noting how many predicted its 'American methods' would fail in London when it opened in 1909. 'A lot of prejudice had to be overcome', Harry noted. 'It has been overcome chiefly by persistent and most ingeniously lavish advertising and by an equally persistent policy of making the place as attractive as possible to the public.' Selfridge's newest idea was an American-style soda fountain. 'I know, among my own acquaintances, women who, if they find themselves within a mile or two of the place in the afternoon, cannot resist going there for an ice cream soda, an almost unheard-of thing among Englishwomen until eighteen months ago.'[80] Harry was delighted.

*   *   *   *   *

During much of 1913, the Robinsons were frequently ill. Headaches, flus, and colds were constant companions. Brad had whooping cough. Florence was often 'in bed', as was Harry. On July 4, he wrote in his diary 'To Office @ 2—fainted in office!' On December 1, Harry was 'in bed till noon with indigestion'.

Harry's articles in The Times ran the gamut from 'House Flies and Disease' to Cup Day at Ascot, the disestablishment of the Anglican Church in Wales, and an exhibition of deer heads. On July 3, 1913, Harry reported that the club scene in London was thriving—even ladies had their own clubs now—but the character had decidedly changed. 'Married men in London now get so few evenings quietly at home that few care to sacrifice them for the sake of going to the club, and domestic cookery has so much improved that to most the club dinner table is less attractive than their own', Harry observed. 'So the latest type of club is little more than a place of sumptuous public entertainment to which the member pays his entrance fee.'[81] Harry himself had forsaken club memberships in his own effort to economize. On August 4, Harry began a second series of his popular 'Studies in Zoological Gardens', starting with giraffes, and moving on to tortoises, camels, kangaroos, crows, ravens, badgers, panthers, penguins, and hyenas, concluding in December. Three supplements occupied much of his time: the Irish Number on March 17 (whose seventy articles were collected and published in book form as *Ireland of To-Day*, edited by Harry); the Russian Number on August 11 ('Russia, indeed, is at the moment such a fascinating problem that what the world needs before everything else is as much truth about it as is possible to get'); and the Pacific Coast Number on December 31, focusing on British Columbia and California.

Such activity led Harry to the inevitable writing to Nicholson on November 12, appealing yet again for more money. 'I told you in our conversation yesterday that I knew that I had done an immense number of hours of work during the year but had made no attempt to count the number of columns or amount of stuff actually printed', he began. Harry did an accounting, and came up with 140 columns of original work, 'more than I thought'. He continued, 'To this must be added all the time given, without producing any original copy, to the Irish Number and Book and all the other Supplements and things on which I have laboured.' The end result? 'I do not think there can be any doubt that if it could somehow be translated into foot-pounds, and so into columns of space, it would very much more than exceed the 200 columns which is necessary to make the £800 which I want to be worth to The Times.'[82]

Nicholson once again called Harry's bluff, doing an accounting of his own for the twelve months to October 31, 1913. Harry, he claimed, filed 106.27 columns, which included 22.17 for special supplements. Take these out, and the total was only 84.1 columns, 'instead of the 125 cols. as per arrangement'. He also noted that Harry had received £200 for the American Railway, Printing, and Shipping Numbers in 1912, and £100 for the Irish Supplement in 1913. So, In addition to his minimum salary of £500 per annum, Harry had been paid an extra £300. 'I can assure you that the amount of work you have been doing for "The Times" in the past year has not in any way been overlooked, and is fully appreciated', Nicholson wrote. But he was not unsympathetic. 'Out of the recent Supplements I had made allowances for further payments to you, and I am now instructing the Accountant to send you a cheque for £200.'[83] So Harry, in the end, was paid nearly £1,000 this year. On December 31, he wrote in his diary, 'Income about £900 and just about spent it.'

Harry's incessant pleas for money meant that the higher-ups now kept a closer watch on him—even Northcliffe. Harry's exhaustive 2,200-word article on 'Thanksgiving Day. An American Festival. Its Origin, History, and Observance' was published on November 27, 1913. 'There are few well-regulated tables from which the traditional dishes, suggestive of the old farm life of the country, the turkey and cranberry sauce, sweet potatoes, succotash, or sweet corn, and pumpkin pie are absent', he reported. 'Nor can a reasonable man want better.'[84] The article, however, provoked a note from Northcliffe himself on November 28: 'Dear Perry Robinson: No one admires your work more than I do, but will you allow me to say, with all respect, that I think your very interesting article on Thanksgiving Day would have been perfect if it had been a column and a stick, instead of nearly a column and three-quarters.' A 'stick' was equal to two column inches, or about 150 words. It is no wonder Harry kept this letter in his private scrapbook.

6

War Correspondent, 1914–1918

At the end of 1917, on a visit home from his service on the Western Front, Harry joined his family and his brother Kay in Cornwall. 'My father was not very well, but in the morning after his arrival he agreed to go out with a picnic up Pentire Head', Brad recalled in his memoir. 'It was a reasonable day but with a cold wind from the West. We settled on the sheltered side of a rough stone wall. While my mother was dishing out for food, Kay looked at his brother and said, "Well?" My father shook his head and said, "No, I can't talk about it." He never even told my mother anything about the horrors. It must have been a fearful burden to carry.'[1]

What would compel a 55-year-old man, not in the best of health, with a young wife and eight-year-old son at home, to go to war? Surely Harry could have remained in London and still have been of great service to *The Times* at Printing House Square as editors digested and packaged the news of the First World War. But in spite of the profound physical and psychological toll, Harry genuinely wanted to go. One wonders if he was anxious to experience the thrill of being a war correspondent that he witnessed in his brother Phil. 'Sometime between the American Civil War and the Spanish–American War, it became understood by many young men that being a war correspondent was the greatest job in the world', Robert H. Patton observed.[2] Harry was not a young man, but many of his journalist contemporaries had had a stint on the front lines, including Richard Harding Davis. Perhaps this was an item on his 'bucket list' that Harry had to check off, however irresponsible it may have seemed as a husband and father. Harry possessed that insatiable wanderlust, and his recent travels may have given him itchy feet. Harry was also, as we have seen, an extreme patriot, and was ready to serve and defend his country. For years he had written about the German menace and the importance of Britain and her Empire (not to mention the United States) to maintain the peace, and he was now ready to join the fight against evil first-hand. Northcliffe and the powers that be at *The*

Times recognized his gift for reportage as well as his loyalty to the newspaper, and so may have overlooked his obvious infirmity. Clearly *The Times* considered him a valuable asset, according to Northcliffe's biographers. 'Northcliffe saw that the new war correspondents would need qualities entirely different from those of Russell, Forbes, Steevens and others who had made their journalistic reputation on earlier fields of battle. To the pen of the ready writer there would have to be joined to the eye of the historian, able to piece together a coherent and accurate picture out of a vast jigsaw of confusing details.'[3] That was Harry.

Whatever the reason, Harry emerged as the oldest war correspondent from any country to cover the entire war, as well as to log the most time at the Western Front. He was in Belgium and the Netherlands in 1914, Serbia in 1915, the French Front in 1916–18, and in Germany at the end of the war. He would write a definitive account of the Battle of the Somme, *The Turning Point*, published in 1917. His occasional articles focusing on the natural world were startling, offering readers rays of hope amid the horror. Harry remained at his post until the end, despite the debilitating effect on his already poor physical health and the severe psychological toll. At war's end, a grateful nation offered him a knighthood.

* * * * *

With Britain's declaration of war on August 4, 1914, the press scramble to cover the action began. Philip Gibbs, representing the *Daily Chronicle*, recalled these early days. 'The War Office kept a little group of distinguished old-time war correspondents kicking their heels in waiting rooms of Whitehall, week after week, and month after month, always with the promise that wonderful arrangements would be made for them "shortly"', he wrote. 'Meanwhile, and at the very outbreak of war, a score of younger journalists, without waiting for War Office credentials, and disobeying War Office orders, dashed over to France and Belgium, and plunged into the swirl and backwash of this frightful drama.'[4] Gibbs, aged 37, was one of them, and was quickly arrested in France. Not so Harry: his permission to enter France was not granted until August 31 by the French Ambassador in London. His official pass stated he was 5 feet 10¾ inches in height—rather above average—and had grey hair and grey eyes. He had a slight build, and wore glasses. Harry crossed to France, then entered Belgium. Like Northcliffe's other correspondents for *The Times* and the *Daily Mail*, Harry was given two hundred pounds in gold to cover initial expenses.[5] He headed into war mourning the death of his best friend, John S. Bradstreet, who died in an automobile accident in Minneapolis on August 10, aged 64.

In 1927, in a letter to Ralph Deakin of *The Times*, who was working on a documentary about newspaper reportage, Harry recalled his initial foray into the fighting. He was especially proud of his coverage, as a 'special correspondent', of the German invasion of Belgium, the fall of Antwerp ('We were first' with the exclusive, he noted), and the refugee crisis in the Netherlands. 'In the first months of the war, I was in Belgium in charge of both The Times and Daily Mail staffs—two Correspondents besides myself, two "interpreters" who were really spies and went in and out of Brussels—then German—unconcernedly', Harry recalled. 'During engagements, I carried a good many wounded Belgians back in my car to the nearest dressing stations; and, at the fall of Antwerp, I got two British nurses and 16 Belgian wounded (besides the British chaplain) out in safety.'[6]

On September 8, Harry sent a postcard to Florence from Ghent, with the note, 'Keep this card for the sake of its date. All my love, B. Sept. 8.14.'[7] That day marked the midpoint of the First Battle of the Marne, a surprise attack by Allied troops against the German Second Army, leading to a German retreat. On the same day, he wrote to Brad, 'Daddy has seen such a lot of soldiers today. Sept. 8. 14.' From Ghent on this day, Harry filed his first story for *The Times*.[8] 'You have already heard that Ghent is safe', Harry began. He reported that the Burgomaster had struck a bargain with the German commander to prevent an enemy occupation: 'fodder for horses, 40,000 litres of petrol, and 100,000 cigars'. As such, there were no German troops in the city. Harry reported on the bizarre scene as the inhabitants ventured out to see what had transpired in fighting on the outskirts. His descriptions of life amid the horror are typical of his descriptive reporting style. 'After the people of Ghent had been assured that immediate danger was relieved from the city they poured out in great numbers along the road to Melle, at the side of which runs the tramway', Harry noted. 'What was yesterday the scene of a hard-fought battle to-day was crowded with what looked like a throng of holiday makers. Boys were picking up shrapnel bullets and fragments of projectiles of all sorts from among the half-dug potatoes and along roadsides. The remnants of the German guns were torn to pieces for souvenirs.' He added that one defenceless farmer had been deliberately shot, and 'there are tales of maltreatment of women which cannot be altogether disregarded'. Harry continued to report from Ghent. 'I have spent one of the saddest afternoons of my life wandering among the ruins of Termonde', he wrote on September 15.[9] For a town of 14,000 houses, fewer than 100 were left standing by the German invaders, a 'deliberate house-to-house visitation of a surrendered and helpless town containing no soldiery'. Germans sprayed a combustible liquid on the floors and set houses alight, resulting in utter destruction. 'There is no salvage whatever', Harry observed. 'Termonde simply is not.' Harry's depiction of the dead and wounded harkened back thirty-one years to his first assignment for the *New York Tribune*, writing about the Brooklyn Bridge disaster.

A unique feature of Harry's reportage emerged from these early days. Amid chronicling the destruction and horror, Harry offered observations of nature, and the war's impact on flora and fauna. The natural world was Harry's touchstone, a reminder of home, a way to relieve stress and, for a moment, escape from the trauma all around him. On September 24, Harry wrote, 'As one moves day by day about this region which has been, and still is, so harried by war, it is a never-ending surprise to see how much of the peaceful life of the country still goes on.'[10] Apart from the absence of horses and young men of military age, the natural world renewed. 'Strips of waste land by the roadside are ablaze with wild flowers, ragwort and milfoil and toadflax and evening primrose', Harry observed. 'The canals are the haunts of gulls and terns and reed buntings. I saw the shell of a farmhouse, burned but a few days ago, crowded with martins gathered presumably for further flight southward.' He concluded, 'Nothing can ever really atone to Belgium for what it has suffered and is suffering. But one can see how quickly when the war is over it will recuperate and build itself richer and happier than ever. It is a land worth fighting for, and it will be doubly endeared to its people hereafter for the sacrifices of these months.'

Harry found himself in Antwerp on September 29, just as the German siege of the city began. 'It is impossible to tell whether the present bombardment signifies a serious attempt to reduce Antwerp, but the attack to-day has undoubtedly been more violent than yesterday',[11] he reported on October 1. He hunkered down and waited for the worst. On October 3, he wrote, 'To one to whom it is new it is an extraordinarily interesting experience to be shut up in a city into which a persistent enemy is trying to batter his way.'[12] Facts were hard to come by. 'Every time a car stops the crowd surges around it, and a word is dropped by one of the occupants is enough to spread detailed narratives of disaster or success through the throng, till a new diversion draws the multitude in another direction', he observed. 'It is amazing with what rapidity rumours travel and grow out of all semblance to their original form.' And into the city poured 'pitiable streams of refugees'.

On October 9, on the eve of the German conquest, *The Times* published Harry's eyewitness account of the siege the day before.[13] A prefatory note read, 'Our Special Correspondent, who stayed in Antwerp after this flight began, describes to-day the hours of waiting for the bombardment.' Harry offered a surreal scene as artillery thunder boomed, the sky filled with white smoke from burning petroleum tanks, and 30,000 people had fled their homes. 'Antwerp itself is an extraordinary place to-day', he wrote. 'This morning the streets were in turmoil. Now they look like those of an English provincial town on Sunday; the shops nearly all shuttered and the pavements almost deserted, save when squads of troops march by. To St. Nicholas the Government has already gone; whether to stay there or to go to Ostend I do not know.' Amusingly, amid the turmoil, Harry rarely missed a meal. 'I went to the famous Restaurant du Grand Laboureur for lunch; the cook had fled, but the *patron* made me an omelette, which the solitary remaining waiter served with the aid of a single boy.' He also visited the Antwerp Zoo, where he saw 'one of the saddest sights of the war—a great open grave with four splendid lions, still limp, lying in it. One was a beast with a truly superb mane. They had been shot, lest in the course of the bombardment their cages should be broken and they should get out.' The zoo director was overcome with emotion when he spoke to Harry.[14]

*　*　*　*　*

Over the next 24 hours, Harry and the remaining inhabitants of Antwerp waited for the denouement. 'We expected it at 10 o'clock this morning', he recalled in his article, 'but apparently the enemy has not yet got his large guns in satisfactory position. His shrapnel is now reaching the inner forts; but he can reach the centre of the town at almost any minute that he pleases. It is a curious sensation waiting for it.'[15]

There are two accounts of Harry's last day, October 8, in Antwerp: his own eyewitness reporting, which was a world exclusive for *The Times*, and a later recollection from a fellow war correspondent, J. M. N. Jeffries. Jeffries was dispatched by Northcliffe to cover the war for the *Daily Mail* with Harry. His memoir, *Front Everywhere*, was published in 1935. Jeffries described Harry as 'a man of presence. He was mistaken for Kipling at times, because of dark, over-hanging brows which, like those of the poet, gathered the whole world of men and women for consideration under their eaves. But he was taller than Kipling. He was one of the caryatids of the *Times;* that newspaper specialising in marble caryatids who will carry any situation with strength and dignity.'[16] He added that Harry boasted of an 'optional accent', whereby he could assume or drop an American accent at will (which is likely). However, Jeffries offered the reader a brief biographical sketch (Harry had died five years earlier, in 1930) that is so wildly inaccurate it calls into question the veracity of Jeffries' eyewitness account. He claimed that Harry supported William Jennings

Bryan rather than William McKinley, for example, and that Harry was nominated to be the governor of an American state by President Woodrow Wilson (who assumed office thirteen years after Harry left America in 1900). Nonetheless, Jeffries' account, while entertaining, may contain kernels of truth.

Harry, Jeffries noted, was the picture of calm as the situation deteriorated and the bombardment began. 'In our present crisis he was unperturbed, though, like myself, he had no vehicle at his disposal. We decided that when we had to leave Antwerp, as we must leave it soon enough, it was no good duplicating our flight. He would go by water, and I by road.' The Dutch frontier was 10 miles away. They made plans to meet at Harry's hotel, the Terminus, in the morning to reassess the situation. '"*Toujours le mot juste*," said Perry Robinson, "you'd better have some more coffee now to keep you awake to-night."'[17]

The next day, October 8, 1914, Jeffries arrived at the hotel:

> His hotel was undamaged, but like all others topsy-turvy. Perry Robinson was nowhere downstairs, so I went up to his room, and had to knock twice before I heard a 'Come in!' in reply. P.R., as we called him for short, had been fast asleep, and only on my entry did he sit up yawning.
>
> It was then about nine o'clock. 'I say, Perry Robinson,' I burst at him, 'don't you know there's been a bombardment?'
>
> 'Yes,' he said, 'I did hear noises during the night.'
>
> 'But didn't you get up?' No, he hadn't got up. 'Didn't you do anything at all?' I asked him.
>
> 'Oh, yes, I took the extra bolster,' he answered (he occupied a great double bed), 'and stuck it down the middle of the bed and shoved my spine well into it. So I felt protected and went off to sleep again.'

While Jeffries admitted, 'I admired his calmness profoundly', he proceeded to advise Harry that 'the city's falling' and they should evacuate. 'I'd better get up, then', was Harry's reply. Jeffries was amazed at what happened next, in a scene straight out of an episode of 'Dad's Army':

> 'I've not had breakfast yet,' said Perry Robinson. 'I told them distinctly last night—you remember—that I wanted to be called at seven, with the particular breakfast I ordered, and no one has been near me till you came. Abominable service! This won't do,' and he seized the hanging bell and pressed it.
>
> The bell rang on and on in some empty corridor, of course without answer. I was surprised to hear it ring: the hotel must have had its own electric system. It rang incessantly and sounded like one of those scientific experiments in which bells ring continuously in vacuums and doubtless prove some theory but cease to be bells.

'Preposterous,' fulminated P.R. in his deep tones, 'I *must* have my breakfast.' I went off in search of the staff and in the end found a reluctant unit. From him and from the stricken kitchens the admirable Perry Robinson wrung exactly the breakfast which he had ordered overnight, and it was no mere affair of coffee and rolls. Then, and only then, did he dress and make ready for departure.[18]

Jeffries bid farewell and good fortune to Harry at the quayside. 'Of course *he* got on board a ship, despite the struggle for places', Jeffries recalled, enviously. 'I had had to abandon my luggage, naturally, and it perished when later in the day the bombardment was resumed and my hotel was struck and set on fire.'

Harry's own account of the experience left out his supposed breakfast tantrum (which does seem somewhat in character). On October 23, having safely returned to London, Harry gave a light-hearted talk to the Crystal Palace Club about his experience in Antwerp. As reported in a local newspaper (saved in Harry's scrapbook), Harry told the gathering, 'I had just one foot on the bed when bang went the first gun. Now I can give you a special remedy for getting to sleep during the bombardment of a town: Play the Dulwich and Sydenham Hill Golf Course. I only remember playing six holes, so I must have fallen asleep.' But he gave a more serious account in a 1924 article in *The Times* on the tenth anniversary of the Antwerp siege:

In the Hotel Terminus, crowded until the preceding day, but rather uncomfortably close to the railway station, which was likely to be one of the first German targets, there were, I think, only two other guests besides myself that night; and with one ear always listening for the noise from without, it was not easy to be hilarious.

I sat writing in my room till late. Having finished and prepared for bed, I glanced at my watch before raising the blinds and throwing up the window for a final look into the night. It was two minutes to 12. I wondered whether, with their punctual habits, the Germans would consider midnight a good moment to begin. The idea was in my mind as I groped my way from the window to the bed, and I was in the act of turning back the bedclothes when the hotel seemed to shake to its foundations. A second explosion, a third, a fourth, then others followed in quick succession, some close at hand, some farther away. There were shouts and the noise of some one running along the passage outside my door. The bombardment had begun.[19]

Harry's eyewitness account of the bombardment was published in *The Times* on October 12, 1914, entitled 'Last Scenes in Antwerp. People Terrified by Bombardment. Flight from the City. Pitiable Condition of the Refugees'.[20] A prefatory note read, 'The following message from our Correspondent, who remained in Antwerp to the last, gives a vivid picture of the terror and misery which oppressed the people during the bombardment by the Germans.' This was an exclusive for *The Times*. Harry's report began, 'Those of us who saw the last of the deserted city on Thursday evening [October 8] will never forget the scene.' Amid a vivid description of a city under siege and the flight of a people by any means possible, Harry focused on two experiences: 'walking through deserted and shuttered streets which were still being bombarded on Thursday afternoon', and 'the spectacle from a lighter anchored in mid Scheldt of the terrific bombardment on Friday night when the whole scene was lighted up by blazing oil tanks and a score or so of minor fires. No more awful picture of the horrors of war could well be imagined.'

Harry noted that as the populace fled every bit of food was stripped from the shops for the journey. 'By noon on Thursday in the few *cabarets* still open near the quays not a slice of bread was to be bought', he wrote. 'The windows of pastrycooks, fruiterers, and grocers were shuttered and every sweetmeat bottle was empty, every shelf bare.' Civic Guards and Allied troops proceeded to destroy 'all sources of comfort to the enemy, stopping the gas and electric light supply, burning stores of grain and materials, sinking lighters in the dock basins, and blowing up forts and bridges'. On his way to the quay Harry encountered the English Colony Hospital, where two nurses and an old man named 'Scotty' cared for sixteen patients, all Belgian soldiers, as bombs fell all around them. 'At great personal risk both nurses went alternately through the bombarded streets to the Red Cross and military hospitals, begging for help in removing the patients to other hospitals, but they could get no help', Harry said. 'At 6 o'clock on Thursday evening I saw them finally get their patients to safety, and too great praise cannot be given them for their devotion.'

Harry boarded one of the last barges (not a tourist boat, as Jeffries claimed) to leave the docks at 7:00 p.m. on October 8, accompanied by an English clergyman, Rev. Cyril Harrison, and his wife—'probably the last British to leave before the entry of the Germans'. From a vantage point in the middle of the river Scheldt Harry and his companions kept watch all night long, witnessing the German bombardment. 'I do not believe that this war will produce an incident more terrific than that night's cannonade as I saw it from the middle of the river before the city', he recalled. 'The danger to us was very slight, but shells flew screaming overhead from both directions. On the right hand the tremendous blaze of burning oil tanks illuminated the city and was reflected blood red on the heavy pall of smoke which covered the sky, while minor fires broke out at various points, forming an almost continuous ring round one third of Antwerp.' After what Harry called 'that hideous night of flames and cannonade while we lay in the river', the barge set out the next morning and floated away from the city. 'The blaze from the oil tanks had burned itself out, and other fires were only sending up spirals of smoke', he wrote, 'but overhead the terrible black pall still hung eclipsing the sun, and it was in eerie twilight we floated down the stream, while the spires and towers of Antwerp slowly receded into the distance.' Along with an unnamed companion, Harry exited the barge and put to shore. 'We made our way—my companion and I—by a devious route to the frontier, where we rejoined the heart-breaking stream of refugees which we had seen on Thursday morning. For some 10 miles we tramped with the refugees, ourselves mere individual units in the great mass, till we reached Bergen-op-Zoom. Thence, still refugees among refugees, we came by train to Rotterdam, arriving after midnight on Saturday morning.'

Harry's article in *The Times* marking the tenth anniversary of the siege added to his story. He noted how, on October 6, the government evacuated to Ostend along with the foreign consuls. 'I had the melancholy pleasure of helping Sir Cecil Hertslet [Consul General in Antwerp] to haul down his consular flag before accompanying him on board to say good-bye', Harry wrote. The final evacuation was seared in his memory.

Figure 15. 'Antwerp, October 8, 1914', this oil painting by the Dutch artist 'J. Snijders' was published in the *The Times History of the War*. The caption states that Snijders painted the scene 'from notes and sketches furnished to him by the Special Correspondent of *The Times*, who spent the night of October 8 on board a lighter anchored in the Scheldt at a spot that would be in the immediate foreground of the picture'. Once owned by Harry, the painting is lost.

'Never in the world's history, probably, has there been so great a migration of people in so short a time', he observed. 'Never in the whole course of the war, before or afterwards, was there such a spectacle as that road afforded when in the course of 24 hours something like a quarter of a million people poured along it into Holland.'

> I found myself, in middle of the throng which moved at foot's pace, close beside a little old man who pushed a small handcart on which, amid a jumble of household goods, something lay covered with a blanket. He motioned to me to keep away from the cart: and then, in explanation, turned the blanket back and showed a little girl whose face was thickly covered with what I took to be, and he said was, smallpox. I can see two small children, each with heavy bundles, leading out of the stream to the roadside, an old woman so frail and shaking that it seemed impossible that she could walk a mile, helping her to sit down upon the bank, easing themselves of their loads, then patting her and talking to her for a while, before helping her again totteringly to her feet to resume their toilsome march. I see a fashionably dressed woman, or girl, in high-heeled shoes and heavy furs (the temptation in every case was, if only one suit could be saved, to take the best), sitting on the bank, holding a small dog on a lead and crying silently without cessation.
>
> People died upon that road and babies were born. And still the procession moved on, always at foot's pace, flowing like some thickly congealed liquid, motor-cars, horse-drawn vehicles, carts dragged by dogs or pushed by hand, cattle and goats and other farm animals, dogs innumerable, old men and toddling children, richly dressed women and beggars, the lame, the sick, and the dying.[21]

All classes, the very poor and the well-to-do, were united in their suffering on that long road to Holland.

Now based in Rotterdam, Harry published his next report, identified as 'our special correspondent lately in Antwerp', on October 13.[22] He had made his way back to Antwerp and wandered about, taking in 'the silence of a deserted city and streets strewn with the wreckage of many buildings', including the English Church of St Boniface. Only a few hundred of the 500,000 residents remained in the city. Hungry (as he always was), Harry looked for food:

> For over an hour I searched—abominably hungry—for some place where I could find anything to eat. Antwerp is a city of *cafes* and restaurants and hotels, and in mid-afternoon I wandered past a hundred eating places unable to get a crust of bread.
>
> Nearly every door was locked and every window shuttered. Here and there, though windows were covered, the door of a cabaret stood open, and I went into the gloom and asked—literally—for bread. It is an absurd thing to

wander about a rich city with plenty of money in your pocket and to be unable to get bread. But it was an hour before I found a tender-hearted woman who went down to her cellar and brought me up two thick slices from her private store, and with them a rapturous tin of sardines.

As the occasional bomb fell, Harry noted, 'Nothing can ever erase the memory of the long, untenanted streets, shuttered and dead, with no sound of moving vehicles, and only now and then a scurrying figure on foot, while all the time the shells sang and crashed from every unexpected quarter.'

*   *   *   *   *

Harry returned home after Antwerp, no doubt in need of a rest and some emotional recovery. He had never witnessed such horror. In January 1915 he resumed his war service, reporting from Amsterdam. After six weeks he was recalled to England again and given a variety of assignments, including a report on the Aldershot School of Cookery, where cadets were trained to run field kitchens. 'An army of 100,000 men needs roughly 800 cooks', Harry reported on March 10. 'Empty biscuit tins and tea canisters, filled with earth, serve well in place of bricks and the oven walls; and dinners are cooked in mess tins—appetizing meat puddings and the like—and onions and potatoes backed in open ovens full of ashes.'[23] There he may have met up with his nephew, Francis Whalley, his sister Mary's son, who was based in Aldershot prior to being dispatched to the Western Front. On April 12, Harry wrote in his diary that he paid a visit to his editor, Geoffrey Robinson, 'and told him I must have holiday. I am overworked and need rest badly'. The stress was taking its toll. William C. Edgar, visiting from Minneapolis for Easter, noticed the change in his friend, as he commented in *The Bellman*. 'It was essentially the same alert, and self-contained Perry Robinson of earlier days that he met again, yet the war had left its mark upon him, particularly in the deep lines of his face. He seemed to have aged greatly and to have become more fragile, nevertheless his energy was unimpaired.'[24] Fortunately Harry was granted a holiday and the family went to Scarborough, where he played a lot of golf. On April 29, he was elated that the cuckoo had returned. 'The cuckoo came to London yesterday, a full week later than his usual date of arrival', he reported in *The Times*. 'So belated was he that one almost began to fear that he would not come at all this year; that, perhaps, his northward route had taken him across the firing line in France, where either his travels had ended or he had been diverted from his wonted path. But there was no need of such dreadful imaginings.'[25]

In spite of the physical toll on its correspondent, *The Times* sent Harry back to war. Of course Harry may have insisted; he wanted to do his part and see the assignment through. The decision was made to send him to Serbia on the Eastern Front. There was a lull in the fighting since the Serbian Army had expelled the invading Austrians and recaptured Belgrade, so perhaps it was seen as a gentler posting for Harry. *The History of The Times* records that Harry spent 'a wasted summer at Kragujevatz—then the Serb headquarters—where there was nothing to see that was worth the expense of telegraphing.'[26] On May 23 he arrived in Niš and checked into the Hotel Serbia, where he wrote in his diary, 'War on bugs!' He dispatched a Red Cross postcard to Brad. 'Though this has a hospital stamp on it, tell Mummie that I am not in the hospital myself, but only came here to get a good dinner—Daddy.' From Belgrade, Harry sent a more explicit card to Brad: 'A lot of houses in Belgrade have been knocked to bits by Austrian guns; but the Serbians fought so well that they have got over 60,000 Austrian prisoners. Since the rest of the Austrians ran away out of the country there has been very little fighting, except shooting at each other across the river, but it will very soon begin again. Kiss Mummy for Daddy.' One gets the sense that Harry was bored and wished he could see more action. 'Times cables me to stay Serbia', Harry wrote in his diary on June 3. 'No news of war—hard work and I am half laid up with malaria.' And he was hungry. 'I am at a place called Kragujevac at the Hotel Takovo, where nobody speaks anything but Serbian', he wrote to Brad. 'I can't read the list of things to eat, so I never know what I have ordered until it comes; and then I always wish I had ordered something else. How I would like some porridge or some strawberries or some cake for tea!'

Harry searched for stories to report for *The Times*. 'The present situation in Belgrade is almost more than Gilbertian', he wrote on July 7. 'After lunch, when you are idle, you go out into the street and look at the enemy and yawn and wonder when he is going to begin.'[27] He admired the young soldiers who manned a solitary little craft nicknamed *The Terror of the Danube*. 'The force is charmingly cosmopolitan', Harry noted. 'The young gentlemen (I cannot, happily, at the moment remember their nationality, for I have not seen them since lunch) who have charge of the Terror of the Danube have great larks with it. They poke their way on dark nights into creeks and passages where they are not in the least expected and annoy the Austrians dreadfully.' Firing its machine gun at the Austrian gunboats, the *Terror* lured a dreadnaught into a minefield, where it floundered. 'The "Terror" next day got a lovely haul of plunder out of her, from machine-gun ammunition and automatic pistols to a gramophone with an excellent stock of records, as well

Figure 16. Harry, age 56 (left), on assignment in Serbia, 1915.

as the Dreadnought's ensign and pennon, three admiral's and one general's flags.'

On July 14, Harry praised the work of 420 British doctors and nurses in Serbia, as well as the young orderlies: 'A year ago they were still undergraduates of Oriel, Corpus, and the House.'[28] Well-liked by the Serbians, the doctors, to Harry, represented the best of young British manhood. 'Undefeated by the difficulties of communication, most cordial friendships have arisen between the bronzed and moustached warriors and the pink-cheeked boys', Harry noted, before he himself was felled by dysentery. Once recovered, he wrote amusingly on August 2 about the Austrian prisoners of war who were put to work in a variety of occupations:

> The cab which takes you about the streets of Nish [*sic*] or Belgrade may be driven by an Austrian prisoner. The prisoners wait on you in clubs and act as orderlies in British, American, and Serbian hospitals. I have met two who used to be waiters in English hotels, one at the Carlton in London and the other in an hotel at Wantage. You see them working in the public parks and repairing high roads. Those who have learned a special trade—as wheelwrights, carpenters, blacksmiths, house-painters, &c.—are given opportunity to practise it in Serbia. They are subjected to extraordinarily little restraint or oversight...

In Nish I visited the old barracks, in which some 400 Austrian officers are confined, and they have absolutely nothing to complain of except idleness. Through the hot days they sit about under the trees and play cards and dominoes. They can buy anything at the canteen—anything that anyone can buy in Serbia—and 'comforts' of all sorts are sent to them by friends. They are all growing fat, and themselves make jokes about the increasing tightness of their uniforms. They are extremely fond of the commandant—as they ought to be, for he is a charming man—and are given any quantity of liberty.[29]

The irony was not lost on Harry, as these prisoners 'were guilty of a savagery as barbarous as anything in which the Germans indulged in Belgium... That the enemy who ravaged and outraged as the Austrians did and who systematically made use of that brutal weapon should be treated with the kindness which the Serbians show towards their prisoners is a striking illustration of the Southern Slav character.' He concluded: 'The Headmaster of Eton could hardly ask a better application of the precept that we should return good for evil.' He elaborated on Austrian savagery in an article written for *The Bellman* and published in November, recounting the assault of Chabatz, with 'the mutilation of women, the burning of people (over one hundred in all) at the stake, the assembling of villagers in the churchyard and the shooting of them in a common grave'. The village was wrecked, but the leading drug store was spared, including the large glass jars containing medicines that lined the walls. The owner, Harry noted, 'was amazed that the Austrians had resisted the temptation to smash so many bottles; but chance led him to examine the contents of the bottles, and he found that they had been carefully mixed, and poison had been introduced into each jar of innocent medicine. It strikes one as being as ingenious a piece of frightfulness as has been perpetrated in all the war—the "spirit of murder working in the very means of life."'[30]

Nature always served to inspire—and console—Harry. 'To British eyes the Serbian landscape has an inexhaustible charm. Continuously reminiscent of England—probably even more of Ireland', he wrote on August 3. 'Serbia is all hill and valley.'[31] Wild flowers were now at their best; 'the Serbian butterflies are enough to drive a British collector mad... Nowhere in the British Isles can we see roadside banks or hedges more lovely—more "English"—than here in Upper Serbia'. But amid the natural splendour were constant reminders of tragedy, 'the dreadful black flags—signals that someone has died there of typhus—which hang over gates and doorways. There are villages were almost every cottage has its flag, and some streets in town look almost as if they were decorated for a Royal funeral.' Harry was reminded of the people of Belgium who had borne their suffering and somehow went about their daily routine. 'In Serbia one marvels at the way in which a people can bear sorrows which would seem to be almost unbearable', he wrote. 'Some time, perhaps, Serbia will have peace; rest from war and freedom from disease. Then there should be no richer or happier part of Europe.'

* * * * *

By the end of August 1915, Harry was recalled from duty in Serbia and made his way home. From Salonika he filed a story about Constantinople, based on a briefing from 'an American friend of many years' standing' who brought 'lugubrious accounts' of the situation there. This could possibly have been William C. Edgar. 'One point on which all are agreed is the terrible character of the Turkish atrocities against the Armenians', Harry wrote on September 16, noting 'a campaign of extermination, involving the murdering of 800,000 to 1,000,000 persons', about which the American foreign minister had just protested.[32] Harry proceeded to Athens, Sicily, Rome, and Paris before arriving in London on September 4, just in time for a Zeppelin raid over the city. One flew directly over Sydenham Hill. 'The Crystal Palace was in fact a useful signpost to the Zeppelins, gleaming as it did in any moonlight', Brad recalled in his memoir. 'Some of the first anti-aircraft guns were sited in its grounds and made a great deal of noise.' During one night-time raid, Brad wrote, his parents ran to his bedroom, but he was not there. 'I was discovered some minutes later beetling around in the garden in my pyjamas and filling the jacket pocket with fragments of anti-aircraft shells which were dropping on the lawns.'[33]

Harry was not home for long. Before leaving for Amsterdam on September 16 he dined with the American Ambassador, Walter Hines Page, along with Sir William Tyrell, Secretary to the Foreign Office. Harry would have known Page from his time as editor of the *Atlantic Monthly*; he was also the co-founder of Doubleday, Page & Co., the distinguished publishing house which included Rudyard Kipling in its stable of authors. That Harry was granted an audience is testimony to his prominence. From Amsterdam, Harry wrote about a visit to the Dutch frontier in the company of friends, including Louis Raemaekers, 'the artist, whose cartoons have been, not in Holland alone, perhaps, the most powerful individual force against Germany since the outbreak of the war'.[34] Harry, who had met Raemaekers during his previous assignment in Holland, would become the young artist's biggest booster, accompanying him to Paris and London. That day they visited Baarle-Hertog, a Belgian enclave in the middle of Holland that the Germans could not access, except for the railway station at the edge of town. 'We were talking to the Dutch sentry at a certain place when he innocently told us that the German over the way had said that there was one man in Holland whom it would be worth 12,000 marks to get across the frontier, and that man was Raemaekers, the artist', Harry wrote on October 9. 'The sentry had no idea who it was that he was talking to; but at parting Mr. Raemaekers sent his compliments to the German with an expression of regret that he could not come across to oblige him.' Harry noted how some villages were literally divided by the war. 'There is one town in the extreme south of the province of Limburg where the frontier goes erratically through the back gardens of many of the houses, and one sees German sentries standing among the peas and potatoes', Harry wrote on October 15. 'Presumably one gets used to soldiers of another country among one's flower-beds, just as one can grow accustomed to strange workmen about the house.'[35]

Harry also took time to talk to the German soldiers on the village lines. 'The soldiers employed on the frontier here are mostly men of the Landsturm, armed with Russian rifles', he wrote on October 22. 'Some we have found gentle and communicative, and I have handled their rifles and ammunition; others have looked like, and I believe were, surly-brutes, who regarded every one on the Dutch side of the frontier with suspicion and animosity.'[36] He shot down the rumour that German soldiers were twice as big and strong as their British and French counterparts. 'Perhaps the German uniform has something to do with the impression of extreme stodginess which these men convey', he noted. 'But they are, in fact, mostly middle-aged men who, however solid, would assuredly not be capable of great activity.' He made a point that 'we heard nothing of any Germans who were impatient to be in the fighting. Many wanted to see their wives and babies, but not one the trenches. Especially have they no desire to see the trenches on what they know as the Yser front, where the furious British soldiers are. The fear of being sent there haunts them like a nightmare.' Clearly, Harry was honest in his reporting which went a long way towards humanizing the ordinary soldier, even the enemy, although articles like these also had strong propaganda value.

On October 18, 1915 Harry wrote a letter to Brad from Amsterdam, in anticipation of his son's ninth birthday on October 21. The poignancy is evident; he was trying to be a good parent despite being away at war. 'I am sending you for your birthday a little Dutch boy's stamp collection', he began. 'As you will see, he used a piece of an old copy-book for a stamp album. I bought it from him in the street.' Harry then offered advice to his young son, a task that, as an older parent, he always found awkward, veering towards a scolding or lecture. 'Now that you are 9 years old you are no longer a child. You are a boy. And you must stop behaving like a child. You must give up crying and you must help Mummie instead of being a nuisance to her', he advised. 'You must be manly and obedient, like a soldier, not a baby any more.' He concluded, 'Remember what I have told you many times: <u>Never tell a lie</u>. <u>Be afraid of nothing; and always be good to Mummie!</u> . . . if you do as I tell you you <u>cannot help</u> being happy. Nobody can give you happiness except yourself. Be a manly, brave, straightforward boy—that is the best thing that I can wish you.' This was not the first letter in which Harry reminded his son about good behaviour; he must have been a handful to his mother, yet what else would one expect of a nine-year-old with an absentee father?

Harry returned home in November with the Raemaekers family in tow. Raemaekers, who had just been elected a foreign honorary fellow of the Royal Society of Literature, was prepping a London show of his editorial cartoons for his Amsterdam newspaper, *De Telegraaf*, in December. On November 16, Harry and Raemaekers lunched with Lord and Lady Northcliffe, a prelude to his cartoons appearing on a regular basis in the *Daily Mail*. According to Brad's memoir, Harry was so impressed by Raemaekers's cartoons that 'my father got through on the telephone to Lord Northcliffe and told him that he had found a man who could be a really powerful propaganda force. Northcliffe took his word for it and arranged (such was the power of a Press baron in those days) for the Admiralty to send a signal to the Royal Navy in Antwerp to convey Raemaekers to England as quickly as possible.'[37] Harry wrote a 5,000-word appreciation of his friend for an oversized album of his cartoons, published at the princely sum of 10 guineas. 'It is doubtful if any artist, any painter or poet, prose writer or cartoonist, has ever exercised so great an influence on so large a number of his contemporaries as Raemaekers exercises to-day', Harry wrote. 'He wields a power which has probably never been matched.'[38] Harry attributed this to Raemaekers's eyewitness testimony as well as to advances in technology, which enabled a wider and faster distribution of his images to the emerging mass market. Harry was as florid in praise for his friend and his vital contribution to the war effort, as he was in displaying his enduring contempt for Germany:

> Raemaekers is a Neutral whose sincerity is transparent. He does not hate Germany because she is German, but because she is foul: because she has broken her own pledged word and the usages of civilized nations, violated and derided the canons of Christianity, murdered mothers and babes, and, stained to the elbows and lips with innocent blood, stands calling blasphemously on God to bless her infamies. It is so that he sees and has

drawn her. Nor is he a friend of the Allies for the sake of France or Great Britain or Russia, but because in this hideous conflict they stand for the Right, and because their overthrow would mean the wreckage of the best of all that man has achieved in centuries. It is this which makes his strength as the strength of ten to-day, and which will ensure immortality to his work.[39]

Harry reminded readers that Raemaekers had a German mother and spoke German fluently. 'He was no professional partisan, no political anti-German, when the war broke out', he explained. 'His cartoons are not the utterance of a Germanophobe. They are the voice only of an enraged and horror-stricken conscience.'[40] In time Raemaekers would move to London with his wife and three young children, settling in a house on Sydenham Hill not far from the Robinsons. Brad said that introducing the Raemaekers into the family circle as playmates was 'one thing which my father did during the war that made a lot of difference to

Figure 17. An original cartoon by Louis Raemaekers, *c*.1916, depicting a distraught Belgian couple cradling the coffin of their child, killed by the Germans. This was a gift from Raemaekers to Harry, his friend and promoter.

Figure 18. Harry and U.S. correspondent Frederick Palmer in the War Correspondents' Mess in Amiens, c.1917. Pencil and chalk drawing by the renowned Scottish artist Muirhead Bone.

Source: © Imperial War Museum/ DACS (Art.IWM ART 2106)

my life as a child (apart from the huge difference made by not having a father at home from the age of seven until 12)'.[41]

*   *   *   *   *

In his diary entry for January 1, 1916, Harry wrote, 'Year begins with war at—I think—its worst.' In fact, this was the year that Harry really went to war, beginning with his arrival at British General Headquarters (G.H.Q.) in France in April. On April 10 he met with Northcliffe in London (noting in his diary, 'I am in khaki!'), then, after a 'horrid' crossing, arrived at G.H.Q. on April 14, proceeding 'into front line trenches'. From this point on, *The Times* would keep Harry at the Western Front until the end of the war, with only a few breaks. Harry's work ethic was praised:

> Robinson was a success at G.H.Q., for he was a hard worker and made himself agreeable to whomsoever he met. Confident that he could write a description of what he had seen which would be no less (and probably no more) readable than anything his colleagues could do, he was ready to hand on material to them; nor did *The Times* suffer from his generosity. He expressed sharp contempt for those who described events they had not seen with their own eyes—a practice too common at that time. On all occasions he tried in the flurry of life at G.H.Q. to keep up the paper's standards of accuracy and fairness.[42]

Harry could write at great speed. He informed Geoffrey Robinson, 'I think all my stuff has to be written at the rate of 1,500 words or more in the hour.'

Harry was one of five official British war correspondents based initially at Château Tilques, a castle-hotel built in 1891 and located outside St Omer, about thirty miles from British G.H.Q. in Montreuil-sur-Mer. Four of the correspondents represented more than one newspaper in an effort to avoid competition and encourage collaboration. Harry wrote for *The Times* and the *Daily News*; Philip Gibbs, the *Daily Telegraph* and the *Daily Chronicle*; William Beach Thomas, the *Daily Mail* and the *Daily Mirror*; and an American, Percival Phillips, who covered the *Daily Express*, the *Morning Post*, and the *Daily Graphic*. The fifth member was Herbert Russell from Reuters.[43] Henry Nevinson, a fellow war correspondent and, like Harry, an alumnus of Westminster School and Christ Church (but four years his senior), claimed that Harry's grouping of rival newspapers was 'unpleasing to his strongly conservative nature, but the leading London papers had been wisely linked together according to their differences in politics'.[44] Gibbs recalled that the appointment of the five correspondents was initially opposed by G.H.Q. 'Staff officers of the old Regular Army were at first exceedingly hostile to the idea, and to

Figure 19. Harry (standing, centre) strikes a pose with his fellow war correspondents in 1916, location unknown. Percival Phillips is seated at left; William Beach Thomas is seated second from right.

us', he wrote. 'They had a conviction that we were "prying around" for no good purpose, and would probably "give away the whole show."'[45] Gibbs insisted the opposite was true: 'We had no other desire than to record the truth as fully as possible without handing information to the enemy...There was no need of censorship of our dispatches. We were our own censors.' In short order the generals realized the importance of working with the press to ensure that the public was informed of the progress of the war—and would support the propaganda effort. All of the correspondents were attached to the British Army and wore the uniform of British officers.

Not everyone was pleased by this cosy arrangement. After the war, C. E. Montague, a journalist for the *Manchester Guardian*, wrote a scathing memoir called *Disenchantment*, in which he blasted the arrangement with the correspondents, blaming Field Marshal Sir Douglas Haig in particular. 'Under his command the policy of helping the Press rose to its maximum', he wrote. 'War correspondents were given the "status," almost the rank, of officers. Actual officers were detailed to see to their comfort, to pilot them about the front, to secure their friendly treatment by all ranks and at all headquarters. Never were war correspondents so helped, shielded and petted before.'[46] Therein lay the problem, Montague observed:

> One of the first rules of field censorship was that from war correspondents 'there must be no criticism of authority or command'; how could they disobey that? They would visit the front now and then, as many Staff Officers did, but it could be only as afternoon callers from one of the many mansions of G.H.Q., that heaven of security and comfort. When autumn twilight came down on the haggard trench world of which they had caught a quiet noon-day glimpse they would be speeding west in Vauxhall cars to lighted châteaux gleaming white among scatheless woods.[47]

Montague concluded that the fighting men read the newspaper dispatches 'open-mouthed', as even a bloody defeat would be couched as 'not quite a good day'.[48]

The war correspondents were not unaware of such criticism. In the December 1917 edition of *The Nineteenth Century,* Harry wrote an article entitled 'A War Correspondent On His Work' which was perhaps intended to respond to public scepticism. Harry was a fervent supporter of Haig, and the Commander returned the favour. Writing to his wife, Lady Haig, on November 18, 1916, Haig noted that he referred all press questions to his intelligence officer, Brigadier John Charteris, with few exceptions. 'I only receive some of the principal ones, like Northcliffe and Robinson of *The Times*, Strachey of the *Spectator*, the *Saturday Review* and such.' Furthermore, he reiterated his policy regarding censorship:

> I tell them all that they can go anywhere, and see whoever and whatever they like—there are no secrets. They can also write what they like, but I beg them to remember that we all have the same objective, viz., beat the Germans—so they must not give anything away which can be of use to the enemy. I must say that the correspondents have played up splendidly. We never once had to complain of them since I took over command.[49]

Harry certainly toed Haig's line (Haig's photograph appeared on the dustjacket of Harry's Somme book, *The Turning Point*). 'The public seems to have formed for itself two widely different pictures of the present-day War Correspondent', Harry wrote in his article. 'There are many people who figure us as breathless young men who dash about, presumably on horseback, among cannon and bursting shells and lines of cheering infantry, seizing and jotting down the impressions of the moment, then hurrying to the nearest telegraph office to send them red-hot to their respective journals.' That, he admitted, was the traditional picture of the legendary correspondents of old, such as his brother Phil. The other picture, Harry noted, is of 'a group of feeble-minded young men who live at some mysterious place known as "headquarters" where official information is served out to us by authority: which information, in transmission, we colour with our own ignoble prejudices—chiefly to the detriment of whatever regiment or unit the drawer of the picture may be most interested in'.[50] Harry insisted that there is more truth in the former than the latter. Speaking for his fellow four accredited correspondents, he wrote, 'That we have not the hard-won military knowledge of the professional soldier is cheerfully admitted, for only one of us has had even a Militia training; but, setting any previous experiences aside, we have in the aggregate seen vastly more of this War than any soldier living.' As such, 'We are getting a little touchy at the comments of writers at home, probably much our juniors, on the subject of our youth and our inexperience of war.' The average age of the quintet was 47, nearer in age to the generals than the infantrymen.[51]

Harry noted that the correspondents worked together on dispatches. 'The Front here is so vast that no single man can possibly be in touch with all of it. We soon decided for ourselves that, so far as the imparting of facts was concerned, we must collaborate and work in harmony, each exchanging daily his news with all the others', he explained. 'For the public good we have stifled that primitive instinct of the journalist to "beat" the other man.'[52] Each correspondent was assigned a Press Officer who accompanied him wherever he went, including the front lines. 'We go nowhere unchaperoned, unless it be to lunch or dine with a friend', Harry noted. 'There is absolutely no restriction on our movements. We walk—or motor—where we will, but, lamblike, a Press Officer comes too.' He felt sorry for these officers. 'They do it with excellent grace and more zest than one might expect from men who have to risk their lives to appease another man's curiosity', Harry wrote. 'The chauffeur we can leave a mile or two behind us on the road (where he sometimes has a more dangerous time than we), but the Press Officer must thread the shell-holes and slimy trenches with us to the bitter end and back.'[53]

Harry explained that the correspondents and their press officers, dispatch riders, and other personnel (a camp of some twenty-seven persons) lived in a château or country house near the Front, never more than two hours' drive from any point of the line from the Somme to the sea. Following an attack the correspondents would meet and share notes, usually around 1:00 p.m. 'All that each man has learned is common property: each in rotation telling his story generally from north to south of the battle-line', Harry continued. 'That done, we then have some two hours or two hours and a half in which to write our despatches so that they may be censored and telegraphed in time for the next morning's papers.' The day after a battle, more in-depth stories were pursued, with analysis. 'It has taken us some time to organise this system, which may yet be capable of vast improvement', Harry concluded, noting 'it has one transcendent advantage. I do not believe that ever before has the public come so near to getting the full truth from the battlefield . . . the reader can rest assured that whatever he reads of news from the Western Front is, with reservations to be explained hereafter, as near the truth as the individual writer can set it down.'[54]

Harry, moreover, expressed no problem with military censorship. 'The broad principles laid down to guide the Censorship are (1) that we must say nothing which will give information or encouragement to the enemy; (2) that we must say nothing which will unduly depress our men; and (3) that we must not criticise the conduct of our military operations. With the wisdom of all these rules we heartily agree',[55] he explained. He admitted that while 'the Army overrates the likelihood of depressing either the troops or the nation' by reporting on Allied defeats and casualties, the correspondents do so anyway, but with care. 'The whole tale of our fighting on the Somme, at Arras, at Messines and in Flanders has been so glorious that we could well afford, if only to heighten the splendour of the victories, to confess to every minor failure', he continued. 'The British public and the world are shrewd enough to know that there must be fluctuations, some taking as well as giving in war, and it is the foam and these swirls and eddies made by obstructions in its course which tell of the strength of a river's current.'[56] At the end of the day, Harry insisted, truth prevailed. 'For the military authorities to tell us how to frame our despatches so as to obtain a certain effect on the readers' minds is as purely absurd as it would be for me to tell an Artillery officer how to use his gun to destroy a given position', he wrote. 'There can be but one common aim: namely, to help to win the War; and the Correspondents' part in it is, by making plain the story of our achievements, to build up the nation's pride in the Army, and to strengthen the general *moral* [sic]. Nothing could do this more surely than would the literal detailed record of every day's achievement. Our despatches are already vastly more truthful, more comprehensively exact, than, I think, the public gives them credit for.'[57] Harry's article in itself certainly had propaganda value.

*   *   *   *   *

Bearing in mind that Harry and his fellow war correspondents collaborated on articles, Harry's reports in *The Times* dealing with the specific details and logistics of attacks and battles are not noteworthy in themselves.[58] What stand out, however, are his in-between articles, when his creative mind and background knowledge, particularly about the natural world, come to the forefront. Harry's diary entries indicate that war correspondents had a lot of downtime at the château between battles. There was an endless stream of visitors, including Northcliffe and Sir Arthur Conan Doyle. John Buchan came to dinner; H. G. Wells stopped in to chat, as did John Masefield. Harry erected a badminton net, explored the surrounding forest, and went fishing. In the January 1931 edition of *The Times House Journal*, the staff publication, a tribute article was published on Harry after his death, referencing his recreational activities at the Front:

> When he was not out with the troops, or talking to soldiers about the chances of the War, or map-reading, or typing his messages—for the most part immediately after the physical and mental strain of a tiring day at the front—he found time whenever he could for the pursuit of his favourite pastime of nature-study, among such birds and beasts and butterflies as were to be found in the country at the back of the front and even on the battlefields in France and Belgium. At one of the châteaux where he and the other correspondents were quartered there was a mill stream running through the grounds, part of which was slack water almost entirely covered by a mass of water-weeds. It was characteristic of his skill as a fisherman that he would sometimes take his rod out with him in a spare half-hour, not for the purpose of catching fish but to practise casting, throwing his fly with extraordinary accuracy into one after another of the tiny open spaces between the weeds. That, to one who has watched him doing it, is a typical example of the thoroughness which he put into every venture that he took in hand.[59]

Not to mention Harry's need to relax and decompress. On May 10, 1916, he wrote about Château Tilques in 'A French Château. Birds and Flowers at the Front'. 'They are charming grounds, well wooded, with stately trees and walks, which wind through shrubberies where rabbits live, and spinneys of young hazel, ash, sycamore, and wild cherry', he noted. Many birds, he added, actually profited from wartime conditions:

> Every house that is blown to bits by shell fire provides an endless choice of fascinating nesting-places for sparrows among the chinks of the ruined walls; and never did starlings have such opportunities for unmolested housekeeping as in the remains of these poor battered churches. As for the guns, they are to the birds, presumably, no more than thunder; and when a shell falls near it is only some new, if startling, natural phenomenon. They have had no experience to breed in them an instinct to be afraid of the booming of big guns.[60]

It was an odd oasis of sorts. 'It is a beautiful place, singularly peaceful and retired; and perhaps seeming all the more peaceful because every now and then one turns from bird's-nesting to listen to the throbbing in the air as it grows louder, and one says to the other, "They are strafing heavily just now"', Harry observed. 'At times, too, one comes out of the trees to where one can have an unobstructed view of the sky where something is humming overhead and one judges from the height, without need of glasses, whether it is a friendly visitor or a Boche', a pejorative for the German enemy.

At the end of June, the correspondents moved into the Hotel Belfort in Amiens to be closer to the action, as the Battle of the Somme was imminent. 'At half-past 7 this morning a great battle began on a front of about 25 miles above and on both banks of the Somme', Harry wrote on July 3. 'Perhaps it will be known in history as the Battle of the Somme.'[61] Watching the nighttime British bombardment of the German line, Harry provided a graphic description of the 'awe-inspiring sight' in distinctly human terms:

> One ordinarily measures the weight of a bombardment by the number of shells that burst in a minute. In this case counting was hopeless. Fixing my eyes on one spot I tried to wink them as fast as the lightnings flickered, and the shells beat me badly. I then tried chattering my teeth, and I think that in that way I approximately held my own. Testing it afterwards in the light, where I could see a watch face, I found that I could click my teeth some five or six times in a second. You can try it for yourself and, clicking your own teeth, will get some idea of the rate at which shells were bursting on a single spot.

The British Army suffered more than 60,000 dead or wounded that day, one-fifth of the attacking force and 14 per cent of the total of the 140 days of the Battle of the Somme. ('The magnitude of the catastrophe, the greatest loss of life in British military history, took time to sink in', noted John Keegan.[62]) Returning to his hotel, Harry lay awake all night, watching the night sky from his window, a 'ceaseless lifting and paling of the Northern Lights'. The next day, as the British troops advanced at Thiepval, Harry observed, 'All the while, above the smoke and mist, two kestrels swung and circled and hovered in the sunlight.'

While Harry mentioned in passing seeing many of the wounded as well as prisoners of war, he did not describe in graphic detail the human cost of warfare. The propaganda reasons are obvious. However, in his 1917 book *The Turning Point: The Battle of the Somme*, Harry was freer to be more explicit about that first day. Wandering the field of fighting from Fricourt to Mametz, Harry described 'a dreadful sight' of destruction and death. 'The work of gathering the dead and preparing them for burial was still going on. Some still lay where they had fallen, full length with their heads toward the German trench', he wrote. 'Others, laid in orderly rows and being very gently and reverently handled, were side by side along a narrow open piece of ground at the village edge, where service was to be read over them later in the day.' Inside the German trenches, where the dead were 'not less pathetic because they were dressed in grey instead of khaki', Harry noted, 'I think the most horrible figure of all was that of a man—part of a man—who lay flat upon the earth, and there was nothing of him above the shoulder blades. War in its details is a gruesome thing.'[63]

'Nobody could possibly be braver than the British soldiers are', Harry wrote on a postcard to Brad on July 13. 'You must be just like them.'

*   *   *   *   *

Harry was fascinated by aeroplanes, invented just over a decade ago, and cited having the chance to fly above the battlefield as one of his main accomplishments as a war correspondent. It was his first time in an aeroplane, and he wrote about the experience in *The Times* on August 1, 1916.[64] 'War nowadays, in most of its aspects, is a terrible, sordid thing. But this fighting of the airmen is more than the warfare of any ancient heroes, and comes nearer to the battling of the old gods than anything men have done or dreamed', he wrote. Harry marvelled at the view as they flew over friendly territory, parallel to the German line. 'What surprised my inexperience most was the wonderful clean-cut neatness of the landscape, with its endless chessboard pattern, as if the whole earth had gone to bed in the sunlight under a glorious patchwork quilt', he observed. 'It is really a much more beautiful world as the birds and the angels see it.' Harry gained a new-found appreciation for the value of observation from the air, the ability to see the enemy position and progress; viewed from above, the ugly trench 'looked as if it were made with a sharp penknife cutting into cardboard'. Harry's giddiness over the 'joy of flight' is apparent:

> They told me that I should hate it when we banked, but they were wrong. It was merely strange and infinitely novel and delightful, while as for the landing, which they said was worst of all, there can be no more gloriously exhilarating thing in life than that steep glide, when the propeller drops its note to a gentle purring, and the machine sweeps, like some fairy motor-car, dropping, with the clutch out, on frictionless bearings down the face of a hill of oil, from cloud-level to tree-level, to grass-level, there to land, with hardly a jar, and bound again and rush across the open space of turf, swinging round in a gentle curve until she stops with her nose to her own hangar like a well-handled horse pulling up at his own doorstep.

In *The Turning Point*, Harry continued the story after his aeroplane landed:

> I have said that the chance of encounter with an enemy machine behind our lines was small; but it happened that that was one of the rare days when the Germans plucked up courage enough to come and had luck and skill enough to avoid our patrols.
>
> As we climbed out of our machine, an officer of the Royal Flying Corps strolled up, and—
>
> 'See anything of the Boche?' he asked.
>
> 'No,' replied my pilot. 'Is he around?'
>
> 'There are five machines reported over and coming this way.'
>
> It was interesting to know that we had been so near to excitement, and I was entirely glad to have missed it. Nor was anything more heard of the enemy machines.[65]

Amid his excitement, Harry also reminded readers that aerial combat was a deadly business. His article on April 29, 1918, regarding an 'extraordinary incident' involving a British aeroplane made headlines around the world. The plane engaged the enemy above Arras, then disappeared from view. It was found 20 miles away, crashed in friendly territory. 'The opinion of experts is that the machine had flown by itself for at least two hours with two dead men in it until the petrol was exhausted, having swung in a great circle over unknown lands and back to behind the starting-place, as boats have been known to sail with sheets made fast and a dead man's hand on the tiller',[66] Harry reported. The *New York Herald* quoted a British flying officer on this so-called 'death flight': 'This incident is quite authentic as mentioned by Perry Robinson ... for upward of two hours the two dead men were in the air before the final crash to earth.'[67]

Back on terra firma, Harry wrote a series of articles on the week-long visit of King George V to the Front, embargoed for publication until after the King had safely departed for home. Harry, ever the royalist, was clearly impressed. 'He has seen, and been seen by, some hundreds of thousands of his soldiers', he wrote on August 17. 'He has spoken with many scores of them, along the roads, going to or coming from the fighting line, on parades, in billets, and in trenches. He has visited battlefields where our guns were roaring, and over which the enemy throws shells every day. He has climbed in and out of trenches which saw desperate fighting in the early days of the battle of the Somme, has gone into German dug-outs and picked up relics of the battle with his own hands.'[68] Crossing into No Man's Land, Harry noted, the King, joined by the Prince of Wales, was 'in places of undoubted danger, where few people care to go unless duty calls them. He was well within range of the enemy's guns.' Harry also reported on a lighter moment, when the King paid a surprise visit to troops billeted in ramshackle barns they nick-named 'The Ritz':

> Some of the men were lying about when the King came among them, unexpectedly, and one man was snoring loudly as he lay stretched out on a wheelbarrow. The noise of the footsteps coming across the cobble-stones disturbed him, and he stretched his arms and sat up blinking, and then saw, in utter disbelief in the truth of what his eyes revealed, the King and the Prince of Wales and a glitter of many 'brass hats.' But the King was wise in going to these places without warning, for he saw the everyday life of his troops without any special preparation of tidying away.

Clearly the royal visit took a lot out of Harry. 'Slept 10 hours!' he wrote in his diary on August 18. 'Back to Amiens after loafing and walking in woods.'

Within days Harry wrote of 'quite the most wonderful spectacle that I have seen in this war—a thing to which no description can do justice and thrilling beyond anything in my experience.' This was the advance on Thiepval in northern France. 'Well hidden ourselves from the enemy's view, we lay in holes',[69] Harry wrote on August 25 with all the *brio* of a *Boy's Own* adventure. When the bombardment began, Harry could barely find the words:

> No description can do justice to it. One could hardly set one's self to describe the end of the world. In the course of my life I have seen many gigantic things, like typhoons and prairie fires and forest fires, and most of the great volcanoes of the world, and some battles, and that last awful night in Antwerp. But merely as a spectacle, for the splendour and the power of it, I doubt if anything ever resembled what went on then for the next twenty minutes. The young officer beside me sat muttering 'Oh, my God! Oh, my God!' For me I wished to shriek, to bite my fingers, to do I knew not what. And all one could do was to drum one's heels on the ground and gasp.

Next came the advance of the troops. 'Our front trench sprang to life. Pouring over the parapets and scrambling as best they could across the uneven shell-pitted expanse of No Man's Land, the khaki figures streamed, not in disorder, but fairly evenly spaced, thin wave behind thin wave. No veterans (but these men were veterans now) could possibly have been steadier and more eager than these troops.'

Apparently around this time *The Times* began to worry about Harry's health, and considered recalling him to London. On August 31, Harry wrote to Geoffrey Robinson, 'A certain professional pride inclines me to stay until the battle is through. I told both Lord Northcliffe and [Military

Correspondent Charles] Repington that I intended to do so, and they both applauded.'[70]

* * * * *

Much as Harry was fascinated by aeroplanes, he was just as obsessed with the arrival of the tank on the battlefield, a key factor in the Allied advance into the German lines on September 16, 1916, resulting in the capture of three villages: Flers, Martinpuich, and Courcelette. He described seeing forty of these 'new armoured motor-cars' which, filled with soldiers, he likened to the fabled wooden horse of Troy in its effectiveness. 'That they were of great service in this attack is undoubted, thrusting themselves with all their spines out, like hedgehogs into a nest of snakes, wherever the enemy's positions were most formidable', he observed. 'I know from German prisoners that the enemy was terrified by them and hates them. They even protest that they are not civilized warfare—and that is a subject on which the German is an authority.'[71] In *The Turning Point*, Harry was even more descriptive. 'We had for some time heard rumours of the monsters which would crawl over trenches and shell holes, butt down houses and eat up trees, trunks and all', he noted. 'But so confidential were all communications on the subject that they justified the official sobriquet which the strange machine had already received, the Hush-hush!' And then he spotted them, 'a herd of forty!'

> It was an entirely incredible scene. No writer of fiction who has set his hero to the hunting of the giant saurians of another age in some impossibly discovered glade of a lost continent ever imagined a spectacle more unbelievable than was that herd of the huge monsters, unlike anything that ever lived on earth, as they shifted and seemed to browse about the meadow before us. A portion of the herd was drawn up in even ranks, like the elephant-lines of some Asiatic army which may have confronted a distant forerunner of Alexander in times long before the commonplace modern elephant of to-day had been evolved. Others moved nosingly about, weaving in and out just as some great brutes might do before settling down for the night. Toad-chimeras; terrestrial whales in crocodile's armour; hybrids, crossed in a nightmare, between behemoth and a she-mastodon: shades of Sinbad, Gulliver and Munchausen![72]

Officially, Harry noted, tanks were called 'his Majesty's land-ships'.

On October 20, 1916 Harry returned home. At Ashmore, the Raemaekers family joined the Robinsons to celebrate Brad's tenth birthday. Harry wrote to *The Times* and raised the issue of his salary, again, claiming he was underpaid. 'I preferred that the letter should not be read by the Press Censors', he explained, which is why he posted it in London. 'You know, I think, that since the war began I have done a good deal of arduous, and sometimes dangerous work', he began. 'In France I am aware that I am receiving a smaller salary than the Correspondents of some, and I believe of all, the other papers which have Correspondents there on the same footing with myself.' Harry suggested that his £800 annual salary be increased to £1,000. 'Whether I have done as good work as the other Correspondents is for The Times to judge, but I have certainly worked as hard and I should be very grateful if you would consider whether I have succeeded in proving myself worth the higher figure to the paper.'[73] The 'Manager', presumably William Lints Smith, replied on October 25. 'The present time is a very bad one, not only for "The Times" newspaper, but for all other newspapers in England. To increase salaries just now is very difficult', he wrote. Nonetheless, the firm acceded to Harry's request, crediting an extra four pounds to his account weekly.[74] Harry noted his pleasure in his diary, adding 'In room working on book all day'. Perhaps his 'instant book' on the war, The Turning Point, was part of his new salary agreement? He would work on the book, on and off, for the rest of the year.

Harry returned to France, but within a month The Times decided to replace him. Even though he had just persuaded his superiors to increase his salary, Harry now demanded a rest, telling the head office on December 7 that he 'shall be unfit for any good or important work here until I have been [relieved]. All the other Correspondents who have been all through it here are either away—like Beach Thomas and [U.S. correspondent Frederick] Palmer[75]—or have had a month or more holiday, like Russell and Philip Gibbs. I am the last rose of summer, and distinctly draggled.'[76] Harry had been in bed for the past week with a bad cold and cough. Unbeknownst to him, his superiors at The Times were well aware of the situation. A Times memorandum dated November 16 stated, 'Perry Robinson is tired, and is very anxious to spend a month or two in Switzerland where his boy has to go for health reasons. I suggest that we allow him to do this and to act as our Correspondent while there.'[77] Brad was scheduled for a thyroid operation in January. A temporary swap of correspondents was agreed upon: Harry would go to Switzerland, relieving Fleury Lamure, who would go to Paris, relieving Gerald Campbell, who would take Harry's place at G.H.Q. Harry left for home on December 20. On December 31, he reflected on a momentous year in his diary: 'A dreadful year, but one in which we had less than our share of the common suffering. I have barely been at home for 2½ months in the year, but my association with Raemaekers and work on the Somme have been to the good. The chief cloud on our private outlook now is Brad's illness.'

Harry's diary entry for January 3, 1917 stated, 'Brad's operation takes place @ 2. F. gone to hospital.' But there was drama the following evening when, Brad recalled in his memoir, 'I was nearly asphyxiated by a heavy snowfall blocking the chimneys of the ward in St George's Hospital at Hyde Park Corner which was blazing with coal fires.'[78]

After Harry met with Northcliffe and delivered the manuscript of his book about the Battle of the Somme to Heinemann (who was becoming Harry's publisher of record), the Robinsons departed for Paris on January 17. There they dined with George Adam, *The Times* Paris correspondent, and the family visited the Swiss Legation for visas. Harry's visa identified him as '*Envoyé spécial des* "Times"', accompanied by 'Mrs. Robinson *et son fils malade, agé de dix ans*'. On January 23 they arrived at their destination: Chalet Bellevue in Château d'Oex, in the canton of Vaud. The choice of Château d'Oex is an intriguing one given its internment camp. Switzerland, officially neutral during the war, agreed to accept 68,000 sick or injured prisoners from both sides of the conflict, assisted by the Red Cross to receive care they could not obtain in an ordinary internment camp. Harry was, in a sense, remaining close to the war effort.

Harry's diary entries reveal that all three Robinsons were, as usual, frequently ill and often in bed. Still, Harry kept busy, as Switzerland was far from a bucolic place due to the war. He filed several stories on German intimidation of the Swiss by closing the frontier, blocking imports and imperiling the country's economic outlook. On March 19, presumably refreshed and restored to good health he left for London to return to duty. Florence and Brad stayed on in Switzerland for another two months, perhaps as Brad was under a doctor's care.

* * * * *

With the entry of the United States into the war on April 7, 1917, Harry returned to the Front and his fellow correspondents at G.H.Q., now stationed at Château Rollencourt in Angres. His first article was published on April 10. Fighting on Vimy Ridge, he noted, 'was like the days of the beginning of the Battle of the Somme again, and the Battle of Arras, if that is what it is to be called, may prove no less disastrous to the Germans'.[79] The opening of the bombardment 'in the grey of dawn was as stupendous a spectacle as anything ever seen in war'. Still, Harry steeled his readers for bad news to come. 'Such a battle as has begun this morning cannot be fought without heavy casualties. We must be reconciled to that in advance. But the enemy will suffer more than we, and we shall break him here as we broke him on the Somme.'

An article Harry wrote on 'Spring at the Front' on May 3, 1917 attracted much attention for the poignant pause it offered from the horrors of war. Once again, this was characteristic of Harry to take a breather and look for signs of hope. 'At last France has some taste of spring', he began. Warmer weather was welcome for the men in the trenches. Harry noted the return of the swallows, and then the first cuckoo. 'A single chiffchaff—plucky little thruster that he is!—was singing impatiently not far behind the battle-line as long ago as on Easter Day, even while our guns thundered the overture to the Battle of Arras, which began on the following morning. It was a very lonely little voice in the wilderness.' With warmer weather came more birds, buds on the trees, meadows yellow with cowslips, and Harry's beloved butterflies, 'not only the hibernated butterflies—brimstones and tortoiseshells and peacocks—which have lived from last autumn, but green-veined whites, which are true children of the present spring'.[80] Harry marvelled at how nature's march would not be deterred, even by war:

> Now that spring is here, one wonders what miracle it will work with all this dreadful area. Nature is wonderfully quick to repair and hide man's ravages...Here, even now, many of the first-line trenches which we stormed on the opening day of the Battle of the Somme are already crumbling in, parapet and parados conspiring together to fill up and obliterate the ugly gash of the trench itself, while the colt's foot and lesser celandine make stars of gold in old shell-holes, which have now lost half their depth.

> For man to reclaim much of this man-made wilderness will be hard and, within the life of modern explosives at least, dangerous work. The earth in many places is so full of unexploded shells and bombs, hidden now beneath the surface, that it would be a perilous task to put a ploughshare through it. But nature, working so patiently and with such little things, has a magic beyond all human reach. In the spring which has begun in these last two days, she has her first chance to show what she can do with the battlefields of last year. Surely she will hide them if she can.[81]

Similarly, Harry juxtaposed the horror of war with hopeful signs of nature when he reported on the opening of the Battle of Messines near Ypres on June 7, 1917, and the 'terrifying' eruption of 600 tons of explosive mines beneath the German positions ('the earth shook like a house of cards...it quaked like jelly'), a noise heard 100 miles away in England. This awful spectacle was but a prelude to what Harry called 'the greatest miracle of all', unveiled at dawn:

> For with the rose flush in the sky the whole bird chorus of morning came to life. Never, surely, did birds sing so—blackbird and thrush, lark, and blackcap, and willow warbler. More of the time their voices, of course, were inaudible, but now and again, in the intervals of the shattering noise of the guns, their notes pealed up as if each bird were struck with frenzy and all together strove to shout down the guns.[82]

Perhaps only Harry with his sensitive eye could have seen this. 'Never, I believe, before can the world have seen such a daybreak', he concluded.

Harry's book, *The Turning Point: The Battle of the Somme*, was published by Heinemann in May 1917, heralded as one of the firm's 'New War Books' including *The British Navy at War* by G. MacNeile Dixon, *Gallipoli* by John Masefield, and even Philip Gibbs's *The Battles of the Somme*. It was published on June 9 by Dodd, Mead in the U.S. Harry essentially stitched together his *Times* articles with a few revisions. In his preface, dated January 11, 1917, Harry admitted, 'This is not an account of the Battle of the Somme which will satisfy military readers. Such an account could not be written yet, even by an expert writer on military affairs, which I make no pretence to be.' Instead, he hoped to provide a consecutive narrative of the battle. 'If I have failed to convey an adequate impression of the magnitude of the achievement of our Army or of the quality of that Army itself, it is because I have not the power', he wrote. 'I do not believe that the Empire yet appreciates at anything like their true value either the splendour of our successes or the heroism of our men.' Reviews were good. *The Graphic* said, 'The shining quality of our new armies makes proud reading.' *The New York Times* observed, 'Mr. Robinson has here told the story of the British part in it as well as it has yet been told, with skill and impressiveness in the writing of the narrative and with an effect so graphic that the reader cannot fail to realize the titanic nature of the struggle in all its terribleness.' The *Chicago Tribune* noted how eager Harry was to acknowledge 'the whole empire in arms. Mr. Robinson is afraid of leaving any one out, of not telling all they did in this monster battle.' The *Times Literary Supplement*, in a review written by Francis Henry Gribble (author of *In Luxembourg in Wartime*), offered praise, even if Harry was a latecomer. 'Mr. Perry Robinson is unfortunate in being a little later in the field with his book on the Somme battle than Mr. Philip Gibbs and Mr. Beach Thomas [*With the British on the Somme*]; but that fact should not prevent anyone from reading what he has written', Gribble wrote. 'The book is full of good stories in all veins, and will take its place as a most satisfactory popular history of one of the most important episodes of the war.'[83]

On May 26, Harry journeyed to Paris to greet Florence and Brad as they made their way from Switzerland. He leased an apartment on the Rue Taitbout for them, so he could stay in closer contact, as Florence's health was not good. 'We landed in Paris the day the Germans started to shell the city with Big Bertha', Brad recalled (the long-range German guns which, John Keegan noted, 'dropped shells into the city, psychologically if not objectively to considerable effect, from a range of seventy-five miles'[84]). Brad hated Paris even more than he did Switzerland. 'The French, as always when they are having a bad time, were disliking foreigners. Even a small boy of 10 like me could be sneered at or robbed', he remembered. 'The only things I really enjoyed were the Parc Monceau and being taken to the Jockey Club. I had my first ice cream in Paris and saw my first film. Both were rather disappointing.'[85] Harry came down to Paris whenever he could (and when he was not busy fishing; he caught his first fish on May 29). He played three sets of tennis at the Racing Club, rather impressive for his age. He was also intent on spending more time with his growing son. During one visit Harry, always a keen sportsman, was concerned that his son could not throw a cricket ball. 'I could only bowl it in round-arm like a girl (of those days)', Brad wrote. 'I had my first lesson in bending the elbow and snapping the wrist with pebbles on Le Havre beach.'[86]

*   *   *   *   *

On July 9, 1917 Harry sent Florence and Brad home to London, where Florence did her part for the war effort, raising money for hospitals and charities. 'My mother, selling Alexandra Roses at Hyde Park Corner, caused a (very tight) inmate at Buckingham Palace to fall off his horse when she tried to fix a posy of the roses to his horse's head', Brad recalled.[87] Meanwhile, back at the Front, Harry on September 29 caught his thirteenth fish and served it to the visiting Geoffrey Dawson (formerly Robinson)[88] for lunch. In between, it was business as usual as he reported on the week-long visit of the King and Queen and the success of the Allies over the summer. 'Though the job be long or short, the Army has perfect confidence that it is better, both man for man and as a fighting machine, than the armies of Germany, and that but one end can come', Harry reported on July 6. 'It is a year with which we can be satisfied.'[89] At Glencourse Wood on August 13, Harry shared that 'Airmen, who are the best authorities, report that they have never seen the ground so strewn and heaped with German dead as is that battlefield... I am using emphatic language in describing this struggle here, but from all accounts the fighting seems truly to have been as intense and desperate as almost seen in a similar area in this war.'[90]

Harry never forgot his dual role of telling the truth but also boosting morale. On September 14, he heaped praise on 'Our Citizen Army... new and untried but one year ago, but no more. These young men come from all backgrounds, yet represent the best of British manhood, and are united in their cause.' Harry was especially lyrical in describing a rare moment of leisure:

A week ago, on the coast, just behind the reach of shells, I watched men out 'in rest' take their horses into the sea, naked men on bareback horses, flesh

Figure 20. Harry (centre) speaking to King George V during a visit to Thiepval, France, on July 12, 1917. At left is Chris Wigram, Harry's press minder.
Source: © Imperial War Museum (Q 5652)

to flesh. There were more than 300 of them; and they went out in a great bow-shaped line cantering, shouting, racing, through the long shallow of the incoming tide till the water rose from hoof to fetlock and fetlock to belly and belly to back, until nothing was to be seen but the horses' heads and part of the neck and men awash to the waists. And then they came back in one glorious race for home, a mass of black shining skin and whirling white arms, all veiled in a smother of foam in which the sun struck rainbows. It was immensely good for the horses; but oh! how good it was for the men! But how came they all to ride, each one like some strange amphibious centaur? What were they before, and how far have they not travelled from their old ways of life and thought? By how much are they not better men?[91]

Harry concluded with a rare opportunity to address readers who had lost loved ones:

I often wish, too that all those who grieve could come out here and see. Nothing, of course, can console—not even the proud companionship of grief at home and the knowledge that 'he' died a hero. But I have often wished that each mourner could come and, mirrored in the others, see what the fallen one looked like when he went about his work, what good fellows his comrades were, of what a splendid whole he was part, and with what amplitude all pride is justified. It is, of course, not possible; nor can we who are out here interpret it. But the time will come when it will be realized more fully than it can be now, when grief will grow less and pride be greater, and above all sense of loss will be sense of gratitude, not merely for the things that have been achieved, but for the new-found qualities of the peoples of the Empire.

On October 5, Harry reported on the 'shattering blow' delivered to the Germans on Passchendaele Ridge, with nearly 4,500 prisoners taken. 'Never has the German army here been so hammered as it has been to-day', Harry wrote. 'Everywhere there is the undefinable thrill of victory, unmistakable and impossible to describe', even among the wounded, 'dreadfully dirty and disreputable to the eye, but every man cheery and full of hearty laughter, knowing we have won. It is good even to be wounded on such a day.'[92]

As winter approached, Harry himself was frequently under the weather. 'Have not been out of doors for 4 days. Cold better', he wrote in his diary on November 16. Still, he maintained a punishing routine, writing up to 2,000 words a day. On December 21, he arrived home for the holidays. The Robinsons journeyed to Bath on Christmas Eve to stay with the Raemaekers. On December 28, Harry met Northcliffe and they visited the U.S. Embassy together. Harry's diary entry for New Year's Eve 1917 is telling. 'Another terrible year in which we have much cause to be grateful that we have suffered so little. Two months in Switzerland for me and 4 for F. and Brad—then F. in Paris this July. Ashmore empty from Jan.–Sept. then let to Lieut. and Mrs. Haven. Brad went to school with Morgan Brown @ Hindhead [St. Edmund's School in Surrey]. F. undergoing treatment by Dr. Sugar, but generally better and stronger than since we were married. My "Turning Point" published and I think my reputation as War Correspondent is good. So, on the whole, for us a good year in the midst of horrors.' Brad, in fact, would miss an entire year of school in 1918 owing to his operation for 'tuberculosis glands'; he and his mother would stay in Cornwall.

*   *   *   *   *

Harry spent the final year of the war at G.H.Q., and working as hard as ever. Intriguingly, Northcliffe sent him a telegram on April 14, 1918: 'Proprietors and staff of The Times desire to congratulate you on your excellent dispatches and trust you will be able to stand the great strain,' a reassuring awareness of Harry's physical state. Henry Nevinson, who stepped in for Philip Gibbs when he took a break, found Harry 'a little rheumatic but otherwise fit for his age'.[93] Harry continued to churn out copy, in colourful fashion. 'Brigades and battalions were handled like pieces of a chess board, so that always there was the thin screen of khaki in the way of the oncoming German waves', he wrote on April 2.[94] A bayonet charge by a Manchester battalion near Bihucourt was described in graphic detail on April 4. German soldiers had forced their way into a section of British trench—to their ultimate regret. 'Manchesters went at them with the bayonet, a regulation charge delivered according to all the rules, and every German in the trench was killed', Harry wrote. 'Later these same Manchesters had another chance to use the bayonet and did it to perfection. "You simply could not keep them away from the Germans when there was a chance fairly to get at them," said an officer in describing it to me. "They were just hungry for it all the time."'[95] At Armentières on April 13, Harry reported on 'Fine British Fighting Against the Odds':

> There is a tale of a most gallant sergeant of artillery who served a field gun alone when it was so injured that at each round he had to prise open the breech with a pickaxe; but he kept on firing point blank on the Germans till they got within 200 yards, and then blew up the gun and got away.
>
> Machine-gunners are also said to have behaved splendidly. Stories are told of a gunner and a gun being buried together by a shell. The man worked his way out, then dug out the gun, and got to work again. And there is the tale of a party of tunnellers who rallied some Portuguese, and, with a handful of Scottish troops, held a section of the line most stubbornly. And there are comic tales, as the one of a German officer prisoner whose pockets were found full of Huntley and Palmer's biscuits, which he had gathered from a dug-out in the forward post as he came through.
>
> But these things are trivial, if most of them are thrilling. The great fact is that our men are fighting splendidly, and whatever gains the Germans are making are made at a fearful cost.[96]

On April 15, Harry reported, 'The Germans continue their ruthless and random shelling of all points they can reach. I understand they have made one direct hit on Amiens Cathedral, but pre-occupation with other parts of the battle area has made it impossible to get there to see. A few nights ago they began suddenly throwing gas shells into an innocent village from which civilians had not departed, with the result that some 50 cases of gas poisoning were caused among the villagers, largely women and children.'[97] Harry was lucky not to have suffered a mustard gas attack himself.

In 1920, in an article for *The Times*, Harry looked back on this period and offered another poignant story. 'A stuffed bird seems a queer object to have a place in the Imperial War Museum; but few things have a better

Figure 21. Harry (right) and his fellow war correspondents examine a dud German 42cm shell, erected in the garden of a home in Houthem, Belgium, September 17, 1917. Captain La Porte of the Belgium Mission is at left; William Beach Thomas stands beside Harry.

Source: © Imperial War Museum (Q 3082)

right to be there than the old stork of the Hotel du Rhin at Amiens',[98] he began. The Imperial War Museum, founded in 1917, was initially housed in the Crystal Palace on Sydenham Hill, Harry's neighbourhood. Harry recalled that during the Battle of the Somme Amiens was the meeting place for the French and British armies, and the center of fraternization was the Hotel du Rhin. Behind the hotel was a garden, sheltered by high walls, featuring a small, round pond, home to a stork and a gull. 'Some members of the hotel staff asserted that they had been there for 13 years; others put it at 27', Harry noted. 'They were great friends. The stork never paced across the grass without the gull pattering close in attendance.' The birds became most animated over passing aircraft:

Aeroplanes interested them most. Before the human bystanders had heard even the throb of an engine, the stork would catch sight of the strange bird in the far-off sky and, with beak pointed heavenward, it would clatter its long mandibles—rat-tat-tat-tat—just like the rattle of a machine-gun. Then the Boche took to bombing Amiens; and at night, when the hotel rocked to the explosions, amid the roar of Archies [anti-aircraft guns], the stork would go on machine-gunning like mad; and officers have been known to lean out of their windows and shout to him: 'Good old bird!' He undoubtedly hated the Boche.

During the great German offensive in March 1918, Amiens was heavily bombed and largely destroyed, including most of the Hotel du Rhin. On March 29 Harry and his fellow correspondents toured the ruins and decided to rescue the birds, returning them to their billet at Château Rollencourt. 'There, turned down in the park, they had a beautiful stream with wide reedy backwaters and shady tree-sheltered lawns to roam in, and they seemed to settle down in happiness', Harry recalled, 'and every night when the German aeroplanes came over on their way to the bombing of Abbeville or some other innocent place, the stork would throw its head back and rat-tat-tat-tat at them as gallantly as ever'. But their idyll was short-lived:

> One day the stork fell ill, being found lying with half-closed eyes in shelter of a bush. He was taken into a warm hut and wrapped in flannel, and every effort was made to induce him to eat or even to swallow a few drops of brandy and water. Perhaps war correspondents and Press officers and the like do not know the right way to doctor storks. Perhaps it was no physical malady, but a broken heart because of the course the war was taking in that dreadful April of 1918. At all events, nothing availed; and in the morning the patriotic bird was dead. That same evening the gull vanished, gone, doubtless, to seek his comrade.

A message was dispatched to G.H.Q. about the famous stork of the Hotel du Rhin. The correspondents suggested it be stuffed and preserved for the new Imperial War Museum. 'Later in the day, a major-general, splendid in scarlet and brass, came all the way from Montreuil and, with all honours, took the stork away with him reverently in his Rolls-Royce car', Harry recalled. 'If there had been a band it would have played a funeral march.'

> Now the stork stands, in a glass case all by himself, with a label telling briefly his history, in the nave of the Crystal Palace. He is a noble bird, gloriously black and white in the full spring plumage of early April. When visitors look at him he peers at them out of his beady eye and is plainly saying: 'Let me see! Did I know you in Amiens in the old days?'[99]

*   *   *   *   *

As summer waned, Harry and the other correspondents knew the tide was finally turning. 'These are great days', he reported on the advance from Arras on August 26, 1918. 'For a correspondent, however, description, and even record, is almost impossible. The sweep of our advance is so rapid that no man can say when our advanced line as a whole may stand at any given moment, for every half-hour brings news that this or that village is in our hands, or that an airman has seen the khaki figures somewhere where we never dreamed that they had reached.'[100] He concluded:

> All this means something—and something very fine. The Army is doing its job. It is an enormous fact that there should be in this universe confidence in all the men in their fellows, and—what is often overlooked—it implies that over all there is extremely competent Staff work and organization going on. It is an old theme, but I doubt whether even yet the Empire understands how fine its armies are.

Harry and the other correspondents followed the Allied advance eastwards in October, resulting in the liberation of Lille. Harry was the first correspondent to reach the city, which had been occupied by the Germans since October 1914. 'It is all true', he reported in a *Times* exclusive on October 17. 'I have returned, after being in Lille for some three hours and having had experiences as extraordinary and moving as possible for a man to go through.'[101] On his journey to Lille he was shocked at how depleted the farms and villages were. 'Though towns themselves are fairly whole, they have been looted of all moveables', he observed. 'Even heavy furniture has been taken away by the human locusts.' He encountered many German prisoners, 'quite ready for surrender and expecting us, with all the rations they can scrape together and their kits packed as if coming on leave'. In Lille, Harry found himself surrounded by a throng of civilians who showered him with kisses—and mistook him for a general:

> The streets for miles were a surging mass of people, chiefly men and women, who had been waiting, nearly delirious with anticipation, since the Germans had gone in the darkness of the early morning. A rumour spread that I was 'the English General,' though whether Sir Douglas Haig, General Birdwood, or General Haking I do not know. It was useless to deny it, for who could argue with a hundred thousand people mad with joy, and on me was poured all the gratitude for its deliverance of the population which has suffered so much through four years.[102]

Harry added that he was draped with tricolour flags and streamers, and 'Fifty times I must with difficulty have saved babies, thrust at me to be touched or kissed, from being trampled under foot. The women struggled to touch or kiss some part of one hand or cheek or clothes—it did not matter.' Harry had never received such attention.

Harry wrote to Geoffrey Dawson on November 10, seeking guidance: 'Have you any especial instructions in case the armistice is signed—as presumably it is about to be?'[103] One senses that Harry wanted to go home, but he was told to follow the Allies into Germany for the occupation. When the Armistice was signed, he was outside Sedan, Belgium, near where he began his service four years earlier. 'It was a marvellous sight and a wonderful memory, and oh, we were glad!' Harry reported on November 12, although the troops made no public demonstration. 'They just stopped firing, and there was no cheering and no excitement. The four years' struggle was over. The four years' noise was at an end. That was all. There was nothing to do except to be glad, and they were glad.'[104] The following day, Harry recorded the sense of disbelief. 'It is all very hard to grasp', he admitted. 'There is an uncanny silence in the air, and it dawns on one that the "tin hat" and gas mask, which have been one's invariable companions for so long, have suddenly assumed the character of souvenirs.'[105] With peace emerged more stories from survivors of German brutality, particularly to English prisoners in Mons. 'More than one saw, only a fortnight ago, an English prisoner shot because he was seen accepting bread from a Belgian woman', Harry continued. 'Another thick-set, black-browed man of the working type cried unaffectedly in describing how English soldiers fell and died from sheer hunger.' Harry offered a strong condemnation of the enemy. 'It must be made impossible for the world to forget what, underneath its veneer of civilization, the German character really is. Many will plead that this will only serve to keep alive hatred. They do not know or understand. Hatred here is necessary and righteous.' Harry's own animus for Germans would not wane, even in peacetime.

In Ghent, Harry reported on November 14 on the triumphal entry of King Albert ('Hardly in my life have I heard such a roar of welcome') and continued to receive reports of German mistreatment. 'But how the people hate the Germans!' he wrote. 'There was the same system of requisitions, fines, imprisonments, and petty persecutions here as elsewhere.'[106] Harry added that 'the German robberies in Ghent have a personal interest for me'. It seems in 1914 Harry left a Gladstone bag in the Hôtel de la Poste, and it was 'bricked up in a cellar' for safekeeping. 'Unhappily, the Germans broke through and opened the bag, and cleaned it of everything of value. I have the bag again, and why they left me so much good leather when it is so scarce I do not understand.'

As instructed, Harry headed east, following the victorious British Army into Germany. He dispatched two postcards to Brad in Cornwall: one, on November 25, from France ('Wish you could see British troops marching across the plain of Waterloo.'); the other, on December 10, from Germany ('I am really sending this card from Cologne which is really on the Rhine! And I <u>do</u> believe I can start back now in a week.'). On

Figure 22. War correspondents stand victorious in Cologne, Germany, on December 16, 1918, after war's end: Percival Phillips, Harry, Philip Gibbs, and William Beach Thomas.

December 16, he reported, 'The curtain has gone up on the last scene of the great drama. This morning the British cavalry crossed the Rhine... Now truly in thankfulness can one pray *Nunc dimittis.*'[107] Harry was bursting with pride. 'Never in all this advance have I seen our troops marching through towns without being struck anew with their splendid looks and bearing, and never have I seen them look finer than to-day.' On

December 17, he paid tribute to the British Army's modesty in victory. 'One can imagine with what pomp the Germans would have surrounded the crossing, let us deprecatingly say, of the Thames', he wrote. 'We do these great things with singularly little fuss, but in their very simplicity and forthright workmanlikeness there is a unique majesty.'[108]

On December 16, Field Marshal Haig assembled the British and Allied war correspondents on the Hohenzollern Bridge, standing beneath the imposing statue of Kaiser Wilhelm II (depicted, Harry wrote on December 18, 'in all his pompousness as War Lord, with his head still turned away from the unpleasant scene going on below'[109]). Harry noted that four of the original five British war correspondents were present: William Beach Thomas, Philip Gibbs, Percival Phillips, and himself, all of whom, he reminded readers, 'had come to the front in August, 1914, and who have been associated with the British Armies in France through all fighting of the last three years'. Haig singled out 'you of the British Press from the beginning of the struggle have carried out your work with complete success. Your despatches have helped to give hope and courage to our families at home and to enlighten the public as to the magnitude of Great Britain's effort in the great cause of Freedom.' He continued:

> Gentlemen, in no previous war have the relations between the Army and the Press been so entirely satisfactory. Perhaps that is one reason why we are at this moment standing on one of the bridges of the RHINE. This is a great moment in the history of the world. I hope that henceforward your efforts may tend towards eternal peace and universal goodwill, and to the still closer union of the peoples represented by the noble soldiers whose deeds in these battlefields you have so ably chronicled.

Harry Nevinson recalled the scene in Cologne. 'Haig had all the correspondents gathered at the entrance to the great Kaiser Bridge over the Rhine, and delivered us a little speech in his best halting English manner, but, in the best English manner also, he inserted at the end the duty of concluding a fair and honourable peace without thought of vengeance', he wrote. 'He then presented each of us with a tiny Union Jack attached to a stick of firewood, so that we withdrew proud as school children after a feast.'[110]

Far away in Cornwall, Florence and Brad marked the end of the war as did many in Britain. 'The tiny ancient church in the middle of St Enodoc golf course has (or had) one very small bell which could just be heard as far away as the 11th green', he recalled. 'We had rung the bell, my mother and I, when war was declared in August 1914, and we rang that bell for peace on November 11, 1918.'[111]

7

World Traveller, 1919–1922

Harry emerged from the First World War with an even higher profile but with broken health. He turned 59 in November 1918, and was praised as one of the leading reporters of *The Times*. But the war took its toll, and one could trace a steady decline in his already-diminished constitution over the next decade. According to Brad, 'Naturally enough, the war did not do my father's health any good. He was in his 60th year before he got home, and his lungs were never much good thereafter.'[1] Indeed, as 1919 dawned Harry was under a doctor's care, in bed with lumbago at the Royal Court Hotel in Sloane Square. 'A poor beginning!' he wrote in his diary. Brad fared no better, as he had chicken pox, and Florence was mourning the death of her brother, Joseph.

With the end of the war Harry presented something of a challenge for *The Times*. As a writer and reporter he had few rivals, but given his shaky health his assignments had to be handled with care. Harry could have served the rest of his career at a desk at Printing House Square, writing and editing copy. But his usual wanderlust would not permit that, nor his hankering to cover grand projects. Besides, Harry was never the stay-at-home family man, much to the regret of his son (and probably his wife, too). So, after a brief visit to France, attending the Armistice Commission meetings and seeing General Pershing, Harry sat down in April 1919 with his superiors at *The Times*. 'I turned my back on the War', Harry recalled, and 'asked not to be sent back to the Rhine'. But travelling the world was still appealing, and Harry 'begged to be allowed to do the Fourth of July Number'.[2] This was a brand new annual supplement dedicated to the United States, tailor-made for Harry. He knew his health would not withstand the rigours of post-war Europe, and wanted to renew his decades-old conviction that the United States and the United Kingdom, together, held the keys to world peace, as shown in their wartime alliance. Northcliffe agreed, convinced that, despite problems with the Treaty of Versailles and its reluctance to join the League of

Nations, America still represented the future. And so, in May 1919, Harry set sail for America.

* * * * *

Harry explained his rationale for the new American Number in a letter to *Times* manager, William Lints Smith. 'Even before the war—long before it—I have persistently maintained that the most important thing in the world for us, next to the consolidation of the Empire within itself, was our relations with the United States', he wrote. 'If anybody doubted the fact before the war, they cannot doubt now.' Barely a decade had passed since the publication of *Twentieth Century American*. Harry insisted that *The Times* should vigorously renew its promotion of the cause in peacetime. 'Not only must we take the lead in it, but the American people must be made to know that we are taking the lead', he continued.

> English friendship (or enmity) is going to be the pre-eminent topic in American politics in the near future. It is almost so now—inextricably mixed up with the Irish question. Our work on the Irish question, in connexion with the American Number, has placed us in a commanding position in America, *so far as that position is known over there*. But we must make it universally known, especially in the West. We must do it, first, because it is just one of those great Causes, which it is the business of *The Times* to champion. We must do it no less for our own profit.[3]

Harry (who had written to Lints Smith after the first American Number was published) was nothing if not forward-thinking. According to *The History of The Times*, 'the instruction of British public opinion regarding the United States, which was an essential element of editorial policy after Versailles, was carried forward in the City pages and trade *Supplements*... the pivot was the importance of true information about American policy in the post-war world'.[4]

Harry sailed from Liverpool on May 7 on the S.S. *Orduña* to New York, via Halifax, skirting the edge of a hurricane. On board he played bridge with the Captain and was pleased to be 'in mufti' instead of khaki for a change. Landing in New York, he embarked on a whirlwind tour, visiting Washington, Chicago, and Minneapolis. His mission was to enlist prominent men in the world of politics, business, and the arts to write authoritative articles for this new supplement. He worked closely with Arthur Willert, still *Times* correspondent in Washington. Harry arrived back in England on June 20 and headed to Ashmore. 'No servants, but very good to be at home', he wrote in his diary. For the next two weeks Harry worked on the American Number, not completing the project until 8:00 p.m. on July 2. The following day, Harry was

'Utterly idle all day. Very tired!' Then on July 4, 'American Number published. Seems all right.'

The twenty-two-page supplement featured fourteen pages of articles, bookended by eight lucrative pages of advertisements from companies doing business in the United States. Harry set the tone with the leading article, noting a new relationship between the United States and the British Empire had emerged from the war, and with it came an enormous responsibility. 'That responsibility is nothing less than the preservation of the peace of the world', Harry wrote. 'With or without the League of Nations, there is no ignoring that it is upon the cooperation of the English-speaking peoples—always strengthened by the association of France—that the maintenance of that peace chiefly rests. Happily, the old tie of blood relationship and of the common inheritance of the same principles and the same ideals still persists to hold us together.'[5] Needless to say, Harry was putting a sunny face on America's post-war stance that was far from ideal. Reinforcing this mission were 'Messages of Greeting and Good Will' in support of 'closer friendship between the English-speaking peoples' received from former President William Howard Taft, Sir Douglas Haig, and Samuel Gompers, among others.

The American Number was comprehensive in its topics, including American finance (A. Barton Hepburn, chairman of Chase National Bank, predicted New York would rival London as the world's banking centre), agriculture, the flour industry (by Harry's old friend, William C. Edgar), prohibition ('Nothing at the moment—not even the Peace Treaty and the League of Nations—occupies so large a place in the minds of the American public as the question of prohibition', Harry wrote), labour unions, immigration, and even the prospect of transatlantic aviation ('Here we stand at the threshold of a new era', predicted Major-General J. B. Seely, war hero). Owen Wister, the popular novelist, mused on the growing acquaintanceship between the two countries despite feuds of old. 'George the Third is more alive with us than with you', Wister wrote. 'It is our school histories that have been keeping his memory green.' Harry certainly knew this from his own experience. Assistant Secretary of the Navy (and future president) Franklin D. Roosevelt wrote on the friendship between the British and American fleets. Of 'the splendid spirit of cooperation', Roosevelt wrote, 'I never doubted for one minute that it would exist from the minute we were able to take our part in the war'.

Regarding the 'Irish Question', which Harry labelled 'Our Chief Stumbling Block', he acknowledged that 'Americans, as well as Irish-Americans, always have been Home Rulers'. Displaying extraordinary fairness, he invited an unnamed Irish contributor to express the

American view on Irish republicanism and the Sinn Fein movement. Harry devoted an entire page to this angry rant, although he did preface it with a note of caution:

> The article, it may be argued, is in some senses manifestly based upon unfair premises. It ignores the fact that the settlement of the Irish difficulty is now essentially an Irish problem, and that, so far as having been indifferent to Ireland during the war, nearly all Englishmen are now Home Rulers and ready to accept and bless any tolerable settlement that the Irish can produce for the political and religious difficulties of their community. It is precisely that sort of omission which gives the article its value as a presentment of American opinion.

A ray of hope for American readers, perhaps, as the Anglo-Irish Treaty was still two years away.

The American Number was favourably noticed in the United States, furthering the aims of both Harry and Northcliffe. 'When the London Times extends hands across the sea, it does so with both hands, and they are strong, beefy British palms', noted the *St. Louis Post-Dispatch*. On July 23, the *Minneapolis Tribune*, Harry's old paper, said this was the first time a foreign newspaper marked the anniversary of the Declaration of Independence in such a fashion. 'This is another result of the war', the paper observed. 'It probably never would have occurred to anybody before the war to do a thing of this kind.' Harry was given full credit. 'Mr. Robinson was just the man to originate and carry through an idea of this kind. He lived long enough in the United States, in one of the great nerve centers (an American daily newspaper office) to have come closely in touch with American life and American affairs.'

*   *   *   *   *

With the inaugural American Number a success, Harry's star continued to rise. Mindful to keep expenses in check (although he always lived above his means), Harry put his Ashmore home on the market after eight years, and moved the family into a flat in Earl's Court. In his memoir, Brad claimed this was done to cut Harry's commute between Sydenham Hill and Printing House Square in the City, although the new route was not that much shorter. In August, he sat down with Lints Smith, who offered him a new assignment: U.S. West Coast correspondent, based in California, which was experiencing a boom. Not surprisingly, Harry turned it down. 'Let me say first that no one could be other than grateful for and flattered by the proposal which you made to me yesterday', Harry wrote to Lints Smith on August 26, 1919. 'At the same time, the proposal distresses me, because I do not see how, under it, I could go to America;

nor, if I did go, could I begin to do the good work that I have dreamed of doing there.'[6] The issue came down to, as it always did, money. The £1,000 salary offered by *The Times* would no longer be sufficient, Harry claimed, as he had to pay for Brad's schooling and life insurance premiums, not to mention income tax arrears (not certain why), and little would be left over for Florence and himself, especially at American prices. Harry would have to supplement his income by writing for American publications and giving lectures. 'It would mean a harassing and hard life', he predicted. 'And the worst of it is that it would make me neglect The Times work.' Harry insisted, however, that he was not ready for retirement. 'To go somewhere and sit down as an invalid, taking no share in the tremendous work that is going on—is a thing against which my whole soul and being rebel', he wrote. 'Purely as a matter of health, I believe that active and hard work is the best thing for me—provided that I am in the right kind of winter climate.' He proceeded to offer a counter-proposal which had three parts. First, given the success of the American Number, Harry wished to start work on the next one. 'I am not sure that any one in the Office understands how very important and how very profitable it can be', he said. 'It alone will pay my (or anybody else's) expenses several times over.' Second, he wanted to return in earnest to reviewing books for the *Literary Supplement* ('less important but quite worth doing from the business point of view'). Lastly, he liked the idea of being an American correspondent again, but did not want to move there, nor be tied down to one specific region such as California:

I propose to go to as many places as possible in the Middle and Further West, meeting the right people and talking to the newspapers (they are extremely glad to be talked to by a War Correspondent of The Times), writing whatever articles I can and ensuring that they are reproduced or discussed in the local papers. It is all very easy; but won't do itself unless somebody goes and does it. Everywhere I would talk of the greatness of The Times and what we are doing for Anglo-American relations and for the Irish question and why... The real returns to the paper will be in the increased prestige in the United States as a whole (I mean not merely in New York and the East) and in the business revenue which will ultimately come out of it.

Harry's proposal is somewhat odd, since his similar stint as a roving American correspondent in 1910–11 ended abruptly and was not a success. What changed? And now, he calculated that he would need £2,000 in salary and expenses to do this job properly—£1,000 more than he was offered in 1910. 'I want to do this thing. I want to prove its value and I do so because I believe it is a bigger opportunity to do really great work for the paper than I or anybody has had—either in the War or elsewhere', he wrote. 'Seriously, this letter will at least show how much in earnest I am. A man does not demur at such a proposal as yours and <u>ask</u> to be given hard work unless he is very keen on his job.' And expects first-class travel and accommodations.

Clearly, this was an ambitious plan, but as the star war correspondent Harry knew he was arguing from a position of strength. Lints Smith responded on August 28 and expressed general agreement, but put the final decision to *Times* director Sir Campbell Stuart. Sir Campbell, however, accepted only part of Harry's proposal. Yes, he could work on the next American Number, and yes he could work in a more suitable climate: if not California, then perhaps another booming region, the French Riviera. But absolutely no more money would be forthcoming.[7] Harry was bound to be disappointed, but his new assignment was a plum. The Riviera, which Queen Victoria had established as the leading holiday centre for the British well-to-do[8] (and therefore *Times* readers), was rebounding after the war. Harry and Florence could live in a salubrious environment over the cold winter months, which would certainly benefit both their constitutions. Harry agreed, and in early November, after receiving the Chevalier of the Legion d'Honneur decoration awarded by the French Republic for his services during the war, he set off for his new home in France.

If Harry's first article from the Riviera, 'Southward Ho! From London to Monte Carlo', published in *The Times* on November 14, 1919 is any indication, he was thoroughly delighted by his new situation (who wouldn't be?). 'As you come to Monte Carlo, the sun is sinking; and the sea is dark purple, the sky clear blue above the horizon, then flushed with rose to the zenith', he wrote. 'Somewhere a bugle is blowing, and less than 24 hours behind you are the slime and sheets of rain, the flapping mackintoshes and soaked umbrellas, of Paris.'[9] The fine weather is a constant mention in Harry's dispatches. 'While the papers tell us daily of snow and rain in Paris and over nearly the whole of France, the Riviera is bathed in unbroken sunshine', he wrote on November 18. 'All day long the sky is blue—the blue of a starling's egg in the morning and of a thrush's egg at noon—and the coast is waking up to its first real season since the beginning of the war.'[10] No wonder a disgruntled reader wrote, 'The gentleman who tells us each week in The Times how the sun is blazing down on him in the Riviera does wisely to remain anonymous, for there must be many envious people tempted to murder him, and none perhaps more so than golfers.'[11]

Harry's daily routine now consisted of travelling between Monte Carlo and Nice, reporting on the towns along the way, thankful that the years of 'hospitals and convalescents and batches of Allied troops—especially Americans—on leave' are over, and making note of the celebrity visitors from Lloyd George to the Shah of Persia. His contempt for Germans continued. 'Hotels have no desire to receive German guests',[12] Harry noted on December 4. 'They would, in any case, be a trifle out of place in the celebration of a Victory season. But Germans were never conspicuously pleasant or well-mannered company at the Casino tables or in the restaurants.' Indeed, Harry offered this holiday message on December 19: 'It would not be a bad Christmas toast for most of the places on the Riviera, Italian or French: "To Absent Enemies : long may they remain so!"'[13] It was not meant to be.

* * * * *

Despite the fine weather, Harry was sick in bed in his Cannes hotel on Christmas Day. 'Nearly burned hotel down with electric hot (water) bottle', he wrote in his diary. 'Everything on bed burned to lower mattress.' Florence joined her husband on January 3, 1920, and promptly fell ill (of course), taking to her bed. A few days later, she was well enough for a visit to Monte Carlo. 'To casino for ½ hour to let F. lose 50 fr.', Harry wrote in his diary. They joined a tennis club, as Florence was quite the player, entering a tournament before falling ill (again) and heading to bed (again).[14]

On March 12, 1920, Harry had momentous news from the Home Office: a knighthood, awarded to him and his fellow war correspondents for their outstanding service. On March 31, John Walter IV, proprietor and chairman of *The Times*, congratulated Harry in a handwritten letter. 'Few war correspondents can have worked harder than you during the last 5 years, and none can have kept more closely to the truth or told it in more delightful fashion', he wrote. 'I am sure that all our friends at Printing House Square will have seen with keen satisfaction that the value of your work is so well appreciated in official quarters.'[15] Harry was one of only 108 Knight Commanders named among the 5,600 Civilian War Honours announced. The *Daily Mail,* announcing the honours on March 31, praised Harry: 'His lucid and vivid description of the different historic phases of the Battle of the Somme are classed among the best literature concerning the tremendous battle.'[16] Making his way north to Paris and on to London, Harry was delighted to be addressed as 'Sir Harry' during a stop in Toulouse.

On April 20, Harry sailed for New York on the S.S. *Vasari* to begin work on the second American Number. Bad weather en route meant a very slow crossing. '14 days at sea!' Harry lamented. 'I've written nearly

100 letters.' Once in New York, he spoke at a dinner of the Council on Foreign Relations at the Hotel Astor, which was covered by the *New York Times* on May 12. 'Sir H. Perry Robinson declared that Americans were never so unpopular in Continental Europe and so little popular in England as they were today',[17] the paper noted. Harry's explanation was quoted in full:

> There are three chief reasons for this unpopularity. First, Europe feels that the United States has not carried out their hopes, which the visit of President Wilson to Europe promised. When President Wilson arrived in Europe it was believed he would set the world in order. That hope has not been fulfilled. The President, it is believed, did his best to carry out his promises.

> In England your unpopularity is largely due to the Irish agitation in the United States. I know that that is being caused by a very small group of Americans.

> Then you are beastly rich. I remarked an example of that when a taxi-driver pulled up his trousers and showed me his socks, saying: 'Those socks cost me $3.25 a pair and they are not worth $1.50.' If a London taxi-driver said that he had paid 15 shillings for his socks, we would say that was preposterous.

The *Times* article was syndicated in newspapers across America, and reaction to Harry's remarks was negative. 'Professedly he is so enthusiastic about us that he describes himself as in spirit more than half American', noted *The Evening News* of Harrisburg, Pennsylvania. 'But whatever may prove to be the effect upon the British lion of his firecrackers in the Times, his present words of cheer sound like the explosion of a bomb beneath the tall feathers of our national bird.'[18] Recounting his taxicab story and the implied accusation of war profiteering, the paper added, 'When he said all this he doubtless smiled; but no ripple of that mirth survives in cold type.' The *English Speaking World* journal, 'published monthly in the interest of American and British unity' and based in New York, was even more critical in its June 1920 edition. 'In other words, we who crossed the sea for pure, neighborly sentiment to save European nations from being burned down to the ground and to help drive away the thugs who were robbing and murdering them, are to blame because we were not also burnt out', the journal said. 'America has asked no compensation, no recognition of rights beyond the privilege of being a friend in need to our neighbors in distress.'[19] Surely Harry would have been distressed that his words were so misunderstood. His remarks even made headlines Down Under. *The Catholic Press* of New South Wales, Australia, on August 5 expanded on Harry's remarks about the Irish. 'Sir Harry urged the suppression of Irish news on the part of the correspondents of the foreign papers as the surest way to settle the Irish question', the paper reported. If true (and it sounds like something Harry, vehemently opposed to Home Rule, would have said), it provoked quite a response:

> One of the correspondents present at that dinner had the manhood to rise in protest against such a suggestion. He declared that he must take exception to the advice of Sir Harry, and that he could not understand how Englishmen could talk about their Magna Charta [*sic*] and in the same breath ask that even the news be smothered in Ireland. He warned the British propagandists of what England suffered in the opinion of the civilised world, from the fact that the news of the Indian massacre had been suppressed for nine months, to her eternal dishonour.

It is intriguing that the *New York Times* did not report this exchange.

No doubt thankful to leave New York, Harry headed to Chicago, then Minneapolis, where he lunched with William C. Edgar and was interviewed by the *Minneapolis Tribune*. 'Former Resident, Now British Knight, Sees Brighter Future for Railroads', ran the headline on May 21, 1920. The article noted that Harry married the daughter of the late Thomas Lowry in 1891, but still neglected to mention the divorce and his

Figure 23. Harry and Florence in Dunster, Somerset, 1922. Harry was 63 years old; Florence, 44.

remarriage. 'There was probably no one man who saw first-hand as much of the great World war as he',[20] the article continued. Not having learned his lesson in New York, Harry harped on about American prices again:

> Sir Harry, at the Minneapolis club yesterday, said that the high prices in this country are terrifying to an Englishman. 'The whole scale of prices here,' he said, 'is very much higher than in England. Wages are found to be extremely high in this country, For instance, a good house cook in England receives $5 a week and that is considered an extremely high wage.' He was impressed with bountiful food supplies found in America. 'More butter has been put before me in a fortnight than I have seen in the last five years,' he said. 'It is delightful,' he added, 'to have sliced bananas before you over which one can pour good rich cream and cover generously with powdered sugar out of a bowl—it's perfectly intoxicating.'[21]

Harry returned to England on June 7, and on June 25, with Florence by his side, he went to Buckingham Palace to be knighted by King George V.[22] They attended several parties that day, then caught a performance of 'Chu-Chin-Chow', the popular musical comedy based on *Ali Baba and the Forty Thieves*.

*   *   *   *   *

Despite the change in his financial situation, and concerns with his own family, Harry was still sought out by his siblings for assistance, as he was the sensible, dependable one. As he prepared to head to Scotland for a summer holiday with Florence and Brad, his eldest (and now widowed) sister, Agnes Hesketh-Biggs, wrote, expressing alarm over their still-troubled sister Valence. With Phil gone, Mary in South Africa, and Kay a penniless squire living in the country, the burden fell on Harry to come to the rescue, yet again. Valence, now 67, was living on her own in London, but dependent upon her siblings for support. 'What can be done for Valence!' Agnes wrote on July 19, 1920. 'If one sends her money, of course, by her own confession, some of it goes in drugs, jaunts, etc.— never in clothes, or necessaries! When I send her clothes she sells all she can.' These included a 'lovely winter coat' ('I longed to keep it for myself—but did not actually need it—so sent it'), a 'lovely silk jumper' ('I had worn it two summers, but it was as good as new'); and even one of Agnes' ivory-backed hairbrushes ('Where is it? She says she has no brush.'). Apparently wealthy Aunt Margaret Pennington had stepped in. 'The "lawyer" through Aunt Pennington forbade me to send her anything convertible into money—but she must have clothes!' Agnes continued. 'I can't help sending what seems necessaries—if she sells these, what can I do?' Agnes pleaded with Harry to speak to Aunt Margaret and her lawyers about this. 'You <u>don't know</u> what a load she has been to us for many years! I wish she could be placed in a Home! It would be the <u>best</u> end, the <u>happiest</u> thing for her! I am far too ill to live with her (as Kay considers <u>my duty</u> to be).' Agnes worried about Valence's mental state. 'She has a much stronger will than I!' she wrote. 'I did spend <u>very much</u> of my time in London with her, she told me she heard voices telling her to <u>kill me</u>. I can <u>never</u> get over the fear and dread of that!' And then there was the drinking:

> Another time when walking with her in London she asked me to buy her some things and while I was paying for them she stepped out of the shop into the dark street. When I went out I could see her nowhere—and as I was turning the corner the door of a pub opened to let someone out and there I saw Valence at the bar drinking! I cried 'Valence!' and she laughed—but the other people moved out of her way and looked shocked.

In a second letter, Agnes added to the story. Apparently the allowance from Aunt Margaret was paid directly to Valence's landlord. 'Can that be true! How can Valence live? Or dress?' she asked. Agnes suspected the strategy was 'to bring her to that point where she will be led into a Home and they hope—but—if I know Valence she never will! In <u>all</u> my letters I beg her to do so! Oh! I wish with all my heart she would!' She repeated her plea to Harry to investigate. 'If you could <u>see</u> her and the lawyer— and find out what he is doing—or wishes to do—and what <u>you</u> think, I should be so glad. It is such a tax on me sending her clothes—indeed many other things—but she <u>must have clothes</u>!'

Did Harry intervene and meet with the lawyer? Was Valence sent to a home? Did Harry continue to offer financial support? No one knows, although Harry did not invite Valence to stay in his home. An oft-told family tale had Valence descending further into madness and fleeing England for Africa, specifically Bulawayo, in present-day Zimbabwe. There she lived quite happily in a barrel on the roadside, greeting passers-by. It's a fantastic, Kipling-esque tale but also quite untrue. Valence died in June 1927, aged 74, in Blean, Kent, quite alone, one assumes.

Preoccupations with Valence did not detract from Harry's summer holiday in Scotland, which was also a working vacation. 'Never before, according to all authorities, was there such a rush to Scotland as has been going on the past 10 days and promises to continue for some time yet', he wrote from Edinburgh in *The Times* on August 4. 'The result, in the tumult of barbarians thus ejected upon them, the Scotsmen accept with tolerant equanimity.'[23] A pleasant travelogue proceeded. 'Strawberries still linger much more abundantly in the shops here than in London.

Also we have 38 minutes more of daylight than you.' He predicted on August 7 that 'Edinburgh will surely have its Parliament again before long', but that it would be a peaceful process. 'There is no danger that, at least in any measurable span of years, the Scottish desire for Home Rule could ever lead to such straits as those into which we have been led in Ireland.'[24] Indeed not. As he travelled about Scotland, he played a lot of golf and ate a lot of pheasant, visiting castles and battlefields and admiring flora and fauna. He lamented at the crowds and the roads choked with motor traffic, including 'sharrabangs', Scottish dialect for a motor coach. 'Certainly there are an astonishing number of motor-cars on the roads', Harry observed on August 21. 'To sit for seven hours or so on the seat of a crowded "sharrabang" must be a pleasure difficult to take other than sadly.'[25]

A curious article by Harry appeared in *The Times Woman's Supplement* (a twice-monthly publication akin to a magazine) published on August 18, 1920. Entitled 'Why not Polo and Racquets? Fresh Conquests Still to be Made and Prejudices to be Overcome by Women in the Athletic World', the article showed Harry to be an equal-opportunity sportsman. Noting that not so long ago ankles had to be covered and women's play was considered immoral, Harry reported that 'since then both women and their skirts have risen in the world'.[26] He had special praise for the French tennis star Suzanne Lenglen (who won Wimbledon in 1919) and the English golfer Charlotte Leitch. 'It will not be surprising if within a dozen years a lady should win the gold championship and another lady arise whom even the best men will not be able to beat at lawn tennis', Harry predicted, no doubt mindful of his own wife's prowess. While football and hockey were thought to be unlikely sports for women due to their violent nature ('It is the physical promiscuousness—the contact of bodies—that revolts'), Harry considered lacrosse 'the field game *par excellence* for ladies'. Then there was polo, where he noted the horses do most of the work. 'There is no apparent reason why women should not produce first-class polo teams— just as, a generation hence, crack jockeys may all be women.' The future was bright, so long as prejudice was overcome. 'As a rule, women are naturally better public speakers than men, largely because women are not equally embarrassed by the publicity', Harry concluded. 'They are accustomed to being looked at. Most of them have been taught from childhood that it is what they are chiefly for.' A sexist remark, granted, but made by a proto-feminist.

Oddly, Harry was not chosen by *The Times* to travel to Antwerp to cover the Olympic Games held in August and September 1920, the first Olympiad since 1912. This may have been at Harry's request, given his experience in Antwerp. Or perhaps his bosses did not want to risk another controversy in his coverage. As it happened, Britain once again placed a distant third in the medal count, behind the United States and Sweden.

*   *   *   *   *

Back in London at the end of September, Florence had surgery for an unknown ailment on September 28. Since she was now Lady Robinson, her predicament made the Court Circular of *The Times* the next day. 'Lady Perry Robinson underwent an operation in a nursing home in London yesterday, and was reported last night to be progressing satisfactorily.' Harry visited her daily for the next month, until her return home on October 26.

For Armistice Day on November 11, 1920 Harry wrote a moving article on 'The Unknown Warrior', a soldier from France whose remains were taken in procession through the London streets on the way to interment in Westminster Abbey. This article was an instant classic and was reprinted many times over the next few years. 'Unknown? His name, indeed, and where he comes from now: such things, perhaps, we do not know, nor do we need to inquire', Harry wrote. 'But him we know, and did know well through four long, terrible, and splendid years. We knew him as he came home on leave... we knew him over there, in his billets... we knew him in the trenches, in the slime and mud and ankle deep in ice-cold water... and he died in many places.'

> All the honour that we can pay him is little for what he did for us. He earned more Victoria Crosses than ever were given to the living. He goes through the streets this morning not as a lowly one uplifted, but as a conqueror and of right. With the grief with which we bow our heads in silence there are mingled rejoicing and gratitude and peace. To future generations the grave to which he is borne will not be a monument of sorrow or the mere tomb of one unfortunate, but the very symbol of strength and gentleness and love of the Justice of the Empire.[27]

Harry received a fan letter from the editor of *The Times*, Henry Wickham Steed. 'In the rush of the last two days I have neglected to congratulate you upon and thank you for your most excellent article on the Unknown Warrior, as I meant to do on the night it was published', he wrote on November 12. 'It is, alongside of the review of Mrs. Asquith's book, one of the finest things we have had in the Paper for a long time. It has been very generally admired and commented upon. So please accept my thanks in the name of all the editorial staff for your splendid work.'[28]

Harry returned to the Riviera, alone, on November 30, where the holiday season was in full swing. On New Year's Eve, he concluded in his diary, 'A goodish, less broken year.' He also listed a number of poems which, he claimed, 'during the year 1920 I have learned by heart, using only the time while undressing at night'. These included:

Francis Thompson, 'The Hound of Heaven' (1893)
Rupert Brooke, 'The Old Vicarage, Grantchester' (1912)
John Milton, 'Lycidas' (1638)
Thomas Gray, 'Elegy Written in a Country Churchyard' (1751)
John Keats, 'Ode to a Nightingale,' 'To Autumn,' and *La Belle Dame sans Merci*' (1820)
Percy Bysshe Shelley, 'Ode to the West Wind' (1820)
Lord Byron, 'The Isles of Greece' (1819)

This was a romantic mix bordering on realism and, as Harry's grandson-in-law (and poet) William Wyndham noted, 'another symptom of his iron self-discipline'.

Harry continued to cast a quizzical and often humorous eye on the Riviera, its people, and customs. On January 17, 1921, he wrote of the game of *la boule* as 'a sad pleasure of the Riviera'. Unlike roulette, this game was played with a larger ball that was spun around a static wheel. '*Boule* is the game played chiefly in casinos on the Riviera where roulette is not permitted', he explained. 'It is a lugubrious game, the players being depressed by the knowledge that the odds are so overwhelmingly against them. That it finds players at all is amazing testimony to the human inability to resist any game of so-called chance.'[29] He concluded, 'At least it can be said of *boule* that it probably never drove a man to suicide. He might lose his temper so as to speak impolitely to his wife or lose his appetite for tea. That is as far as it could go. It is one of the sadder pleasures of the gay Riviera—as impassioned as a cold muffin. As between *boule* and spillikins, for mad excitement give me spillikins.' On March 7, he feasted on *ghianchetti*, whitebait harvested once a year on the Italian Riviera. Harry called it 'an ethereal food which ought to nourish sea-nymphs and young mermaids ... One brief month will seem altogether too short a season for it. But the law is right. Some of the fry must be allowed to grow up, or the world would be left without sardines, a thought to shudder at.'[30]

When not sampling the local delicacies, Harry chronicled the mounting opposition on the Italian Riviera to German tourists, now returning in droves to Bordighera, a favourite holiday spot before the war. Harry's dislike of all things German had not abated since the war. 'People here are much exercised about the new German offensive which is developing on the Italian Riviera front', he reported on March 9. 'The first objective, or "green line," seems to be Bordighera itself; and the shock troops are already here in some numbers. They are undoubtedly shocking.'[31] The local casino had turned a blind eye to prejudice and welcomed the Germans and their money. 'The Casino is, indeed, to all intents and purposes the enemy G.H.Q.,' Harry reports. 'Italians have been disgusted on gala nights at the spectacle of Germans, who are unable to pay reparations, being the chief consumers of champagne and the most hilarious of the revellers.' Harry proposed a boycott. 'While English guests in an hotel cannot demand that Germans be excluded, they can refuse to go to hotels which admit the enemy. Many who wish to return here next year will doubtless do so, but the general hope among the English is that the leading hotels will of their own accord announce that Germans are not acceptable.' Harry quipped that 'one cannot, unhappily, extirpate Germans, like mosquitoes, by, spraying with paraffin', but suggested that isolation might work. 'Germans can, it is claimed, at least be segregated, as it were, in isolation hospitals—lazarets of their own—from which English visitors can keep away', he wrote. 'The alternative is a continuously increasing German infiltration, disgusting both the English and Italian elements, until Bordighera becomes in the future a veritable Boche salient. But that is unthinkable.'

*   *   *   *   *

No sooner did Florence arrive and start playing in tennis tournaments than Harry left her behind. On March 8 in London, Harry met with Northcliffe, and the following day set sail for New York, to troll for contributions for the next American Number. This time around, Harry's travels took him further afield than his usual stops of Washington, Chicago, and Minneapolis. He visited Memphis, Tennessee, and Kansas City, Missouri, before heading to Colorado Springs. There he stayed with his former in-laws, Nellie and Percy Hagerman, dining twice with Percy at the El Paso Club. Circling back to Washington, Harry visited the British Embassy and lunched with the ambassador, Sir Auckland Geddes. He stopped by the White House for the annual Easter Egg Roll, the first since 1916, hosted by the popular new president, Warren G. Harding, and the First Lady, Florence; more than 50,000 children attended. Harding had a famous 'open door' policy for visitors to the White House, and Harry took full advantage, attending the new president's first press reception on March 25, 1921. Oddly, Harry's article did not appear in *The Times* until a month later, on April 20; perhaps the subject matter was not particularly newsworthy. Harry was struck by the friendliness of Harding as much as the rudeness of his fellow journalists. 'To be the President of the United States the Press must be a terrible thing,' he began.

> The throng surged forward through the passage, as passengers crowd to the gang-plank of a steamer and poured into the President's office. Mr. Harding stood behind his desk, on which was a tall glass vase filled with pink roses, facing us, a vigorous and prepossessing figure. There can be no question as to the new President's good looks.
>
> 'Good morning gentlemen!'—with the smile that is already becoming as famous as Mr. Taft's—'good morning. I'm pleased to see you all. My!'—as the crowd still surged in—'we are increasing, aren't we! I shall have to have a raised dais built back here, so that I can see you fellows behind there. I like to look a man in the face when I talk to him.'
>
> After a good deal of shifting and maneuvering for position, the company had formed itself into a ragged crescent before the desk, reaching from wall to wall of the apartment. A rough count showed that there were about 90 persons present, one being a woman.[32]

Harding, Harry observed, was a deft hander of the press. He announced a conference of the Interstate Commerce Commission and the Railroad Labor Board to discuss the problem of high transportation costs which were threatening the railroad companies with debt. Reporters besieged Harding with specific questions, but he simply smiled.

> Some of the questions were useful; some merely silly; some obvious traps in the hope of drawing an admission of personal views from the President. But steadily, with excellent good humour, he clung to his original point. Neither he nor the Cabinet had any views. They had not considered details. Only the large outlines of the problem had been before them; and they had decided to call a Conference to consider it—a Conference of Government agencies only.

'Mr. Harding's qualities in some directions are still unknown', Harry noted. 'But of his affability and tact there is no question. Gradually the heckling—for such it was—died down, and inquisitiveness expressed itself in new forms.'

> The President is notoriously confronted with a prickly problem in the appointment of members of the Shipping Board. Had any appointments, a voice asked from the crowd, been decided on?
>
> 'Now boys,' said the President with winning friendliness, 'this is a nice, fine morning, bright and sunny; why do you wish to spoil it like that?' A general laugh answered him.
>
> 'Was Mexico discussed at the Cabinet meeting at all?' asked another voice. 'No,' said the President shortly, 'And,' after a pause, 'I am looking you right in the eye when I say it.'

Another laugh, and, after a few more scattering and futile questions, the assembly began to disintegrate. There were no 'Good-byes' and no expressions of thanks to the President. The 90 turned their backs on him and filed out as they had come in, leaving him standing behind the desk and the roses, still smiling. He was justified in smiling, for he had borne himself admirably and had won.

Harry said a lesson was to be learned by the headlines in the newspapers the next day.

As has been said, the Press is a terrible thing. How terrible one could gather next day. It was in a town far from Washington then that in a local paper—a paper which serves an agricultural community—I read the headline splashed in huge letters across the front page: 'Harding says Railroad must reduce Rates.' A wicked, wicked headline, seeing how exactly careful he had been to say nothing of the sort, and when one remembers how high, in these agricultural communities, passion can be made to run against the railroads.

One does not wonder that not all Presidents, or all head of departments, have been able to continue the periodical face-to-face meetings with the representatives of the Press.

An early example of what a future U.S. president would call 'fake news', perhaps? Harry was certainly old school when it came to manners, respect for the office of the president, and truthful reporting.

Harry's travels also took him to Cleveland, Ohio ('Cold @ night has given me lumbago!'), and Detroit, Michigan, where he met Henry Ford. They seemed to hit it off, although Ford was unable to write an article in time for the next American Number (in which Harry observed, '"The world owes me a car" is a common catchword in America nowadays, and we have seen how gasoline may be a normal item in the working man's budget', as the Ford Company had just turned out its five-millionth car). Ford did have his assistant send to Harry the second volume of his booklet series on 'The International Jew', this one titled 'Jewish Activities in the United States'. Ford was a notorious anti-Semite, but there is no evidence that Harry shared his views. The series reprinted articles from Ford's personal newspaper, *The Dearborn Independent*, which chronicled what he called 'the Jewish menace'. Ford would be praised by Adolf Hitler in *Mein Kampf*, published in 1925. In any event, Harry was magnanimous in receiving the booklets, writing to Ford on September 21, 'I am really very pleased to have and shall certainly read.'[33] He expressed his thanks for Ford's hospitality while Harry was in Michigan, and hoped he would write an article for the 1922 American Number (he never did).

Harry was able, however, to obtain a glowing endorsement from President Harding for the third American Number, published on July 4, 1921. Harding may have read Harry's sympathetic article on the president's press conference. 'I congratulate the London *Times* and its proprietors on the liberality of view, no less than the enterprise, which prompt them to celebrate the birthday of American Independence by the publication of a special "Fourth of July Edition,"' Harding wrote. 'In the development of civilization, in the extension over ever-widening areas of the earth's surface of the idea of law as the bedrock of liberty, the two great English-speaking peoples have played a part of immeasurable importance.' Harding praised the efforts of the newspaper to further mutual understanding in the supplement, 'in which American questions will be discussed by eminent Americans'. Such understanding, he believed, 'will prove the surest antidote to that unfortunate irritation which is too often caused by the actually unimportant but sometimes aggravating utterances of thoughtless demagogues and irresponsible agitators'. Harding's call for a National Inter-Racial Commission to combat discrimination and promote equality and advancement was praised.

* * * * *

Harry simply could not resist foreign travel, and if it involved a member of the royal family, he jumped at the opportunity—in this case, the nearly five-month goodwill tour of Edward, Prince of Wales (the future Edward VIII), to India. For Harry, this would have been a poignant visit to the land of his birth, a place he left when he was two years old, yet that continued to resonate in his life and his unwavering devotion to the Empire. It also might have fulfilled a wish to emulate his father, Julian, who accompanied another Prince of Wales, also named Edward, on a similar journey a half-century earlier. This particular visit came at a much more unsettled time in the Subcontinent. Mohandas Gandhi and his followers, encouraged by the recent partition of Ireland, hoped for independence for India by leading a non-violent movement of non-cooperation. 'The royal tour during the winter and spring of 1921–22 was designed to reassure the British people that the heart of the Indian empire remained sound and steadfast in spite of the past two years of protest and order', noted Lawrence James. 'Young, handsome and with a breezy informal manner, the prince would win hearts and stiffen that attachment to the monarchy which was the principal bond that held together a scattered and disparate empire.'[34] This was what the prime minister, David Lloyd George, hoped for when he proposed a series of royal tours around the Empire. *The Times* concurred, previewing the prince's trip with a special India Number on November 17, on which Harry worked for several months. 'The visit of the Prince of Wales to India comes at an appropriate moment, when another great stage in the evolution of a system of self-government for the Indian peoples has been successfully inaugurated and is now being closely tested', the leading article stated. 'No phrase is more misleading than "the changeless East," for as he journeys through the Dependency the Prince will contemplate an India unknown to his grandfather, the first King-Emperor.'[35] The supplement (similar in intention to the 1913 Irish Number) sought to present 'a picture of the India of to-day, to show where it has altered, to indicate the traces of past eras which are still visible, and to place on record a careful exposition of the problems which still await solution'. Articles dealt with politics and industry, as well as art, music, architecture, and literature. Kay contributed an article on wildlife (no doubt grateful to Harry for the paid assignment). 'Mention India to a stranger and he thinks at once of tigers and snakes and perhaps scorpions,' Kay wrote. 'Yet of Europeans in India very few ever see a wild tiger, and many never see either snake or scorpion.'[36]

The prince left Portsmouth on H.M.S. *Renown* on October 26, 1921, and arrived in Bombay on November 17. Harry and a party of distinguished guests left London on October 20, arriving in advance of the prince in Bombay on November 4. Among those on board the S.S. *Kaiser-in-Hind* sailing from Marseilles were Sir Alfred Chatterton, Professor of Engineering at Madras and member of the Indian Industrial Commission; Sir Lancelot Sanderson, Conservative M.P. and cricketer who was Chief Justice of the High Court of Judicature in Calcutta; Professor Patrick Geddes, pioneering town planner who taught at Bombay University; and Sir John George Woodroffe, an Orientalist whose work (as 'Arthur Avalon') spread interest in the West of Hindu philosophy and Yogic practices. Also on board was Indian royalty: Sir Jagatjit Singh Bahadur, the ruling Maharaja (Emperor) of the princely state of Kapurthala and the Indian delegate to the League of Nations.[37]

Harry's coverage of the prince's tour toed a fine line between royal reverence and local unrest. A royalist and imperialist at heart, Harry was anxious to promote the British Empire at its best, but as a reporter he could not overlook disruptions, which he either ignored, downplayed, or tried to place in context. His articles were syndicated locally to newspapers including *The Englishman* in Calcutta. Harry, that paper noted on November 14, 'has been famous in journalism as one of the most brilliant special correspondents, and his work during the war in Belgium, Serbia and the Western Front was probably unequalled. Sir Harry Perry

Robinson has represented The Times in many parts of the world, and since the days when he was Captain of Westminster school he has lived a full, active and varied life.' *The Englishman* noted Harry's family ties to India and said that his brother Kay, who contributed a weekly column, 'is one of the most accomplished naturalists in the world, and Sir Harry Perry Robinson shares with him his deep love for natural history'.

Harry previewed the prince's arrival in Bombay with an article on November 15. 'The streets are lavishly beflagged and practically all the prominent buildings are covered with myriads of little lamps on a network of bamboo scaffolding, which should make the illuminations very beautiful', he wrote. 'Of course, there are splutterings of disloyalty and babble of boycotts, but the well informed do not take them seriously. Here, at least, Mr. Gandhi's influence is unquestionably waning, and Bombay will be loyal.'[38] The next day, he reported on a 'staggering and overwhelming' crowd of half a million people who lined the route to catch a glimpse of 'a single slender figure clad in white, slashed across with the pale blue ribbon of the Star of India'. Harry downplayed the opposition. 'While Bombay was thus demonstrating its tremendous loyalty to the Throne, Mr. Gandhi himself, somewhere in the city, is said to have been assisting at a farcical bonfire of imported clothing.'[39] The following week, as the prince left Bombay, Harry acknowledged that disturbances had cost twenty lives, including one Englishman and one American, but he still dismissed claims of widespread mobs and riots. 'The oratory of Gandhi and his fellow non-cooperators undoubtedly set the spark, but from the first it was the mere ruffianism of bands of hooligans such as are to be found in all great cities with a large industrial population', he observed. 'The whole thing is discreditable to the city of Bombay, but to give it a large political significance is preposterous. No one has said that more clearly than Gandhi. What political effect it has had has been entirely disastrous to the Gandhi party, and if any moral is to be drawn it is of the conditions that are likely to prevail if there is no British authority at hand.'[40] Harry walked a fine line in this reportage; he was careful not to exaggerate and overshadow the prince's visit, but also to remind readers of the importance of British rule. On November 18, Harry visited Government House and was presented to the prince by Lord Cromer, who was in charge of the prince's staff for the royal trip. Harry had met the prince previously during his tour of the Somme battlefields with his father.

At each stop on the prince's royal progress of India, Harry filed enthusiastic reports. He could barely conceal his unwavering devotion to royalty and the Empire. In Poona, the prince dedicated the Mahratta War Memorial to men of the Indian Army who served in Europe. After

Figure 24. Edward, Prince of Wales (second row, centre), and his colourful entourage in Delhi, India, in 1922, during his landmark tour of the Subcontinent. Harry is standing in the rear, circled.

the prince left his state chair, Harry reported 'a touching scene' when the crowd pushed forward to make homage (*poojah*) before the empty seat, 'though the Prince himself did not see it'. At the Poona Races, before the Prince of Wales Steeplechase, the prince broke ranks and proceeded to greet the 'natives', proceeding down the line for nearly half a mile. 'It was a scene of extraordinary enthusiasm. He went amid a tempest of hand-clapping and shouts of *Yuvraj ki jai* (victory to the prince), the whole mass swaying after him', Harry wrote on November 23. 'One doubts if ever before in the history of India either a Ruling Chief or an Emperor's son has thus gone on foot to make himself one with the mass of the people.'[41]

Harry's diary entries offer a glimpse of his personal trials behind the scenes. On November 22 he discharged his servants Gawpat and Kandi because they had lost his pocketbook, which contained the keys to his trunk, which held his dress clothes. As a result, he could not attend the state banquet the next evening. Worse still, the pocketbook contained a £200 letter of credit, his return P&O ticket, and his *Times* credentials. On November 29, he dropped and broke his watch. 'No Keys! No Money!!

No Watch!!!' he lamented. On December 15, his beloved Gladstone bag—rescued from the Western Front—was stolen.

Correspondents like Harry travelled with the prince in a special train by day, and bunked at night along with staff and retinue in a 'Prince of Wales's Camp' set up outside whatever palace the prince lodged in that particular evening. Harry wrote about the elaborate travel arrangements in *The Times* on January 13, 1922. 'One of the wonders of the Prince's tour has been the cities of tents which are put up—"built," one is inclined to say—before we arrive, and, we are told, are generally demolished the day after we have left', he wrote. 'The tents stand on each side of wide streets, laid out at right angles, the ground plan of a veritable town.'[42] Harry was impressed by the lavish appointments inside each tent—roughing it this was not.

> Inside, these canvas villas are lined invariably with printed cotton of a soft ochreous yellow stamped with conventional designs in sepia—a pleasant, restful tone, which has doubtless been arrived at from vast experience. The main room may be 20ft. long by 15ft. wide, and off it open two other smaller rooms: a dressing-room, with dressing table, a chest of drawers, and so forth, and a bathroom. The furnishing of the main apartment—except for the bedstead in the middle—something much more than a camp bed—is that of a comfortably-appointed study at home, with writing table, what-nots, and deep easy-chairs; and on the soft carpeted floor heavy rugs are thrown. I have even had tiger skins. But the rugs are always good, and sometimes rich and costly. The tents are always, and lavishly, electric lighted.

> A camp officer with assistants and a staff of countless servants, with one's own servants, make life luxurious. Motor-cars are always waiting to take one anywhere; messengers to go on any errand. Besides the dwelling tents are a post-office tent, a telegraph-office tent, an inquiry tent, a camp doctor's tent, a central club or drawing-room tent, and mess tents for the various grades of European and Indian members of the population. It is a White City of several hundred souls, spreading over a much wider area than a corresponding settlement of bricks and mortar; and it may be occupied for one single night; then it vanishes again.

Harry admitted that 'the ephemerality of the ordinary canvas cities prompts to moralizing', but 'we shall hardly enjoy such sumptuousness again; for India is the only country where it could be'. He was clearly more delighted than embarrassed.

Regarding the postal arrangements, Harry elaborated on these in an article published on March 7. 'One of the miracles of this tour is the postal organization, and the thaumaturgist is a gentleman of the name of Vas Dev (improbable as that may sound) whose laboratory is a cream-coloured post office on wheels on the Royal train', Harry explained.

'Possibly the words Vas Dev are an abbreviation of some magic formula or he may be a reincarnation of Merlin or Cagliostro or the Witch of Endor. Certainly he has much influence with the powers of darkness.'[43] A stamp enthusiast himself, Harry delighted in recounting the organization:

> We arrive in the early morning at the capital of some Native State, and an hour later, the ceremonies of arrival over, repair to our temporary home in the camp. By the time we get there; propped up on each writing-table stands a neat card printed all in gold, with the Prince of Wales's Feathers for crest at the top, informing us precisely at what hours each day the mails for various parts of India and the world will be collected from the brand-new post pillar erected on our doorstep.

> On the trains at odd hours of night and day similar gold-printed missives, crested and beautiful, flutter in upon us in our compartments informing us that 'if the trains arrive on time,' it is expected to distribute the next English mail on the day after to-morrow at 11 a.m. At 11 a.m. on the appointed day a bowing chuprassi steals silently to your tent door with your share of home letters in his hands.

'It is all magic', Harry concluded. 'In Burma the mail reached us faster than we could calculate that trains and ships could possibly have brought it.'

Harry also wrote about the special postmark. 'We have a really lovely cancellation stamp—postmark if you prefer to call it so—large and circular, with the words "Prince of Wales' Camp" on it and the Feathers in the middle. Strange and appetizing tales are told of the enormous prices now asked and paid in philatelic circles for stamps of high denomination cancelled with the similar postmark used on the Indian tour of the King and Queen.' Indeed. 'It is also announced in the Indian Press that in exchange for the proper amount of money Mr. Vas Dev will send to anybody whole sets or partial sets of current Indian stamps duly cancelled with the coveted mark.' Although Harry doubted 'whether any stamp of less than 10 rupees in value can ever be very precious', the end result was clear: 'the Post Office revenue must be profiting considerably; and that—if magicians can consider such sordid things—is probably what Mr. Vas Dev, like a good public servant, is after.' Evidently, Harry himself got in on the act. 'He was terribly conscious of being hard up all the time, and anything that could make him a bob or two', noted Julian Perry Robinson, Harry's grandson. 'He had an enormous collection of special postage stamps of that time with 'Prince of Wales Tour' which he preserved. A constant squirrelling away of things which might be sold later on. He thought they might fetch a fortune.' They did not, and Julian has his grandfather's albums of (unsold) stamps.

* * * * *

Travelling by the royal train from Bombay into the Native States, Harry fell into the rhythm of chronicling the journey while heaping praise upon the prince. In Udaipur the elderly Maharaja defied his doctor's orders and rose from his sickbed to greet the prince. 'The first Rajput chief and the proudest prince in India, who is now 72 and has been 40 years on the throne, would not be withheld from greeting Victoria's great-grandson', Harry reported. 'His own speech was instinct with his own pride and that spirit of devotion to the Throne that has been so signally demonstrated by Udaipur on every opportunity, from the Mutiny to the Great War. The whole episode was very fine, and worthy of the chief who more than any living man represents the spirit and tradition of Old India.'[44] In Jodhpur, the prince participated in the sport of pig-sticking and played eight chukkas of polo, all demonstrating 'the extraordinary fitness of the Prince's condition'.[45] At Gujner Lake in Bikaner, Harry related, 'To-day is Sunday; but for to-morrow morning a great shoot is arranged, and the poor birds are going to have a dreadful time'.[46] Indeed, over the course of the four-day shoot, the prince bagged over 160 birds. The next day, a party of the Sid sect performed a fire dance, leaping onto glowing coals to the wild music of drums for an hour, apparently to no physical harm. 'Personally, I tried merely to toss a single cinder in the air and have burned fingers this morning', Harry relayed. 'Perhaps they are drugged so as not to feel . . . It was a weirdly amazing sight.'[47] In Lucknow, where riots were threatened, the prince's team won the polo cup. 'The same atmosphere of cordiality . . . envelopes him, against which the poison gas of sedition seems powerless',[48] Harry wrote.

On that day, the royal tour passed through Allahabad, where the Robinson family had lived for many years. Harry was pleased to receive an invitation to lunch from the editor and staff of *The Pioneer*, which his father, Phil, and Kay all worked on for many years. Unfortunately, the dinner was not as nostalgic as Harry had expected. 'No one present at that dinner—it was a delightful evening—had ever heard of Julian Robinson', he recalled. 'During the days when we stayed in Allahabad kindly efforts were made in my behalf to find some old resident who might have some recollection of him, but in vain. His fame had passed. It was merely as representative of *The Times* that I was dined so handsomely.'[49] Brad picked up the story in his memoir:

> He naturally assumed that they had invited him as the son of their first Editor, but it turned out that they had no idea of the connexion. One of the staff said he had a chauffeur whose father, he believed, had been coachman to the first Editor. The chauffeur's father was sent for. He was very old and nearly deaf, but eventually he understood that he was being asked how

many sons the Editor had had whose coachman he had been 40 years before. He said once that there were three sons and was told the youngest of the three was there at the table. He ruminated for some time and then said he thought that the Sahib's name would be 'Hari'. This got him a gold piece.[50]

In his article for *The Times*, Harry noted that the reception in Allahabad was subdued due to 'the devices of intimidation and terrorization resorted to by the non-cooperators'. He interviewed a spectator who defied the ban. 'One man casually questioned said, "He is the son of a great King, and will be a great King. I have seen him and I know," and he made the sign of homage (*poojah*) as if to his presence.'[51] When the prince took a week off to go shooting in Nepal, Harry took pains to reassure readers that all was well in the Subcontinent. 'There can be no doubt that the tour has so far been a great success', he wrote. 'The disturbances which coincided with his stay at Bombay and the sulkiness of Allahabad yesterday have been the only two shadows.'[52]

> One does not wish to minimize the present discontent in India and the difficulties of the situation, which are serious enough, but it remains that the extremists are a small minority, and the immense mass of the people are moderate and well-inclined. That mass, when not terrified, has shown every desire to express its loyalty, and I have nowhere been able to hear that any of the stories of the Prince's visit and personality has done other than create great good.
>
> I should like to add that however unfortunate it may be that the present repressive measures should coincide with the Prince's visit here or there, I have heard from no source, whether European or Indian, of any suggestion that the Government should do other than continue to show its determination to govern. The only regret expressed on all sides is the tardiness of this demonstration of authority.

Clearly, Harry endorsed the use of force when necessary. In an article datelined December 15, 1921, but not published in *The Times* until January 5, 1922, Harry further explained the local reverence for royalty. 'We, in our stiff-backed democracy, know nothing of the ritual of homage; and the reverence with which the Prince has been received had been sometimes merely curious, at other very fine and moving', he noted. 'When the Prince shakes your hand, it's like heaven—witness a veteran with a half century of medals on his tunic: "He shook my hand, Sahib, *this* hand. If my father could but have lived to know of his son's honour!"'[53] To Harry, this was a hopeful sign during an unsettled time:

> In spite of the sedition and disloyalty which are rife, and of all the efforts of non-cooperators, it is the homage of India (it is absurd to say that it is all

merely formal and does not arise from the hearts of the people) to the son of the King-Emperor that almost more than any other single impression will remain fixed in one's mind. Reverence for Kingship is a fixed and ingrained habit. Long after India has become a self-governing Dominion, whether the road thereto be long or short, rough or smooth, devotion to the Throne and the Royal House will remain deep-seated in the hearts of the people. Only the grossest misgovernment on our part can ever quench it.

This was a rosy and mildly naive view, even for an imperialist like Harry, and certainly not prophetic.

The royal tour resumed in Calcutta, where the prince was welcomed by a 'vast' throng. He attended Christmas service in the cathedral, where it was announced that the baby son born to the Maharaja of Bharatpur had been named Edwardman Singh in the prince's honour. Harry also had good news: his Gladstone bag had been found. He went shopping in Calcutta but was 'deterred by mosquitoes', which may explain why the New Year found Harry ill, 'bad malarial fever', on board the S.S. *Dufferin*, bound for Rangoon with the royal entourage. As the clock struck midnight, Harry was delirious, while the prince drove golf balls off the deck. 'H.R.H. struck 16 balls past', Harry wrote in his diary. 'A beast of a way to see the New Year in!' Harry's dispatches from Burma were unusually brief, probably because he was too ill to attend all of the activities. 'Though I did not see it myself, I am told that last evening in Rangoon large numbers of Burmese, in the excitement of their enthusiasm, took off their silk headdresses and waved them frantically in the air, which is said to be a quite unparalleled demonstration',[54] he wrote on January 6, 1922. After a visit to Mandalay, the party spent three days at sea, arriving in Madras on January 13.

* * * * *

Harry left the royal party in Madras for a quick trip across the Subcontinent to Bombay, for a surreptitious visit with Lord Northcliffe. Northcliffe had been in Delhi to tour the site of the new capital with its architect, Sir Edwin Lutyens. While there, a Reuters dispatch, reported in *The Times* on January 20, stated that Northcliffe 'expressed astonishment at the rapidity with which political matters were moving. He declined to give interviews to Press representatives.'[55] This was because he wanted to issue a careful but pointed statement on India and the 'dangerous Mahomedan situation', and needed Harry's help to draft it. Summoning Harry in this fashion is another confirmation of Northcliffe's respect and friendship. The article, presumably ghost-written by Harry, was published in *The Times* on January 25, 1922.[56] 'To-day India is turbulent and suspicious, and Mahomedans and Hindus alike, in my opinion, are preparing to make trouble', Northcliffe began. Despite the progress of Bombay and Calcutta—commerce, railways, harbours, roads, education—'almost entirely owing to the cooperation of British initiative with the genius of several native races for business'—Northcliffe noted that 'the outrages on Whites are very similar to those perpetrated in the Mutiny of 1857'. He recounted in detail the murder of William French Doherty, an American engineer from Texas, working in Bombay, who was set upon by a mob of fifty to sixty men ('apparently all Mahomedans') bearing heavy sticks. Beaten and stripped of his clothes and valuables, he lay dead in the hot sun for two hours before a military lorry found him. 'I have given the story in some detail because it is typical of the kind of crimes which the followers of Mr. Gandhi commit, being incited thereto by his so-called non-violent propaganda', Northcliffe explained. 'This case was the worst because the victim was an American quite unassociated in Mr. Gandhi's quarrel with the British Government.' He warned that extremism was on the rise, and that native Indian newspapers were calling for the removal of all white men from India. 'Mr. Gandhi urges what he calls the complete Indianization of India, the natives to return to their native simplicity', he noted, 'but he personally uses fully modern methods, such as trains, the telegraph, telephone, and post, and particularly a rapid motor-car.' Northcliffe predicted the government would have to act soon. 'As in 1857 and 1897, the Indian Government is showing extreme patience. Civilized Hindus and Mahomedans who are loyal to a stable government, who are themselves threatened by the Extremists, and who decline to wear the white caps worn by Mr. Gandhi's supporters, ask me how long the Government will tolerate their intimidation, and the murders, such as that of Mr. Doherty.' In a lighter postscript to this bombshell of an article, Harry mentioned that Northcliffe was the guest at a farewell banquet at Government House, where he was feted by forty-eight leading representatives of naval, military, and civic authorities, and received a 'charming message' from the Prince of Wales. He left Bombay to continue his world tour, stopping in Palestine and Egypt. This was the last time Harry saw Northcliffe, who died seven months later.[57]

In Delhi on February 22, Harry reported with some scepticism on the construction of the new capital. As Northcliffe had done, the prince toured the site with Lutyens. 'There is no doubt that the whole scheme of the new capital is singularly unpopular', Harry wrote. 'This, of course, makes no reflection on the magnificence of the plans designed by Sir Edwin Lutyens, who is now here. It is the scheme itself that has few friends. People who gave the plan their official support at the time have told me that they regret having done so, and that they would oppose it now.'[58] It all augured poorly for the future, Harry warned. 'Only by visiting Delhi can one realize how out of touch it is with all currents of opinion', he observed. 'This is especially unfortunate at a time of such great unrest, when it is so necessary that the Government should have a constant feel of the popular pulse.... Now, when the whole financial situation is so difficult, the expense seems most burdensome.' He added, rather ominously, 'The fragmentary ruins of buried empires which strew this plain are not the best precedent for the sempiternity of our own, and sedition has been quick to make capital of the fact, pointing to the fate of the former Delhi kingdoms as an augury of the approaching end of British rule.' Fortunately for the prince, he had a rapturous welcome in Delhi. 'The demonstrations of enthusiasm of the masses made an extraordinary spectacle', Harry wrote on February 23. 'Neither at his departure from Bombay nor in Burma has the Prince come in such close contact with so vast a concourse of the poorer people of India.'[59]

The Times—and Harry—seemed determined to clamp down on any speculation of trouble in India, but as the royal tour of India came to a close, the political situation unravelled. On March 9, Edwin S. Montagu, Undersecretary of State for India who was sympathetic to reform, resigned, and on March 10, Gandhi was arrested in a government crackdown. Overnight, Harry became a hard news reporter. In his article on March 13, Harry saw Gandhi's arrest as 'the beginning of a trial of strength' and predicted that 'order will be restored...the forces of disorder must, collectively or in detail, be crushed'.[60] Harry noted Gandhi's 'colossal error of attempting to show inhospitality towards a popular Prince when he sought single-mindedly to serve India and study her problems have produced a storm'. Regarding Montagu, 'Indian opinion, so far as I have had the opportunity of testing it, is unanimous in regard to the resignation as a disastrous first-class event', he wrote, as the secretary had a very high public profile and was reform-minded. But Harry admitted that there was rejoicing on the other side, as many believed that 'Mr. Montagu was making the position of the Briton in India impossible'. He concluded with a call for order and tolerance. 'Generous treatment of British officers and civilians, eliminated now and hereafter in the gradual process of Indianization, would pay India tenfold by allaying heartburnings and smoothing difficulties.' In a follow-up article on March 16, Harry offered more perspective, 'after four months in India with rather exceptional opportunities of talking to representative men of all classes'. He said it was 'absurd' to link Montague's resignation with Gandhi's arrest; there was no connection and saying so 'can only tend to encourage sedition mongers'.[61] From his interaction with the people, Harry was convinced that the future was bright, if challenging. 'There is now absolute unanimity in favour of giving the new *régime* every chance, and, what is more, there is a universal desire to help India along the path of self-government and not to obstruct. No single Indian, I believe, yet thinks that India is capable of walking alone. No Englishman wants to do other than help her to a condition when she can. But Indians disbelieve this.' Harry advised that the urgent industrial needs of the country be met, along with better technical training for Indian youth. 'Financial causes and the difficulty of making a living are at the root of most discontents in this world, and it is on the industrial side that the best hope of permanent amelioration of the conditions and the sentiments of the Indian people lies. Both the Home and the Indian Governments cannot take up the matter too earnestly.' Shades of the argument in Harry's novel, *Men Born Equal*. He repeated the warning in his final article on the trip, published on March 17. 'Not less important, perhaps, than anything that has been considered, is that the circumstances attending his visit have called your attention—the attention of the Press, the Parliament, and the people of England—to the seriousness of conditions here as nothing else could have called it,' he wrote. 'England's ignorance of, and indifference to, India is an abiding grievance with both Englishmen and Indians here. It would be futile to expect that the lively interest in Indian affairs now aroused at home would be permanent. But at least it has been aroused. And that is much.'[62]

On March 17, the prince sailed from Karachi for the East. Harry did not join him for the next leg of his tour, which took the prince to Hong Kong, Japan, and the Philippines, among other exotic places (he returned to England on June 20). Instead, Harry departed for home. He had been away four months, and although the trip was exhilarating, he was exhausted. There was little time for a holiday, however, as he was expected in America to solicit articles for the next American Number, which was published on July 4, 1922. Among the many articles was one by Harry on the growing popularity of radio, 'or wireless telephony, or whatever we ultimately decide to call it'.[63] He was astonished to be met, mid-ocean, by a wireless message inviting him to a weekend at a friend's country house.

This would prove to be the last American Number, as its champion, Lord Northcliffe, died on August 14, 1922, aged 57. Harry was among the mourners at the funeral in Westminster Abbey on August 17.[64] As he looked around the Abbey, Harry must have wondered how much of the world he knew was changing, or had already slipped away.

8

Tut Factotum, 1923

Emerging from a gruelling four-month tour with the Prince of Wales in 1922, Harry remained in a prominent position at *The Times*, where he was considered a senior foreign correspondent. At the advanced age of 63, and with his health as fragile as ever, Harry was in a plum position to settle down and contemplate his retirement, particularly since his patron, Lord Northcliffe, had died. But as we have seen, that was not Harry's style, and if a big story came around, coupled with the opportunity to travel, his bags were packed and ready. Little did he know that the scoop of the century was about to drop into his lap, one that would firmly cement his reputation at *The Times*. For whatever reason, Harry's key role in reporting the opening of the tomb of King Tutankhamun has been overlooked, until now.

It is perhaps no wonder why George Edward Stanhope Molyneux Herbert, 5th Earl of Carnarvon, chose Harry to be by his side in Egypt as 'Upper Factotum and Press Agent' (as Harry coined himself in his diary) for the biggest story since the war. With worldwide press interest in their discovery of the royal tomb on November 26, 1922, Carnarvon and his decade-old partner, Howard Carter, were poised to exploit the hoped-for find of the inner burial chamber for maximum publicity and financial gain. Carnarvon was no doubt impressed at how *The Times* handled the 1922 (failed) expedition on Mount Everest (not reported by Harry), for which it had the exclusive worldwide publication rights. In closing a deal with *The Times*, Carnarvon had hoped to limit the expected press frenzy while wrapping the discovery in the shiny veneer of the venerable newspaper. The latter succeeded; the former did not. Harry, moreover, was the most respected reporter on *The Times* staff with considerable experience in foreign locales. Carnarvon would have known Harry by reputation, but whether he had ever personally met him before this time is unknown.

In any event, Harry soon learned he was on the short list for the Egyptian assignment. In December 1922, according to his notes, he met with Carnarvon, who sent him a handwritten list, on his 1 Seamore Place, W.1., letterhead, of recommended reading. The list included James Henry Breasted's *A History of Egypt from the Earliest Times to the Persian Conquest* (1905), which Carnarvon called 'very useful'; Baedeker's *Guide to Egypt* ('Necessary'); and a book written by Carnarvon and Carter, *Five Years' Explorations at Thebes: A Record of Work Done 1907–1911* (1912), which he called 'Dull but only book on Thebes. I think it can still be got.'[1] Harry had his hands full, but he would have enjoyed the academic exercise.

Carnarvon met with Geoffrey Dawson on December 23, and wrote to Carter the following day, detailing his plans regarding *The Times*. He mentioned that he had also met with Harry, but initially believed that 'I could not give all the news first to Times'. Harry may have played a role as a broker for the ultimate *Times* exclusive, urging Carnarvon to reconsider. 'I think the Daily Mail would give more, but the Times is after all the first Newspaper in the world,' Carnarvon decided.[2]

As Harry awaited the finalization of the agreement, he had tea in Dorset with Thomas Hardy (evidently a friend) on January 3, 1923. Hardy would later wish Harry well in a letter on January 11. 'I hope you will not get lost in those underground corridors of the Egyptian tombs—a terrible fate', he wrote. 'The poem by Horace Smith, despised nowadays, called "An Address to a Mummy" is very much to the point in these discoveries of an advanced civilization. I wish you every success out there.' Smith's 'Address to the Mummy in Belzoni's Exhibition' (1829) includes the stanza, 'Speak! for thou long enough hast acted dummy; | Thou hast a tongue,—come, let us hear its tune; | Thou 'rt standing on thy legs, above ground, mummy!'

*　*　*　*　*

Carnarvon signed the exclusive agreement with *The Times* on January 9, 1923 with William Lints Smith representing the newspaper. The contract stated that *The Times* was 'sole agent for the sale throughout the world for news, articles, interviews and photographs concerning all the Chambers connected with the Tomb of Tutankhamen [*sic*] (other than coloured and cinematograph pictures)'.[3] The cost was £5,000 (£300,000 today) and 75 per cent net profits received from the sale of rights to other publications. Item 2 of the agreement concerned Harry:

> The Times shall place at the disposal of the Earl the services of one or more members of the staff of the Times as the Times shall think fit (to be previously approved by the Earl) but such member or members of the Times staff (hereinafter referred to as 'the Times representative') shall be

attached to the Earl's party and be subject to his directions and control and if arrangements can be made shall accompany the Earl's party from England to Egypt and shall be deemed to be a permanent member of the Earl's staff but unless otherwise requested by the Earl he shall confine himself entirely to the newspaper publicity and the Times shall pay the salary of the Times representative and all expenses connected with his journey and his work it being the intention that no expense incurred by or through the Times representative shall fall upon the Earl.

'Heard definitely re Egypt', Harry wrote in his diary on January 10. 'Am to leave London on 19th.'

Following up on this contract item, a memo to Lints Smith from Geoffrey Dawson on January 14 made the case for Harry and not Arthur S. Merton, *The Times*'s Cairo correspondent, as the person to deal with the press. Merton had been reporting on the discovery of the tomb up to this point and was a well-known figure. 'I always thought it very important, for local reasons, that Merton should not be regarded as the principal channel of information under our agreement', Dawson wrote. 'My own view is that Carnarvon, or The Times, or both, should make it clear to the Egyptian Government at once that news will be sent here, for distribution to the Press of the world, by an agent attached to Carnarvon's staff and acting under his instructions.'[4] Dawson was perhaps hedging his bets, knowing how demanding Carnarvon could be, especially when it came to publicity. 'It is obviously convenient that he should be drawn from the staff of The Times; but it is not in that capacity that he is acting', Dawson continued. 'We have seconded him [Harry] at Carnarvon's own request to act as his own Press Agent.' So Harry was placed in the dual role of *Times* correspondent and Carnarvon's PR man, the latter affording him exclusive access. He no doubt relished the rather regal position, and would have found the assignment irresistible. Merton, on the other hand, was perhaps relieved to not only have help with the reportage, but to have escaped the burden of being part of the Carnarvon roadshow. He telegraphed the London office, 'Rooms booked/inform Robinson/welcome prospect with working/can rely my heartiest cooperation interests Times.'[5]

The Times formally revealed the agreement on January 10 in an article written by the day editor, Gordon Robbins. 'We are able to announce that Lord Carnarvon, with the cordial concurrence of Mr. Howard Carter, has entered into an exclusive agreement with *The Times* for the distribution throughout the Press of the world of all news and photographs of his discoveries in the tomb of Tutankhamen [*sic*]', he wrote. 'Neither Lord Carnarvon nor any member of his party will supply news, articles, or photographs to any other individual, newspaper, or agency. No other service will be authorized.'[6] Indeed not. Although *The Times* was said to have ultimately lost money on the deal,[7] it signed up many newspapers and magazines around the world for the syndication service. In London, the *Daily Telegraph* (£600 for news, £50 for photos) signed on, as did the *Daily Mirror* (£350, £100), *Daily Mail* (£350, £100), *News of the World* (£50, £15), the *Manchester Guardian* (£250, £50), and *The Scotsman* (£200, £50), although the *Illustrated London News* and *Country Life* paid £50 for photos only. The contract with *The New York Times* was £2,000 (the New York namesake would later come to an agreement to syndicate throughout the U.S. and Canada). Papers in France, South Africa, Argentina, Slovakia, Sweden, and even *The Englishman* in Calcutta (£200) took the service.[8] This was big business, and one of the first examples of what would come to be known as 'chequebook journalism'.

Harry bid farewell to Florence and Brad in Cornwall on January 16 and headed to London. There he lunched with Carnarvon on January 18, and the next day departed Victoria Station at 10:50 a.m. on the boat train with Carnarvon and his daughter, Lady Evelyn Herbert. They arrived in Marseilles on January 20 and transferred to the S.S. *Adriatic* for the voyage to Alexandria. The Riviera society page of *The Bystander* on January 31 recorded that 'Sir Harry Perry Robinson was dining at the Café de Paris last week with Major and Mrs. Pollitt before leaving in the *Adriatic* for Egypt, where he is to keep the *Times* posted about the unique finds in the tombs of the Kings. Lord Carnarvon, who is going on the boat also, was dining with Major-General Percy Radcliffe,' the former director of military operations for the War Office.

The official party arrived in Alexandria on January 25, and transferred to Cairo. Harry settled into the Continental-Savoy Hotel, where he greeted Merton. The next day, he lunched with Carnarvon and Howard Carter at the Mohamed Ali Club on the banks of the Nile, and met with representatives of the Egyptian press. The latter was a difficult negotiation, as local journalists resented having to receive reports from their own backyard along with the rest of the world. 'The Egyptian Press appears to dislike—or the Government does not wish it—to receive its news from London or through the representative of The Times in Cairo', Harry reported to his superiors on January 26. 'The plan heretofore proposed, under which The Times offered to give the Egyptian Press its full news service for publication simultaneously with its publication in London or elsewhere, without charge, is abandoned.'[9] In its place, Carnarvon agreed to a process whereby the Egyptian Government would brief local journalists directly through the Egyptian Press Bureau. Negotiations were held in the presence of Pierre Lacau, the French

Figure 25. At Luxor station in Egypt, Harry (centre) assumed his usual pose, following closely behind the Earl of Carnarvon and his daughter, Lady Evelyn Herbert.

Source: Bettmann / Getty Images

Egyptologist and philologist who served as Egypt's Director of Antiquities. The Press Bureau would have its own representative on site in Luxor, and, Harry explained, 'Lord Carnarvon will endeavour, personally or through his representatives, to give daily or as often as possible some information to the representative of the Press Bureau for transmission to the Press.' Harry noted that the information would be not be divulged to reporters in Luxor but carried 400 miles north to Cairo for transmission there. 'Lord Carnarvon is entitled to protect himself against any possibility of its publication in Egypt before its appearance in The Times', Harry reassured his bosses. In a handwritten note to Harry on January 28, Carnarvon believed he had scored a victory. 'It seems to me they are in a worse position than they have been so far for they will have to come to Cairo to get old news', he wrote. 'I feel sure that you will have to cable your account from Luxor. It is the only way it can be done. Your stuff ought to reach London a day ahead. I have done my best for you and can do no more.'[10]

On January 28, after an excursion to the Cairo Zoo with Carter in the morning, Harry departed for Luxor with Carter and Carnarvon, settling into the fabled Winter Palace Hotel with the rest of the entourage.

* * * * *

'Very long and complicated time in Cairo, with politics and intrigues of competing journalists. Tired!' Harry wrote in his diary. Unfortunately, the press scrum would only intensify and reach a fever-pitch in Luxor as the tomb opening date approached. The exclusive arrangement with *The Times* did not prevent reporters from other newspapers from coming to Egypt in search of the story, each hoping to outmanoeuvre and out-scoop their arch-rival, *The Times*. Among these were Valentine Williams of Reuters, H. V. Morton of the *Daily Express*, Arthur Weigall of the *Daily Mail*, and H. A. Bradstreet of the *Morning Post*. Harry would collectively refer to this group as the 'Combine'. The *Daily Express*, in a leading article on February 10, branded *The Times* exclusive as 'Tutankhamen [*sic*] Limited', accusing Carnarvon of commercialism and greed. 'The tomb is not his private property. He had not dug up the bones of his ancestors in the Welsh mountains.'[11] Lady Carnarvon was not pleased and had her solicitor fire off a letter to Lints Smith, demanding that *The Times* defend her husband.[12] Meanwhile, Harry telegraphed on February 15 that the Egyptian journalists had rebelled, unsatisfied with the government Press Bureau. On the eve of the tomb opening, they applied for *The Times* service. Harry advised approval, on two conditions: that the majority of the Egyptian morning and evening newspapers request it, and that they refuse to print 'any attacks on Times news service or Carnarvon' in their columns.[13] The *Times* consented, despite a formal protest from the Egyptian Government.

Clearly, Harry shouldered an enormous responsibility. He not only served as Carnarvon's personal press agent, rarely leaving his side and fielding all information requests, but he also had to ensure that *The Times* contract was not violated. Moreover, he was expected to file news stories daily, with the assistance of Merton. And as we know, his health was not good.

Harry's daily diary entries for the next fortnight, until the official opening of the tomb chamber on February 16, followed a pattern. He visited the tomb daily, riding there and back with Carnarvon and Lady Evelyn in their specially imported Ford motor car. They dined together in the evening. Often there was a bridge game (with Carnarvon among the players), with Harry noting his results. He met Merton daily to share notes and/or a meal. Harry marked down how many words he had written each day and transmitted to London. And, more often than not, Harry would remark, 'Very sick at night' or 'Not feeling very well' or 'Feel poorly! Took aspirin.' As there was extreme media interest in the Carnarvons, Harry had his hands full. 'The Carnarvons are rather a nuisance', observed Arthur Mace of New York's Metropolitan Museum of Art. 'He potters about all day, and will talk and ask questions and waste one's time. Lady Carnarvon is not coming out. Lady Evelyn is rather an empty-headed little thing I should think. She and Carter seem very thick.'[14]

Figure 26. Harry is seated in the front passenger's seat in this photograph published in *The Times* on February 9, 1923. The original caption read: 'The motor-car used by Lord Carnarvon and his party for transportation between Luxor and the Valley of the Kings. Lord Carnarvon and his daughter, Lady Evelyn Herbert, are in the back seats. The tomb seen in the background is used as a garage for the motor-car.'

Source: Heritage Image Partnership Ltd / Alamy Stock Photo

Harry's first article in the exclusive arrangement appeared in *The Times* (and in subscribing newspapers) on January 30.[15] This and all subsequent articles carried the tagline '"The Times" World Copyright, by arrangement with the Earl of Carnarvon.' At nearly 1,400 words, the article was a tour de force, covering every detail, from Carnarvon's movements and his meetings with local officials, to a description of the drive from Luxor to the Valley of the Kings. 'It is an extraordinarily interesting trip, because of the varied native life along the road', Harry observed, 'with donkeys, flocks of lop-eared black sheep, goats, women bearing huge loads of forage or water-bottles on their heads, and the numerous wild things—bronze ground doves, crested larks, and painted hoops—which almost allow the car to run over them, and kites which whistle and swirl overhead.' Harry added that the trip by car took twenty minutes, while it was nearly an hour by donkey. The following day, Harry made a special effort to praise Carnarvon, which after all was part of his job. 'It is impossible not to be impressed here with the extremely friendly, even affectionate, attitude of the native Egyptians of all classes towards Lord Carnarvon. Every one knows him, and every one is obviously glad to see him back', he wrote. 'It is a refreshing contrast to the attitude of some Egyptian newspapers elsewhere, which have been assailing him, for political purposes, with the greatest bitterness. The fact is that here the people are well acquainted with Lord Carnarvon, and know especially that he likes them. He likes Egypt and the Egyptians, and is their staunch friend. Mr. Carter also has spent the greater part of his life in Egypt, understands the people, and likes them. And, as always, liking begets liking.'[16] On February 7, Harry noted that Carnarvon and Carter had been swamped by telegrams and requests as 'Tut-mania' swept the globe. 'Among the most recent requests received by Lord Carnarvon have been those from glove-makers, asking for the glove itself or for photographs of it; from seed-merchants, asking for seeds from the tomb; from textile manufacturers, asking for designs for use in weaving; from provision dealers, asking for parcels of mummified foods (apparently they expect them to be tinned); and from shoemakers, asking for the design of the Royal slippers', he wrote. 'Added to these are telegrams from cinema people and photographers, asking for special concessions, and, outnumbering all the others combined, requests for autographs or for some souvenir, such as a bead, a grain of sand, or a leaf from the bouquet. Many of these requests come from children, who write the most enticing letters.'[17] Harry concluded that 'all requests are being treated with great courtesy and patience, but, in the aggregate, they take up considerable time'. And this was even before the burial chamber was revealed.

It is no wonder that a rather anxious Harry wrote to Lints Smith on February 9 about mounting costs. 'The expenses are the Devil', he stated. 'Besides the £100 that I had in London, I have already spent nearly £200 of my Letter of Credit.' Harry said that he had to give money to Herbert Warhurst, photographer, and Harold Moyne, the head messenger, as well as stipends paid to the experts working with Carnarvon and Carter, who provided detailed descriptions of the items being examined and preserved. 'The amount of money that goes in daily boat and donkey hire and postage—especially of photographic plates &c—is horrid', he noted. Then there was the cost of accommodation at the Winter Palace Hotel. Merton had booked two rooms for Harry, one to work in, the other to sleep. Harry had to give one up. He warned Lints Smith that he could not keep expenses much below £50 to £60 a week (as much as £3,500 today). 'I don't think, however, things will be quite as expensive after the critical day—the opening of the next chamber—is passed. I may decide that Moyne is unnecessary. Anyhow, I am doing my best.'[18]

* * * * *

The opening of the tomb on February 16, 1923 was the stuff of high drama. Harry dispatched a report to Gordon Robbins detailing the intrigue surrounding the occasion and the antics of his rival journalists, likening it to guerrilla warfare. This eyewitness account is significant, especially as Harry's key role in the drama has largely been overlooked by historians (owing perhaps to his place in Carnarvon's shadow, and because his colleague, Merton, was better known). It also makes for lively reading. 'After a week of quietness in the usual daily visit to the Tomb by all the Press correspondents and the usual wait on the parapet for general news of the clearing of the various articles from the outer chamber, our rivals began to get restless at getting very little news', Harry began. 'Valentine Williams spent many hours up at the Tomb and generally remained behind in the afternoon after the other Press men had gone back to Luxor, in the hope of finding some channel of information. Finding that I also stopped late, he twice asked me if I would be so kind as to escort Mrs Valentine Williams back to Luxor—apparently an excuse to try and get me out of the way.'[19] Harry declined. He added that he overheard a remark made by Williams to the other journalists 'to do everything possible to break The Times agreement'. He was concerned that Mrs Williams and Arthur Weigall, the Egyptologist representing the *Daily Mail*, who were hosting 'champagne dinners' for Egyptian authorities, were leading the charge to overturn *The Times* agreement. 'Combine against The Times now a real opposition', Harry continued. 'Combine now getting rude and not even a good morning for The Times staff.' He had had enough:

> On the Thursday night [February 15] before the opening of the inner chamber I went out after dinner to find my postal official to get him to hold up the mail for 30 minutes later on the Friday. At a shop he was generally to be found in the evenings, Valentine Williams and Morton were standing at the door talking. As I passed and finding my postal man had not arrived, I strolled up and down. Valentine Williams who apparently had been busy champagne drinking, stopped me and wanted to know why I was following him about—which apparently showed the Combine were getting anxious. To this silly question, I remarked 'Don't be silly, as if The Times would follow you about or even care to know what you were doing; in fact, we have all the information about "Tut" we require and it is hardly likely any information you have is of any use.' Williams was apparently frazzled and went for a night drive with Morton.

Harry's defiance would not have gone down well with the opposition. Unbeknownst to them, Harry knew that the tomb opening would be the next day. He sent a telegram to *The Times* on February 15, advising them

Figure 27. Harry (at right, partially obscured), confers with reporters at the entrance to Tutankhamun's tomb, February 1923.

Source: The Times / News Licensing

to expect dispatches from either Moyne or 'George Stylianos', in an effort to maintain secrecy. Harry was concerned that the Egyptian postal clerks could not be trusted.[20] The prime minister of Greece at this time was Stylianos Gonatas, but Harry may have simply liked the exotic-sounding name.

Harry reported that the press, suspecting something was imminent, mobilized at the tomb entrance on the morning of February 16. Weigall remarked to a friend, 'I'm not leaving that Tomb for the next 48 hours.' In fact, Harry noted that 'all correspondents were sitting on the parapet at 8:45 a.m. and never left their position until 4:30 p.m. Lord Carnarvon and party entered after lunch and the breaking down of the inner chamber could of course be heard from the parapet.' The disinformation, he continued, started to flow—although some of it was intentional:

One of the native workmen collared by the Combine during the afternoon said 8 mummies had been found, another workman said 3 mummies has [*sic*] been found. This confusing information was sufficient to spread all over Luxor that many mummies had been found and the Egyptian Gazette came out next morning with splash headlines of 'Three Mummies Found'. This spurious information specially sent out by Mr Carter as a blind confused our rivals very much, but of course they must have known some sort of shrine had been found by 3 p.m., enough to cable an Evening paper flash that the shrine had been found, but their source of information—an Egyptian official—must have given them a hazy description of the inner chamber, because they described a huge statue of a cat which was about 6 inches high, and a wonderful chariot which was just a broken wreck.

That news flash was by Bradstreet of the *Morning Post*, and its appearance must have disheartened Harry, who wrote in his diary on February 16, 'Fear we have failed.'

In actuality, Harry and Merton had saved the day—and *The Times* exclusive. By the time the rivals returned to the tomb at 5:30 p.m., they were already scooped. 'It was not until after 8.30 that the Combine had got some sort of news to put together and were at the Railway Station as late as 11 p.m. cabling home, whereas I bought down the first story from the Tomb at midday and Mr Merton the remainder at 3 p.m.', Harry reported. 'Throughout this Tomb business, Weigall and Bradstreet were both very annoyed people. Weigall because he thought he was the only authority on the subject. Bradstreet because he had been beaten on the first discovery, hence all their abuse.'[21] Harry noted that they all departed in a huff when copies of the February 17 *Times* arrived at the hotel on February 18, whereupon Bradstreet, in a childish act, 'collared the lot immediately', preventing anyone from seeing them. 'With the exception of Valentine Williams not one of the combine remained to read their "scoops" which they had been talking about for days after the official opening.' The shenanigans continued over the next few days. During the visit to the tomb by the Queen of the Belgians on February 18 during the 'official' opening, 'Mrs Valentine Williams was caught looking over Mr Merton's shoulder looking at his writing pad', Harry reported. 'Merton, noticing this, wrote on his pad, "it is unladylike and rude to look over my shoulder"—exit Mrs Valentine Williams.' In his journal, Mervyn Herbert, former First Secretary of Egypt and Carnarvon's half-brother, also described the situation. His nickname for Carnarvon was 'Porch', short for Lord Porchester, one of the Earl's titles.

> Porch, I think, had a very worrying time at Luxor—not that he disliked it all; some of it amused him quite a lot—But the journalists were beyond belief. The prince of swine was of course Weigall—who is only satisfactory in one way; he looks as complete a cad as he is—in the hotel where we all stayed there were the 2 groups of journalists, the sheep and the goats. The principal of the sheep was physically like one—Sir H. Robinson—who was sent by the Times to do their will and to help Porch—a good old fellow but

not very competent. Weigall and the rest were unutterable—they spied and lied and calumniated as I have not seen it done yet.[22]

Why Herbert would question Harry's competency is uncertain, although he may have resented the access he had to his half-brother.

The 2,750-word article in *The Times* on the tomb opening, written by Harry with the assistance of Merton, began, 'This has been perhaps the most extraordinary day in the whole history of Egyptian excavation. Whatever anyone may have guessed or imagined of the secret of Tutankhamen's [*sic*] tomb, they surely cannot have dreamed the truth as now revealed. Entrance to-day was made into the sealed chamber, and yet another door opened beyond that. No eyes have yet seen the King, but to a practical certainty we now know that he lies there, close at hand, in all his original state, undisturbed.'[23] Harry noted that the official party led by Carter and Carnarvon entered the tomb and began the operation at 1:00 p.m. Harry wrote the account in breathless prose. 'All present then proceeded to take off their coats, for not only was the opening process likely to be lengthy, but the atmosphere was certain to be sultry, to say the least of it', he reported. 'There was a slight hitch owing to the failure of the electric current. The few moments were full of tense suspense, and even those watching from the parapet could sense the suppressed excitement which possessed each of those standing below at the top of the steps on the look out for the signal when they were to descend to experience the moment for which they had waited three months, when before their eyes the crumbling wall would reveal the mystery, that had lain behind it for three thousand years.'

Nearly two dozen people were inside the tomb when Carter and Carnarvon broke through the wall to the burial chamber. Harry may have been one of them; it is not known for certain. But Carnarvon made detailed notes and provided these to Harry, as did the other members of the team, some of whom were quoted directly. From these notes and interviews, Harry, with Merton's help, assembled his report. 'Of what followed I am able to give the following authoritative description', he continued. 'The process of opening this doorway bearing the Royal insignia and guarded by protective statues of the King had taken several hours of careful manipulation under intense heat. It finally ended in a wonderful revelation, for before the spectators was the resplendent mausoleum of the King, a spacious, beautiful, decorated chamber, completely occupied by an immense shrine covered with gold inlaid with brilliant blue faience.' The best was yet to come. 'From the foregoing it will be evident that we have really arrived at the sepulchre of the old Egyptian King, unviolated by robbers and undisturbed through three thousand years', Harry concluded. 'The actual sight of King Tutankha-men [*sic*] where he lies will have to be postponed to some indefinite period. His long and lonely watch is not yet ended.'

* * * * *

Harry remained in Egypt for another six weeks. Although the tomb was closed on February 25, there was much to write about in the array of treasures that were removed for examination and preservation. Each day in his diary Harry tallied up the word count sent to *The Times*, averaging about 2,000 words, all typed from his room at the Winter Palace Hotel. When not writing, he was polishing Carnarvon's own prose for publica-tion. On February 19, the newspaper published a 3,805-word account 'specially written for *The Times* by Lord Carnarvon, which supplements and expands the account sent to you on Friday of that day's extraordin-ary experiences'.[24] Carnarvon's (or Harry's) words were the stuff of high drama. 'I find it most difficult to write about or describe what I saw and felt when I entered the inner chamber of the tomb of Tutankhamen [*sic*], for of a surety I never dreamed I should gaze upon the amazing sight which met my eyes', he conveyed. He assured readers that Tut himself would be revealed. 'The work of dismantling and removing the shrines will require the greatest care and dexterity, and I anticipate constantly increasing interest as we go on, and quickening excitement until we reach the place where I have no doubt the body of the King lies undisturbed. Such a sight as the body of one of the ancient Kings, lying untouched as it was laid there, never yet has been seen by modern eyes.' For a world gripped by Tut-mania, this florid prose was eagerly devoured. In the same article, Harry expressed his delight upon meeting Queen Elisabeth of Belgium as she arrived back at the Winter Palace Hotel. The Queen took an interest in Egyptian history, and supported the Fondation Égyptologique Reine Élisabeth in Brussels, one of the leading centres of Egyptological research in Europe. 'Her Majesty the Queen of the Belgians received me', Harry noted, 'and expressed the profound emotion she had felt at being present at to-day's opening ceremony. Her Majesty still remained wonderstruck at the marvellous objects there exposed to view, and said she thought that the world owed a great debt of gratitude to Lord Carnarvon and Mr. Howard Carter.'[25]

Needless to say, Harry's bosses at *The Times* were thrilled by the worldwide scoop and singled out Harry for special recognition. On February 20, Gordon Robbins wrote to Harry, in a letter which validates his (hitherto obscured) leading role in the operation. 'The first and most important round is over, and you have secured a great triumph for The

Times', he began. 'Last week must have been a terrible one for you to live through, but, believe me, it was almost as anxious for us here.'[26] But the hard work paid off. 'It is clear that you have had almost unbelievable difficulties, and your complete success is all the more astonishing. There is no doubt about it at all. The opposition has been overwhelmed and the battle for The Times-Carnarvon agreement has been won.' Robbins dismissed the feeble efforts of the *Morning Post* and the *Daily Mail* (now controlled by Northcliffe's brother, Lord Rothermere) to claim first news of the tomb opening, noting that *The Times* reports, with Carnarvon's own writings, were 'absolutely decisive' and had been overwhelmingly popular:

> I cannot recall a great news occasion on which the Daily Mail has been so completely beaten. Your big telegrams have been absolutely lapped up by the papers taking the service. Papers like the Manchester Guardian and the Yorkshire Post have given every word and splashed it in the most prominent position in the paper day after day. The New York Times seem thoroughly satisfied with their bargain—so much so that I was constrained at their request to send you an urgent telegram for a special Saturday message. This is not a precedent, and I hope your hard earned day of rest will not be disturbed in future.

Robbins proceeded to convey that *The Times* was doing its best, in leading articles, to defend Carnarvon in the wake of a bitter campaign against him (although he had to admit, 'The opposition, unscrupulous as it has been, has been very clever. It has hardly mentioned The Times, which it knows has a big stick but has concentrated on Lord Carnarvon, who is far away.'). 'The whole business has been horribly unpleasant, but we can realise that it has been ten times more unpleasant for you than for us', he wrote. Robbins then added another round of profound gratitude and noted how Harry's efforts (for telegrams read articles) were affecting the bottom line:

> I personally—and I am sure the Editor shares my view—think you have overcome your obstacles in a perfectly marvellous manner indeed. I know of no other journalist who could have tackled this extraordinary situation with the complete success which you have achieved. You have made the most important contribution to what seems to me to be the biggest new coup brought off by The Times in the last twenty years. Its effect on the fortunes of The Times is bound to be great. The circulation has simply been bounding up, and I have no doubt at all that it is almost entirely due to the Egyptian telegrams. It is a most fortunate thing that these great successes should be happening in the early days of the new proprietorship and the new editorship. During the last few days our circulation has actually been 20,000 above the figure of six weeks ago. The advance is almost incredible.

You can realise what such figures mean in the case of a serious and high priced paper like The Times.

Robbins concluded with a pledge to honour all of the debts to the staff, and wrote, 'We should like Merton to feel that we appreciate very highly his admirably [*sic*] work.'

Harry must have been immensely gratified by Robbins's letter, which represented the high water mark of his career at *The Times*. On the same day, Lints Smith also wrote. His letter was shorter and more businesslike. 'I want to add my congratulations to those you have already received on the great success of your efforts in very difficult circumstances', he began. 'In connection with the service we have very critical clients and in one or two cases the "show" made by the Daily Mail and the Morning Post in particular has made them restless but the majority are perfectly satisfied. I am quite convinced when you were selected for this most important work that we should not be disappointed.' Lints Smith also put Harry's mind at ease about the mounting costs: 'We realise it must be expensive, all the more so because of the competition which has also resulted in restricting the number of papers which have taken the service. But we must go through with it at all costs and I am going to leave it entirely to you to do what is necessary to continue the very effective service.' He hoped for more photographs soon, and concluded, 'I hope you are keeping well in the midst of what must be a very great strain.' Intriguingly, he added a postscript: 'I am not quite sure whether I told you that we shall not be issuing an American Independence Day Number this year. I found when I was in the States that there was no great demand for an annual one on the part of the advertisers.'[27] This was Harry's baby, and he would have been disappointed, but without Northcliffe to champion such a supplement, it was bound to come to an end.

As mentioned, Harry continued to file stories from Luxor, as worldwide 'Tut-mania' was growing. He cleverly relied on experts there such as Professors James Henry Breasted and Jean Capart to contribute personal accounts of their findings, enhancing the exclusivity of *The Times* service. Such access could only be gained directly from Carter and Carnarvon. Apart from detailed descriptions of royal objects, Harry's accounts were distinguished for their humour and interesting asides. On February 20, he noted that a steady stream of visitors and reporters were filing into the tomb, but not into the new opening of the burial chamber. 'It was with considerable trepidation that Lord Carnarvon and Mr. Carter allowed so many persons, not all of the slimmest, to push through the narrow passage between the walls of the chamber and the outer tabernacle yesterday', he wrote. 'Two or three of the least slender, indeed, did stick, and needed help.'[28] But Harry warned readers not to believe unauthorized accounts from reporters peering into the opening. 'The extraordinary stories sent out from unauthorized sources and telegraphed back here have caused immense hilarity at Luxor. Wonderful things seem to have been found, of which the authorities know nothing, and those who have been reading some newspapers much have curious ideas of what really happened.' As an example, on February 21 Harry responded to the fascination over the discovery of the mannequin of the young king. 'Some correspondents appear to consider this to be the figure of the Queen, presumably misled by the fact that the headdress is rather reminiscent of that of Queen Nefertiti in the wonderful statue taken by the Germans at Tell el-Amarna', he noted. 'Others more imaginative have seen a resemblance to Monna [sic] Lisa. What are called "close-up" photographs should be reaching you about now, from which you will see how hard this is on Monna Lisa. Obviously, this figure shows the King as quite a young man. The head is small, and the body is the same, and the features are those of a boy.'[29] Once again, readers were reminded: trust *The Times* for the truth.

On February 24, Harry stepped in to debunk a nasty rumour in the opposing press that Carnarvon was preparing to smuggle Tutankhamun's mummified body (which had not yet been exposed; Carter would uncover the sarcophagus a year later) to England. 'It would be ridiculous if it were not being used to arouse anti-British sentiment among Mahomedans', Harry noted. 'It is being especially employed to work on the passions of the Turks in the matter of the Gallipoli graves. It is an absurd thing that no one seems to have thought it worthwhile to ask Lord Carnarvon what his own real views or intentions are . . . The whole thing is the merest mare's nest.'[30] Indeed, Carnarvon wrote a letter to *The Times* (presumably with Harry's help), insisting that the decision lay with the Egyptians, who could insist that it be removed to Cairo; 'nor do I view with favour the somewhat unwholesome and morbid taste, which some people seem to enjoy, of looking at mummies exposed in glass cases in museums'. Perhaps with a sigh of relief, Harry wrote on February 26 that the tomb had been closed (noting in his diary that he had entered it the previous day). 'To-day has been rather like the farewell performance of an extraordinarily successful play after a tumultuous run', he wrote. 'It is not a final farewell, but only a temporary suspension with a revival promised for the autumn. One thing is certain, and that is, the whole staff both needs, and thoroughly deserves, a holiday.'[31] Harry included: he spent much of the next week in bed with lumbago.

On March 23, *The Times* published Harry's last article from Luxor.[32] An editor's note said, 'The following article has been written in reply to many requests for as exact an account as is possible of the life and personality of the Pharaoh whose name has become a household word since his tomb, with its marvellous treasures, was discovered by Lord Carnarvon and Mr. Howard Carter.' In his overview, Harry was forced to admit how little was known about the boy-king. 'What we do know is that his reign marked the close of, perhaps, the most interesting and picturesque episode not only in Egyptian but in all ancient history', he admitted.

> Could anything, then, be more dramatic, more anomalous, than the present situation? Here we are in possession of scores and scores of the most intimate possessions of the dead king—his furniture, his clothes, his chariots—the things which he daily touched and used and wore. We have his portrait statues and his name is everywhere: his old name in places, his new name in a hundred repetitions on all sorts of articles. His very body, we doubt not, lies, as it was originally laid, almost within arm's reach, inside those tabernacles. But of him, his life, his acts we know of a certainty almost nothing. The tomb seems filled with his living presence; every object touches with memories of him, fresh, almost, as on the day he died. But he himself—his personality, all that he was and did—eludes us: a name, a shadow, a thing of controversy and conjecture.

Harry was, in essence, keeping the story alive for readers hungry for more.

*　*　*　*　*

Harry's last two weeks in Egypt were spent in Cairo. He arrived on March 20 and checked into the Continental-Savoy Hotel, where Carnarvon was staying. Only the day before, Carnarvon had cut himself while shaving, infecting a mosquito bite that would lead to his death three weeks later. In fact, in his diary entry for March 20, Harry noted, 'Lord Carnarvon is very ill. Took charge of Press and all callers.' The next day, he wrote that Carnarvon was better, and had a visit from Carter. For his part, Harry kept a busy social calendar filled with teas and dinners, and visits to the museum and zoo. He spent a lot of time with Merton, no doubt reminiscing over the past six weeks. He had an audience with King Fuad and attended the King's birthday banquet. But hovering over all this activity were concerns over Carnarvon's health. In the margins of his diary Harry scribbled ominous notes: 'Carnarvon ill...Carnarvon worse...Carnarvon very ill—has poor chance of recovery.'

Harry left Egypt on March 30, sailing from Alexandria on the S.S. *Vienna*, destination Venice. He arrived on April 2 and checked into the Hotel Danieli. After a round of sightseeing, including a gondola ride, he boarded the Orient Express on April 4, arriving in London at 11 p.m. the following day. Brad met him at Victoria Station and they headed home to the flat, where Florence was in bed, ill. Harry was furious to learn that his luggage, thought lost, was actually held up by customs in Domodossola, Italy, on the border with Switzerland at the entrance to the Simplon Pass.

Unbeknownst to Harry, in Cairo on April 5 Carnarvon died, aged 56. *The Times* published his obituary on April 6 (not written by Harry), the same day that Harry made the rounds of the office, visiting Stuart, Robbins, Lints Smith, and others. He surprisingly did not note Carnarvon's death in his diary, nor did he mention the growing claims of a Tutankhamun 'curse' as the cause of Carnarvon's demise (Sir Arthur Conan Doyle described 'an evil elemental' brought into being by Egyptian occultism or the spirit of Tutankhamun[33]). *The Times* published Carnarvon's last dispatch on April 7. Considering his ill health from March 20 onwards, this was presumably written or polished by Harry. It contained Carnarvon's final attempt to justify his exclusive agreement with *The Times*:

> The work has been terribly impeded this season by the perpetual stream of visitors. Never in the history of excavation has there been such a thing as a weekly 'Press day,' nor, as far as that goes, has the Press ever before been admitted to the work of an archaeologist. It is to be devoutly hoped that this will not become a precedent for other poor excavators, as work under these conditions becomes almost impossible. There is continual interruption, and the fatigue of the workers is increased many times by the perpetual stream of sightseers. In these circumstances it is very remarkable that we have been able to do even as much as has been done, but had the staff been left in peace and quiet we would be in a far more advanced and satisfactory state.[34]

In retrospect, Carnarvon's desire to limit the press frenzy was a pipe dream, as Harry found out the hard way.

Needless to say, Harry was ready for an extended holiday. After paying a visit to the British Museum to see the just-mounted exhibition on King Tut, Harry bundled the family up and headed to Dorchester for a few weeks. His lumbago was 'rather bad' but he was able to take tea with Thomas Hardy and his wife on April 18. He interrupted his holiday for an overnight trip to London to finally claim his missing luggage at Victoria Station. Ever the royalist, he stopped by York House and Buckingham Palace to sign the congratulations book in honour of the April 26 marriage of the Duke of York to Lady Elizabeth Bowes-Lyon. On April 30, he attended the memorial service for Carnarvon at Highclere Castle.

For the rest of the year, Harry was an office man, assisting where needed at *The Times*. It must have been an adjustment for him, after the excitement and adventure (and stress) of Egypt. He oversaw work on the Swedish Supplement, published on May 29 to mark the Tercentennial Jubilee Exposition in Gothenberg. Harry noted in his leading article that the organizers of this world's fair 'aimed deliberately at giving encouragement to the forces working in Europe for a return to normal conditions. It could not fail, they argued, to contribute something to a restoration of confidence.'[35] Harry's fondness for the country stemmed from his coverage of the 1912 Olympics. Thanks to Sweden's neutrality in the war, he added, 'we get a picture of a vigorous and healthy national life as little touched, perhaps, as that of any country by the poisons which are working in the body of Europe.' Harry's efforts on this supplement earned praise from the new owner of *The Times*, John Jacob Astor. 'I congratulate you most heartily upon the admirable Swedish Supplement to "The Times" of today', he wrote. 'I know the high level invariably maintained in your work for the paper, but I imagine that this time it has, if possible, been surpassed. I am only sorry to learn that much of your heavy task had to be accomplished while you were unwell, and earnestly hope that you are none the worse for the effort. Pray accept my cordial thanks.' Harry must have been pleased. Perhaps, then, it is no wonder that Harry visited Lints Smith and Stuart, the managing director, on June 5 'to talk about salary' (for the umpteenth time), as he wrote in his diary.

Harry's articles for *The Times* ran the gamut from coverage of the annual Harrow Pageant with 3,600 performers ('All of the leading characters have good voices and sufficient dramatic force. If Edward I was less audible than the others, he is, after all, a dying man in a litter, from whom stentorian tones would, perhaps, be inartistic'[36]) and new laws restricting post-war immigration into the United States (a 'new terror' among Americans of 'an overwhelming flood of stricken peoples from all the war-devastated lands pouring in'[37]), to the 'revolution' in the nature of British cats:

> Just as, in twenty years, we have seen a generation of horses arise indifferent to motor-cars, so, almost as quickly, cats have learned to shed their fear of dogs and boys, and dogs—not all dogs yet—have learned that cats are not wild game. In the course of half a century or so, under the benign influence of human kindness and human patronage, they have done almost what it took mankind itself many thousands of years to do: emerged from savagery to civilization, abandoned the lives of hunter and hunted for the ordered ways of a society bounded by the restraints of law and self-respect. It is a wonderful thing; more wonderful than any revolution that has taken place

in human morals; and if the process continues for another generation, to what pitch of insolence cats will attain it is impossible to guess.[38]

Harry was a cat owner himself.[39]

In the autumn, Harry was put on royal wedding duty. On November 3, he attended the marriage of Lady Louise Mountbatten to the Crown Prince of Sweden, held in the Chapel Royal of St James's Palace. Lady Louise, great-granddaughter of Queen Victoria, was the future Queen of Sweden. Her father, Prince Louis of Battenberg, Admiral of the Fleet, renounced his German title during the First World War and changed the family name to Mountbatten. 'While it was a stately and beautiful service it is seldom that a Royal ceremony is invested with an air of charming simplicity', Harry noted of the small affair of just 200 people, including the King, Queen, and Prince of Wales. 'The whole party showed itself evidently on the best of terms with another, as at any happy family affair, all the atmosphere of friendly if—withal, distinctly regal—simplicity continuing to the end.'[40] A week later, Harry covered the nuptials of Princess Maud and Charles, Lord Carnegie, Captain of the Scots Guards and future Earl of Southesk, in the Guards Chapel. Princess Maud was the granddaughter of King Edward VII. 'All brides are beautiful; but the Princess Maud made a Titania among brides—the daintiest of real fairy-tale princesses', Harry gushed on November 13, noting that the princess exited the chapel 'looking radiant on the arm of her tall and soldierly husband.'[41]

*   *   *   *   *

The end of this momentous year found Harry abroad, again, and away from his family at Christmas. Why Harry would accept another foreign assignment defies explanation, especially as his health was as fragile as ever. But Harry was still on the payroll of *The Times* and may have found it hard to say no. True to form, he could never resist another foreign tour which, in this case, involved a particular fascination of Harry's: motor cars. So on December 23 he landed in Algiers to cover the first desert motor-car trip in a newfangled Renault car from Tuggurt (Touggourt), Algeria, to Tozeur, Tunisia. The stunt was the idea of the French Government, to link by car the termini of two railway lines. 'Anxious to again reap the benefits of tourism, French officials rushed to promote North Africa as a tourist destination', noted Philip Scranton and Janet Davidson. 'Prospects for an increase in the number of Anglo-Saxon tourists in the immediate postwar years appeared especially promising.'[42]

Before departing, and perhaps responding to a guilty conscience, Harry wrote another of those long letters to Brad, who was now at

Figure 28. Photographs taken by Harry during the Tuggurt (Touggourt)–Tozeur automobile journey in 1923. At top, Harry wrote on the reverse of the photo, 'The first halt in the desert, Dec. 28. The monument is only a landmark.' Above, he wrote, 'In difficulty, Dec. 30. Clearing a path by shovelling loose sand.'

Repton School in Derbyshire. Brad was 17 and thinking about university. 'I'm very sorry not to see you these holidays because you are growing up fast and I should have liked to talk to you about many things, serious and otherwise', Harry began. The Africa trip came up suddenly, he claimed; 'It can't be helped.' He appealed to Brad that he get along with his mother while they were in Cornwall for the holiday. 'Remember that you and

Mummie will be very much together. You can hardly fail to get on each other's nerves occasionally—for I know you both. But it is your business to see that occurs as seldom as possible', he wrote. 'She is, as you know, the very dearest person, with the most unselfish nature that I have seen in all my life. Be kinder with her and take care of her and make the holiday happy for her, as she will surely try to make it happy for you.' Harry loved his wife, still (at a distance), but mother and son were often at odds.

Awkwardly, Harry then shifted gears, as he usually did when writing to his son, acting more like a tutor than a loving father when he brought up his concerns with Brad's 'lazy' writing. 'I read the essays you sent and there is plenty of promise in the matter of them', he wrote. 'But where do you get your style from? The first business—or essential—of style, which is to say the manner of writing—is, according to all the best authorities therein—who are many and of great diversity of temperament—that it should convey clearly—without sobriety or impediment—to the reader's mind precisely what is desired—or intended—to be said.' Brad's principal offence was a lack of proper punctuation and an overreliance on dashes (rather ironic, since Harry's own writing style included an excessive fondness for use of the em-dash). 'Of course it is much easier to skip along with dashes and things than it is to punctuate properly and make yourself easy to read. "Easy reading is hard writing" is as true as when it was first said', Harry lectured. 'But you must learn to make the reading easy. Once in a generation a man of genius like Henry James can muster an expectation (but never a fortune) by being showier in prose. But break yourself now of what is really a stupid bad habit. If you don't, it will grow on you till you can't break it.' Harry continued, 'I could take your essay and, by breaking it up and punctuating it, make it good enough for anybody to read—or print. For there is good stuff in it; and I congratulate you on that. This lecture is really a compliment to you; and I hope you will take it as such.' Not likely. One wonders if Brad took this criticism as a compliment, or whether he understood how difficult it was for his disciplinarian father to express affection. It certainly would not have boosted his poor self-esteem or his situation at Repton, where Brad claimed his fellow 'inmates' regarded him as 'distinctly odd'.[43]

Miraculously, Harry made it to Algeria. He noted in his diary on Christmas Eve that he 'nearly collapsed on arrival' in freezing Algiers, with 'my breathing very bad'. He added, 'I am very poorly: no breathing. Would not have agreed to come had I known of early rising and long days!' On New Year's Eve he admitted, 'My health undoubtedly gets steadily (and rather rapidly) worse. Am capable of very little.' Still, Harry pressed on, and seemed to enjoy the desert adventure. His first article was published in *The Times* on December 28. The plan was to test a new twelve-wheeled vehicle, invented by Renault, to traverse the loose sand more efficiently than the 'caterpillar type of motor-car'. The organizer of the trip was the Compagnie Générale Transatlantique, which first established a tourist car service in North Africa in 1920. 'It is hoped to accomplish in two days, camping for one night at El Oued, a journey which takes ten days by camel, and thus, by the saving of eight days, making the circular tour through Biskra from Tunis practicable for the ordinary tourist',[44] Harry wrote. The route from Tozeur to Tuggurt was selected because it would connect by car the terminus of the railway line in each country, at that time separated by 160 miles of sand. 'So long as that gulf remained open, tourists could only go south in Algeria to Tuggurt and return by that same door wherein they went; and they could do the same from the Tunisian coast to Tozeur and back', Harry explained.[45]

The 'great experiment', as Harry coined it, set out from Tuggurt before sunrise on December 28, 'a party of 12 in all, including the chauffeurs, a courier, and a finely picturesque armed Arab, who took his duties very seriously, as guard. There must inevitably be a pleasing sense of adventure in starting to do what no one has ever done before; and there cannot help being a certain thrill in pushing out into the unknown desert in the half-darkness of early dawn.'[46] Harry noted that the eleven hours spent in the car each day were far from a pleasure excursion—and that it was bitterly cold. 'Camels, date palms, dry thorn bushes and the thirsty Sahara—they do not conjure up images of cold; but anyone who motors over the desert in December or January will need his thickest under-clothing, a heavy greatcoat and warm muffler—and still he will be cold', he advised. Harry was delighted that each night spent in camp included an 'excellent' chef and receptions by grateful locals, 'with tea-drinking (queer sweet tea, perfumed with mint), and much thumping of drums and firing of muskets'. The new route, Harry noted, 'means very much indeed to these hitherto isolated towns—Guémar, El Wad, Nefta—if it brings them a stream of tourists and keeps them within touch, of ten hours or so, of the railhead on one side or the other'.

The party arrived in Tozeur on December 30 to a rapturous reception. The total travel time was a record eighteen hours: nine hours from Tuggurt to El Wad on December 28, and nine hours from El Wad to Tozeur (after a rest day on December 29). The milestone, however, was bitter-sweet. 'The establishment of the new route not only brings into touch with civilization an area and Arab centres which have heretofore been almost as isolated as they were before the Christian era, but it makes possible new departures into further remotenesses', Harry observed. 'And it makes accessible to the tourist a stretch of as yet unspoiled desert, with its great space and silences, its wonderful light and colour, its widely sundered oases with their palms and pools, its *shots*—or great salt pans—and its mirages. That it means also before long a fundamental change in the life of the desert is certain, for the camel and the motorcar cannot for long exist side by side. There is a certain pathos even in the triumph.'[47] Trans-Saharan leisure travel had begun.

On New Year's Day, a clearly exhausted Harry departed Tozeur by train to Sfax. 'Became ill; sat up all night', he wrote in his diary. In Sfax he changed trains for Tunis. The journey was 'abominable', with 'crawling and endless waits', but he was delighted with Tunis, where he attended a number of parties and receptions. 'Feeling mostly ill all week', he concluded. 'Extremely interesting trip, but quite inept to appreciate it.' From Tunis he sailed for Marseilles, and settled in for another much-needed respite—by himself, again—on the French Riviera.

9

Elder Statesman, 1924–1929

If two gruelling trips to Africa in 1923 broke Harry's health for good, he showed no signs of slowing down in his remaining years. Retirement was out of the question, as there were bills to pay. As 1924 dawned he was in his sixty-fifth year, but looked much older. He may have been weak in body but his mind was as sharp as ever, and his eagerness to make a point was always present. His last years are characterized by a certain feistiness. Harry remained true to his nature as a provocateur, railing once again against the Olympic Games and a culture in which he seemed out of step. He still pursued his grand dream of a U.S.–U.K. alliance, even as he grew cranky and frustrated. The world around him was changing fast, and he was seemingly a man out of place and time.

But first there were family matters to attend to. Settled back in the Bedford Hotel in Beaulieu sur Mer, where he spent most days in bed, on January 27, 1924 Harry wrote yet another long letter to Brad, now in his eighteenth year and facing an uncertain future. Harry once again tried to connect with his son as an absentee father. He suggested that Brad seek out a golfing buddy of Harry's in Cornwall, a Mr Moore. 'For I know no one who would be a better critic than he and no one whose influence—in sportsmanship etc.—might be more wholesome for you', he wrote. 'Try and imbibe a little of his unselfishness and thought for others.' This was the best Harry could offer, as he himself was not around. He proceeded with his usual firm, tough love stance:

> Let me also say this for your comfort: Late starters often travel fast. You have been an unconscionable time getting out of boyhood. Every boy I know—as you know (and you will recognize its truth if you think of them)—has matured in character and outlook on the world faster than you. I am not prepared to say that your lateness is necessarily a bad thing. But you can hang back too long: so long that you'll never make up. I don't think you've done that yet. It is not yet too late. But it is past time that you started: and I think and hope that you <u>have</u> started.

Such words would not have helped Brad's poor self-esteem. Then, as always, Harry moved on to Brad's studies. Brad had written to his father about his recent term at Repton, stating in vague terms that he was 'growing more stable' and 'progressing towards coherence'. Harry was encouraged, but awaited the judgement of the school masters about whether Brad should apply to Oxford. 'If they think it will be good, I agree and will stand the necessary expense', he wrote. 'Let them decide whether you are worth it!' But there were strings attached. 'The old bargain stands: you do your part and I will do mine', Harry wrote. 'But there have been times in the past (you know as well as I) when it has seemed a rather heavy, one-sided job. But you are older now. You know you have my love and every possible desire to keep you and assure your future. Now go on—and I think you have started—and do your bit properly.' The irony is apparent, for Harry himself was not the best student when he was at Oxford. He closed the letter with another word about Brad's writing style. 'Get your thoughts straight and clear and style will come', he wrote. 'Don't try to imitate any more. It will probably only breed affectations. Think clearly and be sure of what you want to say. Then say it so that it will be clear to others.' Harry refused to believe that his son might not have inherited his writing talent.

* * * * *

Harry returned to England in April 1924, in time to attend the opening of the British Empire Exhibition at Wembley by the King on St George's Day. Despite falling ill after eating some 'bad shrimp' on a preview day with Brad, Harry wrote more than sixty articles on the spectacle during May and June, many for a special supplement in *The Times*. 'However shy, as a people, we may be of giving expression to the sentiment which we feel in regard to the Empire, to-day, at least, some openness of pride in the demonstration of the Imperial greatness which Wembley affords is surely permissible',[1] Harry wrote on April 23. On May 6, he covered the visit of the Prince of Wales with Lord and Lady Mountbatten, who loved the model of an Australian gold mine, had tea at Messrs Lyons' Grand Restaurant, and rode the amusements, including the giant switchback. 'The whole party embarked on the exciting journey. The ride was so much enjoyed that the party took a second trip, the Prince sitting in the front seat of the car with Lady Mountbatten. His Royal Highness also experienced the thrills of "The Whip" and came down the great slide of Jack and Jill.'[2] On May 28, the King and Queen visited, accompanied by their Italian counterparts, stopping at *The Times* pavilion and admiring the mock-up of King Tut's tomb, where Queen Mary was presented with a gold miniature of the throne chair. In the 'Gold Coast' section, an African 'native of importance' met King George, but evidently was perplexed by Queen Mary. 'At last the general manager, in despair of otherwise making him understand, said that her Majesty was "the missus of the King." Everyone was amused by this description, and the Queen, laughing, said she had never been so called before.'[3]

Harry was at his most provocative this year when he returned to his favourite subject, the Olympic Games, held in July in Paris. Why Harry was tipped to cover the event when he was passed over for the 1920 Antwerp Games is unknown (he was also not invited to report on the inaugural Winter Olympic Games in Chamonix, France, in January and February 1924, despite being based not far away on the Riviera). We recall that he was an enthusiastic booster of the 1912 Games in Stockholm, although critical of Britain's third-place finish and disregard of athlete training. This time, the climate had changed, along with Harry's attitude. He acknowledged British antipathy to the 1920 Games but was optimistic. 'The British public probably is not anticipating any great triumph for our athletes in either the track or the field events, for it is useless to ignore the fact that we do not take the Games as seriously, or prepare for them as earnestly, as do some other nations', he wrote on July 5. 'None the less, we ought to obtain a good many points in the Stadium. Our material is splendid, and, for the first time, we have something like a properly organized team. One hears complaints of lack of management and control, even here, but these can be largely discounted.'[4] Indeed, when Scottish athlete Eric Liddell (of *Chariots of Fire* fame) set a world record and won the gold medal in the quarter-mile (400 metres), Harry was elated. 'So in one wild minute, what had been the dullest of days was turned into about the most memorable that the Olympic Games have ever seen', he wrote on July 12. 'After Liddell's race everything else is trivial.'[5]

But it was all downhill for Harry's Games from there. Alarmed by outbursts of nationalistic pride, Harry heaped scorn on biased judges and unruly spectators. A rugby football match between the U.S. and France featured a near-riot among rival spectators; Harry noted that 'the immense superiority of the American team as a whole' was widely envied and resented. In the 'fancy diving contest', French spectators threatened to throw the judges into the pool when the American women won all of the medals; French fans booed whenever 'The Star-Spangled Banner' was played (which was often).[6] Then there was the case of the Italian fencer, Oreste Puliti, who challenged the Hungarian judge, Gyorgy Kovacs, to a duel ('the approved Fascist manner', Puliti said), after he and his Italian team members were disqualified. They did not duel to the death.[7] The last straw for Harry was the boxing match on July 18 between Harry Mallin, the British middleweight champion, and the Frenchman, Roger Brousse, in the quarter-finals. The judges awarded the bout to Brousse, but the decision was reversed when Mallin showed the bite marks on his chest, inflicted by his opponent. Mallin went on to win the gold medal, with furious reactions from French spectators. Such biased judging, Harry insisted, was experienced by other countries as well. 'The refereeing, it should be said, is extraordinarily lax; many things are permitted which would never be tolerated in England; and representatives of some of the countries are disposed to take the largest advantage of the fact', Harry wrote on July 19. 'Partisan feeling in the audience also runs at times very high. On one occasion, when the audience booed a decision in favour of an American, it looked very much as if there might be serious trouble, for there was a large contingent of able-bodied Americans in the hall who showed their resentment of the hostile attitude of the crowd towards their man.'[8]

The same day, Harry wrote in his diary that he began his 'funeral oration' for the Olympic Games. His article was published on July 22. 'To write this article is like delivering the funeral oration of the Olympic Games', he began, 'not of these particular Games only, which will come to a natural end in the course of a week or so, but of the whole Olympic movement.' Harry was desperate to avoid any threats to peace: the horrors of the war were still fresh in his mind, and the Olympics—which did not prevent the First World War—were in his sights.

> The ideal which inspired the re-birth of the Games was a high one—namely, by friendly rivalry and sport to bind together the youth of all nations in a brotherhood so close and loving that it would form a bulwark against the outbreak of all international animosities. The events have shown that the world is not yet ripe for such a brotherhood. There has for a long time been profound and widespread misgiving whether the Games had not in practice served to inflame animosities rather than to allay them.[9]

Disagreeable incidents had cropped up at previous Olympiads, Harry admitted, but 'at Paris we have had the first real test under the new order; and even those who came here most full of hope are completely disheartened'.

> The fact is that it has once more been demonstrated with dreadful clearness that the Games exacerbate inter-national bitternesses instead of soothing them. It is useless to attempt to create a brotherhood of sport which will react to the improvement of political relationships so long as these political relationships are permitted from the outset to embitter and demoralize the sport. Before Olympic Games can do any good, all nations must learn

equally to regard sport and politics as two separate and independent spheres, which at present not all nations seem to do.

Harry did emphasize, however, that the British and American athletes were models of sportsmanship and virtue. 'No one, it is to be feared, will feel justified in again appealing to the British public to support the sending of a full team to another Olympiad', he concluded. 'Saddest of all, perhaps, must be the view of one section of Frenchmen. It is Baron Pierre de Coubertin to whom the revival of the Games is chiefly due. It is pathetic that it should be in Paris that they should receive their grievous blow.'

The Times backed Harry, its star correspondent, in a provocative leading article entitled 'No More Olympic Games' on the same day. 'The message which we publish to-day on the subject of the Olympic Games was evidently written under a profound sense of disappointment. Even those who went to Paris most full of hope are completely disheartened. In the opinion of our Special Correspondent who has described the Games, they have shown that the world is not yet ripe for the ideal which was the basic object of their revival.'[10] The editors agreed that 'Miscellaneous turbulence, shameful disorder, storms of abuse, free fights, and the drowning of the National Anthems of friendly nations by shouting and booing are not conducive to an atmosphere of Olympic calm' and concluded, 'The peace of the world is too precious to justify any risk— however wild the idea may seem—of its being sacrificed on the altar of international sport . . . The death-knell of the Olympic Games has, in fact been sounded.' The following day, Harry made a bold statement that the judging was tainted: 'It was not an Englishman who had said earlier to me that every British, American, and Italian competitor started with five marks against him because of the Ruhr',[11] referring to the controversy over the recent French occupation of the German Ruhr Valley. He dismissed this accusation, but added that the fact such a statement was made 'throws a flood of light on the whole situation'. He repeated his conclusion: 'In so far as the Olympic Games contribute to International harmony they are a good institution and deserve encouragement. In so far as they tend to create friction and animosity between nations, they are bad. No intelligent person of any nationality can possibly have watched the course of events in the present Olympiad without being convinced that nothing has been generated except International ill will.'

Harry was more measured in his next article. On July 24, 'Olympic Games. A Possible Solution' was published.[12] One wonders if he was advised by his superiors to tone down the controversy and extend an olive branch. 'Amid a great deal of miscellaneous clamour aroused by my articles in *The Times*, and by the leading article thereupon, attention is now being concentrated on the problem of the curtailment of the programme of the games (to which I have referred more than once), even to their limitation to the Stadium sports—*i.e.* the track and field events, alone. In this form, it is urged, they may be usefully continued with advantage to the cause of sport and without engendering international friction.' Harry believed that 'corps-a-corps' contests like fencing, boxing, and wrestling, held in smaller venues, only asked for trouble, so Olympic events should be limited to track and field, swimming and diving, and rowing. Harry reiterated that 'no one would feel justified in appealing to the British public for support to prepare another team for the whole present Olympic programme'.

> It would be much easier to produce our team on the limited scale; and it may well be that the severity of the lesson of Paris may produce a chastened and healthier atmosphere four years hence. The British Olympic Committee, on whom, of course, there is great pressure, will beyond doubt strongly urge our continued participation on this restricted scale; and without assuming any airs of superiority we have to remember that we have taught sport to the world, and that while we have our Henley, Bisley, Lord's, Hurlingham, Wimbledon, and Stamford Bridge, other nations are less fortunate, and the Olympic Games represent to them almost the whole of International sport.

He concluded, 'It should be added that the feeling is so strongly against the organization of national *claques* in the Stadium and the waving of national flags, both of which have helped to intensify feeling in the past, that they are likely to be forbidden in the future.'

Harry's stand seemed both unreasonable and unattainable. There were too many vested interests in the other sports, as well as a desire for international competition and amity, to risk curtailing the Olympics. Even Eric Liddell, whose 'outstanding qualities of dash, pluck, and endurance' made him 'one of the most wonderful athletes produced by any country', was quoted in *The Times* on July 26 as being opposed to the idea; he was sure that Britain and America could not withdraw over judging, as 'the definition of a sportsman was that he accepted the decision of the referee, whatever it may be'.[13] In fact, the reaction to Harry's articles and *The Times* stance was largely negative. The *Manchester Guardian* was dismissive, stating 'It seems to have been tacitly agreed on this side of the Channel to ignore, at least until the formal ending of the Games, the severe criticisms that are being made in England and America of the management and conduct of the Olympic Games and the charges of incompetence and gross partiality brought against certain judges...It is claimed, apparently with truth, that the criticisms are greatly exaggerated.'[14] A leading article in *The Observer* stated 'Sportsmanship has a way of developing good will. In spite of "incidents," the Paris Olympiad did much to promote a friendly reunion of nations. We expect to see its successor obtain better results under more favourable conditions in 1928.'[15] In America, the *New York Times* referenced Harry's articles and outed him as the author, the 'famous war correspondent' who 'makes the flat accusation that instead of building up a brotherhood of sport among nations the games tend to inflame animosity.'[16]

Harry noted in his diary on July 22, 'Talk with Ld. Cadogan. Angry.' This was an understatement. Gerald Oakley Cadogan, the 6th Earl Cadogan, was chairman of the Council of the British Olympic Association and a member of the International Olympic Committee. In a letter published in *The Times* on July 25, Cadogan admitted that he and his colleagues did not deny 'that there is a great deal of truth in what your Correspondent writes, but many of his statements of fact are not as yet established by evidence'.[17] He assured readers that 'prompt and drastic action was immediately taken by the Executive Committee of the International Olympic Council to investigate, take evidence, and, if necessary, punish the offenders. Until their decision is made known it is difficult to see how your Correspondent's ill-timed and ill-advised attack can do anything but harm.' Cadogan defended sending a British contingent to the Paris Games. 'The British Olympic Association sent a full team to the Olympic Games in Paris, with a view to encouraging and helping every sport to which large sections of the English people are devoted, and it is not their fault if in isolated instances the federations of certain sports have failed to carry out their duties.' But he proceeded to condemn Harry, fanning the flames:

> I feel certain that the writer's un-English and unsportsmanlike strictures on the Belgian referee's handling of the Mallin–Brousse fight will be read by every true British sportsman with disgust. The writer's regrettable references to the Italian incident and its possible dangerous results are unpardonable, and, by giving prominence to tittle-tattle of this kind, have done much to complicate a situation that is both delicate and unfortunate. He professes to believe that the Games 'exacerbate international bitterness,' but I can assure him that his unhappy article has 'exacerbated international bitterness' far more than all the regrettable incidents put together, and to an extent that he possibly never foresaw when he penned it.

These were strong words. Cadogan concluded that 'in spite of the writer's doleful prophecy that the Olympic Games are at an end', the opposite was true: 'These great meetings can, under the firm hand of the

International Olympic Committee, continue to be carried on for the physical and moral advancement of all nations.' In a postscript, Cadogan lamented that *The Times* editorial board had sided with Harry, and injected politics into the argument and the threat to world peace. 'It is the first great aim of the International Olympic Committee to govern sport solely from the standpoint of sport and sport only, and in the deliberations of that Committee politics play no part', he wrote. 'In England this position has always been upheld by the rulers of our great sports, and I feel that a great English newspaper's attempt to introduce politics and to justify its strictures on political grounds is most deplorable.'

Needless to say, *The Times* could not let this attack on itself and its most famous special correspondent go unanswered, and Harry was allowed to respond below Cadogan's letter in the same edition. Cadogan's letter, he insisted, 'leaves untouched the one central fact—namely, that the Games here have given rise to displays of intense international ill-feeling. It is, of course, absurd to accuse me (or *The Times*) of allowing politics to intrude into the domain of sport when the whole tenour of my articles has been to deplore just that intrusion. Equally absurd is it to accuse either *The Times* or myself of hostility to international sport. It is the defacing of it here that has been so lamentable.'[18]

Harry was undoubtedly distressed by this very public tête-à-tête while the Olympics were still going on. 'A horrid week because of my controversy with Lord Cadogan', he wrote in his diary. He also noted on July 25 that Cadogan had promised him an apology. On the next day, Harry wrote, 'Ld Cadogan says he did not know how to get apology to me! Started new series of complaints.' That began on July 29, two days after the Olympics concluded, with a new letter in *The Times* from Cadogan. He refused to back down. 'I have to-day received a statement from the Executive Committee of the International Olympic Council that they have thoroughly sifted the whole matter, and cannot find a shadow of evidence that there is one word of truth in the rumour that your Correspondent has thought fit to publish',[19] he said. Cadogan did not dispute Harry's right to comment on the incident, 'but we do complain that his hostility to the movement has carried him to the extent of publishing idle gossip without taking the trouble to verify the truth of so grave a charge'. Clearly on a roll, Cadogan further attacked Harry's insistence that he did not inject politics into his argument:

> Your Correspondent still denies that he has dragged in politics to justify his strictures on the Olympic Games. Let him read the following statement, copied from his letter of July 23:—'But what is one to say of the Italian-French (and Hungarian) *imbroglio* in the fencing? A very distinguished representative of a Continental nation on the International Olympic

Committee told me that the Italian attitude was entirely political. "They are dreaming," he said, "of the old Roman Empire." On the other hand, it was not an Englishman who said earlier to me that every British, American, and Italian competitor started with five marks against him because of the Ruhr.' I shall be surprised if after reading this quotation, your Correspondent will again deny that he dragged in politics as an argument against the Olympic Games.

Cadogan concluded that Harry's opinion was only that; but for his part, Cadogan wrote, 'I do not for a moment believe that politics or international hatred entered into their excited demonstrations.' He added that both Harry and *The Times* had fanned the flames of international disgust. 'I repeat that your Correspondent's hasty and ill-advised article has done more to exacerbate "international bitterness" than all the regrettable incidents that have occurred in all the Olympiads that have ever been held', he wrote, 'but in proof of this let him read the comments of the French Press on his article, which contain such remarks as this: "*The Times*—the enemy of France."'

Clearly, this was getting personal, but Harry once again wrote a rebuttal, which was published in *The Times* underneath Cadogan's letter. 'Where the International Olympic Council looked for evidence in its "thorough sifting" of my statement, I cannot imagine. They did not sift me, and this is the first I have heard of their inquiry',[20] he stated.

> The accusation about my introducing politics is as absurd as when Lord Cadogan first made it. It is like accusing a clergyman of introducing sin because he denounces it. Nor should Lord Cadogan resort to the quotation of a couple of my sentences without their context. International ill-feeling based on politics spoilt the Games, and I am afraid that Lord Cadogan will have difficulty in finding anyone who will deny it outside the small circle of officials. Inside that circle one can understand the desire to put the best aspect on the Games—in fact, to 'whitewash' them; and in view of the pressure of the atmosphere in which our representatives have moved in these last few days much may be forgiven them.

In the end, Harry's crusade was for naught. The *Buffalo Courier* in New York captured the mood of America in a leading article condemning Harry, noting that 'Not a season passes without incidents at our baseball grounds which are every bit as bad as anything that happened in Paris. But we are not considering or suggesting the abandonment of baseball... [The Olympic Games] are an international institution which we can not afford to relinquish merely because all conduct at them is not of the Utopian standard.'[21] That was the consensus. *The Times* reported on July 31 of a meeting of the Executive Committee of the International Olympic Council in Paris, held on July 28. France was praised for a splendid Games, and Cadogan was quoted as saying, 'The British Olympic Committee completely disassociated itself from the remarks which had been made concerning the organization of the Olympic Games in Paris.'[22] Vandalism in the stadium and the theft of flags as souvenirs were regretted, and two resolutions were passed, asking the host countries of the boxing teams to punish offenders, and for the Olympic Committee to take action on the judges of the walking race. Cadogan, to his credit, did acknowledge the anti-Olympic mood and suggested that a 'drastic reduction' be imposed on the size of future Olympic programmes, 'to eliminate some of the sports more prone to overtly nationalistic displays'.[23] Only four sports were dropped from the 1928 Olympics in Amsterdam: rugby, tennis, polo, and shooting.

During a much-needed respite in Scotland over the summer, Harry wrote the last word on the controversy for the September 1924 edition of *The Nineteenth Century and After*, entitled 'England and the Olympic Games'. He toned down his rhetoric for this article, no doubt because Britain was not likely to withdraw from the 1928 Games in Amsterdam and future Olympiads, even if the incidents at Paris 'helped to increase our national distaste for the Games'. Harry acknowledged that 'the world no longer looks to Britain as the leading athletic nation. That position has passed, and rightly passed by any standards that the world can judge by, to the United States. Considered merely as an advertisement, the investment of the United States in the Olympic Games has been almost fabulously profitable.' Moving forward, he repeated earlier calls for 'improving the physique of our growing boys and men. To rail at professional training is like saying that we must not have professional doctors or nurses or masseurs, professional barristers or solicitors.'[24] Until that is done, Britain must expect more third-place finishes, as in Paris.

Harry, clearly exhausted, had thrown in the towel, but was also making the best of a bad situation. Obviously, after what he had experienced during the war, he was on guard against any activity that threatened amity between nations.

*   *   *   *   *

On December 8, 1920 Harry and Florence left for a holiday in Paris; 'F. racing home for trunk left behind'. After a few days Florence returned home and Harry headed to the Riviera, and his base at the Hotel Grande Bretagne in Nice. 'Saw the New Year in alone from my room', he wrote in his diary on December 31, then offered a surprising admission: 'I have notified The Times that I cannot go on as I am and the future is very uncertain.' He also noted that he earned more than £143 from 'casual writing' in the year, to supplement his income, including £7 from the *Nineteenth Century and After*, £8 from *Country Life* for an article on 'Birds of Egypt', and £100 from Raemaekers (reason unknown).

Brad's future weighed heavily on Harry's mind as he saw his own health decline, and therefore his earnings potential. 'Brad is in his last year at school and has tried twice unfailingly for scholarships' to Oxford, he noted in his diary. So on New Year's Day 1925, Harry wrote another of those very direct father–son letters, this one the most explicit yet. Brad had written to his father of something unpleasant that had happened at Repton involving his fellow students. 'This letter is for you and not for your mother: you can read to her parts of it—or all—as you see fit', Harry began. From what Harry described as 'beastliness at Repton' it is unclear whether Brad was the victim of bullying, had had a homosexual encounter, caught a venereal disease—or all three. The implication is that Brad had been traumatized, and may have considered dropping out of school, which Harry would have considered unthinkable. So he turned whatever happened into yet another long-distance teaching moment for his 18-year-old son. First, he offered some perspective. 'There is, of course, a certain amount of dirt and lust at all schools, because a certain proportion of boys are born that way or are subjected to horrid influences when they are young', he explained. 'The human race, after all, is not very far removed from its brute ancestry and the bestial strain is not yet bred out yet.' However, he refused to generalize, and wrote from personal experience. 'I have no patience at all with most of the nonsense that is talked about our public schools', he wrote. 'The whole of the well-bred male population of the British Isles goes through them; and the result is a larger—and incomparably larger—proportion of clean-minded gentlemen there is to be found in any other country.' Harry blamed the actions of a few vocal opponents. 'Like the sex-obsession in so many novelists (to which it is very closely allied) the tendency to gloat over the supposed immorality of the schools is a fad of the moment, and I hope a passing one', he claimed. 'Things are written, or told, by men who were themselves nasty-minded boys: hole-and-corner boys who were of no use at all to the school and who did not like it nor did it like them. They have their message.' Harry insisted they represented a 'small minority', the 'few, dirty ones' whose claims are 'magnified in the imaginations of frightened mothers and hysterical women'.

Harry urged restraint and perspective. 'Sometimes, I know, a whole House at any school may go wrong through the influence of a bad set of boys at the top', he wrote. 'But it is not the rule, and it is difficult for it to happen, in school or House, with good Masters who can judge boys.' He admitted there might be 'plague-spots' at Repton but 'I trust and believe that the body as a whole is sound'. He insisted that Brad soldier on through 'the evil':

> Now that you have come in contact with the evil, you are old enough and clean enough in yourself to keep free from infection. Your business is to do all you can to build up the healthy anti-toxin spirit in which the germs cannot thrive. And don't, I beg of you, don't join the band of those who think evil; the 'muck-rakers' who, being dirty themselves, suspect and see dirt everywhere. Believe in the Good and you will not only help the Good to be and increase but you will keep good yourself. There is no worse trait in a man than to be always seeing evil in his fellows. Human nature is a far better and more beautiful thing than many people would have us believe.

Clearly, Harry was desperate that his son not head down the wrong path. Having raked through this muck, he abruptly changed tack in his letter, and turned to his favourite pastime: critiquing Brad's writing style. Brad had written a letter from Oxford, enclosing one of his entrance examination papers for his father to see. 'It contained several bad mistakes in spelling!' Harry observed. 'Did you spell "week" (it says) as "weak" in your exam papers and call Balliol College "Baliol"?' He went on. 'I didn't like your "pungent aphoristic remarks." This showed an intellectual conceit which might well put any examiners off badly. You have that intellectual conceit. It shows often in your letters. I can see you admiring yourself for the beautiful way you do it. Examiners don't like that—nor does anyone else.' Harry did not mince his words. 'May the year that is starting be a happy one and may it build you up and strengthen you and make you a better man', he concluded. 'It is worth using well. It won't come again—the year when you step out from school.'

* * * * *

Harry spent his usual three months on the Riviera, where the highlight was a January 9, 1925 article in which he proposed the banning of gambling. 'What would, beyond doubt, be best for the Riviera and for humanity would be to wipe out the gaming tables altogether', he proposed. 'Monte Carlo is an entrancing spot: the daintiest and best-managed little city in the world. But no glamour or sophistry can conceal the fact that its influence is flagrantly anti-moral.'[25] If only, he wished, a millionaire like a Rockefeller or a Henry Ford could come in and endow the principality, it would be a place of wonder. 'It ought to be the permanent home of the League of Nations, the happy centre of peace for all the world.' Instead, the other Riviera towns resented Monte Carlo's siphoning off of the tourists and their cash. Needless to say, Harry was becoming *persona non grata*, at least in Monte Carlo.

In April 1925, Harry's three-part series 'As England Sees It' began in *The Landmark*, the monthly journal of the English-Speaking Union, based in New York.[26] This series, intended mainly for American readers, could be considered Harry's last attempt—better yet, last gasp—to bring about his life's work, to draw the U.S. and Britain closer together, a personal crusade launched thirteen years earlier with his book *Twentieth Century American*. These new articles represented Harry's argument at its purest, most refined, and most powerful, and reflected changes in the world since the war. He no doubt watched events unfolding in Germany, a challenging time for the fledgling Weimar Republic. The editor's note stated, 'Sir Harry Perry Robinson, during the last 44 years of his life, has spent an equal amount of time in the United States and Great Britain. As he is also a Chevalier of the Legion of Honour of France, he is well qualified to write impartially on international affairs.' In his preface to the series, Harry wrote, 'The world is threatened, in the not very distant future, with another war like, but worse than, the last. The United States and Great Britain can prevent it if they choose; and they, working in conjunction, are the only power, under Providence, that can prevent it. These articles are an appeal to the English-speaking peoples to face their responsibilities and get together.'

In the first instalment, 'The British Empire', Harry made an appeal for understanding. Britain was not a part of Europe, as Americans tended to lump her. 'The Channel still remains a vastly wider gulf than the Atlantic', he wrote. 'Americans cannot see that England is not part of Continental Europe. The British Isles become part of the background. Physically we seem to you to be one with the mainland. Politically also you regard us only as one item in the European mess.' Instead, Harry argued (like a modern-day Brexiteer):

> We regard ourselves as nothing of the sort. We are of another breed, with different character, standards and ideals. Our kinship is with those who have gone out from us across the sea: with Canada, with Australia, with South Africa—and with you. The British Empire—the British Isles, Canada, and South Africa, and the rest—is a great coherent unit as distinct from, and as unsympathetic with, the policies of Europe as the United States itself.

Harry neglected to mention India and Ireland, perhaps mindful of current tensions in both countries. Kinship extended to the United States, Harry insisted, particularly as America and Britain shared the same commitment to democracy (although Britain, Harry noted, was 'unhampered' by a written constitution). 'Did you ever hear of an English-American citizen or an English-American vote?' Harry asked, restating a point from *Twentieth Century American*. 'Irish-American,

German-American, Italian-American, Papuan-American, perhaps, South Sea Islander-American, if you like; but never an English-American, for the mere reason that an Englishman in America coalesces naturally: just disappears into his environment—and *is* an American.' Therein lay the reason Harry took to the U.S. when he arrived in 1883. 'When we beg you to stand with us to save the world, we are not inviting you to "take sides" in the domestic quarrels of Europe', Harry insisted. 'We are as detached from them as you are. We look at them, if from much closer at hand and with fuller knowledge, in the same light as you. They make us as mad as they do you.' He concluded, 'We have shaped the present fabric of the world; and in our hands its future rests. In taking care of that future we have simply got to work together cordially and without jealousy. We can prevent the next war if we will.'

In Part II, 'Our Navies', in the May 1925 issue, Harry condemned as 'wicked talk' suspicions that Britain was not adhering to the terms of the recent multinational Washington Naval Treaty, which sought to curtail a naval arms race by imposing limits to the building of battleships. Not only was this untrue, Harry insisted, but the world was in debt to Britain:

> Great Britain had 100 per cent and more superiority for the best part of a century; and did it do any harm? The only effect it had in the United States was that it immensely benefited American trade, because the British navy kept the highways of the sea tidy and safe for commerce. It was the policeman of the world. Now we are sharing the job between us. It is not the same job as it was, because the world has progressed and the seas are (except in Chinese waters) reasonably safe anyhow.

Harry's great vision was that the world's navies would operate as one: not an Anglo-American navy but an English-speaking one. But he knew such talk would arouse mistrust:

> Let me say that I have not lived for nearly twenty years in the Middle West, more or less mixed up in politics, without learning that anyone who talks in this way lays himself open to most harrowing suspicions. It is impossible that a Briton should desire American co-operation save from some base ulterior motive. Roosevelt understood when he said that any American who wished to be a success in high society had better be an Anglo-maniac; but any society man who went into politics had to be an Anglo-phobe.

Harry was fond of the former Naval Secretary (and future U.S. president), who had contributed to a *Times* Fourth of July Number. But Harry could dream. 'Suppose that, instead of the British Empire, it called itself the Free Empire, which is what it is—this great association of liberty-loving white peoples on all the continents', he wrote. 'I wonder whether the

American people would not listen with a friendlier ear to its proposals than they lend now to the proposals which come to it labelled "British."'

In the third and final article, 'The Power of the United States', in the June 1925 edition, Harry threw down the gauntlet: America was the new Rome!

> Most Englishmen regard the present power of the United States as a temporary and eccentric phenomenon. Accidentally produced by the War, it has produced a situation rather bewildering, a trifle grotesque— perhaps a little irritating—which will, however, pass. Things will straighten themselves out in time, something like the old order will be restored. Certainly it will pass; as Rome passed, and Babylon; as the British Empire will pass; as roses pass or mosquitoes. But anyone who supposes that the rise of the United States is any less significant or likely to be more temporary than the rise of Rome or of England is, I believe, mistaken. It marks one more definite stage in the evolution of humanity.

To Harry this was predestined, with no little thanks to the 'dominating Anglo-Saxon stock'. 'Looking back, we can see how the world, the very forces of Nature, seem to have been preparing for the cradling and nursing of the Republic', Harry observed. 'Just so, the whole world shaped itself for the coming of the dinosaurs. Given the antecedent process, nothing else was possible.' He proceeded to praise American charity. 'My own opinion—as is that of most people who know anything about it—is that the Rockefeller Foundation is about the most splendid thing that has happened to humanity since, at all events, the birth of Christ', he proclaimed (a remarkable statement indeed). 'American charity for the relief of all distressed peoples of all parts of the world has been, and is, magnificent and will doubtless continue to flow in an ever-widening stream.' This generosity was overshadowed by the anti-American attitudes of much of the British and European press, due to American policy since the war. 'Politically, the world, learning from its press, still believes that by throwing over the Wilson policies the United States betrayed mankind', Harry wrote. Don't believe everything you read, he insisted: 'You must not blame the world. You cannot expect the mass of people in any European country to follow and understand the drift and currents of thought in the United States or the underlying motives of your policies.'

Harry concluded the *Landmark* series with a dramatic appeal to America to take its rightful place in the world. 'Now the United States really is the biggest in the world, and most of her things are, in their mind, the biggest too', he wrote. 'We have to measure you by hitherto unknown standards. In you the evolution of human society has taken another definite step—a step which, however uncertain it may look at present, will ultimately be seen to be, as always, upwards.' That step, he insisted, was to join Britain in crusade to 'abolish war', once and for all:

> Trashy films and jazz bands, murders, divorces and bootlegging—the things which the world knows America best by to-day—are but wild oats: the effervescences of an aboundingly vigorous adolescence which has not yet found itself. Humanity looks and waits for something bigger from America now. You abolished slavery. You have come near to abolishing poverty. Will you not kindly abolish war?

> A new 'Great War' for which the last was but a dress rehearsal looms not very far ahead. One thing only can stop it; but that thing can stop it to a certainty. If it is known clearly that the United States and the British Empire together will not tolerate it—that our united might will be thrown immediately into the scale against the aggressor—there will be no war. Every part of the Empire stands ready and eager to enter into a joint engagement: Canada, Australia, South Africa, New Zealand, Newfoundland, and Great Britain.

Harry admitted that talk of alliances which 'entangle' was not popular, especially in the United States which had rejected the League of Nations. But he warned that America would be entangled well enough in the next war, unless it acted now. 'The only sure road to disentanglement is to stop the war from coming', Harry insisted.

> If the military clique in Germany had been certain that Great Britain would stand by France, the war would assuredly have been postponed and might thereby have been ultimately avoided altogether. If it had been known that the United States would come in (Great Britain remaining neutral) the war might have been postponed; for at that time in Germany the military power of America was ranked lower than that of England. But if it had been certain that both Great Britain and the United States would be against Germany from the start, then there would have been no war.

> The same situation is shaping itself anew, and it is up to us, acting in concert, to let it be known *in advance* that we will not tolerate another world war.

> 'In time of peace prepare for war' was the old motto. 'In time of peace prevent war,' is a better one.

One could sense the desperation in Harry's writing, a yearning to convince the reader, once more, that this was the only way forward. There is no evidence that Harry's *Landmark* series was reported by the American press nor sparked public debate. Still, it is remarkable that, in spite of world events, Harry's insistence that partnership between Britain and America was crucial to world peace never wavered. He remained an optimist to the end of his life, five years later. One wonders how Harry would have regarded the policy of appeasement and the subsequent outbreak of the Second World War, as well as the stubborn isolation of the United States during its first two years. Would he have been surprised that the world was seemingly caught off guard by the German menace, once again?

*   *   *   *   *

Although fees from freelance writing such as for *The Landmark* and *Country Life* supplemented his income, Harry still could not make ends meet, and he was concerned about looming university fees for Brad. On April 16, Harry visited Lints Smith and asked a extra favour: would the company help him by paying his income tax arrears? Lints Smith took pity on Harry and agreed, making an exception to the company rule. This would have heartened Harry when the bad news came that Brad had failed for the third time to obtain a scholarship to Oxford. But help came quickly from an unexpected quarter: Harry's aunt, Margaret Pennington. Now 97 years old but in full control of her faculties, she offered to pay £100 a year (£6,000 today), a sizeable sum, for Brad to attend Oxford. Florence and Harry met her on May 18 and accepted the generous offer. Brad would start at Oriel College in the autumn.[27]

Harry and Florence spent July in France, where Harry wrote travel articles on Paris, Deauville, and the Norman Coast. The family holiday was in Boxford, Suffolk, where Harry rented a rectory for six weeks. Heading west, Harry wrote travel articles on the New Forest, Glastonbury, and Bath. He deemed his holiday 'excellent' when it came to a close on September 20. On October 9, he saw Brad off at Paddington Station as he headed to Oxford at last.

Buckingham Palace found itself in Harry's debt when the Prince of Wales returned to London at the end of his latest foreign tour, his fourth, this time to Africa and South America. 'To Victoria to meet the P of Wales @ 3. Telephoning Buckingham Palace and L. Stamfordham re error in King's message', Harry wrote in his diary on October 16. Lieutenant-Colonel Arthur John Bigge, 1st Baron Stamfordham, was the private secretary to George V. Apparently Harry had seen the King's message in advance, and it contained an omission, neglecting to mention that the accounting of countries and places visited over the years by the prince had also included Japan, the continuation of the trip to India which Harry covered in 1921–2. Harry alerted the Palace, and the corrected message from the King was distributed to the press, dated October 16, 1925:

The warm-hearted affection of the welcome given to our dear Son in London to-day has greatly added to the joy and thankfulness which the Queen and I feel in his safe home-coming. His return marks the completion of those missions to the different Dominions of the Empire undertaken six years ago, and including visits to the United States, Japan and South America. I know that the millions who have been associated with him in these many countries will join with us in thanking God for the protection granted to him and his companions in their eventful and world-wide travels.

Privately, Harry was concerned he might have been overzealous, and on October 21 left a card at the Palace 'to apologize' to Stamfordham. The private secretary sent a personal note on October 23. 'Thank you for leaving your card upon me: but I am sorry you should have thought there was any necessity for apology, in fact I am very grateful to you for what you did in rectifying the mistake made here in not including Japan with the United States in those countries visited by the Prince of Wales outside the British Empire. Yours very truly, Stamfordham.' Harry would have been delighted.

The end of the year saw more economy measures for the Robinsons. Harry took a loan on his insurance policy, yielding £195 12s. 4d. He and Florence moved to a smaller flat, from 1B The Mansions, Earl's Court Road, SW6, to 26 Bramham Gardens, Kensington, SW5. Harry noted in his diary on October 31, 'Bad attack @ station on way home; nearly collapsed', and 'very feeble' the next day. But the news from Oxford was good; Harry did not mention Brad's studies in his diary, but 'Brad 2nd in Long Jump and 3rd in High in Fresher sports'. Before he left for the Riviera on December 6, Harry wrote to Brad, once again imploring for peace between him and his mother. 'This letter is all about your mother', he began. 'She has been having a very hard time and is going to have it, with all the work connected with the Flat and all. She will work much too hard and hustle much too much; and she will have more headaches.' It was up to Brad to ease her burden. 'You can't stop her from over-working and wearing herself out for others—for you and for me especially', he wrote. 'But you can show her that you love her, and help her as much as you can and make it a little easier for her. And I trust you—and charge you—to do your best.' Harry's tone seemed more suitable for a nine-year-old than a man of 19. He then asked another favour. 'Make her go with you to the Mikhara Pearl place—she will know all about it—and get herself a Christmas present', he suggested. 'She can get something that she will really love to have for 30/- or £2; and if she can't, she must spend more. Let her understand that these are my orders to you. And be as gentle and kind as you can to her on your own account.' Cultured pearls from Japan at this time were becoming very popular in the West.

Unfortunately for Harry, the Riviera was gripped by a cold spell. 'Not well—and alone', he wrote in his diary on Christmas Day. The first snow in twenty years had fallen. 'We do not consider it our snow', Harry wrote on January 22, 1926. 'We do not know what to do with it; even the small boys do not know enough to make snowballs, but they only kick the strange stuff about and shout.' Florence arrived on February 2, her arm in a sling following an injury when she fell off a bus. Brad joined them in Cannes for his spring break. 'Putting: Brad won cup and I did best round', a proud Harry recorded on April 6. On April 17, the Kiplings came to supper.

The Robinsons returned to London on April 25, 1926, and none too soon, as a General Strike was looming. When industrial action was called by the Trades Union Congress on May 3, bringing the nation to a veritable standstill for nine days, *The Times* was determined to continue to publish when its printers walked out. Harry headed to Printing House Square to pitch in and produce an abbreviated version of the newspaper. Strike action, as we have seen, was anathema to Harry, and with memories of the Pullman Strike still fresh in his memory he was no doubt the first to volunteer to assist *The Times* in need. It was, in a sense, his last stand against trade unionism. 'Am working as Reader in Office', he recorded, 'from 3 pm till the paper's out', usually 2 o'clock in the morning. In a leading article in *The Times* on May 7, the editors called for solidarity in resisting the strike action: 'Let all good citizens whose livelihood and labour have thus been put in peril bear with fortitude and patience the hardships with which they have been so suddenly confronted. The laws of England are the people's birthright.'[28] Although the strike officially ended on May 12, workers were slow to return, and normal operations at *The Times* were not resumed for another week. In fact, staffing levels were so dire that Harry summoned a reluctant Brad to leave Oxford and come to work at *The Times* on May 13 (as Brad recalled in his memoir, 'to do my duty'). The situation must have been desperate for Harry to interrupt Brad's studies, or perhaps he thought a life lesson was on offer. 'It was the only newspaper published every night throughout the Strike, and it was distributed by the private cars of London subscribers and trustees', Brad recalled. 'I was given the job of feeding the cars into the confines of Printing House Square as their particular parcels were made up. Of course I was useless at this—the superior chauffeurs paid no attention to a very young man squeaking at them. My shift was 9 PM to 3 or 4 AM, with half an hour's break for a meal in the middle.'[29] On May 16, Harry noted, 'To Office @ 3 for last time.

Home @ 12.' *The Times*, noting that 'the nation has gone through a searching ordeal and it has stood the proof', offered hope for the future: 'The first and greatest lesson of the strike is the absolute need of this willingness in employers and employed to work together for their common good... Nothing has been more marked in the strike itself and in the settlement than the readiness of employers and employed to understand each other's attitudes and each other's difficulties.'[30] Harry would have agreed, along with the editors' view that 'there is no place in wholesome democracy for the alien bogy of Communism, and that the "class-consciousness" preached by a handful of extremists has taken no root among us'. This overly rosy view was perhaps thought necessary to restore calm after the storm.

The following week, Harry journeyed to Oxford to speak to Brad about his future. What transpired is uncertain; perhaps Harry worried that Brad was not applying himself to his studies. 'He did not approve of the way I was spending my time at Oxford', Brad admitted in his memoir. 'It was not that I was bringing opera companies over from Paris, nor indeed that I was doing anything extravagant'—a reference to his grandfather Julian's antics at Cambridge. 'My friends, I suppose, were anti-Establishment, like many young intellectuals are. I remember he particularly disapproved of my attitude to the General Strike of 1926—which I said was no business of mine.'[31] With a cavalier attitude like that (no doubt observed while Brad was in London), Harry would have indeed been alarmed. Still, father and son watched cricket together, and Harry, staying in his old rooms in Christ Church, dined at High Table.

Brad recalled a happier memory of his father in the summer of 1926, during one of Harry's excursions outside of London to Epping Forest, 'the most princely pleasure ground of London' just beyond 'the unlovely barrier of the East End and the wilderness of bricks and mortar which is for ever thrusting northward and eastward from the City',[32] Harry wrote. 'We took a train from Fenchurch Street to Loughton on the southern side of the Forest', Brad wrote in his memoir.

> When we got out at Loughton, lo and behold a horse-drawn Victoria in the station yard! The coachman was surprised to get a fare in the middle of a weekday morning. We settled into it—that most elegant of carriages—and were slowly drawn up into the Forest. My father recalled a pub at a junction on that way in and directed the coachman to it. There it was, sitting there peacefully on that stretch of road as it had no doubt done since Barnaby Rudge.
>
> The innkeeper was happy to give us lunch in the garden, and after some soup and cutlets, he brought a tower of a cheese—nearly the whole of a Cheddar round. My father helped himself and then said 'Ah, here's an old

London spectacle for you' and shewed me the cheese squiggling with cheese mites. They didn't matter, he told me—just shake them out. Certainly it was a very nice cheese to eat.

The emotionally fragile Brad, unused to spending quality time with his father, recalled the day with a somewhat pathetic fondness. 'I don't know why I remember it so well, it isn't the cheese mites so much, I think, as just the pleasure of sitting face-to-face with my father in that Victoria and seeing the famous Forest. I spent many, many hours in the Forest later on, walking all over it.'[33]

Surprisingly, Brad and Florence joined Harry for Christmas on the Riviera, at the Grand Hotel de Cimiez in Nice. This, despite Florence's health which had deteriorated in the autumn, along with Harry's. 'F very bad—and did myself in trying to lift her', Harry recorded on September 9. On October 26, 'F collapsed @ breakfast.' And on December 31, 'F's attacks seem to be growing worse. Still, we have much that is good!' Harry sublet his flat in London while they were away, which supplemented his income.

The Riviera was changing fast. 'Everybody expects the coming season to be more tumultuous than ever', due to the huge building boom and a shortage of labour, and those pesky prices again, Harry wrote on November 29 in a season preview. The worst development? 'A new feature of the season is the extent to which Germans are returning to the French Riviera', Harry observed. 'The *boche salient* which, soon after the war, thrust down to the coast at San Remo and Ospedaletti has been successfully enlarged to include the whole Riviera, and the enemy seems well dug in. The suggestion has been made that the Promenade des Anglais should be renamed the Promenade Locarno, and the Quai des Etats-Unis the Quai de Thoiry.'[34] Naturally, the increased German presence was not to Harry's liking. His position with *The Times* had also changed on the Riviera: he was writing fewer articles. 'Am busy with new scheme by which I correct and forward the notes from all Riviera Correspondents', he recorded on January 1, 1927. Harry had become a kind of prose polisher, which would have reduced the pressure on him to write articles. A fine thing, too, as he was often in bed with the flu, as was Florence after one of her frequent 'attacks'. Still, he found time to write about birds, lamenting on January 12 that the French consume all shapes and sizes of feathered friends, even magpies, jays, and larks. 'The cause of bird protection in England has no more militant advocate than the present writer: to no one do these small draggled masses of feathers seem more pitiful', Harry wrote, admitting, 'The French in any case are not inclined to accept British authority as final in gastronomic matters.'[35] He found some solace in his beloved butterflies: 'The butterflies of the Riviera (we are not speaking of human beings) go some way to compensate for the lack of bird life.'[36]

*　*　*　*　*

Returning to London at the end of April, Harry's preoccupation—one could say obsession—for the rest of 1927 concerned Auction Bridge, the variation of whist which Harry had enjoyed and played since his first days in Minneapolis. Auction Bridge (the third evolution of whist, first played in 1903) was now under threat by the new game of Contract Bridge, popular in the United States,[37] and Harry was not pleased (a rarity for him, as he loved all things Yankee). One day after the death of his last surviving sister, the troubled Valence, aged 70, on May 13 (which he did record in his diary), Harry wrote an impassioned letter to *The Times* on the subject of 'majority bidding'. He was responding to an article that the London-based Portland Club, long the world's authority on the rules of bridge and whist, was favouring American rules rather than the long-standing British ones. 'If this is authoritative, it will be a great disappointment to nearly, if not quite, all those players who have had any extensive experience of the game as played under the two systems', Harry wrote. 'As a Bridge-lover who, year after year, in Great Britain, the United States, and on the Continent, has played as impartially under the two sets of laws as, perhaps, anybody, I hope I may be allowed to make a few remarks.'[38] He was despondent. 'Bridge will still be the best of games, but it will be a poorer game that it is if the change is made.' Many letters ensued from members of various London clubs, impassioned and evenly divided. Some thought Harry wrong; others did not want to be stampeded into accepting Yankee rules. Harry responded with another letter to *The Times* on May 25. 'Let us concede that it may be desirable to have one common code', he granted, but suggested playing both sets of rules for one year before making a final decision. 'My personal belief is that then the English game would be retained. I have yet to meet the English player who, after playing for a while under majority bidding in a foreign country, was not anxious to get back to his own laws. The Portland Club is too august and responsible a body to allow itself to be "rushed." '[39] A reader replied that the English game was played in America before America 'improved' it, and that, besides, Contract Bridge would be replacing Auction Bridge soon—and it did. Harry threw in the towel in a final letter on September 22. 'There is more or less general resignation to the inevitability of a change which is more or less generally disapproved', he wrote. 'We seem to be accepting with our eyes open the game which we do not believe to be the better.'[40] He agreed to become the new Auction Bridge reporter for *The Times*, filing occasional columns.

Harry's other preoccupation in 1927 was his son. 'Provost of Oriel advises that Brad be taken down!' he wrote in his diary on June 6. Brad was finishing his second year. This would have been a great blow to Harry, and an embarrassment before his generous aunt, Margaret Pennington. Nothing else was mentioned on the topic, but Brad offered some perspective in his memoir. He claimed that his father's 'worries deriving from the manners and morals of the post-war period were at their sharpest in sending his son as a Close Exhibitioner to Oriel College, Oxford. In fact, he considered his son's progress at Oxford was so irregular and unconventional that at the end of the boy's second year he notified the College that he wished to withdraw his son and forgo the Exhibition.'[41] Harry's diary entry begs to differ: Brad's poor academic performance appears to have been the cause. 'I might have become a musician at one time', Brad recalled. 'I played the piano at school concerts (and sang), and my parents said they would give me a piano if I got a scholarship to Oxford. I did not get a scholarship, so I did not get a piano and no longer had the school piano to play on. So I gave it up and took to listening instead.'[42]

The question was, what to do now with Brad, who was approaching his twenty-first birthday. Over the summer, Harry encouraged his son to

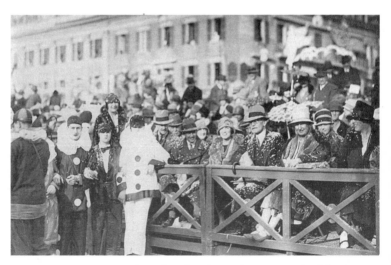

Figure 29. Harry, age 67 (seated, right of centre), at Carnival celebrations in Nice, France, in 1927. Florence is seated at far right.

try his hand as a freelance journalist, determined once again that he follow in his footsteps. 'The first piece for which I was paid was an item in the <u>Evening Standard</u>, beginning, "The Dimorphotheca are very fine just now in Kensington Gardens"',[43] Brad recalled. Then Harry did what most fathers would have done: he obtained a job for Brad at his place of work. On October 10, 1927 Harry marked in his diary, 'Brad went to work @ Times.'[44] This was risky at best, and Harry's relief was palpable when he wrote in his diary on October 14 that Brad completed his first week and 'got his first £20 salary'. On his twenty-first birthday, October 21, Brad moved out of the flat to live on his own, sharing an apartment with a friend, E. B. Noel, at 107 Comeragh Road, W14, nearly two miles west of Bramham Gardens. Clearly, times were changing fast for Harry and Florence as parents, as they spent a rare Christmas together on the Riviera at the Grand Hotel de Cimiez in Nice. It would be their final holiday abroad.

* * * * *

Harry would look back on 1928 as his last good year. 'My own health broken badly: am in my 70th year and begin to feel it!', he wrote on December 31, 1927. In fact, Harry received a heavy emotional blow at the start of the year, when his brother Kay died on January 20, 1928, aged 72. Harry idolized his older brother and they remained close throughout their lives. Emotionally, Harry would realize that he was now the only surviving sibling, and in failing health himself. Harry wrote Kay's obituary, which was published in *The Times* on January 23. He gave a nod to his other brother, Phil ('who first introduced Englishmen in India, other than professed sportsmen or naturalists, to the fascination of its wild life'), and acknowledged Kipling's debt to Kay, before lauding Kay's achievements in natural history as a journalist, lecturer, and founder of the British Empire Naturalists' Association. 'He was a very bold, if undisciplined, thinker, and with a curiously wide and intimate knowledge of natural history as an observer and field naturalist he combined a great tenderness and gentleness towards life in all forms', Harry observed. 'There are many thousands of people in all parts of the world who will feel that in his death they have lost a much loved teacher and friend.'[45] Surprisingly, Harry and Florence did not return from the Riviera to attend Kay's funeral on January 26; Brad represented them.

Harry continued to be plagued with money woes, and dependent on the good graces of *The Times* to make ends meet. On March 16, he wrote to Lints Smith from Nice. 'On the First of April I have to pay the last instalment—£129—of the ghastly income tax arrears', he wrote.

'I do not know whether The Times is disposed to continue to the end its generosity of the last two years, but I need hardly say that I shall be very grateful if it is.'[46] Lints Smith responded on March 27, with a mixture of sympathy and diplomacy. 'I know you will not misunderstand me when I say that it would be quite impossible to pay the Income Tax of members of the staff; in fact, we have a definite rule against it', he wrote. 'Yours is the only exception I have made during my term of office, but I do not feel justified in making further payments. I will, however, on this occasion authorise a contribution of £100 (£6,100 today) towards the amount, and I enclose a cheque.'[47] Harry would have been pleased, but also worried about the future.

Sitting out coverage of the 1928 Olympics in Amsterdam (no surprise), Harry's last hurrah for *The Times* was shepherding the War Graves Memorial Number, scheduled for publication on the tenth anniversary of the end of the First World War. This required Harry to dust off his skills honed during the many American Numbers, soliciting letters and articles from generals and commissioners far and wide. The supplement would mark the accounting of the work of the Imperial War Graves Commission, established by royal charter in 1917 with the Prince of Wales as its president. By 1928 more than 500 cemeteries on the Western Front had been built, with memorials designed by Sir Edwin Lutyens, among others, and with Kipling serving as the literary adviser for the inscriptions. Kipling collaborated closely with Harry on the herculean project, which he described in a letter to Harry as 'an amazing drama, and the biggest bit of concrete work since the Pyramids that man has ventured upon (Compare cubic contents of Cheops' Pyramid with stones set and handled &c &c.)'. He added it was also 'the largest bit of gardening undertaken in any country' and the effort 'has dealt with as many races and sorts of people as are in the Empire—also with wild beasts from Giraffes down'.[48]

'Working every day on correspondence about the War Graves Number—an awful job!' Harry, emotionally drained, recorded on August 13. The contributors also found the job taxing, as expressed in letters kept by Harry. Vice-Admiral Sir Herbert Richmond, writing on 'The Sea Services', considered his article 'most disappointing to myself... Burn the confounded thing if you like—I shall not be hurt'. General Sir Ian Hamilton, who wrote about Gallipoli, sympathized with Harry's job. 'I feel I can't go wrong in thanking you for you took all the trouble of using my very inadequate contribution. I wish it had been better, but these things can't be got by wishing. They just "come off" or they don't.' Maurice Baring returned proof corrections to his back-page epic poem, '*Per Ardua* 1914–1918'. He had cut lines to save space, as requested, and told Harry to 'please set up as you think fit'. But he insisted that other corrections be restored, in particular seven lines that Harry himself had excised. 'I think these lines give lift to the poem', Baring wrote. 'This is not only my opinion but that of three others to whom I have shown the poem. One of them was Ronald Knox who is highly fastidious and who said the same thing of his own accord. He felt this very strongly.' The stanza Harry wished to cut was the fourth:

> Now it grows dark, and like a tawny shield
> The full moon rises on the misty field,
> And veils the drowsy world with silver bliss.
> The spectral poplars tremble at her kiss.
> 'Oh! why? Oh! why?'
> Is the murmured cry,
> 'Must men go to war on a night like this?'

To appease Baring, and fit everything, a smaller font was used than in the rest of the Number, making the poem somewhat harder to read. On September 24 Sir Fabian Ware, vice-chairman of the commission (who spearheaded the original campaign) returned corrected proofs of the entire Number, noting that Kipling had sent a couplet, 'Their name liveth for evermore', for the cover, but insisted his name not be used.

Harry completed work on the War Graves Number on October 7, one month early, then stayed in bed for two days. On November 9, Lints Smith wrote to express his appreciation. 'I wish to place on record our deep gratitude to you for the conception and execution of something worthy and worth while. The Times, in my opinion, has never in its history done anything finer in the way of Supplements. To give you some slight tangible recognition of your work I have pleasure in enclosing a cheque for £100.'[49] The extra income would have been welcome. Harry had just 'sold £610 5% War Loan for £629. 4. 0.', as noted in his diary, and consulted 'Sotheby's book expert to see my Kiplings', to appraise a set of autographed volumes for sale at auction.[50]

One could regard the War Graves Number, published as a supplement to *The Times* on November 10, as the capstone of Harry's remarkable career in journalism, as well as a monument to a glorious imperial era that was fast coming to an end. Twenty pages in length, booklet sized, heavily illustrated, and printed on better paper, this was intended as a keepsake. Harry presumably wrote the introduction, entitled 'An Empire's Gratitude', which provided an overview of the Number, 'intended as a tribute to the Million British Dead, and as a record of their burial places. To preserve the idea and the reality of freedom not only for the British Empire, not only for the Empire and its Allies, but for all the world, men of the British Empire took their lives in their hands. A million and more lost their stake, to win a greater prize.' He was quick to add 'There were women, too. They might not do battle as men did battle; but they also took, in thousands, their lives in their hands for the tending and helping of the men who fought, and of them also many paid the price.' Harry paid tribute to the work of the Imperial War Graves Commission and its president, the Prince of Wales. 'Honourable burial and exact record for every man and woman who fell in the War service of the Empire were the ideal; and this Number gives an account of the toil, the pertinacity, the ingenuity, the sense of honour, with which the Commission has realized that ideal to an extent that must often have seemed beyond hope.' The graves that were recorded, he added, would be tended to. 'The graves of those who died in their beds at home may some day be neglected: the dead soldier's never. And this has been made possible by the Governments and peoples of France, of Belgium, and of other countries, who, by the gift in perpetuity of the land for those British cemeteries, have made each a little bit of England, of Canada, of Australia, of India, of all parts of the Empire, so that every man of them all lies buried, in a sense, at home.' Recognition was also paid to those who had no graves, who died either on land, or at sea, or in the air—and also to those who survived. 'In honouring the dead, let us not forget the living. Besides these million, there are other millions who were not called upon to make the final sacrifice, but were no less ready to die.'

The War Graves Number, which was subsequently published in book form, included messages from the Queen and the prime minister, Stanley Baldwin, as well as articles by officials of the regions concerned or by officers who had fought in that part of the world, including Lord Lloyd on Egypt, and Admiral Lord Jellicoe on the war at sea. Kipling wrote (but without a byline) 'The Silent World. Battlefields of France and Belgium. The Gathering in of the Dead' and 'An Epitaph'. Harry was responsible for 'The Million Dead. Distribution of Cemeteries, Graves, and Memorials', a listing of locations around the world, noting the half-million identified graves, and the additional half-million casualties with no known grave. The table of the deceased, Harry wrote, 'accurate as it can be made up to date, is of profound and pathetic interest.'

*   *   *   *   *

Harry and Florence spent the Christmas holidays in Minehead, Somerset. As he noted in his diary, 'The first winter I've not gone abroad since the War.' His health continued to decline in the new year. February 5,

1929: 'To hospital to be x-rayed in am.' April 30: 'Dr. Liddon called to offer me private sacrament.'[51] June 15: 'Am very far from well.'

On June 18, Geoffrey Dawson collected Harry to go to lunch with Harry's old friend from his Chicago days, Charles Dawes. Dawes, the former vice president of the United States under President Calvin Coolidge, had just taken up his new post as Ambassador to the Court of St James. Intriguingly, *The Times* asked Harry to write Dawes's obituary for the file, which he completed on August 16 (Dawes did not pass away until April 23, 1951). On October 8, Harry's friend and former colleague, Harold Begbie, died. He was only 58. Harry's obituary was published in *The Times* the next day. Mentioning Begbie's stint as a newspaper reporter and, later, editor of 'a short-lived weekly paper, the *V.C.*', Harry noted that Begbie had grown disenchanted with journalism. 'He could not reconcile himself to the difference between the "news" value and the intrinsic value of events as he saw them', Harry observed, 'giving when he retired from daily journalism the characteristic reason for his withdrawal that if he went on he should come to feel that "nothing in the world—not God or religion—was worth more than 1,200 words"'.[52] Perhaps Harry, nearing the end of his own life, felt the same way.

Later that month, Harry sat down with Lints Smith for a discussion about his future. He was just shy of his seventieth birthday, and well aware of diminishing returns on his part. Lints Smith would have wanted to treat his legendary correspondent with compassion and dignity. It would appear that Lints Smith proposed a new assignment, with Harry moving permanently to his favourite holiday destination, Minehead (a better climate than London), and becoming a *Times* correspondent from the country. Harry had lunch with Geoffrey Dawson to discuss the idea, then wrote to Lints Smith. 'When you made certain proposals to me the other day as to my future connexion with The Times, I expressed my recognition of the generosity of the terms proposed: and I meant it', Harry replied in a letter on October 29, 1929. 'At the same time, I was taken aback, being conscious of the extreme difficulty of adjusting myself to the change just at this time.'[53] That change, he noted, 'will involve a change in my whole way of living: the giving up of this Flat and, probably, the retirement altogether from London. Also I must add to my income by writing for other publications.' Noting he had the lease of his London flat until April 1930, he asked if his current arrangement with *The Times* could be maintained until then, after which he would move to Minehead. Harry noted that 'with my much improved health, I have been able to be a good deal of use to the Paper this summer and was beginning to have hopes that I would really be earning my salary again. Perhaps I never could; but in any case I shall do the best I can.' He

Figure 30. Harry (right) and Brad in Minehead, Somerset, May 1929. Marked as the last photo taken of Harry. Harry was 69; Brad, 23.

did file a number of articles in the course of the year, including a lengthy article on the evolution of London daily newspapers for the Printing Number, published on the day he wrote the letter. Harry concluded, 'I hate pleading like this in my own behalf, as, I think, few men could hate it.' *The Times* agreed to his proposal.

'Saw New Year in with F. in my room with mulled claret', Harry wrote in his diary on December 31, 1929 from the Beaconwood Hotel in Minehead. 'A mixed year. I'm better than a few years ago, but still feeble and old. F. and Brad on the whole have both been well.' Harry had spent the last ten days in bed.

Epilogue

1930

On April 2, 1930, Harry wrote to Geoffrey Dawson from the hotel in Minehead, presumably to announce his retirement, as indicated the year before. Dawson must have responded favourably, for Harry wrote again on April 30. 'Your letter confirms a formula which I have been in the habit of using in all parts of the world for many years past, namely, that whatever anybody may think of me or of any other individual representative of the Paper, The Times itself is always a gentleman.'[1] This did not mean Harry stopped writing altogether for *The Times* during his final year. There was the occasional bridge column and reviews for the *Literary Supplement* on natural history. In his last, regarding *The Life of the Ant* by Maurice Maeterlinck on December 4, Harry was fascinated by the 'regurgitative charity' of ants as they shared food between them, which Maeterlinck claimed promoted mutual respect and unity among the bugs. 'If this peculiar habit seems an unheroic basis on which to rear the whole framework of life higher and happier than any that we can know', Harry wrote, 'we can at least pay tribute to the genius of the artist who has dared to attempt so stupendous a task and has almost succeeded in making the picture which he draws convincing.'[2]

Remarkably, Harry took on a book commission in the summer of 1930. He was approached by the Employers' Liability Assurance Corporation to write a history to mark the firm's fiftieth anniversary. Founded in response to the Employers' Liability Act of 1880, a forerunner of workmen's compensation, the corporation was the first to offer accident insurance to employees while on the job. Harry would have endorsed this development as it benefited both employer and employee, an extension of themes he had explored nearly forty years earlier in *Men Born Equal*. As Harry wrote, 'Employers were acknowledged to be humane and generous, but the workmen objected to having to depend on humanity and generosity. They wanted their rights established and to be put on the same footing as the rest of the public.'[3]

The Employers' Liability Assurance Corporation, Ltd 1880–1930 was published by Waterlow & Sons Limited, intended for private distribution as a souvenir. At 177 pages, it was illustrated with photographs and reproductions of historical documents. Harry noted in his diary on September 23, 'withdrawing my name, making book anonymous', but it was not. In the book's foreword, Sir Joseph G. Broodbank, chairman, paid tribute to Harry: 'The Directors deem themselves fortunate in having been able to persuade Sir H. Perry Robinson to undertake the writing of their story, and they feel sure that its interest must be enhanced by the skill and charm with which he tells it.'[4] That Harry had the stamina to complete this task is remarkable. According to his diary, he earned an advance of £90 in July, and the balance of £210 when the book was published in October, a tidy sum of £300. This certainly helped, as his earnings from *Times* articles now averaged only about £20 a month. A gala dinner was hosted by the corporation at the Savoy Hotel on November 21, but by then Harry was too ill to attend.

* * * * *

'Getting better but still shaky and can't smoke—since Sept. 5!!', Harry recorded on October 26. On November 11, his penultimate article for *The Times* was published: 'Bridge. What is a Professional?'[5] Harry condemned the recent 'Test Match' held between British and American teams, another attempt to popularize American rules. He also soured on the proposal to arrange a Davis Cup-like competition between the two countries annually. Even when exasperated, Harry could still be humorous:

> Not that the prospect of Davis Cup Competitions at Bridge has not attractive features, for the countries to enter would be likely to be numerous and varied. It would probably not be long before the Cup found its way to the Near East, and, once it was safely lodged in, say, Belgrade, Jerusalem, or Constantinople, Western Europe and the United States between them would have a hard time getting it back. It would, not impossibly, be more likely to continue its journey towards the sunrise, to find ultimately a more or less permanent home in Nanking. At inventing inconspicuous methods of conveying information between partners the Chinese should be incomparable.

Harry's last diary entry for the year was on November 17: 'Brad is out of The Times', part of a dismissal of 15 per cent of the staff. This would have been a heavy blow, making Harry even more anxious about his son's future. On November 19, Florence took over the daily entries in the diary, calling Harry by her affectionate nickname, 'Billie' (origin unknown). Her scribbles offer a rare glimpse into her elusive personality and the obvious love she had for her husband. On November 24, she wrote to Brad, asking if he could take over Harry's bridge articles. November 25 was Florence's birthday. 'Billie sad about it. Rather worse. He tried to shave—very exhausted after.' On November 27, she wrote to Brad that Harry had a high fever as well as pneumonia in his right lung. 'Billie seriously ill. Is so sweet and dear to nurse.' On November 30, Harry's seventy-first birthday, 'He didn't remember it but is not despondent.'

Harry made his first appearance in the 'Invalids' column of *The Times* on December 5: 'The condition of Sir Harry Perry Robinson, who is lying ill at Minehead, Somerset, with pneumonia, is stated to be grave.' On December 13: 'The condition of Sir Harry Perry Robinson is causing anxiety.' On December 20: 'Sir Harry Perry Robinson, who is lying ill at Minehead, was in a critical condition last night.' In fact, on that day, at 5:45 a.m., Harry died, in the presence of both Florence and Brad. 'Very quietly', she wrote. 'We were both with him.' On December 23, they took him to Bristol for a private cremation. 'Service very nice at 2 o'clock. I felt awful at leaving him there', Florence noted. In a letter to Lints Smith on December 24, Brad apologized for the private ceremony. 'I am afraid we must have caused the Social Dept. much inconvenience by giving no notification of where or when the funeral would be', he wrote. 'But my father so strongly wished that it be entirely private, without flowers or any one present except my mother and myself, that we said nothing about it. He was cremated at Bristol yesterday.'[6] Harry's wish for a private funeral is somewhat surprising, although he must have been self-conscious about his new living arrangements. Florence and Brad did give their blessing to a memorial service arranged by *The Times* and held on January 5, 1931, at St Bride's Church in Fleet Street. Florence was too ill to attend, but Brad did.

'The marriage between my father and my mother was undoubtedly a good one', as Brad observed in his memoir. 'My father was invariably very kind to my mother, and she was not merely devoted to him but adored him. Nevertheless, it is the case that in the miserable days after my father's rather sudden death (of pneumonia in a hotel in Minehead) my mother remarked to me "it wasn't always easy—he could be a very difficult man". What she meant, of course, derived in part from their very different backgrounds.' Florence would have also referred to Harry's strong character and disciplinarian nature when it came to, as we have seen, childrearing, household accounts, and, especially, grammar.

*   *   *   *   *

The Times published a lengthy obituary of Harry on December 22, written by Harry's fellow correspondent at the Western Front, Sir William Beach Thomas. Little wonder it was at times intensely personal, quite affectionate, and moving. 'In him this journal loses an exceptionally able and valued contributor, and one who had gained the regard and affection of all his colleagues', Beach Thomas wrote. 'Perry Robinson's articles were compact of good history, as well as personal observation and inference, and enlivened with a delightful humour. Moreover, they bore triumphantly the severe test of republication in book form.' Not surprisingly, he recounted stories from the war years. 'He was the oldest of the official correspondents in France, but certainly not the least courageous or the least energetic', he noted. 'He underwent many hardships, especially in long daily journeys. Courage and persistence were two of his master qualities.' Oddly, Beach Thomas made no mention of Harry's time with Carter and Carnarvon in Egypt, nor of his stint as a book publisher. 'After the War he continued to do admirable work for *The Times*. His knowledge, both theoretical and practical, of games and sport, especially of lawn tennis, golf, fishing, and, latterly, bridge, proved especially valuable, and his powers of vivid description showed no sign of failing', he continued. 'In later years the state of his lungs compelled him to winter in warm places, though he continued to work with undiminished zeal.'

As a bonus, *The Times* ran an 'appreciation' from the American Ambassador, Charles Dawes, at the end of the obituary. Dawes recalled his work with Harry in 1896, during the McKinley presidential campaign. 'I knew him so well in the days when we were both young that the recalling of them when I heard the news of his death made me live over again that crowded and active period in our two lives when our hopes and ambitions were as boundless as they were unrealizable, but our physical energy commensurate with them both', he recalled. 'He had a long and distinguished career since those days when we parted long ago, but I shall always think of him as he was then, when for us "half the world was good, and the other half unknown."'

The condolence letters poured in, Florence noting that she had received a hundred by Christmas Day. John Jacob Astor, *Times* proprietor, wrote, 'During my years at The Times, your husband has been one of its outstanding figures, and in addition to my admiration for his great abilities, I had come to hold him in warmest personal regard. The Times has suffered the loss of a most distinguished correspondent, and all at Printing House Square that of a friend who was universally respected and beloved.' This sentiment was echoed by William Lints Smith: 'The staff of The Times mourn with you the loss of your husband. He was not only a distinguished member of the staff but also a popular colleague.' Louis

E. Hinrichs, Financial Correspondent for *The Times* in New York, remembered that 'very early in my acquaintance with him I discovered how kind he could be—this was when he came here to edit one of the special American number of the Times—for no older man could have done more to help a younger colleague.' Intriguingly, Hubert Walter, a *Times* colleague stationed with Harry at the Western Front, recalled his friend as a straight arrow: 'He was particularly valuable to the Paper during the dreadful Northcliffe regime as one of those members of the staff who never allowed himself to be driven into the sensationalism dear to N's heart and destructive of all honest journalism.' Walter was presumably referring more to the *Daily Mail* than *The Times*. From America, John Crosby, president of the City Council in Minneapolis, had been friends with Harry since 1890. 'How well I remember how I looked up to him, a man of standing and accomplishments, a trifle older than myself, in the world of the small Minneapolis of 1890 or thereabouts!' he wrote. 'I shall always think of him as typical of the best of Englishmen, and what a splendid type that is!'

In a letter to Florence dated January 9, 1931, W. R. Williamson, secretary of *The Times* Publishing Company, Ltd, informed her that the board of directors had met and passed the following resolution: 'That the Board expresses its deep sympathy with Lady Perry Robinson and Mr. J. B. Perry Robinson on the death of Sir Harry Perry Robinson, and desires to place on record its appreciation of the valuable services he rendered to The Times during his thirty-four years' association with the paper.' This was an error: Harry was associated with the paper for twenty-four years. And there was more good news: Lints Smith wrote to Florence on January 19 with a remarkable offer:

> We do not as a rule give allowances to widows of former members of our staff. I placed before the Board of Directors, however, the special circumstances of your case and also a record of the yeoman service rendered to The Times by your late husband, and it was unanimously decided to make you an allowance at the rate of £250 a year. The duration of this agreement will be at the discretion of the Company, but I do not think that this qualification need give you any uneasiness. The existing arrangement will continue until the end of January, so that the new payment will take effect as from February 1 next.[7]

A delighted Florence thanked Lints Smith on January 22; her emotional response is revelatory, as few of Florence's letters exist:

> Your letter is a very kind one to me. I am much touched by it and I am indeed most grateful to you and the Board of Directors for their generosity in conceding to this. I most gratefully accept it. Indeed, I do not know what

I would do without it as since the War I have had no money of my own—
and have been entirely dependent on my husband for everything—even the
clothes! For the last two years I have been in rather bad health and cannot
imagine what there is I could do to support myself—but I shall certainly try.
May I ask you to give the 'Board of Directors' my very grateful thanks for
their exceedingly kind offer to me. And I hope soon you will let me thank
you personally for your kindness to me.[8]

One recalls Florence's dependence upon her husband from the 'contract'
signed by her and Harry, early in their marriage, to limit expenses. It is
unclear whether this annual payment continued for the next thirty years,
until Florence's death in 1961. On February 12, Harry's will was probated: 'Effects £656 9s. 9d. Net pers., £411.'

There is the sense that, after Harry's removal from the scene, Florence
was left utterly at sea, unable to cope on her own. This is perhaps not
surprising for a woman who adored her husband and who, during
twenty-five years of marriage, was often ill and left all of the decisions
to him. Fortunately Brad, who seemed to have a love–hate relationship
with his mother, rose to the occasion, although money remained tight.
They left London and together moved into a cottage in Bray, Berkshire.
Brad held a variety of odd jobs to support himself and his mother before
joining the Ministry of Information in 1939, which brought him to
Palestine. There he married Marguerite Elaine Downing, and they had
two children, named after the grandparents Brad never knew: Julian
(b.1941) and Harriett (b.1945). Brad's book, *Transformation in Malaya*,
recounting his fact-finding assignment there, was published in 1956.

Harry's granddaughter, Harriett, recalled Florence living with her
family for a while. 'All I remember is an old lady who was very with-
drawn. She didn't come up with any stories as grannies do', she reminisced, through a child's eyes. 'Granny had a black cigarette holder and
nicotine-stained fingernails, and the only thing she wanted to do was to
play bezique. She never talked about anyone. Daddy was a responsible
son but felt rather burdened by the maintenance of her. There was no
money.' Florence eventually entered a nursing home in Kent, where her
grandson, Julian, recalled she ruled the roost. '"Lady Perry Robinson"
had a real cachet. I can imagine her being tyrannical', he noted. Julian
suggested that Florence's demeanour 'was a reflection on her husband
who was tyrannical with his moral outlook and insistence on deference',
stories that Julian would have been told by his (usually bitter) father
Brad. Harry was strict and 'old school', yes, but 'tyrannical' seems
extreme; from all indications Harry was a loving and devoted husband.
Florence died on April 14, 1961, aged 82.

*　*　*　*　*

Figure 31. Florence, age 75, with her grandchildren, Harriett and Julian, *c.*1953. Both of Brad's children were born after Harry's death.

It is tempting to wonder how Harry, a journalist for forty-eight of his seventy years, would have written his own obituary and accessed his importance in the grand scheme of things. Intriguingly, on March 18, 1930, nine months before his death, he began writing his memoir, which he entitled 'Some Robinsons', and may have been intended as a testament. The sixty-eight extant pages cover the family tree on both sides, his parents and their life in India, and his own childhood in England. This was a project Harry had considered for some time, and had consulted his siblings and Aunt Margaret Pennington for reminiscences over the years.

The typescript is bookended by two very telling anecdotes. Harry opened the memoir with this one:

> How small I was, I do not know, but certainly quite small. In the room were several grown-ups, some of them not of the immediate family—not my parents, brothers or sisters, but probably cousins and aunts and such—when one of them said:
>
> 'Indifference to one's family is a Robinson idiot's <u>inkresy</u>.'
>
> It puzzled me a good deal. Who was the Robinson idiot? I should like to know him. And what was inkresy? Doubtless something to do with ink-erasers. And the sentence fascinated me, not merely because when first enunciated it had met with the evident approval of the company, but by reason of its mystery and the very ring of it. It sounded important and redounded somehow.

I used to repeat the sentence to myself when alone in corners of the garden and in my room at night; and years passed before I learned that idiosyncrasy was a single word and what it meant, and probably years before it was borne in upon me how extraordinarily true the statement was.[9]

This was a remarkable admission for Harry. Now in his seventy-first year and with mortality on his mind, he may have harboured regrets over not being a less indifferent and more attentive husband (both times) and father (once), and a better provider. As we have seen, wanderlust and ambition got the better of him over the years, drawing him away from his family. Yet in terms of his own siblings, notably Phil, Kay, and Valence, and his parents, Harry was certainly not indifferent to their needs, keeping in touch and responding to calls for help.

The typescript ends abruptly with a fond memory of his father, Julian, when Harry was 13:

I seem to see my Father as he was in 1873 clearly. He accompanied me to London to oversee my outfitting for Westminster. Where we stayed I do not know; but we lunched, I think, daily at the East India United Service Club in St James' Square and it was at this time, as we walked the streets together, that he told me such things as I have already quoted about his father. I remember his opening my eyes to the beauty of the Banqueting Hall of Whitehall and to the dignity of the porch of St Martin's Church in contrast with the mass of the National Gallery adjoining. As we stood in front of Northumberland House— so soon to be swept away he told me the story of Sydney Smith (if... [typescript ends][10]

The genuine affection between father and son as conveyed in 'Some Robinsons' is striking, considering how Harry struggled to connect with his own son—that 'Robinson idiot's inkresy' to family, perhaps. There's little doubt that Harry's sugar-coated depiction of his happy childhood and the love he had for his parents and siblings would have been a revelation to Brad, offering a more sympathetic view of his stern and often unapproachable father.

Whether Harry intended to complete his memoir with a full account of his own life is unknown. If he had, he would have recorded an impressive number of accomplishments of genuine historical import-ance. He inherited from his father and brothers a talent for writing, interpretation, and observation which stood him in good stead through-out his life. In America, as a young immigrant, he founded a journal (*The Northwestern Railroader*) at age 28 and rejuvenated another (*The Railway Age*). He published two short stories in the most prestigious literary journal, and wrote a provocative novel. He proposed an alternative to the trade union for railway workers, organizing them into a voting block with genuine influence. He befriended a U.S. president, and enjoyed a national profile as an industry spokesman and pundit. In England, he rose through the ranks at *The Times* to become a respected foreign correspondent, reporting from North America, Europe, Africa, and Asia. He fostered discussion on both sides of the Atlantic of what was coming to be known as the 'Special Relationship'. He was the oldest and longest-serving correspondent in the Great War, writing a well-received book and earning a knighthood. As the tomb of Tutankhamun was revealed, Harry was present, recording the excitement for an avid reading audience around the world. Clearly, this was a full and influential life.

Harry would also look back on his fair share of disappointments. His personal life was a minefield of marital, parenting, and financial woes. His divorce from Mary, whether or not the union was sound and loving, was a blow. The death of their two young children was the near-ruin of Mary and had a lasting psychological impact on Harry. It is remarkable how Harry rebounded, refusing to succumb to depression and despair. He married again, this time for love. He tried to be a good husband and father, despite his advanced age, broken health, and financial problems. Professionally, Harry's stint as a book publisher was a colossal failure, despite the fact that, thanks to him, Jack London was introduced to the world. A promising return to America as a *Times* correspondent ended abruptly. Harry's personal crusade against the Olympic Games was another misfire, despite the backing of his newspaper.

The modern reader will marvel—and despair—at how many issues that Harry grappled with a century ago are still discussed—and unsettled—today. As an immigrant in the United States he faced discrimination (as many do today) but persevered. He obsessed about world peace, desperate to avoid another war, insisting to his death that an alliance between the United States and Britain, the two great Anglo-Saxon nations, was vital (it remains so). He despised Germany and her hegemony over Europe; might he have welcomed Brexit? (one thinks so). Future Olympic Games would not prevent war, nor would they be free from controversy and violence. Harry abhorred organized labour (as many do), but was progressive in his insistence that workers and bosses can find mutually beneficial solutions without the interference of outsiders. He was passionate about the natural world and the environment (most are), eager to promote knowledge while condemning the destruction of animal habitats. He condemned racism and was a proto-feminist in his promotion of women in sport. He was a fervent royalist (many are) but committed to the Empire (long gone). However, Harry was not blind to the problems of the 'White Man's Burden' in India, for example, and knew that change was coming. Would he have approved of the evolution of the Empire into a peaceful commonwealth of friendly trading partners with the British sovereign at its head? (most assuredly).

Seeking Harry's epitaph, we could look to the address by the Rev. A. Taylor at Harry's memorial service on January 5, 1931: 'To do faithfully the duty of the moment was...the guiding aim of his life.' Harry never left his post. Taylor continued, 'It is true that he was for ever seeing new paths to walk in, new adventures to be undertaken, and ever ready to buy them at the price of study and devotion. The sincerity and simplicity with which he dealt with each in turn had a great deal to do with endearing him to the many friends by whom his loss will be lamented.'[11] That was Harry, always on the run, seeking the next path (life), reinvention, and opportunity. But success came at a high personal price, as Harry often preferred his own company to that of others, even his family. Brad, who had a troubled relationship with his father, wrote in his memoir that 'the dominating factor was a sense of <u>duty</u>. It took precedence over all other motives and considerations. It was an inescapable obligation. If my father said it was my duty to go and see Aunt Emily, that was the end of the argument; there was no escape.'[12]

Perhaps Harry was trying to make amends for this tendency towards isolation when he admonished himself in his memoir. 'This shameful family "inkresy" makes me singularly ill fitted for any such task as this', he wrote. 'Cursed with full measure of it myself, I never asked or learned of my own family, and as all my relatives seemed to have even larger share of it than myself, they never told me anything. Truly an "idiot's inkresy". Yet I should do something to save names that I love and, as I firmly believe, names of men who had some of the qualities of real greatness from complete oblivion.'[13]

Sir Harry Perry Robinson—immigrant, journalist, author, publisher, junior kingmaker, war correspondent, pundit, peacemaker, and provocateur—in spite of all his flaws, had 'real greatness' himself, which (hopefully) has now been rescued from complete oblivion.

Notes

In these notes, extracts from the unpublished memoirs 'Some Robinsons' by Harry P. Robinson and 'Stuff & Nonsense' and 'Robinson Purview' by John Bradstreet Perry Robinson, in private family archives, are cited without author name and published with permission. 'TNL archive' refers to documents in the Times Newspapers Ltd archive, News UK and Ireland Ltd. Published with permission of *The Times*/News Licensing.

PREFACE

1. *Albuquerque Morning Democrat-Journal*, September 15, 1896, 1.

INTRODUCTION

1. 'Some Robinsons', 6–7. Harry began this memoir in March 1930, nine months before his death. Sixty-eight pages of the unpublished typescript survive, covering the family tree on both sides, his parents and their life in India, and his own childhood in England.
2. Ibid.
3. Ibid., 23, 27.
4. Ibid., 25.
5. Mrs Frederick Pennington, 'LIVE TO BE 100 IF YOU CAN! The Age When Everyone is Kind—I Remember the Days Before the Polka—My Dance With Shelley', *Sunday Express*, July 1, 1928. In 1854 Margaret Sharpe married a merchant, Frederick Pennington, who served as a Liberal Member of Parliament for Stockport. They lived at Broome Hall in Surrey, where the couple hosted the leading lights of the day, including Disraeli and Gladstone. Margaret was an early supporter of women's rights and a campaigner for suffrage. She died in 1929, aged 100.
6. 'Some Robinsons', 31.
7. Ibid., 35–6. Harriett's younger brother, John Edward Sharpe, a Captain with the 46th Bengal Infantry, was killed at Fort Sialkote on July 14, 1857, during the Mutiny.
8. Ibid., 37–8.
9. Ibid., 39.
10. Ibid.
11. Charles Allen, *Kipling Sahib: India and the Making of Rudyard Kipling* (London, 2008), 50–1.
12. See Brahma Chaudhuri, 'India', in J. Don Vann and Rosemary T. VanArsdel (eds), *Periodicals of Queen Victoria's Empire: An Exploration* (Toronto, 1996), 182.

13. Lawrence James, *Raj: The Making and Unmaking of British India* (New York, 1997), 356.
14. 'Some Robinsons', 2.
15. Ibid., 41–2.
16. 'Stuff & Nonsense', 39. Brad's 85-page manuscript, dated October 1989, covered episodes in the lives of his father and uncles, as well as his own childhood.
17. Bernard Ellison, *H.R.H. The Prince of Wales's Sport in India* (London, 1925), 25.
18. William Howard Russell, *The Prince of Wales' Tour: A diary in India; with some account of the visits of His Royal Highness to the courts of Greece, Egypt, Spain, and Portugal* (London, 1877), 504.
19. 'Stuff & Nonsense', 36.
20. 'Some Robinsons', 5–6.
21. Ibid., 21.
22. Ibid., 14.
23. Ibid., 56.
24. Harry P. Robinson, 'Echoes from Bow Bells', *The Bellman*, May 23, 1908, 570. Harry wrote often about his childhood and family in his monthly column for this Minneapolis-based journal during the years 1906–9.
25. English translation of the Latin by the Rev. Monsignor William V. Millea, who noted, 'Robinson was a capable Latinist, but some of the references were obscure'.
26. 'Stuff & Nonsense', 40. The Nondescripts was 'not the top-notch one, but more of a friendly XI, who socialised as much as played', according to Judith Curthoys, archivist at Christ Church.
27. 'Some Robinsons', 26–7.
28. Ibid., 25.
29. Harold Spender, *The Fire of Life: A Book of Memories* (London, 1926), 13.

CHAPTER 1

1. Robinson, 'Spokane Falls', *The Northwest*, July 1884, 15.
2. 'Stuff & Nonsense', 38. By way of comparison, in Devonshire, Leopold Grey sent his son, Frederick, to North America in 1890 in search of opportunity. 'In the early eighties lads who preferred exercise to examinations looked abroad for work, and parents who feared their failure in competitions agreed with them', he wrote in the preface to his son's memoir (F. W. Grey, *Seeking Fortune in America* (London, 1912), v).
3. See Rowland Berthoff, *British Immigrants in Industrial America, 1790–1950* (Cambridge, MA, 1953), 5–7.
4. Ibid., 132–3. According to Charlotte Erickson, 'All these circumstances—the ease of obtaining employment without special qualifications, the friendliness of the American community toward British immigrants in such jobs, and the positive attitudes of the immigrants themselves expressed towards

America—were favourable to assimilation in a new society' (Charlotte Erickson, *Invisible Immigrants: The Adaptation of English and Scottish Immigrants in Nineteenth-Century America* (London, 1972), 404).

5. Thomas Greenwood, *A Tour in the States & Canada: Out and Home in Six Weeks* (London, 1883), 158.

6. Robinson, 'Echoes from Bow Bells', *The Bellman*, September 25, 1909, 1134–5.

7. Richard Kruger, *The Paper: The Life and Death of the New York Herald Tribune* (New York, 1986), 148, 153.

8. Hamil Grant, *Two Sides of the Atlantic: Notes of an Anglo-American Newspaperman* (London, 1917), 17.

9. Richard Haw, *The Brooklyn Bridge: A Cultural History* (New Brunswick, NJ, 2005), 21.

10. Ibid., 27.

11. *New York Tribune*, June 1, 1883, 2. Newspaper articles at this time did not as a practice carry bylines which identified the author.

12. Ibid.

13. *St. Paul Gazette*, c.1889; clipping saved in Harry's scrapbook.

14. *New York Tribune*, May 31, 1883, 1.

15. Ibid., 2.

16. Matthew and Hannah Josephson, *Al Smith: Hero of the Cities* (Boston, 1969), 25. One year later, P. T. Barnum put to rest any fears that the Brooklyn Bridge was unsafe by marching 21 elephants across the span, including the famous 'Jumbo'.

17. Robinson, 'Echoes from Bow Bells', *The Bellman*, February 12, 1910, 208.

18. Berthoff, *British Immigrants*, 130. F. W. Grey left Devonshire for North America in 1890, seeking his fortune across Canada and the U.S. He did not have an easy time in Chicago and New York. 'It is a fact that among a certain class of people in the States that the instant they find you are English they immediately drop all other topics of conversation to refer to the time "we licked you badly," or to discuss the degeneracy of the House of Lords, or some other topic which they think will be of interest to you. At first I used to get very angry and try to argue with them, but later I gave this up, and found the only position to take was one of superiority, and say in so many words, "How can people be so ignorant of facts, so dense as to talk such utter rot? Yet they look intelligent."' (Grey, *Seeking Fortune*, 136–7).

19. Robinson, 'The Log of the "Mayflower"', *The Landmark*, September 1920, 266.

20. Phil Robinson, *Sinners and Saints: A Tour Across the States, and Round Them, with Three Months Among the Mormons* (Boston, 1883), 1.

21. Jan Taylor, 'Marketing the Northwest: The Northern Pacific Railroad's Last Spike Excursion', *Montana: The Magazine of Western History*, 60/4 (2010), 19.

22. *New York Tribune*, August 26, 1883, 2.

23. Ibid.

24. *New York Tribune*, August 27, 1883, 5.

25. *New York Tribune*, September 2, 1883, 1.
26. Ibid.
27. Nicholas Mohr, *Excursion Through America* (Chicago, 1884), 68.
28. Robinson, 'Notes by the Way. An English Journalist's Observations on the Northern Pacific', *The Daily Oregonian*, September 12, 1883, 3. This was one of Harry's freelance articles written during the Villard trip, presumably for extra money.
29. Ibid.
30. Ibid.
31. *New York Tribune*, September 12, 1883, 4.
32. *New York Tribune*, September 9, 1883, 1.
33. Robinson, 'Notes by the Way'.
34. *New York Tribune*, November 4, 1883, 13.
35. Robinson, *The Twentieth Century American, Being a Comparative Study of the Peoples of the Two Great Anglo-Saxon Nations* (New York, 1908), 227.
36. *Independent Record* (Helena, Montana), September 28, 1883, 5.
37. Robinson, *Twentieth Century American*, 70.
38. Mark Twain, *Roughing It* (New York, 1984; first published 1872), 541.
39. See Edgar C. Duin, 'Settlers' Periodical: Eugene Smalley and the Northwest Magazine', *Minnesota History*, Spring 1952, 29–34.
40. Undated clipping from newspaper in Walla Walla, Washington Territory, *c.* January 1884, pasted in Harry's scrapbook.
41. Robinson, 'Walla Walla: The Wheat Metropolis of Eastern Washington', *The Northwest*, February 1884, 2.
42. *The Courier-Journal* (Lexington, Kentucky), January 20, 1884, 5.
43. Eugene V. Smalley, 'The Coeur d'Alene Stampede', *Century Magazine*, October 1884, 841–7.
44. Jerry Dolph and Arthur Randall, *Wyatt Earp and Coeur d'Alene Gold! Stampede to Idaho Territory* (Coeur d'Alene, 2008), 93.
45. Robinson, 'The New El Dorado: The Rush to the Gold Fields of Coeur d'Alene Mountains', *The Northwest*, April 1884, 15.
46. *New York Tribune*, March 30, 1884, 3.
47. *New York Tribune*, April 20, 1884, 3.
48. *New York Tribune*, May 4, 1884, 3.
49. Ibid.
50. Robinson, 'Panning Out Gold: Cleaning Up of a Coeur d'Alene Placer', *The Northwest*, June 1884, 7.
51. Smalley would agree. In the May 1884 edition of *The Northwest* he wrote about the current state of the Coeur d'Alene stampede (with advice from Harry, no doubt), and despite the obvious hardships, encouraged readers to try their luck. 'We see no reason why any stout, adventurous young fellow who wants to knock around the world a little and see the life of a Rocky Mountain mining camp should not go to these new diggings. If he is industrious and decent, saving his earnings and keeping out of whiskey saloons and gambling houses, he can hardly fail to make money during the

rush and excitement, whether the placers turn out well in the end or not. In case the gold gives out, he can take up a claim on the neighboring plains of Idaho and Washington and turn farmer or stockraiser' ('The New Gold Mines', 8). Bear in mind that Villard and the Northern Pacific Railroad were Smalley's backers, and Villard had a good deal to gain by encouraging rail traffic in the region.

52. *New York Tribune*, July 13, 1884, 4.
53. Robinson, 'Echoes from Bow Bells', *The Bellman*, January 11, 1908, 36.
54. Penny A. Peterson, 'Great Homes of Minneapolis: The Judd Home', *Lake Area News*, June 1991, 25.
55. Robinson, 'John S. Bradstreet and His Work', *The Bellman*, May 18, 1907, 598.
56. Robinson, 'Minneapolis: A Year's Growth of the City by the Falls of the Mississippi', *The Northwest*, January 1885, 10.
57. Bradstreet, a frequent traveller to the Far East, became best known throughout the United States for a line of furniture and decorative objects based on a Japanese wood-carving technique called *jin-di-sugi*. See Sarah Sik, 'John Scott Bradstreet: The Minneapolis Crafthouse and the Decorative Arts Revival in the American Northwest', *Nineteenth-Century Art Worldwide*, Spring 2005.
58. Robinson, 'Yarns of an Old Miner: "3-7-77"', *The Northwest*, February 1885, 14–15.
59. Harry kept one of these '3-7-77' signs in his scrapbook, given to him by Senator Wilbur Fisk Sanders of Montana during the Villard trip. The meaning of the numbers is disputed. They could represent the dimensions of an average grave, 3 feet by 7 feet by 77 inches. Or they could imply March 7, 1877, the first meeting of the Masonic Lodge in Bannack, Montana, whose members were the original Vigilantes. Today, officers of the Montana Highway Patrol wear arm patches with the legend '3-7-77'.
60. *St. Paul Globe*, September 27, 1885, 3.
61. *Minneapolis Tribune*, May 16, 1885, 4.
62. *Minneapolis Tribune*, May 18, 1885, 3.
63. *Minneapolis Tribune*, May 19, 1885, 4.
64. *Minneapolis Tribune*, May 25, 1885, 4.
65. *St. Paul Globe*, November 2, 1886, 3.
66. Robinson, 'The Crime of Christmas Eve', *The Northwest*, December 1885, 18–20, and January 1886, 15–16.
67. Robinson, 'The Curse of Indian Mill', *The Northwest*, Holiday (December) 1886, 25–7.

CHAPTER 2

1. *St. Paul Globe*, February 26, 1887, 5.
2. Jocelyn Wills, *Boosters, Hustlers, and Speculators: Entrepreneurial Culture and the Rise of Minneapolis and St. Paul, 1849–1883* (Minneapolis, 2005), 204.
3. *Minneapolis Tribune*, January 8, 1888, 1.
4. *St. Paul Globe*, January 24, 1888, 4.

5. *St. Paul Globe*, February 24, 1889, 13.
6. *Minneapolis Tribune*, May 19, 1889, 1.
7. See David C. Smith, 'The Makwa Club's Lake Calhoun Toboggan Slide', Minneapolis Park History, https://minneapolisparkhistory.com/2012/11/09/makwa-clubs-lake-calhoun-toboggan-slid/, November 9, 2012.
8. *Minneapolis Tribune*, January 22, 1888, 6.
9. *Minneapolis Tribune*, April 1, 1888, 6.
10. See 'Naturalization Records', U.S. National Archives, https://www.archives.gov/research/naturalization/naturalization.html.
11. Berthoff, *British Immigrants*, 141.
12. Note that at this time the accepted spelling for 'employee' in the United States was 'employe'.
13. *The New York Times*, November 2, 1888, 3.
14. *St. Paul Globe*, January 25, 1891, 4.
15. *St. Paul Globe*, January 31, 1891, 4.
16. Lake Harriet was adjacent to Lake Calhoun in Minneapolis, where the Makwa Toboggan Club built its slide. Thomas Lowry—Harry's future father-in-law—constructed a lakeside pavilion on his property there; it was destroyed by fire in 1891.
17. Secretary of State James G. Blaine, who served under President Benjamin Harrison.
18. Ironically, on August 10, 1910 a Northern Pacific derailment west of Glendive killed two and injured thirty.
19. Harry also published his first—and last—poem in *St. Nicholas* a year later, in the March 1891 edition. Entitled 'The Turtle and the Katydid', the rhyme began '"Dear Turtle," chirped the Katydid, "what makes you walk so slow?" | (They're sadly ungrammatical, are Katydids, you know.)'
20. See Mary Lethert Wingerd, *Claiming the City: Politics, Faith, and the Power of Place in St. Paul* (Ithaca, NY, 2001), 13–15.
21. *St. Paul Globe*, March 29, 1891, 5.
22. *Minneapolis Tribune*, March 29, 1891, 4.
23. *The Northwestern Miller*, April 17, 1891, 500.
24. *The New York Times*, May 9, 1891, 4.
25. *St. Paul Globe*, April 30, 1891, 4.
26. *Chicago Tribune*, July 15, 1891, 1. Minneapolis and St Paul never consolidated into a single city. Despite the 'Twin Cities' moniker, they remain independent municipalities with defined borders. Minneapolis still has the larger population, while St Paul is the capital of the state of Minnesota.
27. *Minneapolis Tribune*, May 5, 1891, 4.
28. *St. Paul Globe*, May 10, 1891, 11.
29. Quoted in the *Minneapolis Tribune*, May 17, 1891, 5.
30. *The Inter Ocean*, September 5, 1891, 10.
31. *Minneapolis Tribune*, September 24, 1891, 13.
32. *St. Paul Globe*, September 24, 1891, 8.
33. *Minneapolis Journal*, undated clipping in Harry's scrapbook.

34. *Minneapolis Tribune*, September 24, 1891, 13.
35. *The Inter Ocean*, September 24, 1891, 1.
36. Julian Ralph, *Our Great West: A Study of the Present Conditions and Future Possibilities of the New Commonwealths and Capitals of the United States* (New York, 1893), 12.
37. John J. Flinn, *Chicago, The Marvelous City of the West; A History, an Encyclopedia, and a Guide* (Chicago, 1891), 367.
38. William Cronon, *Nature's Metropolis: Chicago and the Great West* (New York, 1991), 294.
39. *The Inter Ocean*, December 13, 1891, 18.
40. Ralph, *Our Great West*, 19.
41. Ibid.
42. Robinson, 'John S. Bradstreet and His Work', 598–9.
43. Robinson, 'A Railway Party in Politics', *North American Review*, May 1893, 552–60.
44. *St. Paul Globe*, May 16, 1893, 4.
45. *The Inter Ocean*, May 7, 1893, 28.
46. General Nelson A. Miles, 'The Lesson of the Recent Strikes', *North American Review*, August 1894, 188.
47. Wade Hampton, 'The Lesson of the Recent Strikes', *North American Review*, August 1894, 194–5.
48. Samuel Gompers, 'The Lesson of the Recent Strikes', *North American Review*, August 1894, 205–6.
49. Harold C. Livesay, *Samuel Gompers and Organized Labor in America* (Boston, 1978), 7.
50. The so-called 'Panic of 1893' launched the worst financial crisis in U.S. history to date: stock prices declined, 500 banks closed, 15,000 businesses failed, and numerous farms ceased operation. About 19 per cent of the workforce was unemployed at the panic's peak.
51. Robinson, 'The Lesson of the Recent Strikes', *North American Review*, August 1894, 195.
52. Ibid., 200–1.
53. *Minneapolis Tribune*, August 12, 1894, 12.
54. *Chicago Tribune*, August 25, 1894, 12.
55. Quoted in *The Rock Island Argus & Daily Union* (Illinois), November 24, 1894, 2. In Harry's scrapbook there is an undated, unattributed clipping related to this controversy, in verse: 'Harry P. Robinson, he slashes away at Wright, Carroll D., for his report on the strike at C., and Harry P. Robinson, he swears he lies like a heathen Chinee.'

CHAPTER 3

1. Anita Clair Fellman, 'The Fearsome Necessity: Nineteenth Century British and American Strike Novels' (Ph.D. dissertation, Northwestern University, August 1969), 164.

2. Letter, Herbert R. Gibbs to Harry, August 9, 1894; Houghton Mifflin Company correspondence and records, Houghton Library, Harvard University, Cambridge, Massachusetts.

3. Houghton Mifflin reader's report, August 3, 1894; Houghton Mifflin Company correspondence and records, Houghton Library, Harvard University, Cambridge, Massachusetts.

4. Robinson, *Men Born Equal* (New York, 1895), 3–4.

5. Ibid., 4–5.

6. Ibid., 111.

7. Ibid., 98.

8. Ibid., 348.

9. Ibid., 364–5.

10. Ibid., 365.

11. Ibid., 366.

12. *Minneapolis Tribune*, February 27, 1895, 6.

13. *The Inter Ocean*, February 23, 1895, 10.

14. *Chicago Tribune*, March 2, 1895, 5.

15. *Minneapolis Tribune*, May 26, 1895, 5.

16. *Chicago Tribune*, December 21, 1895, 2.

17. Source: Harper & Brothers Records 1817–1929, Columbia University, New York.

18. *Atlanta Constitution*, October 6, 1895, 17.

19. Letter, Rudyard Kipling to Harry, March 7, 1896, in *The Letters of Rudyard Kipling*, Vol. 2 (Iowa City, 1990), 234–5.

20. Source: Harry's scrapbook.

21. [Robinson], 'The War on the Wage-earner', *The Railway Age*, July 17, 1896, 1.

22. Charles G. Dawes, *A Journal of the McKinley Years* (Chicago, 1950), 92.

23. Robert W. Merry, *President McKinley: Architect of the American Century* (New York, 2017), 137.

24. See Merry, *President McKinley*, 136; Hal R. Williams, *Years of Decision: American Politics in the 1890s* (New York, 1978), 121; and Karl Rove, *The Triumph of William McKinley* (New York, 2015), 374.

25. Quoted in *The Times*, December 22, 1930, 17.

26. Robinson, *Twentieth Century American*, 282.

27. *Albuquerque Morning Democrat-Journal*, August 14, 1896, 2.

28. *Minneapolis Tribune*, August 9, 1896, 7.

29. *Minneapolis Times, c.* August 1896, clipping in Harry's scrapbook.

30. *Chicago Tribune*, August 13, 1896, 12.

31. Published by *The New York Times*, September 8, 1896, 2.

32. *The Inter Ocean*, September 20, 1896, 1. McKinley had good reason to praise the railroads. In his journal, Dawes recorded on September 11, 'At lunch with Mr. Hanna who handed me an envelope containing 50 one thousand dollar bills—being the contribution of a railroad to the Republican campaign fund. Deposited a check for a similar amount from another source. These will be

the largest contributions of the campaign.' (Dawes, *Journal*, 97). Fifty thousand dollars in 1896 would be worth $1.5 million today.

33. See also Richard J. Jensen, *The Winning of the Midwest: Social and Political Conflict, 1888–1896* (Chicago, 1971), 287.

34. *St. Louis Dispatch*, September 29, 1896, 6.

35. *The Inter Ocean*, October 2, 1896, 3.

36. Robinson, *Twentieth Century American*, 280–1.

37. Unnamed newspaper clipping in Harry's scrapbook.

38. Bryan had referred to the moneyed East, and New York City in particular, as 'the enemy's country', which was denounced by his Republican opponents as prejudice common to the sectional strife of the Civil War.

39. Rove, *Triumph of William McKinley*, 367–8.

40. Robinson, 'The Railway Vote in the Campaign', *North American Review*, January 1897, 123.

41. Ecclesiastes 9:10: 'Whatever your hand finds to do, do it with all your might, for in the realm of the dead, where you are going, there is neither working nor planning nor knowledge nor wisdom.'

42. Harry was not a 'colonel' in the military sense. This was presumably an honorific title used among railroad executives or prominent representatives like Harry. In the *Kansas Weekly Capital* newspaper on October 24, 1899, Harry is referred to as 'Colonel Harry P. Robinson' in an article on establishing uniform railroad rates of transportation.

43. Letter, Ralph Deakin to Harry, February 3, 1927; TNL archive.

44. 'Stuff & Nonsense', 34.

45. *St. Paul Globe*, February 6, 1897, 5.

46. Letter, John Addison Porter to Harry, December 28, 1897; William McKinley Papers, Library of Congress, Series 2, Vol. 107, 300.

47. *Sound Money* (Chicago), October 1897, 1.

48. *Chicago Tribune*, March 23, 1901, 1.

49. McKinley did indeed speak at Harry's rally, held in Chicago on October 20, 1898. He told the assembled railway workers, 'You carry the commerce of the country, you carry the rich treasures of the country from the Atlantic to the Pacific, and you carry daily and hourly the freightage of humanity that trusts to your integrity, your intelligence, and your fidelity for the safety of their lives and protection from injury, and I congratulate you from the bottom of my heart that in this great system, so interwoven with the everyday life of the citizen, in the everyday history of the republic, we have such splendid character and such high intelligence' (*Chicago Tribune*, October 21, 1898, 12).

50. Robinson, 'The American Presidency—Mr. McKinley and Mr. Roosevelt', *Good Words*, November 1901, 771.

51. Phil Robinson, 'How I Landed in Cuba', *Good Words*, October 1898, 678–84.

52. The will was witnessed by Percy Loveridge, who may have been related to Annie. A possible clue about Annie Loveridge comes from the *Statesman Journal* of Salem, Oregon. The newspaper reported on the death of Eliza Annie (née

Loveridge) Sexton in Dallas, Texas, on November 21, 1943. She was born in London in 1875 and came to America in 1902, where she married William Sexton, a native of Suffolk who 'had come to the United States five years before to prepare for her arrival'. They lived for a time in Oregon. This woman would have been 24 years old when Julian died; this Annie might well have been his caretaker, or something more.

53. *Minneapolis Tribune*, October 13, 1899, 7.

CHAPTER 4

1. William C. Edgar, 'Under Two Flags', *Minneapolis Tribune*, February 2, 1931, 4.

2. Letter, Ralph Deakin to Harry, February 3, 1927; TNL archive.

3. Five years after writing 'Stuff & Nonsense' Brad wrote a second (also unpublished) memoir, a 17-page tract called 'Robinson Purview', dated October 29, 1994. He claimed that after McKinley's election in 1896, Harry rented a cottage in Virginia, where he wrote his novel *Men Born Equal* (published in 1895). This was false. Brad proceeded, 'When he came back to his family, he found that his wife, at the persuasion of her brothers, had become a drug addict. In those days there was virtually no cure or treatment for addiction, and the Courts regarded it as a justification for dissolving a marriage.' Brad claimed they divorced (untrue), and Harry left for England. He added, 'There was one child of the marriage, a daughter who lived to be 14 in a mental hospital.' This was also untrue. Brad must have heard these stories from Harry or his mother Florence, or perhaps the years (Brad was 88 in 1994) had dulled his memory.

4. 'Robinson Purview', 6.

5. In *The Savage Club* by Aaron Watson (London, 1907), Phil was described as one of the most popular members. 'Although born in India, he was an Englishman to the core. Phil was a fine figure of a man, as an Irishman would say, carrying the energy and sprightliness of youth, and also its playfulness, far past middle age. His face was browned by exposure to hot suns. He had been almost everywhere. He had edited a newspaper in India, where he had also been chased by a wild boar. He had visited Salt Lake City, and had traversed the American continent from end to end. It was his habit to disappear from the haunts of men in London, and to return in a few weeks, or a few months, looking hardier and browner, but in other respects unchanged, from the fashion of his clothes to the heedless hilarity of his temperament' (205).

6. Robinson, 'Echoes from Bow Bells', *The Bellman*, January 19, 1907, 64.

7. *Minneapolis Journal*, March 23, 1901, 7.

8. Intriguingly, Mary may have been employed at the Northwestern Hospital for Women and Children, founded in 1882 by a group of society ladies including her mother, Beatrice Lowry. The new hospital, managed by women, served disadvantaged women and children, and included a nursing

school (Goodrich Lowry, *Streetcar Man: Tom Lowry and the Twin City Rapid Transit Company* (Minneapolis, 1978), 78).

9. *The Bourbon News* (Paris, Kentucky), July 1, 1902, 3.
10. Edgar, 'Under Two Flags'.
11. Source: William Isbister and Co. Ltd, Company documents, National Archives, Kew, UK.
12. Special Resolution, William Isbister & Co. Ltd, October 19, 1901: Company documents, National Archives, Kew, UK.
13. Quoted in *The New York Times*, February 15, 1902, 32.
14. Letter, Harry to Jack London, February 18, 1902, Huntington Library, San Marino, CA: JL 17246. For a fuller description of Harry's relationship with Jack London, see Joseph McAleer, *Call of the Atlantic: Jack London's Publishing Odyssey Overseas, 1920–1916* (Oxford, 2016).
15. Letter, Harry to Jack London, April 3, 1902, Huntington Library, San Marino, CA: JL 17246.
16. Letter, Jack London to George Brett, November 21, 1902, Huntington Library, San Marino, CA: JL 11060.
17. Letter, Jack London to Harry, April 28, 1902, Huntington Library, San Marino, CA: JL 13337.
18. Letter, Harry to Jack London, March 31, 1903, Huntington Library, San Marino, CA: JL 17255.
19. Letter, Brett to Jack London, May 27, 1903, Huntington Library, San Marino, CA: JL 2994.
20. Letter, Harry to Jack London, August 24, 1903, Huntington Library, San Marino, CA: JL 17258.
21. 'The Strenuous Life' is the name of a speech given by then-New York Governor Theodore Roosevelt in Chicago on April 10, 1899, as a framework for the betterment of individuals and society in the new century. 'I wish to preach, not the doctrine of ignoble ease, but the doctrine of the strenuous life, the life of toil and effort, of labor and strife', he said, 'to preach that highest form of success which comes, not to the man who desires mere easy peace, but to the man who does not shrink from danger, from hardship, or from bitter toil, and who out of these wins the splendid ultimate triumph' (*Chicago Tribune*, April 11, 1899, 1).
22. No date; clipped and saved in Harry's scrapbook.
23. Edgar, 'Under Two Flags'.
24. Minutes, Extraordinary General Meeting, William Isbister & Company Limited: Company documents, National Archives, Kew, UK.
25. Robinson, 'Echoes from Bow Bells', *The Bellman*, December 25, 1909, 1474.
26. *Times Literary Supplement*, November 4, 1904, 342.
27. Court documents, Mary Robinson vs Harry Perry Robinson, State of Minnesota, County of Hennepin, Case # 93611, Box # 131; Centralized Records Center, Minneapolis, Minnesota.
28. *Minneapolis Journal*, February 4, 1905, 7.
29. *Minneapolis Tribune*, April 21, 1905, 8. Schwyzer was featured in *Men of Minnesota: A Collection of the Portraits of Men Prominent in Business and*

Professional Life in Minnesota, published in 1902 (his new father-in-law, Thomas Lowry, was also included). Given his prominence, one wonders if Schwyzer and Harry had ever crossed paths. Schwyzer (d.1951) went on to have a storied career as a physician. He rose to be chief of staff of North-western Hospital, and was one of the founders of the American College of Surgeons.

30. Harry kept a daily diary, faithfully, from 1905 until his death in 1930. These pocket-sized annual diaries, written in pencil, survive, with the exception of the years 1918 and 1922. It is not known if he kept a diary prior to 1905, although he did keep scrapbooks of newspaper clippings, letters, and ephemera.

31. 'Stuff & Nonsense', 31.

32. Ibid., 34.

33. *The Times*, February 16, 1905, 4.

34. Source: TNL archive. Bell scribbled on Harry's letter, 'We have nothing to do with any new paper.' Harry's mistook an advertisement in *The Times* for the new evening newspaper, the *Evening Standard and St. James's Gazette*, which was pitched to *Times* readers as a second newspaper they should take.

35. *Times Literary Supplement*, July 21, 1905, 231.

36. Robinson, *The Life Story of a Black Bear* (London, 1905), ii.

37. Ibid.

38. Ibid., 68.

39. Ibid., 93–4.

40. Ibid., 140.

41. Ironically, one of the acts at the circus at the London Hippodrome in November 1905 was a giant black bear which walked upright like a man. 'Like all bears it has a real sense of humour and is the clown', observed *The Tatler*.

42. Robinson, *Black Bear*, 203.

43. Although in October 1905, one month after Harry's novel was published, Roosevelt wrote an article in *Scribner's Magazine* about hunting black bears, which he observed, were not 'formidable brutes ... None of the bears shot on this Colorado trip made a sound when hit; they all died silently, like so many wolves' (*Washington Post*, September 22, 1905, 12).

CHAPTER 5

1. Regarding Harry's pen name, Brad offered an interesting anecdote of his father: 'A small but striking instance of his versatility was the Motor Car competition in *Pearson's Magazine*. The magazine offered a first prize of a motor car with a second prize of a motor cycle and the third prize of a bicycle for a verse saying what you thought of motor cars. When the prize-giving was announced at some hall in London, only two winners arrived. The first prize-winner was my father in his own name; third was J Blundell Barrett who was my father too' ('Stuff & Nonsense', 41). Harry promptly sold the car to Charles Burgess Fry for £280, no doubt needing the cash.

2. Robinson, *Essence of Honeymoon* (London, 1911), 32.

3. Ibid., 68–9.

4. Brad wrote in his memoir about Bob, 'the old English sheepdog from whom I had learned to walk, clinging to his woolly sides. He had appeared in Cambridge market when my parents had bicycled in to get some ribbons. My mother saw him looking miserable with an old countryman also looking miserable, and she insisted on going up speaking to them. My father guessed what would happen, and it did. Bob travelled back to Shelford with them, crossing along beside the bicycles, and when he got in he saw a leg of mutton on the kitchen table, and the leg disappeared in a flash, and Bob stopped looking miserable.' ('Stuff & Nonsense', 3).

5. Ibid., 95–6.

6. Ibid., 98–9.

7. Ibid., 311–12.

8. Source: Harper & Brothers Records 1817–1929, Columbia University, New York. By way of comparison, Sir Gilbert Parker's novel *Northern Lights*, published by Harper's in 1909, sold more than 30,000 copies by 1911, while Edith Nesbit's children's novel *The Enchanted Castle* (1909) sold fewer than 1,300 copies.

9. See Charles Feinstein, 'New estimates of average earnings in the United Kingdom, 1880–1913', *Economic History Review*, 43/ 4 (1990), 603–4.

10. *Minneapolis Tribune*, March 17, 1907, 13.

11. Robinson, 'Echoes from Bow Bells', *The Bellman*, April 13, 1907, 436.

12. Andrew Duncan Campbell, *Unlikely Allies: America and the Victorian Origins of the Special Relationship* (London, 2007), 1.

13. The book's dedication issued a challenge: 'To those readers, whether English or American, who agree with whatever is said in the following pages in laudation of their own country, this book is inscribed in the hope that they will be equally ready to accept whatever they find in praise of the other.'

14. H. G. Wells, *The Future in America: A Search After Realities* (London, 1906), 257.

15. Robinson, *Twentieth Century American*, 91–2, 93.

16. Ibid., 8.

17. Ibid., 6–7.

18. Ibid., 113.

19. Ibid., 36–7.

20. Ibid., 51.

21. Ibid., 59.

22. Ibid., 130.

23. Ibid., 182.

24. Ibid., 74.

25. Ibid., 226.

26. Ibid., 337.

27. Ibid., 373.

28. Ibid., 302.

29. Ibid., 304–5.
30. Ibid., 430–2.
31. Robinson, 'Echoes from Bow Bells', *The Bellman,* August 10, 1907, 162.
32. Robinson, 'Echoes from Bow Bells', *The Bellman,* November 23, 1907, 576.
33. Robinson, 'Echoes from Bow Bells', *The Bellman,* January 23, 1909, 96.
34. Robinson, 'Thomas Lowry', *The Bellman*, February 13, 1909, 193–4. Thomas Lowry may have died before learning the good news that his daughter, Mary, was pregnant. She gave birth to a son, Werner, on September 19, 1909. Like Harry, Mary had only one surviving child.
35. 'Stuff & Nonsense', vii–viii.
36. *The Times,* May 15, 1909, 6.
37. *The Times,* December 11, 1909, 7.
38. Georges Cuvier (1769–1832), French naturalist and zoologist.
39. Letter, Charles Frederic Moberly Bell to Harry, January 8, 1910, TNL archive. Arthur Willert (1882–1973), Washington Correspondent for *The Times*, was just 28 years old when he took up his assignment in January 1910. Like Harry, he would be knighted for his journalistic services during the First World War.
40. Letter, Harry to Moberly Bell, January 9, 1910, TNL archive.
41. *The History of The Times*, Vol. IV, Part I (London, 1953), 22–3.
42. Intriguingly, while Harry was away Florence took Brad to meet her father, whom she had not seen since her wedding, and would never see again. 'I suspect it was a piece of deviousness on my mother's part', Brad recalled in his memoir. 'The thing I remember best about the visit was the dripping toast. We had tea in the kitchen, and I sat on a bench at a scrubbed kitchen table, and my mother's father, who was off duty that afternoon, sat at the end of the table and looked at me. Except that he didn't really say anything, he was quite nice to me, that I was not much accustomed to big black beards or to grandfathers. I caused my mother some embarrassment for some time afterwards by frequently demanding at home when we were going to have to have dripping toast for tea.' ('Stuff & Nonsense', 31–2).
43. *The Times,* May 24, 1910, 33.
44. Ibid., 34.
45. Ibid.
46. *The Times,* May 24, 1910, 37.
47. Ibid., 39.
48. *The Times,* December 1, 1910, 4.
49. *The Times,* October 28, 1910, 5.
50. *The Times,* November 8, 1910, 5.
51. *The Times,* December 2, 1910, 5.
52. *Honolulu Star-Bulletin*, September 5, 1910, 1.
53. *The Times,* December 22, 1910, 5.
54. In his memoir, Brad recalled his governess, who was the daughter of a neighbouring vicar in Cambridgeshire. 'I am not sure that she really enjoyed America', he wrote. 'She was a handsome, tall girl with red hair and a flashing

eye, and I think she found American men too "forward." My parents always said she could have made a very good marriage in the States, but she would have none of it and eventually married a sergeant in the British Army.' He also remembered 'the mysterious occasion when we were invited to the White House, I think at Easter, and rolled eggs down the lawn' ('Stuff & Nonsense', 5). The annual Easter Egg Roll would have been hosted in 1911 by President and Mrs Taft.

55. Memorandum dated September 29, 1910, and sent to Harry by Moberly Bell on October 3; TNL archive.

56. *The Times*, April 19, 1911, 8.

57. *The Ogden Standard*, May 2, 1911, 6.

58. In his book, Phil found that most Mormons he met condoned polygamy but few practised it. When challenged, however, many Mormons rose to its defence. Phil used some colourful metaphors to describe polygamy. In one, it was a tame hedgehog, but one which rolled itself into a ball and armed its prickles when confronted. Another involved a monkey. 'I remember once in India giving a tame monkey a lump of sugar inside a corked bottle. The monkey was of an inquiring kind, and it nearly killed it', Phil wrote. 'Taking polygamy to be the bottle, and the Gentile to be the monkey, it appears to me that the only alternatives in solution are these: Either smash the whole thing up altogether, or else fall back upon that easy-going old doctrine of wise men, that "morality" is after all a matter of mere geography' (*Sinners and Saints*, 92–3).

59. *The Times*, May 1, 1911, 8.

60. *The Salt Lake Tribune*, May 8, 1911, 4.

61. 'Stuff & Nonsense', 5.

62. Letter, Reginald Nicholson to Harry, July 11, 1911; TNL archive.

63. 'Stuff & Nonsense', 6.

64. Ibid., 7.

65. Ibid., 7–9.

66. Ibid., 10.

67. *The Times*, July 9, 1912, 5.

68. *The Times*, July 19, 1912, 12.

69. *The Times*, July 9, 1912, 5.

70. *The Times*, July 29, 1912, 10.

71. In 1912, Olympic athletes faced strict rules regarding amateurism. The American athlete Jim Thorpe, who won the gold medal in the pentathlon and decathlon (and whom King Gustav V declared the world's best athlete) was stripped of his medals in 1913 when it was revealed that he had played semi-professional baseball. His medals were reinstated posthumously in 1983. Olympic rules were relaxed over time, and today professional athletes are allowed to compete alongside amateurs.

72. *The Times*, July 29, 1912, 7.

73. *The Times*, July 30, 1912, 6.

74. *The Sun* (New York), September 1, 1912, 8.

75. *The Times*, September 19, 1912, 10.
76. *The Times*, August 18, 1913, 7.
77. *The Times*, September 10, 1912, 25–6.
78. Letter, Harry to Reginald Nicholson, October 8, 1912; TNL archive.
79. Letter, Reginald Nicholson to Harry, October 10, 1912; TNL archive.
80. Robinson, 'Westminster Chimes', *The Bellman*, March 15, 1913, 331.
81. *The Times*, July 3, 1913, 11.
82. Letter, Harry to Reginald Nicholson, November 12, 1913; TNL archive.
83. Letter, Reginald Nicholson to Harry, November 14, 1913; TNL archive.
84. *The Times*, November 27, 1913, 11.

CHAPTER 6

1. 'Stuff & Nonsense', 12.
2. Robert H. Patton, *Hell Before Breakfast: America's First War Correspondents Making History and Headlines, from the Battlefields of the Civil War to the Far Reaches of the Ottoman Empire* (New York, 2014), xv.
3. Reginald Pound and Geoffrey Harmsworth, *Northcliffe* (London, 1959), 483. William Howard Russell (1820–1907) covered the Crimean War for *The Times* and is often credited as the first war correspondent. Archibald Forbes (1838–1900) and George Warrington Steevens (1869–1900) followed in his footsteps.
4. Philip Gibbs, *Adventures in Journalism* (New York, 1923), 232–3.
5. J. Lee Thompson, *Politicians, The Press, and Propaganda: Lord Northcliffe and the Great War, 1914–1919* (Kent, OH, 1999), 23.
6. Letter, Harry to Ralph Deakin, April 25, 1927; TNL archive.
7. 'B' refers to 'Billie', which was Florence's nickname for her husband, explanation unknown.
8. *The Times*, September 10, 1914, 7.
9. *The Times*, September 15, 1914, 12.
10. *The Times*, September 24, 1914, 7.
11. *The Times*, October 1, 1914, 6.
12. *The Times*, October 3, 1914, 8.
13. *The Times*, October 9, 1914, 6.
14. Harry revealed in a follow-up article in *The Times* on February 26, 1915, that the killing of the lions proved unnecessary, as only a single shell fell in the zoo, 'killing nothing more than a vulture. None the less the precaution was intelligible; for the Antwerp Zoo immediately adjoins the Central Station, which it was assumed would be a mark for the German gunners; and the lions, if they had got out, could not have been trusted to discriminate between the peaceful citizens of Brussels and more legitimate enemies' (11).
15. *The Times*, October 9, 1914, 6.
16. J. M. N. Jeffries, *Front Everywhere* (London, 1935), 173.
17. Ibid., 176.
18. Ibid., 179–80.

19. *The Times*, October 9, 1924, 15.
20. *The Times*, October 12, 1914, 9.
21. *The Times*, October 9, 1924, 15.
22. *The Times*, October 13, 1914, 8.
23. *The Times*, March 10, 1915, 7.
24. Edgar, 'Under Two Flags'. While in England, Edgar was introduced by Harry to his friend, the Dutch artist Louis Raemaekers, who agreed to draw two new cartoons for exclusive publication in *The Bellman* in August 1915. Edgar praised Raemaekers as 'a master of pictorial irony'. Edgar later visited Harry at the Front before returning home.
25. *The Times*, April 29, 1915, 11.
26. *The History of The Times*, Vol. IV, Part I, 229.
27. *The Times*, July 7, 1915, 7.
28. *The Times*, July 14, 1915, 7.
29. *The Times*, August 2, 1915, 3.
30. Robinson, *The Bellman*, November 13, 1915.
31. *The Times*, August 3, 1915, 3.
32. *The Times*, September 16, 1915, 7.
33. 'Stuff & Nonsense', 8.
34. *The Times*, October 9, 1915, 5.
35. *The Times*, October 15, 1915, 7.
36. *The Times*, October 22, 1915, 7.
37. 'Stuff & Nonsense', 42.
38. Robinson, 'An Appreciation', in Louis Raemaekers, *The Great War: A Neutral's Indictment* (London, 1916), xv. It is somewhat ironic that Harry, who claimed he had turned down an offer to be the American Ambassador to the Netherlands, would in the end become one of the biggest boosters of the Dutch and the talented Raemaekers during the war.
39. Robinson, 'An Appreciation', xxix–xxx.
40. Ibid., xvii.
41. 'Stuff & Nonsense', 42.
42. *The History of The Times*, Vol. IV, Part I, 229.
43. Charles E. W. Bean, the official war correspondent for the Australian forces, commented on his British counterparts to the New York-based *Editor & Publisher* on November 6, 1919 (37). 'Perry Robinson, the Times correspondent, always gave a straight story, but he hated the Germans tremendously', he wrote. 'Philip Gibbs, of the Daily Chronicle, a pale, ascetic man, was an indefatigable writer of high-class material; brilliant, sincere, and accurate...His story in the morning paper was cast in the same mold as his chat at the afternoon tea of the previous afternoon...W. Beach Thomas of the Daily Mail was a tall, spectacled athlete, of rather academic appearance, an old Oxford half-miler. Thomas was a fine correspondent, always keen on his work and willing and anxious to assist his colleagues.'
44. Henry W. Nevinson, *Last Changes, Last Chances* (London, 1929), 138.
45. Gibbs, *Adventures in Journalism*, 247–9.

46. C. E. Montague, *Disenchantment* (New York, 1922), 123.

47. Ibid., 124.

48. Ibid., 126.

49. Robert Blake (ed.), *The Private Papers of Douglas Haig 1914–1919* (London, 1952), 180. The exception would be *The Times*'s military correspondent, Charles Repington, often the subject of Haig's ire and eventually fired by Northcliffe. See A. J. A. Morris, *Reporting the First World War: Charles Repington, The Times and the Great War, 1914–1918* (Cambridge, 2015).

50. Robinson, 'A War Correspondent On His Work', *The Nineteenth Century*, December 1917, 1205.

51. Ibid., 1205–6. Philip Gibbs wrote in his book, *The Battles of the Somme* (London, 1916), 'We have had more experience of war than most men will have, I think, for another fifty years. In our own mess we are critics and prophets and judges, and I fancy we could give a point or two to the experts at home, and, with any luck, later on, may do so. Now in the war-zone we are but chroniclers of the fighting day by day, trying to get the facts as fully as possible and putting them down as clearly as they appear out of the turmoil of battle' (xxvi).

52. Robinson, 'War Correspondent', 1206–7.

53. Ibid., 1207.

54. Ibid., 1208–9.

55. Ibid., 1209–10.

56. Ibid., 1213.

57. Ibid., 1214–15.

58. Harry's articles appeared with the byline, 'Our Special Correspondent', with the dateline 'War Correspondents' Headquarters', in *The Times* and the *Daily News*. Overseas in America, in newspapers subscribing to *The Times*'s syndication service, he was identified as 'Perry Robinson'.

59. 'Sir Harry Perry Robinson. An Active and Varied Career', *The Times House Journal*, January 1931, 104.

60. *The Times*, May 10, 1916, 11.

61. *The Times*, July 3, 1916, 9.

62. John Keegan, *The First World War* (New York, 1998), 295.

63. Robinson, *The Turning Point: The Battle of the Somme* (London, 1917), 23–5.

64. *The Times*, August 1, 1916, 9.

65. Robinson, *The Turning Point*, 107–8.

66. *The Times*, April 29, 1918, 9.

67. *New York Herald*, April 30, 1918, 2.

68. *The Times*, August 17, 1916, 7.

69. *The Times*, August 25, 1916, 7.

70. Letter, Harry to Geoffrey Robinson, August 31, 1916; TNL archive.

71. *The Times*, September 18, 1916, 9. In the same article, Harry observed the ruins of a church and graveyard, 'a thing obscene and terrible . . . sticking out of the edges of the shell holes are the bones of those who once occupied the

graves'. In the midst of this horror, Harry spied a statue of the Virgin Mary, intact on its pedestal, 'her robes still blue and pink and gold embroidered in spite of two months of exposure to the weather, and in spite of all the smoke and gas fumes which have swept over her; and her face is still serenely beautiful... It was very horrible, very wonderful, to stand there in the grey of the dawn, amid a clamour and fury as if the world was truly coming to an end and all around you the graves had already given up their dead—and then to turn to the sweet Virgin in her blue and pink and gold with the infinite patience and eternal pity on her face.' Although the son of a clergyman, Harry was not known to be a spiritual man, at least not outwardly, so these observations are telling.

72. Robinson, *The Turning Point*, 175–6.

73. Letter, Harry to The Manager, *The Times* Office, October 21, 1916; TNL archive: MAN/1/.

74. Letter, The Manager, *The Times* to Harry, October 25, 1916; TNL archive: MAN/1/.

75. Frederick Palmer (1873–1958) was the sole American correspondent attached to the British press group. In his book *My Second Year of the War* (New York, 1917), Palmer recalled his fellow journalists with affection, including Harry: 'Robinson with his poise, his mellowness, his wisdom, his well-balanced sentences, who had seen the world around from mining camps of the west to Serbian refugee camps.' His hope for Harry after the war was, 'May Robinson have a stately mansion on the Thames where he can study nature at leisure.' (403–4).

76. Letter, Harry to Geoffrey Robinson, December 7, 1916; TNL archive.

77. 'Memorandum on the possible replacing of Perry Robinson by Campbell at British G.H.Q.', November 15, 1916; TNL archive.

78. 'Stuff & Nonsense', xii.

79. *The Times*, April 10, 1917, 7.

80. *The Times*, May 3, 1917, 9. A history of the Skylight Club in Minneapolis offered an anecdote about Harry: 'In one of the "hush" periods of the War, when news was discouraged, he and a colleague sought in vain in a congenial French district for specimens of the large and surpassingly beautiful purple emperor butterfly. Robinson, feeling sure that they were to be found on the continent, sent to London for some female emperors and set them in a cage in the garden of the Press Château. Within 24 hours he was rewarded by the appearance of several male emperors' (Bergmann Richards, *The Skylight Club* (Minneapolis, 1965), n.p.).

81. In *The Times* in 2008, journalist Simon Barnes referenced Harry's article: 'It touches me very deeply: the thought of this dauntless journo, writing his dispatches from hell, and, momentarily distracted, looking up and saying to himself: "Ah, that's the first willow warbler this year." These birds, these flowers, these scraps of life held a staggering significance for those who were there—so much so that we commemorate them to this day' (*The Times*, November 8, 2008, 27).

82. *The Times*, June 8, 1917, 7.

83. *The Times Literary Supplement*, May 3, 1917, 208.

84. Keegan, *First World War*, 406.

85. 'Stuff & Nonsense', 13.

86. Ibid., i.

87. Ibid., xiii.

88. Geoffrey Robinson, editor of *The Times*, changed his surname from Robinson to Dawson in 1917 to allow him to inherit the family estate, Langcliffe Hall in North Yorkshire, from his aunt, Margaret Dawson.

89. *The Times*, July 6, 1917, 7.

90. *The Times*, August 13, 1917, 6.

91. *The Times*, September 14, 1917, 5.

92. *The Times*, October 5, 1917, 8.

93. See Angela V. John, *Journalism and the Shaping of the Twentieth Century: The Life and Times of Henry W. Nevinson* (New York, 2006), 157–9.

94. *The Times*, April 2, 1918, 7.

95. *The Times*, April 4, 1918, 7.

96. *The Times*, April 13, 1918, 6.

97. *The Times*, April 15, 1918, 9.

98. *The Times*, November 26, 1920, 15.

99. What happened to the stork? There's no reference to it in the collections of the Imperial War Museum today, and curators are unaware of its fate.

100. *The Times*, August 26, 1918, 7.

101. *The Times*, October 17, 1918, 6.

102. *The Times*, October 19, 1918, 7.

103. Letter, Harry to Geoffrey Dawson, November 10, 1918; TNL archive.

104. *The Times*, November 12, 1918, 7.

105. *The Times*, November 13, 1918, 7.

106. *The Times*, November 14, 1918, 5.

107. *The Times*, December 16, 1918, 8.

108. *The Times*, December 17, 1918, 7. Harry could be charitable when it came to the enemy. 'Sometimes one catches the eye of a man or woman which is ablaze with hatred. How could it be otherwise?' he wrote in *The Times* on December 18, 1918 (8), after touring the region outside Cologne. 'But I have met with no single discourteous word or gesture in Germany. Half the people seem curious and the other half indifferent. The children cheer the British troops, and not seldom women wave their hands.'

109. *The Times*, December 18, 1918, 8.

110. Nevinson, *Last Changes, Last Chances*, 149–50.

111. 'Stuff & Nonsense', 14.

CHAPTER 7

1. 'Stuff & Nonsense', 43.

2. Letter, Harry to William Lints Smith, August 26, 1919; TNL archive.

3. Ibid.

4. *The History of The Times*, Vol. IV, Part II, 1105–6.

5. *The Times*, July 4, 1919, v.

6. Letter, Harry to Lints Smith, August 26, 1919; TNL archive.

7. Letter, Lints Smith to Harry, August 28, 1919; TNL archive.

8. 'The British predominated on the Riviera to such an extent that when the writer Alexander Dumas asked an innkeeper what the nationality of the guests who were just arriving was, he said that they were all English, but he was not sure if they were Germans or Russians' (Michael Nelson, *Queen Victoria and the Discovery of the Riviera* (London, 2001), 6–7).

9. *The Times*, November 14, 1919, 15.

10. *The Times*, November 18, 1919, 15.

11. *The Times*, November 21, 1919, 6.

12. *The Times*, December 4, 1919, 17.

13. *The Times*, December 19, 1919, 15.

14. In his memoir, Brad wrote about his mother's tennis prowess and her frail health. 'I cannot now recall how it happened that my mother found herself playing the first match of a lawn tennis tournament at Cannes against Helen Wills, the Wimbledon champion', he wrote. Wills won her first Wimbledon doubles title in 1924, and singles title in 1927. 'She said the champion was very nice to her and let her win a few points, but after the first set my mother retired. She was well into her forties at the time, but she was extraordinarily strong and vigorous, and even when she was 60 she played a lot of tennis and used to run the legs off young women 30 or 40 years junior. Yet all her life she used to have an extraordinary seizure which caused her without warning to fall flat on her face and for several minutes to be unconscious and then to go rigid as she came round. Naturally this could be highly embarrassing. I remember her doing it as she and I walked up the aisle at the Guards' Chapel! About every three weeks she also had two or three days of acute migraine' ('Stuff & Nonsense', 68–9).

15. Walter (1873–1968) was the direct descendant of John Walter I, the founder of *The Times* in 1785.

16. *Daily Mail*, March 31, 1920, 7.

17. *The New York Times*, May 12, 1920, 2.

18. *The Evening News* (Harrisburg, Pennsylvania), May 18, 1920, 10.

19. *English Speaking World*, June 1920, 13.

20. *Minneapolis Tribune*, May 21, 1920, 23.

21. Julian Perry Robinson, Harry's grandson (born after Harry's death), was pleased to learn of 'the probable origin of my odd pleasure in eating sliced bananas with cream and sugar'.

22. Sir Philip Gibbs in *Adventures in Journalism* described the scene with King George V. 'He gave me the accolade, put the insignia of the K.B.E. round my neck, fastened a star over my left side, and spoke a few generous words. I should be wholly insincere if I pretended that at that moment I did not feel the stir of the old romantic sentiment with which I had been steeped as a boy,

and a sense of pride that I had "won my spurs" in service for England's sake. Yet, as I walked home with my box of trinkets and that King's touch on my shoulder, I thought of the youth who had served England with greater gallantry, through hardship and suffering to sudden death or to the inevitable forgetfulness of a poverty-stricken peace' (275–6).

23. *The Times*, August 4, 1920, 8.

24. *The Times*, August 7, 1920, 8.

25. *The Times*, August 21, 1920, 8.

26. Robinson, 'Why not Polo and Racquets? Fresh Conquests Still to be Made and Prejudices to be Overcome by Women in the Athletic World', *The Times Woman's Supplement*, August 17, 1920, 59.

27. *The Times*, November 11, 1920, 15.

28. Steed refers to Percy Lubbock's review of *The Autobiography of Margot Asquith*, published in the *Literary Supplement* on November 4, 1920. Lubbock was not impressed. 'Mrs. Asquith is no story-teller, it is not her line; she lacks the seeing eye and the vivifying phrase. And yet she elects to write a book that is all story-telling, all an attempt to reproduce the brilliant phantasmagoria in which she lived. She persistently makes the mistake of presenting her conversations with people of interest in the form of dramatic dialogues, with stage directions—'Jowett (smiling)...Margot (indignantly)...'

29. *The Times*, January 17, 1921, 8.

30. *The Times*, March 7, 1921, 13.

31. *The Times*, March 9, 1921, 15.

32. *The Times*, April 20, 1921, 11.

33. Letter, Harry to Henry Ford, September 21, 1921; Benson Ford Research Center, The Henry Ford, Dearborn, Michigan.

34. Lawrence James, *Raj: The Making and Unmaking of British India* (New York, 1997), 491–2.

35. *The Times*, November 17, 1921, v.

36. *The Times*, November 17, 1921, x.

37. While Harry was away, Remembrance Day on November 11, 1921 was the first to sell red poppies in support of the Royal British Legion charity, headed by Lord Haig. More than 8 million were sold. A special pamphlet, 'Remembrance Day—Poppy Day', was also sold to raise money. It included a reprint of Harry's 'The Unknown Warrior' article; the poem 'In Flanders Fields' by Colonel John McCrae; and the suggestion for a war memorial by Louis Raemaekers depicting a soldier crucified. 'Sir H. Perry Robinson has contributed an appreciation of the Unknown Warrior as he was known in different phases during the war and a record of some of his glorious achievements on many fields', *The Times* noted on November 10. Copies of the pamphlet were autographed by Lord Haig and later sold for charity.

38. *The Times*, November 15, 1921, 10.

39. *The Times*, November 18, 1921, 10.

40. *The Times*, November 25, 1921, 10.

41. *The Times*, November 23, 1921, 10.

42. *The Times*, January 13, 1922, 11.
43. *The Times*, March 7, 1922, 11.
44. *The Times*, November 28, 1921, 10.
45. *The Times*, December 2, 1921, 10.
46. *The Times*, December 5, 1921, 10.
47. Ibid. On December 5, 1921, Harry's sister, Agnes, died in London from 'arteriosclerosis and exhaustion'. Harry did not mention this in his diary, nor was there any update on Valence's situation.
48. *The Times*, December 12, 1921, 10.
49. 'Some Robinsons', 3–4.
50. 'Stuff & Nonsense', 38–9.
51. *The Times*, December 13, 1921, 10.
52. *The Times*, December 15, 1921, 11.
53. *The Times*, January 5, 1922, 9.
54. *The Times*, January 6, 1922, 9.
55. *The Times*, January 20, 1922, 10.
56. *The Times*, January 25, 1922, 10.
57. *The History of The Times* expounded upon Northcliffe's travels. 'In January, 1922, while on the world tour that ended with a fatal illness, he seized upon the anger of Moslems as the most explosive ingredient in the whole mixture, and the paper was easily able to relate this diagnosis to its general attack on the Coalition over policy in the Near East. "I am shocked," said Northcliffe, "at the change in demeanour and acts towards Whites by both Hindus and Mahomedans, and especially Mahomedans, who were formerly most friendly."' (Vol. IV, Part II, 855).
58. *The Times*, February 22, 1922, 12.
59. *The Times*, February 23, 1922, 11.
60. *The Times*, March 13, 1922, 12.
61. *The Times*, March 16, 1922, 12.
62. *The Times*, March 17, 1922, 13. Overall, Harry thought the prince did as best he could in the face of the Gandhiite opposition. 'All that could be done to outweigh the evil the Prince did. For that the credit is his. In India itself, I believe, the great preponderance of opinion would be that his visit has done much good.'
63. *The Times*, American Number, July 4, 1922, vii.
64. Intriguingly, Harry noted in his diary on October 27, 1924, 'To Office @ 5 to receive Northcliffe legacy: £259. 6. 0' (£15,000 today), a not insignificant sum—and another sign of Northcliffe's affection.

CHAPTER 8

1. Letter, Earl of Carnarvon to Harry, no date, *c.* December 1922; TNL archive.
2. T. G. H. James, *Howard Carter: The Path to Tutankhamun* (London, 2008), 278.
3. Contract between The Times Publishing Company Limited and The Right Honourable George Edward Stanhope Molyneux Herbert, Earl of Carnarvon, dated January 9, 1923; TNL archive.

4. Memorandum from Geoffrey Dawson to William Lints Smith, January 14, 1923; TNL archive.

5. Telegram, Arthur S. Merton to *The Times*, January 14, 1923; TNL archive.

6. *The Times*, January 10, 1923, 11.

7. See Ben Macintyre, 'How *The Times* dug up a Tutankhamun scoop and buried its Fleet Street rivals', *The Times*, November 10, 2007, 41.

8. 'Luxor—Service of News and Photographs', listing; TNL archive.

9. Extract from Harry's letter, dated January 26, 1923; TNL archive.

10. Letter, Earl of Carnarvon to Harry, January 28, 1923; TNL archive.

11. Thomas Hoving, *Tutankhamun: The Untold Story* (New York, 2002), 155.

12. *The Times* denounced the accusations in a leading article on February 17, congratulating Carnarvon and Carter on their discovery. 'Their congratulations will be the warmer by reason of the discreditable and unfounded aspersions which have been cast in certain quarters upon Lord Carnarvon's work. He has been charged with creating a monopoly in the news from Luxor, and even with "commercialism." No charges could be more false. He supplied the news through *The Times* solely because that was the best way, and, in fact, the only practical way, of supplying it fully and independently to all newspapers throughout the world who wished to take it. The nature of the work compelled him to distribute it through an agent. Had he attempted to do it himself, it would have swamped his labours as an archaeologist. The imputation of "commercialism" is without the shadow of foundation' (*The Times*, February 17, 1923, 11).

13. Telegram from Harry to *The Times*, February 15, 1923; TNL archive.

14. T. G. H. James, *Carter*, 283. Harry's close personal role with Carnarvon may have been the reason why Harry and Howard Carter were apparently at odds, according to family accounts. Harriett Wyndham, Harry's granddaughter, noted that, after Harry's death, Florence destroyed all correspondence with Carter. 'My impression was that she probably didn't want to have anything said that she felt would make her husband look not in good stead', she recalled. 'My father [Brad] always said, "Oh he [Carter] was a horrid man."'

15. *The Times*, January 30, 1923, 11. While Harry has traditionally been given credit for writing the dispatches from Luxor and the tomb, the marked-up copies of the original *Times* newspapers at the Times Newspapers Ltd archive label these as written by Arthur S. Merton. It would appear that Harry and Merton collaborated on most of these articles. We know from Harry's diaries that he was writing and filing hundreds of words each day. Moreover, Harry himself noted of the opening of the tomb, 'I brought down the first story from the Tomb at midday and Mr Merton the remainder at 3 p.m.' If, therefore, Merton was telegraphing the balance of the story, his name was presumably attributed to the entire article. Certainly Harry received credit from his superiors at *The Times* for both his reporting and the success of the mission, and the articles from Luxor are written in Harry's descriptive, enthusiastic style.

16. *The Times*, January 31, 1923, 10.

17. *The Times*, February 7, 1923, 11.

18. Letter, Harry to William Lints Smith, February 9, 1923; TNL archive.

19. Harry, undated report to *The Times*; TNL archive.

20. Telegram, Harry to *The Times*, February 15, 1923; TNL archive.

21. Harry, undated report; TNL archive.

22. T. G. H. James, *Carter*, 290.

23. *The Times*, February 17, 1923, 10.

24. *The Times*, February 19, 1923, 12.

25. The diary entries of Arthur C. Mace, the Egyptologist from the New York Metropolitan Museum of Art, are amusing in its descriptions of the players. On February 21, he wrote, 'The Queen of the Belgians came and spent a long time going over everything in the laboratory. She's embarrassingly keen on everything, proposes to come over again on Sunday to see us open a box. The Prince is rather bored with the proceedings, and glad to get away for a quiet chat and a cigarette.' On March 9, he complained that the Queen had just paid her fourth visit. 'To tell you the truth we are all getting very bored with her... she stayed till twenty past five. Royalties haven't much consideration for other folk' (T. G. H. James, *Carter*, 288–9). Mace was present at the opening of the burial chamber, and his death in 1928 is often attributed to the Tut 'curse'.

26. Letter, Gordon Robbins to Harry, February 20, 1923; TNL archive.

27. Letter, William Lints Smith to Harry, February 20, 1923; TNL archive.

28. *The Times*, February 20, 1923, 12.

29. *The Times*, February 21, 1923, 12.

30. *The Times*, February 24, 1923, 10. Identifying the Allied war dead and maintaining cemeteries on the Gallipoli peninsula were fraught with controversy among the Turkish people for many years following the war.

31. *The Times*, February 26, 1923, 10.

32. *The Times*, March 23, 1923, 13.

33. Paul Collins and Liam McNamara, *Discovering Tutankhamun* (Oxford, 2014), 84. Only six of the twenty-two-odd people present when the burial chamber was opened would die within the next ten years, and of those, only a few in unexpected, 'curse-worthy' circumstances. Interestingly, Harry's death in 1930 has never been attributed to the curse (but could easily have been), perhaps because he had been in uncertain health long before arriving in Egypt.

34. *The Times*, April 7, 1923, 11.

35. *The Times*, May 29, 1923, 5.

36. *The Times*, June 25, 1923, 17.

37. *The Times*, July 3, 1923, 15.

38. *The Times*, August 7, 1923, 13.

39. An aside: on July 23, 1923 Mary Schwyzer, Harry's first wife, died in Minneapolis, aged 51. She was buried the next day in Lakewood Cemetery, beside her father and her two children with Harry. There was no mention of her death in Harry's diary. She was survived by her husband Gustav (d.1951) and their son Werner (d.1976).

40. *The Times*, November 5, 1923, 19.

41. *The Times*, November 13, 1923, 15.

42. Philip Scranton and Janet F. Davidson, *The Business of Tourism: Place, Faith and History* (Philadelphia, 2007), 41–2.

43. 'Robinson Purview', 6.

44. *The Times*, December 28, 1923, 8.

45. *The Times*, January 11, 1924, 11.

46. Ibid.

47. Ibid.

CHAPTER 9

1. *The Times*, April 23, 1924, 15.

2. *The Times*, May 6, 1924, 9.

3. *The Times*, May 29, 1924, 16.

4. *The Times*, July 5, 1924, 8.

5. *The Times*, July 12, 1924, 14.

6. Mark Dyreson, 'Paris 1924', in John F. Findling and Kimberly D. Pelle (eds), *Encyclopedia of the Modern Olympic Movement* (Westport, CT, 2004), 85.

7. See Sheldon Anderson, *The Politics and Culture of Modern Sports* (London, 2015), 86.

8. *The Times*, July 19, 1924, 5.

9. *The Times*, July 22, 1924, 14.

10. *The Times*, July 22, 1924, 15.

11. *The Times*, July 23, 1924, 14.

12. *The Times*, July 24, 1924, 6.

13. *The Times*, July 26, 1924, 8.

14. *Manchester Guardian*, July 24, 1924, 7.

15. *The Observer*, July 27, 1924, 10.

16. *The New York Times*, July 23, 1924, 13.

17. *The Times*, July 25, 1924, 15.

18. Ibid.

19. *The Times*, July 29, 1924, 8.

20. Ibid.

21. *Buffalo Courier* (New York), July 26, 1924, 6.

22. *The Times*, July 31, 1924, 14.

23. Matthew P Llewellyn, *Rule Britannia: Nationalism, Identity and the Modern Olympic Games* (New York, 2012), 166.

24. Robinson, 'England and the Olympic Games', *The Nineteenth Century and After*, September 1924, 415, 418. When Baron Pierre de Coubertin, founder of the modern Olympic Movement, published his memoirs in 1931, he dismissed the controversy at the 1924 Games and blamed it on a handful of disgruntled reporters: 'What importance therefore do you expect me to attribute to the petty examples of shortsightedness that lie behind the predictions of gloom? During each Olympiad, I read that it will be the *last*

because—Because, if you really want to know, the reporter (one has to see facts as they are) was poorly accommodated, was overcharged in a restaurant or because the telegraph or telephone did not work as it should. This is only human.' He might have had Harry in mind. (Pierre de Coubertin, *Olympic Memoirs* (Lausanne, Switzerland, first published 1931, repr. 1979), 136.)

25. *The Times*, January 9, 1925, 15.

26. Robinson, 'As England Sees It', *The Landmark*, April 1925, 199–204; May 1925, 263–6; June 1925, 335–40.

27. An aside: Mary Whalley, Harry's sister, died in South Africa on June 11, 1925, aged 76. While Harry did not note this in his diary, he did record that Mary had left him the sum of £2 in her will, which Harry used to purchase a new umbrella. Mary was a notorious figure in her own right. At the turn of the century, she separated from her Indian civil servant husband, Paul Whalley, with whom she had three children, and moved to South Africa, where she was an ardent Unionist during the Boer War. In 1909 she collaborated on a book with A. Eames Perkins (her suspected lover) called *Of European Descent*. As self-proclaimed 'Imperialists', their intention was to shine a spotlight on 'an insidious danger which is threatening family life in this Colony of South Africa'; namely, 'the races must NEVER be allowed to marry and produce subsequent "half-caste" children', who they coined 'Eur-african'. There was only one answer, the authors concluded: segregation, enforced through 'Purity of Race Associations'. Harry never mentioned his sister's book and would not have shared her extreme views on what came to be known as apartheid.

28. *The Times*, May 7, 1926, 3.

29. 'Stuff & Nonsense', x.

30. *The Times*, May 18, 1926, 9.

31. 'Stuff & Nonsense', 43.

32. *The Times*, August 10, 1926, 15.

33. 'Stuff & Nonsense', x–xi.

34. *The Times*, November 26, 1926, 15.

35. *The Times*, January 12, 1927, 15.

36. *The Times*, March 8, 1927, 19.

37. See Richard L. Frey (ed.), *The Official Encyclopedia of Bridge*, 3rd edn (New York, 1976).

38. *The Times*, May 14, 1927, 8.

39. *The Times*, May 25, 1927, 12.

40. *The Times*, September 22, 1927, 10.

41. 'Robinson Purview', 10.

42. 'Stuff & Nonsense', 71.

43. Ibid., 44.

44. 'At my father's suggestion The Times agreed to take me on just before my 21st birthday', Brad recalled in 'Stuff & Nonsense' (44). 'For the first three years all went well, and I enjoyed the work (mainly Assistant Foreign News Editor)', he noted, but 'at the start of my fourth year things began to go

wrong. The "Great Slump" of 1929–1931 caused the Fleet Street proprietors to agree to an all-round dismissal of 15% of their staff, on the basis of "last in, first out". I rather doubt if I was "last in", but they pushed me out in the week my father died. (In those days, of course, there were no Trade Unions to look after white-collar workers).'

45. *The Times*, January 23, 1928, 17.
46. Letter, Harry to William Lints Smith, March 16, 1928; TNL archive.
47. Letter, William Lints Smith to Harry, March 27, 1928; TNL archive.
48. Letter, Kipling to Harry, June 25, 1928. See Thomas Pinney, editor, *The Letters of Rudyard Kipling*, Vol. 5 (Iowa City, 1990), 441–2, and Philip Longworth, *The Unending Vigil: A History of the Commonwealth War Graves Commission, 1917–1967* (London, 1967), 126.
49. Letter, William Lints Smith to Harry, November 9, 1928; TNL archive.
50. Harry did sell his 37-volume New York edition of Kipling's writings. Intriguingly, when the set came up for auction again at Sotheby's in 1966 (according to the *Battle Creek Enquirer* (Michigan), on April 6, 1966), the highlight was a letter tucked inside from Kipling to Harry, attaching the poem about the 'Rudyard' and 'Kipling' stations on the Soo Line, which Harry had published in the *Railway Age* in 1896. See Chapter 3.
51. An aside: On April 29, 1929, Harry's aunt, Margaret Pennington, died, two months shy of her 101st birthday. Florence went to the funeral. She left an estate worth £33,583 1s. 11d. (around £2 million today) to her son, Frederick, and two daughters. The library of the Zoological Society received a gift of several hundred paintings of Indian birds and mammals. There is no evidence that Harry received a bequest; his aunt had already been unduly generous to Brad.
52. *The Times*, October 9, 1929, 16.
53. Letter, Harry to William Lints Smith, October 29, 1929; TNL archive.

EPILOGUE

1. Letter, Harry to Geoffrey Dawson, April 30, 1930; TNL archive.
2. *The Times Literary Supplement*, December 4, 1930, 1031.
3. Harry Perry Robinson, *The Employers' Liability Assurance Corporation, Ltd 1880–1930* (London, 1930), 7.
4. Ibid., viii.
5. *The Times*, November 11, 1930, 17. One additional article by Harry was published in *The Times* after his death: 'Bridge. Conventions at Contract' on December 24, 1930, 11.
6. Letter, John Bradstreet Perry Robinson to William Lints Smith, December 24, 1930; TNL archive.
7. Letter, William Lints Smith to Lady Perry Robinson, January 19, 1930; TNL archive.
8. Letter, Lady Perry Robinson to William Lints Smith, January 22, 1930; TNL archive.

9. 'Some Robinsons', 1.
10. Ibid., 68. Northumberland House, home of the Dukes of Northumberland, was located on the Strand from 1605 until 1874, when it was demolished. Sydney Smith (1771–1845) was an Anglican minister and humorist who championed parliamentary reform and Catholic emancipation.
11. *The Times House Journal*, January 1931, 104–5.
12. 'Stuff & Nonsense', 1.
13. 'Some Robinsons', 4.

Bibliography

Allen, Charles, *Kipling Sahib: India and the Making of Rudyard Kipling* (London: Abacus, 2008).

Anderson, Sheldon, *The Politics and Culture of Modern Sports* (London: Lexington Books, 2015).

Berthoff, Rowland, *British Immigrants in Industrial America, 1790–1950* (Cambridge, MA: Harvard University Press, 1953).

Blake, Robert (ed.), *The Private Papers of Douglas Haig 1914–1919* (London: Eyre & Spottiswoode, 1952).

Burrows, Edwin G., and Mike Wallace, *Gotham: A History of New York City to 1898* (Oxford: Oxford University Press, 1999).

Campbell, Duncan Andrew, *Unlikely Allies: America and the Victorian Origins of the Special Relationship* (London: Hambledon Continuum, 2007).

Chaudhuri, Brahma, 'India', in J. Don Vann and Rosemary T. VanArsdel (eds), *Periodicals of Queen Victoria's Empire: An Exploration* (Toronto: University of Toronto Press, 1996), 175–200.

Collins, Paul, and Liam McNamara, *Discovering Tutankhamun* (Oxford: Ashmolean Museum, 2014).

Coubertin, Pierre de, *Olympic Memoirs* (Lausanne, Switzerland: International Olympic Committee, 1931; repr. 1979).

Cronon, William, *Nature's Metropolis: Chicago and the Great West* (New York: W.W. Norton, 1991).

Davis, Richard Harding, *With the French in France and Salonika* (New York: Charles Scribner's Sons, 1916).

Dawes, Charles G., *A Journal of the McKinley Years* (Chicago: Lakeside Press, 1950).

DeForest, Walter S., 'The Periodical Press and the Pullman Strike: An Analysis of the Coverage and Interpretation of the Railroad Strike of 1894 by Eight Journals of Opinion and Reportage', M.A. Thesis, Madison, WI: University of Wisconsin, 1973.

Dolph, Jerry, and Arthur Randall, *Wyatt Earp and Coeur d'Alene Gold! Stampede to Idaho Territory* (Coeur d'Alene, ID: Museum of North Idaho, 2008).

Dyreson, Mark, 'Paris 1924', in John E. Findling and Kimberly D. Pelle (eds), *Encyclopedia of the Modern Olympic Movement* (Westport, CT: Greenwood Press, 2004), 79–88.

Duin, Edgar C., 'Settlers' Periodical: Eugene Smalley and the Northwest Magazine', in *Minnesota History* (Spring 1952), 29–34.

Edgar, William C., 'Under Two Flags', *Minneapolis Tribune* (February 2, 1931), 4.

Ellison, Bernard C., *H.R.H. The Prince of Wales's Sport in India* (London: William Heinemann Ltd, 1925).

Erickson, Charlotte, *Invisible Immigrants: The Adaptation of English and Scottish Immigrants in Nineteenth-Century America* (London: Weidenfeld & Nicolson, 1972).

Feinstein, Charles, 'New estimates of average earnings in the United Kingdom, 1880–1913', *Economic History Review*, 43/4 (1990), 595–632.

Fellman, Anita Clair, 'The Fearsome Necessity: Nineteenth Century British and American Strike Novels', Ph.D. dissertation, Northwestern University, August 1969.

Flinn, John J., *Chicago, the Marvelous City of the West; A History, An Encyclopedia, and A Guide.* (Chicago: Flinn & Sheppard, 1891).

Frey, Richard L. (ed.), *The Official Encyclopedia of Bridge* (3rd edn, New York: Crown Publishers, 1976).

Fyfe, Hamilton, *Northcliffe: An Intimate Biography* (New York: Macmillan, 1930).

Gay, J. Drew, *The Prince of Wales in India, or, From Pall Mall to the Punjab* (New York: R. Worthington, 1877).

Gibbs, Philip, *Adventures in Journalism* (New York: Harper & Brothers, 1923).

Gibbs, Philip, *The Battles of the Somme* (London: William Heinemann, 1916).

Goldblatt, David, *The Games: A Global History of the Olympics* (New York: W.W. Norton, 2016).

Gower, F. Leveson, *Bygone Years: Recollections* (London: John Murray, 1905).

Grant, Hamil, *Two Sides of the Atlantic: Notes of an Anglo-American Newspaperman* (London: Grant Richards, 1917).

Greene, Julie, *Pure and Simple Politics: The American Federation of Labor and Political Activism, 1881–1917* (Cambridge: Cambridge University Press, 1998).

Greenwood, Thomas, *A Tour in the States & Canada: Out and Home in Six Weeks* (London: L. Upcott Gill, 1883).

Grey, F. W., *Seeking Fortune in America* (London: Smith, Elder & Co., 1912).

Hale, Julian, *The French Riviera: A Cultural History* (New York: Oxford University Press, 2009).

Hamilton, Ulf, 'Stockholm 1912', in John E. Findling and Kimberly D. Pelle (eds), *Encyclopedia of the Modern Olympic Movement* (Westport, CT: Greenwood Press, 2004), 57–62.

Hapke, Laura, *Labor's Text: The Worker in American Fiction* (New Brunswick, NJ: Rutgers University Press, 2001).

Haw, Richard, *The Brooklyn Bridge: A Cultural History* (New Brunswick, NJ: Rutgers University Press, 2005).

Hobson, Harold, Philip Knightley, and Leonard Russell, *The Pearl of Days: An Intimate Memoir of The Sunday Times 1822–1972* (London: Hamish Hamilton, 1972).

Hoving, Thomas, *Tutankhamun: The Untold Story* (New York: Cooper Square Press, 2002).

Jackson, Holbrook, *The Eighteen Nineties* (London: Grant Richards, 1913).

James, Lawrence, *Raj: The Making and Unmaking of British India* (New York: Little, Brown, 1997).

James, T. G. H., *Howard Carter: The Path to Tutankhamun* (London: Tauris Parke Paperbacks, 2008).

Jeffries, J. M. N., *Front Everywhere* (London, Hutchinson & Co., 1935).

Jensen, Richard J., *The Winning of the Midwest: Social and Political Conflict, 1888–1896* (Chicago: University of Chicago Press, 1971).

John, Angela V., *War, Journalism and the Shaping of the Twentieth Century: The Life and Times of Henry W. Nevinson* (New York: I.B. Tauris, 2006).

Josephson, Matthew and Hannah, *Al Smith: Hero of the Cities* (Boston, MA: Houghton Mifflin, 1969).

Keay, John, *India: A History* (New York: Atlantic Monthly Press, 2000).

Keegan, John, *The First World War* (New York: Vintage Books, 1998).

Kruger, Richard, *The Paper: The Life and Death of the New York Herald Tribune* (New York: Alfred A. Knopf, 1986).

Livesay, Harold C., *Samuel Gompers and Organized Labor in America* (Boston, MA: Little, Brown, 1978).

Llewellyn, Matthew P., *Rule Britannia: Nationalism, Identity and the Modern Olympic Games* (New York: Routledge, 2012).

Longworth, Philip, *The Unending Vigil: A History of the Commonwealth War Graves Commission, 1917–1967* (London: Constable, 1967).

Lowry, Goodrich, *Streetcar Man: Tom Lowry and the Twin City Rapid Transit Company* (Minneapolis, MN: Lerner Publications Company, 1978).

Lubow, Arthur, *The Reporter Who Would Be King: A Biography of Richard Harding Davis* (New York: Charles Scribner's Sons, 1992).

McCullough, David G., *The Great Bridge* (New York: Simon & Schuster, 1972).

Macintyre, Ben, 'How The Times Dug Up a Tutankhamun Scoop and Buried its Fleet Street Rivals', *The Times* (November 10, 2007), 38–41.

McAleer, Joseph, *Call of the Atlantic: Jack London's Publishing Odyssey Overseas, 1902–1916* (Oxford: Oxford University Press, 2016).

Men of Minnesota: A Collection of the Portraits of Men Prominent in Business and Professional Life in Minnesota (St Paul: The Minnesota Historical Company, 1902).

Merry, Robert W., *President McKinley: Architect of the American Century* (New York: Simon & Schuster, 2017).

Metcalf, Barbara D., and Thomas R. Metcalf, A *Concise History of India* (Cambridge: Cambridge University Press, 2002).

Minneapolis City Directory (Minneapolis, MN: C. Wright Davison and Minneapolis Directory Company, 1883–1891).

Mohr, Nicholas, *Excursion Through America* (Chicago: Lakeside Press, 1973; first published 1884).

Montague, C. E., *Disenchantment* (New York: Brentano's, 1922).

Morris, A. J. A., *Reporting the First World War: Charles Repington, The Times and the Great War, 1914–1918* (Cambridge: Cambridge University Press, 2015).

Nelson, Michael, *Queen Victoria and the Discovery of the Riviera* (London: I. B. Tauris, 2001).

Newman, John J., *American Naturalization Processes and Procedures, 1790–1985* (Indianapolis, IN: Indiana Historical Society, 1985).

Nevinson, Henry W., *Last Changes, Last Chances* (London: Nisbet & Co., 1928).

Palmer, Frederick, *My Second Year of the War* (New York: Dodd, Mead, 1917).

Patton, Robert H., *Hell Before Breakfast: America's First War Correspondents Making History and Headlines, from the Battlefields of the Civil War to the Far Reaches of the Ottoman Empire* (New York: Pantheon Books, 2014).

Pennington, Mrs. Frederick, 'LIVE TO BE 100 IF YOU CAN! The Age When Everyone is Kind—I Remember the Days Before the Polka—My Dance With Shelley', *Sunday Express* (July 1, 1928).

Peterson, Penny A., 'Great Homes of Minneapolis: The Judd Home', in *Lake Area News* (Minneapolis) (June 1991), 25.

Pound, Reginald, and Geoffrey Harmsworth, *Northcliffe* (London: Cassell, 1959).

Raemaekers, Louis, *The Great War: A Neutral's Indictment* (London: Fine Art Society, 1916).

Raemaekers, Louis, *The Great War in 1916: A Neutral's Indictment. Sixty Cartoons* (London: Fine Art Society, 1917).

Ralph, Julian, *Our Great West: A Study of the Present Conditions and Future Possibilities of the New Commonwealths and Capitals of the United States* (New York: Harper & Brothers, 1893).

Richards, Bergmann, *The Skylight Club* (Minneapolis, MN: privately printed, 1965).

Robinson, Edward Kay, *In the King's County* (London: Isbister & Co., 1904).

Robinson, Edward Kay, *My Nature Notebook* (London: Isbister & Co., 1903).

Robinson, Harry P., 'A Railway Party in Politics', *North American Review* (Vol. 156, No. 438, May 1893), 552–60.

Robinson, Harry P., 'As England Sees It', *The Landmark* (April 1925), 199–204.

Robinson, Harry P., 'A War Correspondent On His Work', *The Nineteenth Century* (December 1917), 1205–15.

Robinson, Harry P., 'England and the Olympic Games', *The Nineteenth Century and After* (September 1924), 412–19.

Robinson, Harry P., *Essence of Honeymoon* (New York: Harper & Brothers, 1911).

[Robinson, Harry P.], 'Federal City: Being a Remembrance of the Time Before St. Paul and Minneapolis Were United', (Minneapolis, MN: privately printed, 1891).

[Robinson, Harry P. (ed.)], *Ireland of To-Day* (London: John Murray, 1913).

Robinson, Harry P., 'Medusa', *Westward Ho!* (November 1891), 15–25.

Robinson, Harry P., *Men Born Equal* (New York: Harper & Brothers, 1895).

Robinson, Harry P., *Of Distinguished Animals* (London: William Heinemann, 1910).

Robinson, Harry P., 'On a Mountain Trail', in *Western Frontier Stories: Retold from St. Nicholas* (New York: Century, 1907); first published in *St. Nicholas Magazine* (New York: Century), Vol. 17, No. 5, 371–4.

Robinson, Harry P., 'Organized Labor and Organized Capital', *Journal of Political Economy* (Vol. 7, No. 3, June 1899), 327–51.

Robinson, Harry P., 'Our Navies', *The Landmark* (May 1925), 263–6.

Robinson, Harry P., 'Some Robinsons', unpublished memoir, 1930.

Robinson, Harry P., 'The American Presidency—Mr. McKinley and Mr. Roosevelt', *Good Words* (November 1901), 765–74.

Robinson, Harry P., 'The Crime of Christmas Eve', *The Northwest* (December 1885), 18–20; (January 1886), 15–16.

Robinson, Harry P., 'The Curse of Indian Mill', *The Northwest* (Holiday (December) 1886), 25–7.

Robinson, Harry P., *The Employers' Liability Assurance Corporation, Ltd. 1880–1930* (London: Waterlow & Sons, 1930).

Robinson, Harry P., 'The Fastest Railroad Run Ever Made', *McClure's Magazine* (Vol. 6, No. 3, February 1896), 247–55.

Robinson, Harry P., 'The Gift of Fernseed', in *The Atlantic Monthly* (February 1889), 231–55.

Robinson, Harry P., 'The Gold Heart', in *The Atlantic Monthly* (September 1889), 303–14.

Robinson, Harry P., 'The Humiliating Report of the Strike Commission', *The Forum* (January 1895), 523–31.

Robinson, Harry P., 'The Lesson of Recent Strikes', *North American Review* (Vol. 159, No. 453, August 1894), 195–201.

Robinson, Harry P., *The Life Story of a Black Bear* (London: Adam & Charles Black, 1910).

Robinson, Harry P., 'The Power of the United States', *The Landmark* (June 1925), 335–40.

Robinson, Harry P., 'The Railway Vote in the Campaign', *The North American Review* (January 1897), 122–5.

Robinson, Harry P., 'The Story of the Late War in Europe', *Scribner's Magazine* (November 1895), 545–56.

Robinson, Harry P., *The Turning Point: The Battle of the Somme* (London: William Heinemann, 1917).

Robinson, Harry P., *The Twentieth Century American, Being a Comparative Study of the Peoples of the Two Great Anglo-Saxon Nations* (New York: G.P. Putnam's Sons, 1908).

Robinson, Harry P., 'Yarns of an Old Miner', *The Northwest* (February 1885), 14–15.

Robinson, John Bradstreet Perry, 'Robinson Purview', unpublished memoir, 1994.

[Robinson, John Bradstreet Perry], *Repton Sketches* (London: Ernest Benn, 1928).

Robinson, John Bradstreet Perry, 'Stuff & Nonsense', unpublished memoir, 1989.

Robinson, John Bradstreet Perry, *Transformation in Malaya* (London: Secker & Warburg, 1956).

Robinson, Phil, *Birds of the Wave and Woodland* (London: Isbister & Co., 1895).

Robinson, Phil, *Bubble and Squeak: Some Calamitous Stories* (London: Isbister & Co., 1903).

Robinson, Phil, 'How I Landed in Cuba', *Good Words* (October 1898), 678–84.

Robinson, Phil, *In Garden, Orchard and Spinney* (London: Isbister & Co., 1898).

Robinson, Phil, *Sinners and Saints: A Tour across the States, and Round Them, with Three Months among the Mormons* (Boston, MA: Roberts Brothers, 1883).

Robinson, Phil, Robinson, E. Kay, and Robinson, H. Perry, *Tales by Three Brothers* (London: Isbister & Co., 1902).

Roth, Michael P., *Historical Dictionary of War Journalism* (Westport, CT: Greenwood Press, 1997).

Rove, Karl, *The Triumph of William McKinley* (New York: Simon & Schuster, 2016).

Russell, William Howard, *The Prince of Wales' Tour: A Diary in India; With Some Account of the Visits of His Royal Highness to the Courts of Greece, Egypt, Spain, and Portugal* (London: Sampson Low, Marston, Searle & Rivington, 1877).

Scranton, Philip, and Janet F. Davidson, *The Business of Tourism: Place, Faith and History* (Philadelphia, PA: University of Pennsylvania Press, 2007).

Sik, Sarah, 'John Scott Bradstreet: The Minneapolis Crafthouse and the Decorative Arts Revival in the American Northwest', *Nineteenth-Century Art Worldwide,* 4/1 (Spring 2005), http://www.19thc-artworldwide.org/spring05/64-spring05/spring05article/301-john-scott-bradstreet-and-the-decorative-arts-revival-in-america.

'Sir Harry Perry Robinson. An Active and Varied Career', *The Times House Journal* (London) (January 1931), 103–5.

Smalley, Eugene V., 'The Coeur d'Alene Stampede', *Century Magazine* (October 1884), 841–7.

Smith, David C., 'The Makwa Club's Lake Calhoun Toboggan Slide', Minneapolis Park History (November 9, 2012), https://minneapolisparkhistory.com/2012/11/09/makwa-clubs-lake-calhoun-toboggan-slid/.

Smith, Vincent A., *The Oxford History of India* (4th edn, Oxford: Oxford University Press, 1981).

Spear, Percival, *India: A Modern History* (Ann Arbor, MI: University of Michigan Press, 1972).

Spears, Timothy B., *Chicago Dreaming: Midwesterners and the City, 1871–1919* (Chicago: University of Chicago Press, 2005).

Spender, Harold, *The Fire of Life: A Book of Memories* (London: Hodder & Stoughton, 1926).

Spraker, Jean E., 'A Century of Carnivals in St. Paul', *Minnesota History* (Winter 1985), 322–31.

Taylor, Jan, 'Marketing the Northwest: The Northern Pacific Railroad's Last Spike Excursion', *Montana: The Magazine of Western History,* 60/4 (2010), 16–35.

The History of The Times, Vol. IV: *The 150th Anniversary and Beyond: 1912–1948,* Parts I and II (London: *The Times,* 1952).

'The Prince of Wales Camp Postmarks 1921–1922', *Global Philately* (November 19, 2012), http://globalphilatelic.blogspot.com/2012/11/the-prince-of-wales-camp-postmarks-1921.html.

The Prince of Wales' Eastern Book: A Pictorial Record of the Voyages of H.M. S. 'Renown' 1921–1922 (London: Hodder & Stoughton, 1922).

The Times History of the War, 22 vols (London: *The Times,* 1914–22).

The Times: Past, Present, Future: To Celebrate Two Hundred Years of Publication (London: *The Times,* 1985).

Thompson, J. Lee, *Politicians, The Press, and Propaganda: Lord Northcliffe and the Great War, 1914–1919* (Kent, OH: Kent State University Press, 1999).

Twain, Mark, *Roughing It* (New York: Library of America, 1984; first published 1872).

Villard, Henry, *Memoirs of Henry Villard, Journalist and Financier, 1835–1900,* 2 vols (Boston, MA: Houghton Mifflin, 1904; repr. New York: DaCapo Press, 1969).

War Graves of the Empire: Reprinted from the Special Number of The Times, November 10, 1928 (London: *The Times* Publishing Company, 1928).

Watson, Aaron, *The Savage Club: A Medley of History, Anecdote and Reminiscence* (London: T. Fisher Unwin, 1907).

Wells, H. G., *The Future in America: A Search After Realities* (London: Harper & Brothers, 1906).

Whalley, Mary Frances, and A. Eames-Perkins, *Of European Descent* (Cape Town: J.C. Juta & Co., 1909).

Wheeler, George, *India in 1875–76. The Visit of the Prince of Wales. A Chronicle of His Royal Highness's Journeyings in India, Ceylon, Spain, and Portugal* (London: Chapman & Hall, 1976).

Williams, R. Hal, *Realigning America: McKinley, Bryan, and the Remarkable Election of 1896* (Lawrence, KS: University Press of Kansas, 2010).

Williams, R. Hal, *Years of Decision: American Politics in the 1890s* (New York: John Wiley & Sons, 1978).

Wills, Jocelyn, *Boosters, Hustlers, and Speculators: Entrepreneurial Culture and the Rise of Minneapolis and St. Paul, 1849–1883* (Minneapolis, MN: Minnesota Historical Society Press, 2005).

Winstone, H. V. F., *Howard Carter and the Discovery of the Tomb of Tutankhamun* (London: Constable, 1991).

Wingerd, Mary Lethert, *Claiming the City: Politics, Faith, and the Power of Place in St. Paul* (Ithaca, NY: Cornell University Press, 2001).

Zed, Rajan, 'Coverage of Mahatma Gandhi in *The New York Times* and *The Times* (London), 1924–1947', M.S. dissertation, San Jose State University, California, May 1996.

Index